LIBERTY OF CONSCIENCE

Liberty
of
Conscience

In Defense of America's Tradition of
Religious Equality

Martha C. Nussbaum

A Member of the Perseus Books Group
New York

Copyright © 2008 by Martha C. Nussbaum

Published by Basic Books
A Member of the Perseus Books Group

Designed by Timm Bryson
Set in 11.5 point Bulmer MT

Library of Congress Cataloging-in-Publication Data
Nussbaum, Martha Craven, 1947–
  Liberty of conscience : in defense of America's tradition of religious equality / Martha Nussbaum.
    p. cm.
  ISBN-13: 978-0-465-05164-9 (alk. paper)
  ISBN-10: 0-465-05164-2 (alk. paper)
  1. Freedom of religion—United States. I. Title.
  BL640.N87 2008
  323.44'20973—dc22

                        2007038176

10 9 8 7 6 5 4 3 2 1

In memory of Philip Quinn, 1940–2004

CONTENTS

1

INTRODUCTION

A Tradition Under Threat

Every year, at Thanksgiving, thousands of small American children dress up like Pilgrims. Grave in tall hats and buckled shoes, or starched bonnets and aprons, they proudly act out the story of that courageous band of settlers who fled religious persecution in Europe, braving a perilous ocean voyage and the harsh conditions of a Massachusetts winter—all in order to be able to worship God freely in their own way. Those who survived feasted with the native inhabitants and gave thanks to God.

We cherish and celebrate this story, but we too rarely reflect on its real meaning: that religious liberty is very important to people, and that it is often very unequally distributed. The dominant majority in England did not have to run risks to worship God according to their consciences. They established an orthodoxy, an official church, that favored them and subordinated others. In the England from which the Pilgrims fled, people were not equal citizens, because their rights were not equally respected by the government under which they lived. The Pilgrims were not expelled from England, as the Jews had earlier been expelled, but they were living in a condition of subordination. Something very precious had been withheld from them, and it was to recover that space of both liberty and equality that they crossed the ocean in three small vessels.

The lesson of the first Thanksgiving is easy to forget. Indeed, the early settlers themselves soon forgot it, establishing their own repressive orthodoxy, from which others fled in turn. People like exclusive clubs that rank them above others. My mother's ancestors came over on the *Mayflower,* and some of my relatives were obsessed with triumphal genealogizing, as they marshaled the evidence that they belonged in the exclusive and socially prominent Mayflower Society, while others did not. The Pilgrims' quest for freedom, centuries later, had become elite Americans' quest for superiority. Nor was religious toleration in a healthy state among the Pilgrims' descendants, as the exclusion of Jews (and, often, Roman Catholics) from local private schools, country clubs, law firms, and prestigious social events indicated. When I later married a Jew and converted to Judaism, the Pilgrims' descendants did not applaud my choice to worship God according to my own conscience.

People love in-groups that give their members special rights. Equality, and respect for equality, are difficult for human beings to sustain. Particularly in the area of religion, which seems so vital to the salvation of individuals and the health of the nation, it is very tempting to think that orthodoxy is a good thing and that those who do not accept it are dangerous subversives. This sort of in-group favoritism, however, is what the laws and traditions of our country utterly reject. This is a country that respects people's committed search for a way of life according to their consciences. This is also a country that has long understood that liberty of conscience is worth nothing if it is not equal liberty. Liberty of conscience is not equal, however, if government announces a religious orthodoxy, saying that this, and not that, is the religious view that defines us as a nation. Even if such an orthodoxy is not coercively imposed, it is a statement that creates an in-group and an out-group. It says that we do not all enter the public square on the same basis: one religion is the American religion and others are not. It means, in effect, that minorities have religious liberty at the sufferance of the majority and must acknowledge that their views are subordinate, in the public sphere, to majority views.

I. A Tradition of Fairness

The dominant American political tradition repudiates this style of thinking, so common in the world's history. Citizens, we believe, are in fact all equal. We have not just rights, but equal rights. The state may not create a two-tiered system of citizenship by establishing a religious orthodoxy that gives rights to the nonorthodox on unequal terms. As Justice Jackson put it in a famous opinion holding that Jehovah's Witnesses may not be compelled to recite the Pledge of Allegiance in school (which their religion forbids, as a form of idolatry): "If there is any fixed star in our constitutional constellation, it is that no official, high or petty, can prescribe what shall be orthodox in politics, nationalism, religion, or other matters of opinion or force citizens to confess by word or act their faith therein. If there are any circumstances which permit an exception, they do not now occur to us."[1]

Our commitment to religious equality did not emerge immediately or easily. The colonial period saw intense and painful differences about religious matters, and much intolerance. Gradually, however, the sheer experience of living together with people who differed in belief and practice gave rise to a consensus: the future constitutional order must be dedicated to fair treatment for people's deeply held religious beliefs. The framers of our Constitution reflected long and well about these matters, and they carefully wrote protections for religious fairness into the document they framed. The Constitution as a whole makes no reference to God, not even the vague and general reference to a Creator that Jefferson thought acceptable in the Declaration of Independence. Article VI states that "no religious Test shall ever be required as Qualification to any office or public Trust under the United States." And the First Amendment states: "Congress shall make no law respecting an establishment of religion, or prohibiting the free exercise thereof." The freedom of religion and a prohibition against setting up any religion as the national orthodoxy are the first two protections for citizens' rights mentioned in that all-important amendment.

Throughout America's history, those clauses have been understood to guarantee all citizens both religious liberty and religious equality: no religion will become an orthodoxy that undercuts any citizen's claim to equal rights. Many difficult questions of interpretation have arisen, but on the whole Justice Jackson is right: a shared understanding of religious fairness has been a "fixed star" of our tradition.

To say that there is a shared understanding and that a noble tradition has on the whole prevailed is not to say that it has not often been assailed. Religious fairness has periodically endured challenges throughout our history, some subtle and some less subtle, some apparently benign and some violent. People aren't always content to live with others on terms of mutual respect. So the story of the tradition is also a story of the attacks upon it, as different groups jockey for superiority. What has kept the tradition alive and healthy is continual vigilance against these attacks, which in each new era take a different concrete form.

This book concerns both the tradition and these periodic attacks, and its purpose is both to clarify and to warn. Without vigilance, our "fixed star" may not be fixed for much longer. Religious fairness has always encountered temporary threats. No doubt it will encounter others in the future—because the tendency to exalt one's own group as the good, orthodox group and to demote others is lamentably common in human life. Fear of strangers, demonization of new or unpopular groups, panics about the future of the nation—all these, from time to time, have caused Americans to diverge temporarily from our fundamental constitutional commitment to equal citizenship and equal liberty in religious matters. It was one of those panics that led several states to mandate the recital of the pledge, expelling children who refused to recite it for religious reasons. For a time, even the U.S. Supreme Court went along. Jews, Mormons, Jehovah's Witnesses, Seventh-Day Adventists, atheists, members of nontheistic religions such as Buddhism or Taoism, Native Americans, Santeria worshipers—all these have suffered religious disabilities at the hands of the majority. Constant watchfulness has been required to protect liberty and equality from various social pressures. Many of these threats, however, were local rather than nationwide, and many were short-lived. On the whole, despite such lapses, our judiciary has been a reliable guardian.

The current threat to religious fairness is not local, and it is not likely to be short-lived. In that way, it is less like the temporary uproar over Jehovah's Witnesses and the pledge and more like the long sad history of anti-Catholicism that is the ugliest blot on our national commitment to religious fairness. Anti-Catholicism was violent, and the current threat is not, or not yet, violent. We are not beating small children because they refuse to say the Protestant version of the Ten Commandments in the public schools, as happened in the mid-nineteenth century, and we seem to have reached a shared understanding that government-orchestrated sectarian religious observances in the schools are utterly unacceptable. Nonetheless, watchfulness is needed. An organized, highly funded, and widespread political movement wants the values of a particular brand of conservative evangelical Christianity to define the United States. Its members seek public recognition that the Christian God is our nation's guardian. Such an agenda threatens to create, once again, in-groups and out-groups, defining some citizens as dominant members of the political community and others as second-class citizens. It threatens to undermine the very idea that all citizens, no matter what they believe about the ultimate meaning of life, can live together in full equality.

We are living in an era of unprecedented religious diversity in America. The two most rapidly growing religions in our nation are Hinduism and Buddhism, the former through immigration from India, the latter through a combination of immigration and conversion. An increasing number of Americans, moreover, define their religion as eclectic and do not attach themselves to a particular conventional denomination. (Such was the case, as well, at the time of the Founding: only between 8 and 17 percent of the colonists belonged to a recognized church.[2]) Propositions that might have seemed the common ground of all the religions (the singleness of God, the concern of God for human beings, the very existence of a deity) are now newly divisive—not simply dividing religious people from atheists and agnostics, but dividing monotheists from religious polytheists, and theists from members of nontheistic religions (Buddhism, Taoism, Confucianism, and in some interpretations Unitarian/Universalism). Fairness is a tall order among so much diversity, and sensitive thought about apparently unproblematic statements is badly needed.

Instead, we all too often have a push in the opposite direction, a push to institutionalize Christian evangelical fundamentalism and its near relatives as our state religion. It is alarming when a Justice of the U.S. Supreme Court argues, as Justice Scalia recently did, that it is perfectly all right for government to endorse monotheism publicly, giving polytheism and nontheism a secondary status.[3]

Equally shocking are the many ways in which the rhetoric of important political officials highlights Christianity, implicitly suggesting the inequality of non-Christians. Examples abound. Here are just a few of the more disturbing:

- John Ashcroft, former attorney general, regularly asked his staff to sing Christian songs before work began in the morning.
- While he was a sitting U.S. senator, Ashcroft characterized America as "a culture that has no king but Jesus."
- The "faith-based initiatives" program, a major conduit for federal welfare funding, permits the religious institutions (most of them Christian) that dispense federal funds to refuse aid to people of a different

religion *even in programs* (like health care and job training) *that have a purely secular purpose.*

- The idea that we are a holy nation with a divine mission has been omnipresent in the second Bush administration's rhetoric on the war in Iraq. A typical example is President Bush's statement that "the author of freedom is not indifferent to the fate of freedom," a comment that not only seeks to wrap controversial policies in a mantle of sanctity, but also neglects the fact that many Americans do not believe in an anthropomorphic God who is the "author" of freedom.

- Lt. General William Boykin, a former head of U.S. Army Special Forces who is involved in the search for Osama bin Laden, said in a speech in June 2003 that radical Muslims hate the United States "because we're a Christian nation, because our foundation and roots are Judeo-Christian and the enemy is a guy named Satan."

- Alan Keyes, Republican candidate for Senate in 2004 in the state of Illinois, claimed in a televised debate that voters should choose him because Jesus opposes his opponent, Barack Obama (who won the election). (Obama's appropriate riposte was that he was running to be the senator from Illinois, not the minister from Illinois.) After his loss, Keyes refused to make a concession speech or to speak to Obama, characterizing the contest as one of "good" versus "evil."

- President Bush has recently endorsed the move to require the teaching of "Intelligent Design," a view of the universe with sectarian religious roots, in science classrooms alongside the theory of evolution.[4]

The effect of all this is to suggest that those who do not share the particular religious values of the current administration are less than fully American and less than fully equal.

The Supreme Court remains in a relatively healthy state where issues of religious liberty are concerned. Indeed, we can see clear signs of progress in the Court's ability to understand the strange and initially alarming in religious matters, although there remain difficult issues about the level of protection that religious minorities deserve from the courts. Where the public establishment of a state religion is concerned, our recent tradition has been more tumultuous, and the Court at present is deeply divided. Particularly worrying is the stance recently taken by Justice Thomas concerning the all-important Establishment Clause of the First Amendment.[5] He holds that it applies only to acts of the federal government, thus freeing the states to adopt policies that favor some religions over others, and religion over nonreligion. The doctrine that the Bill of Rights applies to state as well as federal government had its origin after the Civil War. Called "incorporation," it is the view that the Fourteenth Amendment applied key provisions of the Bill of Rights to the states. (Prior to that time, citizens were protected from tyranny at the hands of state government only by individual state constitutions.) At the time, the doctrine of "incorporation" was controversial, and some history scholars contest that history today. Incorporation, however, is settled law. For many years Americans have relied on the fact that the Bill of Rights protects us against abuses at the hands of state as well as federal government. When, in 1960, the state of Maryland revoked the appointment of a state official because he refused to declare his belief in God, both the public and the Supreme Court were very clear: this is a shocking violation of a basic constitutional guarantee.[6] Thomas's view, however, implies that a state can, with no constitutional barrier, call itself a "Christian state," order Christian prayer in state-run schools, require Christian oaths of state officials, even decide to fund only Christian schools. His radical doctrine removes vital protections for equal rights on which Americans rely every day.

Justice Thomas, while denying that the Establishment Clause applies to the acts of state government, at least accepts "incorporation" for the Free Exercise Clause (as well as the speech and press clauses of the First Amendment). In other words, he still believes that it would be constitutionally impermissible for a state to deny Jews, or Muslims, or Buddhists the right to practice their religion freely. Even that deeply traditional idea, however, has been denied by another judge whom the Bush administration has made a linchpin of its program for remaking the federal judiciary. Janice Rogers Brown was recently confirmed to a seat on the Federal Court of Appeals for the District of Columbia Circuit—a court second only to the Supreme Court in influence and prestige—as a result of the deal through which Democrats made concessions to Republicans in order to avoid the "nuclear option" (removal of the traditional right to filibuster). Janice Rogers Brown is radical in many areas, but on the "incorporation" of the Bill of Rights she is a true extremist. In a 1999 speech, she said that the arguments against the idea that the Bill of Rights applies to the states are "overwhelming," and that the Bill of

Rights is "probably not incorporated"—contrary to a century and more of Supreme Court precedents. At her hearing before the Senate Judiciary Committee, she hedged, saying that she had spoken hastily and would now give the matter further study. But she still called incorporation "anomalous."[7] Judge Brown did not invent these radical notions. They have been marketed aggressively by the religious right, and there are many younger thinkers like her out there.

The religious right has been active for many years, at least since the 1980s. Recently, however, the threat posed to our tradition has, for several reasons, become more acute. First, the growing religious diversity of the U.S. raises new issues of fairness, making statements endorsing monotheism, for example, more evidently problematic than they were before. To endorse monotheism in the face of this diversity is to make a statement that was not intended by many eighteenth-century references to a monotheistic God. Second, the efforts of the religious right to "mainstream" some of their chosen doctrines have taken time, and have only recently begun to bear fruit at the level of appellate adjudication, as years of subsidized scholarship has finally succeeded in moving positions that were once considered marginal to the center of the political spectrum.

The distressing change in our recent political life is further spurred, as bad changes so often are, by fear. When people feel fear and insecurity, it is easy for them to demonize those who are different, seeking safety in solidarity. This search often takes the form of seeking to define the nation as one under God's protection. After the great national trauma of the Civil War, in 1861, a Baptist minister wrote to the Secretary of the Treasury, Salmon B. Chase, saying that the war had been caused by God's anger because He was not recognized on our currency. The Secretary of the Treasury agreed, as did Congress in 1864. As a result, the words "In God We Trust" were added to our coins. (They did not appear on paper money until 1957.) During the Cold War, Americans terrified by the threat of communism and nuclear war rallied around the idea that we ought to add the words "under God" to the Pledge of Allegiance. Prior to 1954, the pledge had read simply, "one nation, indivisible, with liberty and justice for all." The political debate surrounding that addition focused on the importance of distinguishing the U.S. from "godless communism."

Now we are in the midst of another war that inspires great fear and that appears to have no end: the "war on terror." This time the enemy has been linked in the public mind with an extremist interpretation of Islam. As more and more Muslims enter the U.S., the rhetoric of war makes people wonder whether they are trustworthy citizens. Fear makes people ask whether all religions should really be treated equally. Other fears concern the future of the family in an era of change. As women's growing economic independence makes many less dependent on traditional marriage, as many people choose to live together without the benefit of marriage, as gays and lesbians live openly in our communities and raise children, people fear that society is losing its moorings and seek to return it to traditional religious values. As always, fear makes people ask whether equal treatment should really apply to all citizens— or only to citizens who hold religious and moral views similar to their own. The current eagerness to declare religious foundations for our nation is an understandable reaction to more general global and domestic insecurities, but it is also dangerous, threatening the commitment to equality that holds us together. It has been greatly fueled by the rhetoric of the Bush administration. It is difficult to say whether our judicial tradition will respond appropriately now, as it has in the past.

Many citizens of goodwill, who would be horrified by the repression of minority religion or by the very suggestion that all citizens do not have equal rights, see the trend toward public endorsement of a religious national identity as innocuous, or even good—because they do not see the way in which it is connected with unequal liberty and unequal standing in the public domain. Many if not most Americans think that religion is enormously important and precious, and they do not like being told by intellectuals that they should not bring their religious commitments into the public square. Even "separation of church and state" sounds to them like an idea that marginalizes or subordinates religion, asking it to take a backseat, when people think that it should be in the driver's seat. Many people think, then, that defenders of the continued separation of church and state are people who have contempt for religion.

These people are right about something: religion is enormously important and precious. Not every American believes this personally, but all ought to be prepared to see, and respect, the importance of religion for many, if not most, of their fellow citizens. I myself believe religion important personally as well: I am a committed Jew whose membership in a Reform Jewish congregation is an important part of my life and my search for meaning. It is certainly supremely annoying when intellectuals talk down to religious people, speaking as if all smart people are atheists. Philosopher Daniel Dennett is particularly guilty of this. In an op-ed piece in the *New York Times*, he coined the term "brights" for nonbelievers, suggesting very clearly that the right name for believers was "dummies."[8] In his popular new book *Breaking the Spell*[9]—whose very title drips contempt—he contrasts religious people with philosophers, as if there were no such thing as a religious philosopher. I am a philosopher, but I and many of my professional colleagues disagree with Dennett personally: we are ourselves religious people. Almost all, furthermore, would disagree with Dennett about respect for others: we think that people's religious commitments should be respected, and that it is simply not respectful to imply that religion is a "spell" or that people who accept such beliefs are dummies. Michael Newdow, the plaintiff in the Pledge of Allegiance case[10] (and in a new similar case recently decided in California) is similar to Dennett: a proud atheist who has evident contempt for religious beliefs and religious people. Many Americans of goodwill associate the very idea of the "separation of church and state" with this sort of smug atheism. They therefore prefer the idea that we are a godly nation; at least they see nothing wrong in public statements of this idea. I sympathize with them up to a point, sharing their reaction to arrogant public atheism and with some people's use of the language of separation to express it.

Indeed, the story this book will tell is one in which religious fairness faces threats from both the "right" and the "left," from arrogant secularism as well as from aggressively insular forms of Christianity. Particularly during the second phase of intense anti-Catholicism, in the period after World War II, left-wing intellectuals played a key role in denigrating Catholics as bad citizens and in promoting an approach to the legal tradition that was, in its extreme form, deeply unfair both to Catholics and to other people committed to educating their children in religious schools. The phrase "separation of church and state," which does not appear in our Constitution and plays no role in our early tradition of religious fairness, attained currency during the first wave of anti-Catholicism in the nineteenth century, and was resurrected during the second, to express a doctrine that denied the religious schools some forms of protection from the state that ultimately seemed to most Americans both fair and decent. The issue of aid to religious schools is a profoundly difficult one, but we can say with confidence that it is one on which some parts of the left went wrong, and we can also conclude that leading figures on the left, at that time, used the idea of "separation" in a way that went astray from the tradition's central commitment to fairness and equal respect. It seems to me that there is little point in simply adding to the swelling chorus of alarm over "the religious right." The helpful thing is to produce a good analysis of religious fairness. But any such good analysis entails, I believe, that there are errors on the left as well, and that we should be, and remain, vigilant about them.

Insofar as "separation of church and state" is a good idea, it is good because of the way it supports equal respect, preventing the public realm from establishing a religious doctrine that denigrates or marginalizes some group of citizens. Nobody really believes in separation taken literally across the board. The modern state is ubiquitous in people's lives, and if we really tried to separate church from state all the way, this would lead to a situation of profound unfairness. Imagine what it would be like if the fire department refused to aid a burning church, if churches didn't have access to the public water supply or the sewer system, if the police would not investigate crimes on church property, if clergy could not vote or run for office. Such proposals seem horribly unfair, because the state is providing all these forms of support for everyone else. So, we can't use the bare idea of separation to guide us: we need other guiding ideas to tell us how far and when separation is a good thing.

Our legal and judicial tradition, on the whole, knows these things well, although there was a brief era when the separation idea acquired a momentum of its own and things became unbalanced. Discussion in the general public realm seems to me more confused on this question. Liberals of good faith attach themselves to the rhetoric of separation, without asking seriously why and how much separation really is good or fair. Meanwhile, there are some leading figures who speak on these matters who seem animated by the same aversion to religion that motivated the left-wing intellectuals of the 1950s, when they tried to convince people that the U.S. was facing a Catholic takeover that would destroy our democratic traditions. We hear something like this hysteria today, and it is important for liberal intellectuals to eschew it.

Seen in its right relation to the idea of fairness, the idea of separation of church and state does not express what the left sometimes uses it to express, namely contempt for, and the desire to marginalize, religion. Our tradition has sought to put religion in a place apart from government, in some ways and with some limits, *not* because we think that it has no importance for the conduct of our lives or the choices we make as citizens, but for a very different reason. Insofar as it is a good, defensible value, the separation of church and state is, fundamentally, about equality, about the idea that no religion will be set up as *the* religion of our nation, an act that immediately makes outsiders unequal. Hence separation is also about protecting religion—minority religion, whose liberties and equalities are always under pressure from the zeal of majorities. Protecting minority equality in religious matters is very important because religion is very important to people, a way they have of seeking ultimate meaning in their lives. If religion were trivial, it would not be so vitally important to forestall hierarchies of status and freedom in religious matters.

Americans disagree about how much separation is required by a commitment to equality. Nobody thinks that the fire department should not help the burning church, and most people agree that, on the other side, the state should not subsidize religious instruction or introduce sectarian religious observances. Both in the funding area and in the area of public displays and ceremonies, however, there is much disagreement about how much separation is constitutionally required. Such dispute must be settled by values other than the bare value of separation.

To be sure, there are and have been since the Founding other plausible arguments in favor of the separation of church and state. Separation is partly sheer insulation, since the founders thought that the machinery of government would be likely to corrupt true religion, producing lifeless bureaucratic established churches, such as those they had observed in Europe. They believed, furthermore, that churches ought to be free to manage their own affairs, and that they would not be free if they were deeply involved with government. On the other side, they also thought that the machinery of government needed to be insulated from the divisive influence of religious bickering. They had seen that in Europe too. These arguments have merit: in many nations with an established church we do see religion becoming a lifeless bureaucracy, and we also sometimes see government impeded by bickering among religious factions. More basically, however, separation is about equality and equal respect.

Still, why should we really find it objectionable to speak of America as a nation protected by God? We might grant that there should be no hierarchies *among* the different religions and yet believe that a general reference to God is totally fine, excluding nobody. There are, however, subtle difficulties here. First of all, we should remember that even an apparently nonsectarian reference to God is in fact sectarian and excludes many people. Most obviously, it excludes atheists. More subtly, it excludes polytheists and members of nontheistic religions. More subtly yet, it includes many believing members of monotheist religions who do not hold that God offers special protection to favored nations. Maybe these people believe that God is remote and not personally involved in human affairs. Maybe they believe that God's primary way of being involved is to look for justice and righteousness, not to take a particular flawed group of humans under a protective wing.

Long ago, people did not notice some of these exclusions, because very few members of nontheistic and polytheistic religions were in America—apart from the Native Americans, whose religious concepts few Americans took very seriously, since most of them, culpably, had contempt for Native Americans. Judaism, Islam, and the various forms of Christianity were all people thought they had to deal with. New immigration—and new recognition of the equal dignity of Native Americans—have brought new demands for respect and equal treatment.

But nonetheless, can't public, governmental references to faith, or even to a particular faith, go hand in hand with toleration and protection of minorities? Yes, perhaps—but only in a country where people do not care very much about religion or the values that divide people along religious lines. Some of the established churches of Europe create few troublesome inequalities because people do not pay very much attention to them and because there are few religious differences that inspire real passion. This is especially likely to be true in nations that allow little immigration—not a particularly admirable policy in a world in which so many people are fleeing persecution and starvation. In most other European countries, moreover, recent immigration, especially from Muslim countries, has challenged the toleration that goes with benign establishment, and has shown it to be, in many cases, a thin veneer, undergirded by insufficient respect for people who have nonmajoritarian practices and ways. Used to the idea that citizens are all alike, many Europeans have thought little about how to live with people who are different. I have had frustrating conversations with entirely admirable Italians who find nothing problematic in the presence of a crucifix at the front of a public school classroom, with French colleagues who defend the ban on the Muslim headscarf and the Jewish yarmulke in French public schools, with Dutch journalists who favor banning the wearing of the Muslim burqa in public places.

The American constitutional tradition offers insight into these cases—insights not only helpful to Americans seeking self-understanding, but helpful, as well, to European nations newly grappling with religious difference. This tradition suggests that the Italian crucifix represents a dangerous form of religious establishment, dangerous because it announces to young impressionable children from minority religions (including Protestant Christianity) that they do not enter society on equal conditions so long as they cling to their religion. The legal banning of the burqa (if the law passes) would be a similar subordinating establishment.[11] Our tradition also suggests that the French law is an unjustified incursion into an area of religious self-expression that the law ought to protect for all citizens. Once again, this restriction of liberty also threatens equality, since it bears more heavily on Muslims and Jews (whose religions require articles of apparel that the new French law forbids) than on Christians (who are not required to wear the large crosses that the law also forbids, and who are permitted to wear small crosses). The French tradition of coercive assimilation (as earlier, in policies concerning the assimilation of the Jews) neglects the insight expressed in George Washington's letter to the Quakers, when he said, "I assure you very explicitly, that in my opinion the conscientious scruples of all men should be treated with great delicacy and tenderness: and it is my wish and desire, that the laws may always be as extensively accommodated to them, as a due regard for the protection and essential interests of the nation may justify and permit."[12] No essential state interests are at stake in the headscarf controversy. If Washington was prepared to allow Quakers to refuse military service, a very important public function, why are the French so unwilling to allow Muslims and Jews to wear religious articles of dress? The French policy seems to express a refusal of the "delicacy and tenderness" that is owed to other people's "conscientious scruples."

When I contemplate these cases, I feel considerable pride in the U.S. tradition, which seems to me to have struck basically the right balance between the need for neutral institutions and the needs of people of faith. How terrible it would be, then, if that admirable American tradition were undermined in a time of widespread public uncertainty and fear.

Like many Americans, I have seen these questions from the perspective of the dominant majority. As a girl I went to church on Sunday, celebrated Christmas, and never had to worry about missing school when I did. Like many other Americans, however, I have also seen things from the side of the minority.[13] As a convert to Judaism, I found that I suddenly had to wrestle with questions about whether to attend (or, later, to hold) classes on Jewish holidays, since those were never public holidays. As a Reform Jew, I also understood the more difficult struggles that Orthodox students and faculty routinely face, since their rules for holiday observance are stricter. It is not surprising that my temple, among the oldest Jewish congregations in Chicago (about 160 years old), has an ongoing project to study, and support, the separation of church and state—under the leadership of congregation member Abner Mikva, a distinguished retired federal judge. Religious minorities know what the denial of that separation usually leads to: the imposition of the ways of the majority on all—or, at least, the public statement that the majority is orthodox, who "we" are, and that the minority are outsiders.

As a scholar whose work concerns issues of economic development, focusing on India, I also have an acute awareness of the struggle of much newer minorities, Hindu, Buddhist, and Muslim, in the U.S. political context. I understand that for many Hindus the words "under God" in the Pledge of Allegiance are problematic because, as polytheists, they do not like the implication that a single god presides over the fate of the nation. Polytheism has so often been denigrated as a low-level or barbarous type of religion that this exclusion carries a particular connotation of inequality. (One of the great acts of the late Pope was his public recognition that Hinduism, as well as Judaism and Islam, offers a legitimate route to salvation.) Hindus are even more troubled by public displays of the Ten Commandments, a sacred text that is shared (though in different forms) by Judaism, Christianity, and Islam. A Hindu group submitted an amicus brief asking the Supreme Court to declare one of these public displays unconstitutional. Muslim citizens have their own, more obvious struggles. Although anti-Muslim feeling in the U.S. has not caused as great an assault on civil liberties as might have been feared after 9/11, and though President Bush has made numerous commendable efforts to express respect for Islam and to distinguish Islam from terrorism, the danger of intolerance is there, increased by Americans' considerable ignorance of Islam, even though it is a religion on the rise here.

I approach these questions as a scholar of constitutional law, but also, and more fundamentally, as a philosopher. Philosophical ideas were important to the Founding, and thinking about some of the philosophical texts that formed its backdrop helps to clarify the underlying issues. I take an independent interest in these philosophical ideas as good ideas to think with, not just ideas that had a certain historical and political influence. But I will also be arguing that the constitutional tradition is best read as embodying at least some of these ideas, in some form.

Law is more piecemeal than philosophy, and it is constrained by many things other than the philosophical truth: by the facts of the case at hand, by the legal precedents (which may or may not be clear or well argued), by the fact that a court is always a plurality of people with different views, and a majority opinion has to seek consensus among these views. Often, too, there are both majority (or plurality) and concurring opinions that offer different reasons for the outcome, so even respect for precedent is a highly complex matter. We should therefore not expect the legal tradition to be tidy, and, in this area above all, it certainly is not. Philosophical ideas can mislead if they make us think that there is more unity than there is, or ignore important strands of reasoning that diverge from the one that seems most philosophically interesting. Judiciously used, however, philosophical reconstruction can illuminate some of the grand themes of a tradition in ways that help us see what has been accomplished, and what still remains to be done.

II. Two Cases: Mrs. Sherbert and the Pittsburgh Courthouse

Why do I claim that both of the "religion clauses"—the so-called Free Exercise Clause ("Congress shall make no law . . . prohibiting the free exercise [of religion]") and the so-called Establishment Clause ("Congress shall make no law respecting an establishment of religion") are centrally about equality? Consider these two cases, one decided under the Free Exercise Clause and one under the Establishment Clause.

Adell Sherbert worked in a textile factory in South Carolina. All the employers in her town had similar policies for working hours. After Mrs. Sherbert had been a good employee for many years, the policy changed, during a time of economic stress and competition. Instead of working five-day weeks, employees were now expected to work six-day weeks. Saturday was the added day, and that was true of all the employers in the area. Mrs. Sherbert, however, was a Seventh-Day Adventist, for whom it was religiously forbidden to work on Saturday. She tried to find similar work elsewhere in the region, but all employers required Saturday work. Not surprisingly, there was none who chose to close on Saturday and to remain open on Sunday, because most workers and managers were Christian. Mrs. Sherbert resigned and sought unemployment compensation. She was denied by the state of South Carolina on the grounds that she had refused "suitable work." She went to court, arguing that the state had impermissibly impeded her free exercise of religion.

In a famous judgment in 1963, the U.S. Supreme Court agreed.[14] They held that benefits could not be made conditional on a violation of a person's religious scruples: this was just like fining someone for Saturday worship. In other words, the denial of benefits was a violation of Mrs. Sherbert's *equal* freedom, as a citizen, to worship in her own way. Free exercise does not mean simply that nobody can come and put Mrs. Sherbert in jail for her nonstandard religious practices. It means, as well, that the conditions of liberty must be the same for all. The Court held that no person may suffer a "substantial burden" to their religious liberty without a "compelling state interest"— which clearly did not exist in this case.

Workplace arrangements are always made for the benefit of the majority. The holidays observed, the workdays chosen—all are tailored to suit the local majority, in this case Christian. There is nothing inherently wrong with this— *so long as* care is taken to prevent this convenient arrangement from turning into a fundamental inequality in freedom and respect. The Free Exercise Clause, the Court held, guarantees that equal freedom.

The Allegheny County Courthouse stands on public property in downtown Pittsburgh. In the late 1980s, the county set up two holiday season displays. The first, inside the courthouse, consisted of a crèche (Nativity scene), donated by a local Roman Catholic organization, and labeled to that effect. Placed on the grand staircase of the courthouse, with no other displays around it, the Nativity scene bore a sign—carried by an angel above the manger—saying "Gloria in Excelsis Deo," Glory to God in the highest.

The second display was outside on the courthouse lawn. It consisted of a Hanukkah menorah eighteen feet tall, standing next to the city's forty-five-foot decorated Christmas tree. At the foot of the tree was a message from the mayor saying that the display was a "salute to liberty." (In fact, the menorah is a symbol of liberty, since the holiday of Hanukkah commemorates the Maccabees' courageous rebellion against oppression. It is difficult to say whether a Christmas tree represents liberty, but it is such an all-purpose symbol that the mayor can probably declare this without implausibility.) Local residents took both displays to court, charging that they violated the Establishment Clause.

The Court obviously considered this a very difficult case.[15] Ultimately a split Court judged that the first display violated the Establishment Clause and the second did not. The crucial question they asked was whether each display communicated the message that the county was giving its endorsement to a particular set of religious beliefs and practices, thus threatening equality. The first display seemed to the majority to communicate such an endorsement: the religious Christian display stood alone, in a position of special prominence and honor. The second display was different: the fact that more than one religion was honored, and that the theme connecting the tree with the menorah was that of liberty, a theme that could include all citizens, whatever their religion or nonreligion, meant to at least the Court's center that the people of Pittsburgh would not be likely "to perceive the combined display of the tree, the sign, and the menorah as an 'endorsement' or 'disapproval . . . of their individual religious choices.'"

We can grant that this is a difficult case to decide, and we can even differ about whether it was correctly decided, while yet agreeing about the immense importance of the principle involved. What my Italian friends don't understand about the message sent by a crucifix in front of a public school classroom is what the Court sees very clearly in *Allegheny:* some religious symbols, set up by government, threaten the equal standing of citizens in the public realm. They attach the imprimatur of orthodoxy to Christian observance, while demoting the beliefs and practices of others. Our "fixed star" is that no such orthodoxies are admissible.

The Free Exercise Clause and the Establishment Clause are difficult to interpret and even more difficult to relate to one another. We shall see many examples of these difficulties. But a central thread that connects them, directing some of their most important applications, is this idea of a government that does not play favorites.

III. Concepts

Many different, though related, ideas are present in the tradition we shall be examining. Different writers—and different judges—stress different concepts and connect them to one another in different ways. So it is useful to begin with a "concept map," laying out the key ideas and suggesting some key connections—and questions.

- **Liberty.** Liberty, or the free exercise of religion, means being able to follow one's own conscience in matters of religious belief and—within limits set by the demands of public order and the rights of others—religious conduct. One thing that the religion clauses do is to protect areas of liberty within which people can hold different beliefs *and also* exercise religious conduct. What are the areas of liberty, what are their limits, and what is the pertinent notion of liberty? How does the tradition understand, and justify, religious liberty?

- **Equality and equal respect.** Closely linked to the idea of liberty is the idea that all citizens are equal, or, in Madison's words, that they all enter the polity "on equal conditions." In fact often in the debates we hear of "equal liberty of conscience," not just "liberty." The philosophical tradition is very keen on this idea, and it is a linchpin of the relevant notion of religious freedom: we want not just *enough* freedom, but a freedom that is itself *equal*, and that is compatible with all citizens being fully equal and being equally respected by the society in which they live. One way of thinking about why establishment is bad, from Madison to Justice Sandra Day O'Connor (whose important opinions in this area draw particular attention to the theme of equality), is that it is a violation of that civic equality, equality of standing in the public realm.

- **Conscience.** In the tradition we hear a lot of talk about "liberty of conscience," "equal liberty of conscience," and so on. I shall argue that the argument for religious liberty and equality in the tradition begins from a special respect for the faculty in human beings with which they search for life's ultimate meaning. This faculty was held to be present in all human beings in such a way as to make human beings equal: anyone who has it (and all humans do) is worthy of boundless respect, and that respect should be equally given to high and low, male and female, to members of the religions one likes and also to members of religions one hates. Conscience is precious, worthy of respect, but it is also vulnerable, capable of being wounded and imprisoned. The tradition argues that conscience, on that account, needs a protected space around it within which people can pursue their search for life's meaning (or not pursue it, if they choose). Government should guarantee that protected space. (The relationship between conscience and religious conscience is controversial and will be a topic of debate within the tradition.)

- **Protection of minorities from domination by majorities.** From the colonial period onward, our nation has been keenly aware of the danger that majorities will tyrannize over minorities in religious matters. Many of them persecuted minorities themselves, the early settlers tried to figure out how there could be a government that did not do this. This issue is closely connected to issues of equality and equal respect, but it involves a particular way of thinking about equality: as involving not formally similar treatment but, rather, the removal or prevention of hierarchies. Sometimes making minorities fully equal requires treating them differently, giving them dispensations from laws and customs set up by the majority. Mrs. Sherbert was given a break that no Christian who refused Saturday work would get, because the Court was aware that the workplace put her in an unequal position vis-à-vis the majority; they sought to remove that hierarchical arrangement. A lot in the tradition can be well understood if we think from the point of view of such beleaguered minorities.

- **Neutrality.** Neutrality, in religious matters, is the idea that the state does not take a stand on these matters, or takes a stand that is studiously neutral, favoring or disfavoring no particular conception, not even religion over nonreligion. This idea is closely related to the idea that all citizens are equal and should be shown equal respect, but it is not the same idea. Sometimes, as in Mrs. Sherbert's case, treating someone as fully equal requires special attention to that person's (minority) needs, to compensate for the fact that law and workplace arrangements are always made by majorities in their own interest.

- **Establishment.** An "establishment of religion" means that government has put its stamp of approval on some particular religion or group of religions, creating an official orthodoxy. What is wrong with that? Are establishments bad only insofar as they are malign, infringing on liberty? Is there anything else wrong with them? Are they a direct threat to equality the minute they exist?

- **Separation.** The idea that there should be a "separation of church and state" is mentioned a lot, but I argue that it should be seen as posterior to the ideas of equality and liberty. The prominence of the bare idea of separation in current debate is a source of confusion, since separation, when not further interpreted through other concepts, may suggest the idea of marginalizing religion or pushing it to the periphery of people's lives.

- **Accommodation.** Accommodation means giving religious people a "break" in some area, for reasons of conscience—a dispensation from laws of general applicability, such as the military draft, or rules about years of schooling, or, as in Mrs. Sherbert's case, the rules that govern state unemployment compensation. The guiding idea is that reasons of conscience are very important. In some cases, where public order and safety are not jeopardized, they may take precedence over laws that apply to all, so that people will not be forced to violate their conscience. This idea has also been around since the Founding; it is the idea that George Washington mentions in his letter to the Quakers, assuring them that he understands the conscientious reasons that lead them to refuse military service. How is accommodation related to the constitutional text and tradition? Is it ever constitutionally required, or only an attractive option? Who gets it, and why? How is accommodation linked to both liberty and equality? Finally, doesn't it have a problematic relationship to neutrality, and perhaps also equality, if the reasons for which people win it always have to be religious? What happens to nonreligious people who have deep ethical commitments, or commitments to family? (What if Mrs. Sherbert had had an elderly mother to care for, and good care was unavailable on Saturdays?)

We shall trace the complicated interweavings and resonances of these concepts—but with a particular "fixed star" to guide us. My contention will be that a key thread holding all the key concepts together is the idea of equality, understood as nondomination or nonsubordination (which might sometimes require differential treatment). A major part of not being subordinated will be to have equal standing or status in the public realm. Thus this conception is highly sensitive to dignitary affronts in the symbolic realm, even when they entail no material disadvantage.

The idea of equality has to be supplemented by an independent idea of the worth of liberty of conscience, since we might have been equal by all (equally) lacking religious liberty (as philosopher Thomas Hobbes urged, in the seventeenth century). That idea, in turn, rests on a view about the preciousness and vulnerability of conscience. But liberty is only fair if it is truly equal liberty.

As for neutrality, it is usually a good way to preserve the equality of citizens, but not always: sometimes differential favorable treatment is required, thus accommodation. Accommodation is a form of nonneutrality that sometimes seems required by equality. And yet there remains always the question: why is it "free exercise of *religion*" that gets the breaks, when citizens have so many things to care about, and so many ways, both religious and nonreligious, of arranging their most fundamental conscientious commitments?

In the area of nonestablishment, many concepts are at play, including those of neutrality and liberty (noncoercion). But a major thread is the rejection of a state orthodoxy, of words and acts that subordinate.

Finally, separation does have some ancillary purposes (protecting religion from government and government from religion), but it is valued primarily on account of the equality it protects.

IV. Principles

The tradition combines these concepts in a distinctive way. We can map their intersections in terms of six normative principles, all amply recognized in our constitutional tradition and in the philosophical works related to it:

- **The Equality Principle.** *All citizens have equal rights and deserve equal respect from the government under which they live.*
- **The Respect-Conscience Principle.** *Respect for citizens requires that the public sphere respect the fact that they have different religious commitments* (and, as time goes on, at least some of this gets extended to their nonreligious commitments in the area of life's ultimate meaning and ethical basis), *and provide a protected space within which citizens may act as their conscience dictates.* If a government says that it respects all its citizens, but shows (in its arrangements and statements) a callous disregard for their most fundamental beliefs and practices, then respect is just an empty posture. *If respect for persons is to be equal, this consideration for the conditions in which conscience oper-*

*ates must also be equal: all citizens enter the public square "on equal
conditions."*

Notice that respect does not require either the public sphere or individual
citizens to approve of the theological and ethical claims of any particular religion. Indeed, in order to avoid endorsing one religion over another, or religion over nonreligion, the state will wisely seek to avoid making public
statements of either agreement or disagreement. It won't say that the Roman
Catholics are right, and it also won't say that they are wrong about ultimate reality and the Buddhists are right. To say such things is to establish a public orthodoxy. The hope is that public institutions can be founded on principles
that all can share, no matter what their religion. Of course these institutions
will have an ethical content, prominently including the idea of equal respect itself. But they should not have a religious content.

Respect for fellow citizens does not mean saying or believing that their religious views are correct, or even that all religions are valid routes to the understanding of life. If it did, the Respect-Conscience Principle would be hard for
religious people to accept, since many religions teach the superiority of that
religion to other religions and nonreligion. Some religious, especially today,
do hold that other religions are valid routes to understanding, but others do
not. The Repect-Conscience Principle just means respecting them as human
beings with their own choices to make in religious matters, and a right to make
those choices freely. Accepting the principle, then, in no way implies skepticism or indifference. As Roman Catholic philosopher Jacques Maritain wrote
in an essay entitled "Truth and Human Fellowship":

> There is real and genuine tolerance only when a man is firmly and ab-
> solutely convinced of a truth, or of what he holds to be a truth, and when
> he at the same time recognizes the right of those who deny this truth to
> exist, and to contradict him, and to speak their own mind, not because
> they are free from truth but because they seek truth in their own way, and
> because he respects in them human nature and human dignity and those
> very resources and living springs of the intellect and of conscience which
> make them potentially capable of attaining the truth he loves.[16]

That is the view of respect that animates this book. (I prefer the term "respect" to Maritain's "tolerance," which seems too grudging and weak.)

Finally, this principle does not imply that *all* religions and views of life must be (equally) respected by government: for some extreme views might contradict, or even threaten, the very foundations of the constitutional order and the equality of citizens within it. If people seek to torture children, or to enslave minorities, citing their religion as their reason, their claims must be resisted even though they may be sincere. If they simply *talk* in favor of slavery or torture, their freedom to speak must be protected, up to the point at which speech becomes a threat. They will not, however, be able to present their ideas in the political sphere on an equal basis with other ideas, since the Constitution (in the case of slavery) and the criminal law (in the case of torture) forbid the practices they recommend. So: *people* are all respected as equals, but actions that threaten the rights of others may still be reasonably opposed, and opinions that teach the political inequality of others, while they will not be suppressed, will still be at a disadvantage in the community, since their advocates would have to amend the Constitution to realize their program.

Here we encounter a danger: people who don't like another religion sometimes feel, and say, that it is like these bad things, even if it isn't: comparisons of some new religion's practices to child sacrifice and slavery abound when people are gearing up to discriminate against others.

- **The Liberty Principle.** *Respect for people's conscientious commitments requires ample liberty.* The Respect-Conscience Principle cannot be satisfied by a regime of equal constraint (in which nobody has much religious freedom): understanding what conscience is like and what it needs, we see that it requires substantial (and equal) religious liberty, including liberty of belief and speech, liberty of religious practice (within limits set by the rights of others), and the liberty of religious bodies to organize their own affairs (again within some limits).
- **The Accommodation Principle.** The Equality Principle, the Respect-Conscience Principle, and the Liberty Principle, taken together, suggest that *sometimes some people (usually members of religious minorities) should be exempted from generally applicable laws for reasons of conscience.* The scope of this principle is much de-

bated within the tradition, but it is clear that some accommodation is necessary in order to protect minority equality.

- **The Nonestablishment Principle.** The Equality Principle and the Respect-Conscience Principle require a further principle: *The state may make no endorsements in religious matters that would signify an orthodoxy, creating an in-group and out-groups.* Whether this principle is compatible with any form of state aid to religion, or any form of public display including religious elements, must be thrashed out.

- **The Separation Principle.** The Equality Principle, the Respect-Conscience Principle, the Liberty Principle, and the Nonestablishment Principle can be implemented only if we accept the principle that *a certain degree of separation should be created between church and state: on the whole, church and state have separate spheres of jurisdiction.*

This is a distinctively American combination of principles. Most European traditions have been happy with establishments that preserve ample space for religious liberty. They have been content to send signals to minorities that the community's form of life is structured by the majority religion, and they don't think that this creates a problem for the equality of citizens—or, if they do see a problem, they are willing to live with it. Minorities will not be persecuted, but they are expected to assimilate and conform. Thus debates about the emancipation of (giving political rights to) the Jews, in the eighteenth and early nineteenth centuries in Germany and France, focused on the idea of a semicoercive assimilation as the price of equal liberty. There was no doubt that Jews would get no breaks in connection with their distinctive religious requirements: if the law required them to testify on a Saturday, or to show up at work on Yom Kippur, that is what they would have to do, or face the penalty. The fact that the usual way of doing things created unequal burdens for Jews who wanted to live in accordance with their conscience was not regarded as a problem. If they wanted political rights, they would have to hold them at the sufferance of the majority. This has been the dominant European tradition. At the same time, the European tradition also sees no problem with curtailing liberty, sometimes unequally, as the French headscarf case shows. Current problems that many European nations are experiencing should, I believe, lead them to study and consider adopting the subtly different American conception.

The American law of religion is not a tidy area. It does not look the way a philosopher usually likes an argument to look: neat, well articulated, each step connected to the one before by a convincing path of reasoning. Instead we have lots of different people with different ideas. No responsible scholar could claim to do more than to highlight some issues that seem to lie at the core, and even that claim is open to reasonable disagreement. Nonetheless, the contrast with Europe, in connection with my set of principles, makes some of the key structural features of the American tradition clear, and clearly distinctive.

V. Dangers

People love homogeneity and are startled by difference. When the Quakers first turned up, saying "thee" and "thou" and refusing to take their hats off in court, people thought them very ominous, and it was perhaps only their small numbers that insulated them—in the New World at least—from persecution. Roman Catholics have always seemed strange to Protestants: their rituals, their celibate clergy, their allegiance to the Pope—all of this has made Americans wonder whether they can be good fellow citizens. The issue of the Pope's role in politics was for a long time used to sideline Catholics in American politics. My father had a stranger basis for his view that Catholics should not be permitted to live in our neighborhood: given their large numbers of children, he argued, they would drive up the property taxes we paid to support the public school system. (He didn't take into account the fact that Catholics typically did not send their children to public schools.) People find all sorts of speciously plausible reasons for keeping people who look and act differently at bay. Jews are even more obviously different, because many Jewish men wear yarmulkes, and the dietary laws often make it difficult for Jews to dine with non-Jews. The history of anti-Semitism is full of elaborate myths embroidered on the fabric of these differences: that Jews smell different, that they are sexual predators, that matzohs are made from human blood.

Still, after a time in the U.S., we reached a position in which it was generally agreed that Protestants (including Quakers and Baptists), Catholics, and Jews should all enjoy equal rights and equal religious liberty. Early court cases, as we'll see, defended the sacrament of the confessional as essential to Catholic worship, Saturday prayer as essential to a good Jewish life. For many years, Jews and Catholics still suffered widespread social discrimination and discrimination in private employment. For example, most large law firms did not hire Jews until the 1960s, and no Jew was president of an Ivy League college until the 1970s,[17] although at present all but one of them have or have had Jewish presidents. (Brown, the sole exception, has an African-American female president, so we may safely conclude that the omission of Jews is an accident. It was very likely the first to have its Board of Trustees chaired by a Jew.) Quakers, Jews, Catholics—members of all these religious groups stopped being startling, and fears that the fabric of the community would decay if they were fully included have largely fallen away. Other strange people slipped into the American consciousness with little opposition—in particular the Amish and the Mennonites, who did and do seem very odd to most people, but who keep to themselves and make a lot of money, thus not imposing a drain on the public treasury—as a Supreme Court opinion giving the Amish a substantial dispensation pointed out.

Because Catholics were so much more numerous than Jews and because most of them arrived as new immigrants from countries in Southern and Eastern Europe, they faced intense persecution for a long period of time. This persecution had elements of class and race bias, but it tended to focus on the alleged incompatibility of the Catholic religion with good democratic citizenship. It is to be hoped that this era of persecution is now at an end—as it seems to be, given the lack of public alarm over the fact that, for the first time in our history, the U.S. Supreme Court now has a majority of Catholic members.

The gradual acceptance of Jews, Catholics, and others in American life did not, however, mean that Americans had lost their fear of people whose religious observances look strange. Jehovah's Witnesses, arriving in the late nineteenth century, encountered enormous animosity. Their habit of going door to door with religious literature, their refusal to recite the Pledge of Allegiance, and their German origins all made people suspicious that a subversive "fifth column" had entered the nation. Around the same time, the Mormons encountered perhaps the most irrational and violent resistance ever to greet any religious minority. Their unfamiliar religious text, their strange prophet, their practice of polygamy—all this caused a true panic, fueled by competition over control of crucial western territories. The military repression of the Mormons, and the series of court cases that denied them substantial parts of religious freedom and the freedom of speech, shocked people all around the world: John Stuart Mill, in England, refers to this example scathingly in *On Liberty*.

Even today, the Mormons seem strange to many Americans and are the object of contemptuous denigration. The scare-image of polygamous sexuality—bizarrely compared to child sacrifice in one Supreme Court case that we'll study later—has long been used to marginalize and subordinate them, and many people still think of Mormons in ways tainted by that panic.

The list goes on. Santeria worshippers who sacrifice animals as a part of their worship found that special laws in one city were introduced to forbid them—not because people objected to the killing of animals, since other equally painful forms of slaughter were permitted, but because local citizens did not want to live next to Santeria worshippers and believed that such laws would drive them away. Native American religions still encounter both incomprehension and contempt. Native American ideas about communal sacred land, about the use of peyote in sacred ceremonies, about the danger of photography to a child's young spirit—all these, for the most part, meet with scoffing—even, in some cases, from the Supreme Court. Hindus and Muslims, relatively recent arrivals (because of discriminatory immigration policies in the first half of the twentieth century), are just beginning to fight similar battles.

This history tells us that our Constitution is always threatened—by people's fear of the different, and their desire to keep the different at bay. Firm protection for equal liberty is particularly important in the face of these common human failings.

Another threat comes from sheer selfishness, from people's desire to lord it over others and establish their own superiority. Religious orthodoxy is one very convenient way for people to win a competitive struggle for status and prestige. If your church is the orthodox one and mine belongs to a minority, that seems to make you better than me. Such comparisons happen all the time in informal social life. As a child in an elite Philadelphia suburb, I learned by observation that the Episcopalian and Presbyterian religions were the "in" religions. Those churches were large, opulent, and centrally located. Those people wore expensive clothes. When from time to time I had a friend who was Methodist or Baptist, I felt ashamed or even slightly contaminated when I visited those smaller churches set in unfashionable neighborhoods, and participated in the strange service without a fancy organ. Without exactly being taught, I had learned that I (an Episcopalian) was better than they were. I think I even believed that there was something a little dirty about those churches and those forms of worship, as if bugs and worms would turn up there. One motivation for my conversion, as well as for writing this book, was, and is, remorse and self-criticism about that early experience of shame. What a terrible way to feel about a fellow classmate, much less a friend. And what a terrible way to build a society. People, however, have such experiences all the time. It is very hard to be human and to avoid them completely. (One of the good things about religion, as Immanuel Kant said, is that it gives people a group of like-minded strivers with whom to fight their battles against competitive self-love.) Once again, then, we need vigilance about our constitutional tradition if we are to combat these universal human weaknesses.

VI. History and Law

This book is above all a work of philosophical analysis, which identifies and assesses salient features of our legal tradition and argues that the values that survive philosophical scrutiny are also well embedded in our traditions of precedent, albeit with much backsliding and much untidy diversity of analysis. It also, however, focuses a good deal on colonial history and history at the time of the Founding. How and why is history important to this project?

As a philosopher, I have always focused on the close analysis of historical texts, and I have found my own ideas emerging best in conversation with such texts. My use of Roger Williams in this book is motivated, in part, by the feeling that ideas of great importance do in fact emerge from a confrontation with his writings. But since I am also making claims about the existence of a distinctively American tradition of thought about religious liberty, history also has the more direct relevance of showing where and how that tradition got started, how it was contested, how it grew and was disseminated—how it happened that we Americans ended up with a tradition that is in many respects different from that of Europe. (Here the Williams influence derives more from his political practice and his extensive correspondence than from his philosophical books, which, published in England, may not have been widely read in the colonies.) The legal tradition, moreover, is itself very historically self-conscious, where the religion clauses are concerned, so it seems right to go back behind the brief references to history in this or that Supreme Court opinion and to try to lay out the main arguments that really were influential in the seventeenth and eighteenth centuries.

In this book I do not argue for a preferred view of constitutional interpretation, and therefore I do not try to convince readers that this or that is *the* right way to connect eighteenth-century history to present-day matters of interpretation. Some constitutional scholars hold that the text of the Constitution contains general values that should be interpreted in the light of many factors. Factors that have been seen as relevant to interpretation include the general goals and purposes that the text seems to embody, a good reflective understanding of the concepts involved in the text, the tradition of precedent, and the public meaning of the text at the time it was written. Some legal thinkers, who are called "originalists" or "textualists," believe that the public meaning of the text at the time it was written is the main factor in determining its meaning.

Most textualists do have respect for precedent, so they don't think that the original meaning is the only thing to take seriously. Moreover, where the Bill of Rights is concerned, most textualists grant that we have to talk about two different times: the time when the amendments were drafted and the time, after the Civil War, when they were "incorporated." So the question of textual meaning itself becomes complex.

I do not myself espouse textualism, but I do not argue against it in this book. Apart from its other difficulties, salient among which is the difficulty of ascribing a determinate meaning to a text that is the work of a plurality of people with differing views, it seems to me to embody an odd kind of contradiction, since the founders were characterized by an intense dislike of tradition-bound ways of thinking and had little sympathy for the view that the past should have authority over the present. This dislike of being governed by the past was so ubiquitous among the new Americans that Alexis de Tocqueville, attempting to characterize the "Philosophical Method of the Americans," wrote:

> To evade the bondage of system and habit, of family maxims, class opinions, and, in some degree, of national prejudices; to accept tradition only as a means of information, and existing facts only as a lesson to be used in doing otherwise and doing better; to seek the reason of things for oneself, and in oneself alone; to tend to results without being bound to means, and to strike through the form to the substance—such are the principal characteristics of what I shall call the philosophical method of the Americans.[18]

So insofar as originalism is commended as a way of being respectful of the framers' intentions,[19] it seems a dubious method at best.

Given the influence of textualist views about the history of the religion clauses, however, it seems important even for someone who is no textualist to assess some of the historical claims made by textualists, since these claims are often influential in recent Supreme Court debates. One further use of history in this book is to scrutinize a variety of historical claims about the meaning of the idea of nonestablishment, the idea of liberty of conscience, and so forth. I believe that several currently fashionable theses about the meaning of the religion clauses can be called into question by this sort of historical scrutiny. Of course they could not be disabled in such a manner had they been defended in a nontextualist way, as the best way of analyzing the concepts contained in the text, or the best way of making sense of the Constitution's underlying goals and purposes. Since, however, they were defended only by appeal to history, dismantling that defense disables them. If they are to be resurrected, new arguments of a different type will have to be provided for them.

So I attempt to prescind from divisive issues about how textual meaning, history, and the analysis of general goals and concepts ought to figure in constitutional interpretation. What about the larger relationship between the legal tradition, as best interpreted, and what is right or good?

This book traces a distinctively American tradition of thought about religious matters, and words like "our tradition" and "the American tradition" will show up often in it. One might easily suppose, then, that I am saying we should care about this tradition simply because it is ours. That reading of my enterprise would, however, be in error. As my remarks about Europe show, I believe that good normative arguments can be given for the approach I favor, independently of the fact that it has on the whole been ours. I think that this tradition offers a great deal to the nations of Europe, who have on the whole had a different tradition. It is right at times for nations to interpret general values differently, as befits their special history and problems. Thus a free-speech right that suits the U.S. well (permitting anti-Semitic demonstrations and speech) is probably too permissive for Germany, with its particular history, and Germany is probably right to impose restrictions on anti-Semitic speech. But in the religion area I think it would be all to the good if Europe learned at least some lessons from the U.S. tradition. Hence I cannot and do not hold the view that traditions are good just because of one's own belonging to them. It is also clear that our own tradition has had blind spots and flaws, which we can diagnose only with normative concepts and arguments to guide us. Indeed, as will soon become clear, the tradition of thought that I value has continually been contested and opposed by other less promising, though equally American, ideas.

Traditions help thought. Many of the principles mentioned here have been understood more adequately over time, as they have been tested against a wide range of cases. A philosophical rule formulated in full detail in advance could not have given nearly as good guidance, I believe, as (by now) does our unfolding and incremental legal tradition. So there is a nonincidental connection between the fact that it is a tradition that we are studying and the fact that it gives good answers to a wide range of concrete questions. On the other hand, many traditions, and many aspects of our own, are wrongheaded and unjust. So we can only say what is good about this one if we hold it up at every point against some general goals and conceptions that we are seeking to embody in concrete laws and institutions. Only those goals ultimately tell us why Mrs. Sherbert had a powerful argument. Certainly the legal tradition did not tell us that, since her case led to an altogether new result, though one rooted in some general values recognized in the past. Only such goals, again, will ultimately help us understand how to think about the two displays in Allegheny County. Tradition offered little, since tradition had frequently been obtuse before, when public displays communicated a message of disendorsement and inequality, and constitutional law had been pulled in two directions on such questions, the proper interpretation of the text being highly disputed.

Conveniently enough, the general goals and concepts against which I am holding the tradition up are also deeply embodied within it, or so I believe. This makes the enterprise of historical study take on a particularly close and intimate relationship to normative inquiry. But it can also generate confusion. So it is important to say that the purpose of the book is to commend this tradition because of its depth and ethical value (on the whole), not because it is American. If there are readers who find an additional reason to love it in the fact that it happens to be ours, they are welcome to embrace it for that additional reason.

Constitutions do many things in liberal democracies. One especially important thing that they do, however, is to protect vulnerable groups and people from the tyranny of majorities. Given the fact that we are all weak and all liable to fear, contempt, and the deforming lust for inequality, we need the "fixed star" of our constitutional tradition to guide us. That is why current threats to it must be identified, criticized, and resisted.

2

LIVING TOGETHER

The Roots of Respect

*Sixthly, it is the will and command of God that
(since the coming of his Sonne the Lord Jesus) a
permission of the most paganish, Jewish, Turkish,
or antichristian consciences and worships, bee
granted to all men in all Nations and Countries.*

ROGER WILLIAMS, *The Bloudy
Tenent of Persecution* (1644)[1]

*Your Selvs praetend libertie of Conscience, but
alas, it is but selfe (the great God Selfe) only to Your
Selves.*

ROGER WILLIAMS, LETTER TO THE GOVERNORS OF
MASSACHUSETTS AND CONNECTICUT (1670)

The first half of the seventeenth century saw bloody explosions of religious violence in both Britain and continental Europe. Most early American colonists came to the New World in flight from religious persecution. In Britain, the civil wars were raging. King Charles I was executed in 1649, in a

34

struggle in which religion, though not the only issue, was one salient cause of hostility. Puritan Oliver Cromwell's brief tenure as Lord Protector (1653–1658) temporarily ended the persecution of Puritans and lessened that of Quakers and Baptists. More surprisingly, Cromwell allowed Jews to return to England after their long banishment, influenced by the arguments of Portuguese-Dutch Jewish thinker Menassah ben Israel, who visited England in 1655. As a Puritan obsessed with the destruction of idolatrous images of God, Cromwell clearly already felt an affinity with the Jewish ban on representation. (The many smashed heads of stone images of saints and angels around England still testify to Cromwell's anti-idolatrous zeal.) Cromwell, however, was far from having a general policy of toleration: other persecutions (of Anglicans and Roman Catholics) quickly took the place of the old.

The end of the period of civil war did not bring a commitment to religious peace. People who had suffered from one another's violence did not conclude that they needed to find ways to live together on terms of mutual respect. Instead, as before, each side sought to make its own orthodoxy prevail, subordinating the religions they saw as erroneous and heretical. At the Restoration (1660), the established Anglican Church shored up its power through policies of intolerance toward all other churches and worships. King Charles II showed some personal favor to policies supporting religious liberty, but his inclinations found little immediate expression in England itself. Hemmed in by an intolerant parliament, Charles learned to confine his experiments in religious fairness to the New World—focusing in particular on the strange royal colony of Rhode Island.

Meanwhile, on the Continent, the Treaty of Westphalia (1648) brought an end to the century's bloody wars of religion, but in a way that was not reassuring to religious minorities. The treaty's stated principle, *cuius regio, eius religio* (whoever's region it is, his shall the religion be), allowed local rulers to establish a chosen religion in each domain, persecuting internal dissidents. Even the wise Dutch philosopher Hugo Grotius, one of the main founders of modern international law, who made eloquent arguments against the policy of using religion as a ground for aggressive wars against other nations, had no objection to the persecution of minorities within one's own—despite the fact that he himself was first imprisoned and then smuggled into exile for his allegedly heretical beliefs; he wrote his famous work *On the Law of War and Peace* (1625) at the court of Louis XIII of France.[2]

In this situation, many minorities who cared about their religion chose to emigrate. The Pilgrims famously tried Holland first, rejecting it only after they saw that their children were growing up speaking a foreign language. In 1620, their three storm-tossed vessels landed at Plymouth. Other Puritans came to the New World directly from Britain, a decade or so later. By the 1630s, Massachusetts contained several thriving settlements, including those at Boston, Salem, and Plymouth.

Life was tough for the new settlers of Massachusetts Bay. They responded to hardship by trying to gain God's favor for their new colony—which required, as they saw it, establishing and sternly enforcing a religious orthodoxy.[3] By punishing, or banishing, those who disobeyed in word or deed, they hoped to cast impurity from their common life. The idea that a good community would be one that allowed all people to seek God in their own way took root only gradually and with great struggle.

This chapter traces that struggle, focusing on the life and ideas of one of the century's great apostles of religious liberty and fairness, Roger Williams, founder of the colony of Rhode Island and seminal writer about the persecuted conscience. American writings about religious liberty were in conversation with similar work in England, and there are striking similarities between the arguments used in Williams's two most influential books (published in England in 1644 and 1652) and those used later and more famously by John Locke. Nonetheless, the American tradition has some distinctive features that ultimately proved valuable in forging our constitutional heritage. We should not focus only on the eighteenth-century arguments of the framers, ignoring this prior, and distinctively American, tradition, quintessentially embodied in Williams's *The Bloudy Tenent of Persecution* (1644).

The tradition Williams inaugurated contains, first, a distinctive emphasis on the importance of a mutually respectful civil peace among people who differ in conscientious commitment. The vulnerability of all Americans in the perilous new world they had chosen led to a recognition (which came much slower in Europe, if indeed it has come at all) that people with different views of life's ultimate meaning and purpose really needed to learn to live together on decent terms if they were to survive at all. Williams dramatizes this idea from the start by making his work a dialogue between two friends called Truth and Peace, in which Truth acknowledges the deep importance of finding a way to live on terms of mutual respect with people whom one believes to be in error.

The second distinctive feature of the American tradition is a personal, and highly emotional, sense of the preciousness and vulnerability of each individual person's conscience, that seat of imagination, emotion, thought, and will through which each person seeks meaning in his or her own way. The experience of both solitude and space that the wild world conveyed to its new inhabitants brought with it a picture of human life as a risky and lonely quest. The idea that we are all solitary travelers, searching for light in a dark wilderness, led to the thought that this search, this striving of conscience, is what is most precious about the journey of human life—and that each person—Protestant, Catholic, Jew, Muslim, or pagan—must be permitted to conduct it in his or her own way, without interference either from the state or from orthodox religion. To impose an orthodoxy upon the conscience is nothing less than what Williams, in a memorable and oft-repeated image, called "Soule rape."

This idea that each person's inner and intimate searching is a precious living thing that must be respected by laws and institutions went well with the idea that we have to learn to live together on terms of mutual respect. Conscience, and its strivings, were the proper object of that respect. The free conscience, and the civil peace it requires, became the foundation of America's distinctive approach to religious liberty and equality. The equal status of religious minorities was its most persistent concern.

I. This "wild and howling land"

Life in New England was fragile and exposed. If people did not die on the voyage to the new land, they knew well that they might die shortly in it, whether from starvation, disease, or cold, or at the hands of the native inhabitants, whose claims to the land they utterly ignored.[4] On the dubious authority of a land claim made by James I, they grasped for security, alleging that the land was their own because Englishmen first discovered it—something that Roger Williams called a "solemne publick lye." He added the sarcastic comment, "Christian kings (so calld) are invested with Right by virtue of their christianitie to take and give away the Lands and Countries of other men."[5] The Puritan settlers' campaign to make themselves secure by denigrating and depriving the "pagans" was a bad early sign of other persecutions to come.

The world around them really was alarming. The wind, the seas, the forests, the deep snows—all this was very strange to people accustomed to life in England, whether urban or rural. "But oh poore dust and Ashes," Roger Williams wrote of himself and his fellows, "like stones once roling downe the Alpes, like the Indian Canoes or English Boats loose and adrift, where stop we until infinite mercy stop us."[6] In his remarkable *A Key into the Language of America*, a study of Indian life and languages written during a sea voyage back to England in 1643, Williams ponders the Indians' ability to coexist with impermanence and constant vulnerability in "this wild and howling land." He finds it astonishing that the Indians do not mind picking up and moving on to a new place, whenever climate, or insects, or sheer inclination moves them. "I once in travel lodged at a house, at which in my returne I hoped to have lodged againe there the next night, but the house was gone in that interim, and I was glad to lodge under a tree."[7] This sense of life as utterly transient, as requiring reinvention at every moment, deeply shaped the new Americans' culture and, ultimately, their religious sensibilities.[8]

The Indians may have made their peace with transience; the Puritan settlers, used to a very different sort of existence, resisted. To keep the "howling land" at bay, they found it prudent to shore up the structures of order within their communities, seeking comfort in homogeneity and discouraging spontaneous outbursts of personal will. New England child-rearing practices strongly discouraged expressions of autonomy, suppressing the usual crises of human maturation, the search for identity that is a commonplace of childhood, and especially adolescence, in many cultures.[9] Historian John Demos concludes that "New England children encountered in earliest life a strenuous resistance to their deepest autonomous strivings" as they heard "from all sides the Puritan message of 'peace,' of 'harmony,' of submission—with its corollary warnings against anger and the open assertion of self."[10]

Meanwhile, the public religious life of the community focused intently on constructing and enforcing orthodoxy of religious belief, expression, and practice. Orthodoxy was comforting to storm-tossed people. It seemed to mean shelter, an absence of storminess within.

Enforcing orthodoxy, however, required the suppression of dissent. John Cotton (1595–1652), pastor of the First Church of Boston, one of Massachusetts's most influential religious leaders and Roger Williams's lifelong intellectual adversary, wrote copiously in defense of religious persecution, arguing that it was necessary for civil order. It was also God's will, he said, in order to separate the diseased element of society from the healthy element. As he and

Williams wrangled endlessly about whether people diverse in faith could co-exist peacefully in civil society, Cotton maintained again and again that the wholesome parts of a community cannot but be corrupted by the presence of heretics and dissidents, unless those people are brought to judgment, punished, and, if unrepentant, banished. Such people are like Satan in our midst. Even if they behave peaceably like ordinary citizens, they will be covert enticements to sin. In works such as *Democracy as Detrimental to Church and State* (1636) and *The Way of the Churches of Christ in New England* (1645), Cotton defended a stringent and exclusive picture of theocratic community. This same view is the basis for his book-length attack on Williams, *The Bloody Tenet Washed and Made White in the Blood of the Lambe: being discussed and discharged of bloud-guiltinesse by just Defence* (1647).[11]

Cotton's rhetoric is animated by an intense hatred of sin and a fervent desire to distance his people from it. His emphasis on people's inherent sinfulness neglects the equally central Christian idea that human beings are made in the image of God. Williams repeatedly charges him with neglect of the Christian virtues of "meeknesse and gentlenesse toward all men" (BT 92). Cotton's pro-persecution position—the intellectual doctrine that Williams calls "the bloudy tenent of persecution"—fights, Williams says, against the "spirit of Love, Holines, and Meeknes by kindling fiery Spirits of false zeale and Furie" (BTY 494). Williams's summary conveys an accurate sense of the spirit as well as the content of Cotton's pro-persecution arguments.

Sometimes the desire to keep sin at bay did not content itself with persecution and banishment. The vivid sense of Satan's presence in the community found frequent expression in the hunting of witches. Both Massachusetts and (the similarly Puritan and even more orthodox) Connecticut,[12] throughout this period, experienced repeated upheavals over allegations of witchcraft and trials of alleged witches. We tend to remember only the famous case of Salem, made mid-twentieth-century metaphor in Arthur Miller's *The Crucible*. But Salem, though extreme, was not atypical: the hunting and trying of witches was a common phenomenon throughout the seventeenth century, both in New England and in Europe.[13] In New England, the typical accused—Satan's alleged ally in the community—was a person unusually vulnerable, by low socioeconomic class and/or unpleasant personality.[14] The most typical sort of accuser—the witch's alleged victim—was, more surprisingly, not a pubescent girl, although Salem has made this case famous. Far more common were accusations by young adult men just setting out in the world to make a life for themselves, and not yet married.[15] (Marriage in New England tended to be late for men, whose fortunes had to be securely established first.) Young men were perhaps the most insecure group in Massachusetts and Connecticut society—expected to become financially secure, but not yet confident in their control over the necessary things of life. In their remarkable and detailed allegations of attacks by a witch, who is said to torment their bodies and control their actions, such young men externalize their own vulnerability. They are not insecure because life is hard: no, it is someone else's fault, the doing of some stigmatized outsider. If only this person can be removed from the community, they will have the secure control they seek. As Demos says, "The entire situation is complex and keenly felt—and *vulnerability* is right at the heart of it."[16]

As we shall see, Americans have a recurring tendency to seek the comfort of orthodoxy during times of stress. Minorities often suffer from these anxious impositions of order. Cotton's seductive metaphor of a taint or stain in our midst that must be removed if we are to resist corruption is still with us. Continual vigilance is required lest anxiety triumph over the spirit of love and peace. That is why the Puritan experience, and Williams's response, are so important to ponder. When we find ourselves strongly inclined to use Cotton's purifying rhetoric, we should at least consider the possibility that what we fight in others is actually something about ourselves that is difficult to bear, some loneliness and harshness about human life that make us feel small, afraid, and victimized.

Williams shows us a different way of living with uncertainty, a way involving civil peace and equal respect for each person's conscience. Moreover, although Williams's personal influence was uneven, the general spirit of his writings became the dominant ethos of the colonies, as ideas of religious liberty and fairness gradually took hold even where Williams's name would have brought nothing but scowls. He pointed to features of human experience that were vivid to the new settlers in any case; thus people who did not revere him ultimately discovered the wisdom of his position on their own. By the time of the Founding, America had evolved considerably, if not under Williams's direct influence, at least in the spirit of his life and work. During a period in which there were fifty prosecutions for witchcraft in Massachusetts and forty-three in Connecticut (where orthodoxy was even more severe), there were no such trials in Rhode Island, the colony that Williams founded.[17]

II. "To ship my selfe all alone in a poore Canow": Williams's Rhode Island

Roger Williams is typically remembered as a religious and political leader rather than as a thinker—an odd kind of zealot bent on purity, who managed to found and successfully run a colony. If his ideas are remembered at all, he is identified with one (uncharacteristic) phrase he used once in a letter, the "wall of separation" between religion and state, rather than for his careful and extensive arguments about the evils of persecution, the primacy of individual conscience, and the appropriate jurisdictions of the civil and the religious spheres. Although he is a systematic thinker of considerable originality, his ideas are rarely set out with care, and the relationship of those ideas to those of more famous seventeenth-century philosophers, Locke in particular, is rarely appreciated—although his important writings of the 1640s anticipate Locke's 1689 *A Letter Concerning Toleration* in every major point.[18]

Some who invoke Roger Williams's name neglect his voluminous philosophical writings. Thus, it is often said that Williams is primarily concerned to protect religion from the impurity of state power and that he is not concerned about protecting the state from the churches, or about protecting individuals from domination in religion's name. One source of this error is Mark Howe's influential *The Garden and the Wilderness*. Citing only one passage in one letter, Howe writes, "When the imagination of Roger Williams built the wall of separation, it was not because he was fearful that without such a barrier the arm of the church would extend its reach. It was, rather, the dread of the worldly corruptions which might consume the churches if sturdy fences against the wilderness were not maintained."[19] Howe draws large conclusions from this claim: that the First Amendment is best read as protecting churches from state interference, and that much of our Supreme Court jurisprudence has therefore been mistaken, insofar as it construes the amendment also to prevent churches from overreaching in the public domain. Howe's idea about Williams has even made its way into the best casebook on religion and the First Amendment (although the book does not endorse his larger theory of constitutional meaning).[20]

Howe's claim about Williams, however, is so inaccurate that a reading of only a random few of the nine hundred pages he wrote on the topic of religious freedom (to which we can add close to a thousand pages of letters, most on this topic) would quickly refute it: Williams is concerned above all with the individual soul or conscience, which he wishes to free from persecution both by churches and by state officials acting in religion's name, so that it can find its own way to God. In the process he has a great deal to say about the danger that churches will overreach in the public domain, and a great deal to say about the need to keep the political domain free from religious orthodoxy.

An equally odd error about Williams, though from a writer who has a deep understanding of some of Williams's work, is the claim that Williams's dominant emotion is a "longing for the purifying inferno."[21] Although Williams does of course inveigh against the errors and corruptions of Cotton and his other opponents, his standard posture is that of a gentle and civil defender of the vulnerable soul. The attitudes he recommends and loves are those of mercy, gentleness, meekness, and civility; these words recur with obsessive frequency throughout the two philosophical dialogues that constitute his major works. The interlocutors of these dialogues are Truth and Peace—both of whom he loves and who evidently love one another. His very address to his audience is entitled "To the Merciful and Compassionate Reader" (BTY 33). His letters again and again urge the settlers of Providence to drop their quarrels and to adopt the spirit of peace. In both letters and treatises he repeatedly alludes to the goodness of people who go wrong in religious matters, appealing to us to respect them; the Indians in particular earn his deep admiration. It is Williams's opponents, not he, who wish to consign erring mortals to the fiery inferno. The "Bloudy Tenent," or bloody philosophy, is theirs, and he seeks to show how ugly and destructive it is. One may add that throughout his correspondence with some very angry and uncivil individuals, Williams invariably preserves a respectful and gentle tone. To friends he expresses love; to enemies he speaks with civility. Even when the foul-tempered Mrs. Anne Sadleir is consigning him and his friend Milton to a fiery hell, he tells her gently of his warm memories of her father's kindness.

Why is Williams so misunderstood? Locke's *Letter*, some sixty pages long, is ubiquitously read. In general what is written about it is accurate. Williams's works, both more original and, in some ways, more profound in their grasp of human psychology, are either ignored or grossly distorted. One reason for the difference is that Locke is famous for other philosophical achievements that on the whole interest philosophers more than does the subject of religious toleration. If he had not made great progress in the theory of knowledge and the theory of the social contract, we probably would know nothing about the *Letter*. Williams, by contrast, was obsessed throughout his life with this one topic and made no other philosophical contribution, his other intellectual contribution being his analysis of Narragansett language. The second reason is, surely, style. Locke writes succinct and beautiful English. His argument unfolds with no repetition. Williams's works, by contrast, are somewhat hastily organized cascades of argument. Rather like the Roman philosopher Seneca, but writing at much greater length, he does not hesitate to make a good point many times, hoping to wear down the reader's resistance. This trait helps explain why he is read without that gift for patience and attentive silence that Williams imputes to his Indian friends.[22]

Recent work on Williams has begun to undo these wrongs. Timothy Hall's *Separation of Church and State: Roger Williams and Religious Liberty*[23] gives Williams his just position in the history of thought and contains a fine treatment of many aspects of Williams's ideas, particularly his relationship to Locke's writings, several decades later. Hall, however, does not give the theme of impartiality and fairness the importance it clearly has for Williams. He also tends to attribute Williams's philosophical conclusions to the influence of his own peculiar religious beliefs. Williams, however, nowhere alludes to these beliefs in arguing for liberty of conscience—nor should he, since it is his considered position that political principles should not be based on sectarian religious views of any sort. It seems to me to be an advantage in a reconstruction of Williams's thought if it can show him to be consistent with his own principles, and this is easy to do, since Williams does not in fact use his own religious views as premises in his philosophical arguments.

But since Williams was a leader as well as a thinker, and since his work needs to be assessed in the context of his life and career, we must first recount his story.[24]

Williams was born in England, probably in 1603, to a prosperous merchant family. He grew up in London, near the Smithfield plain, where religious dissenters were sometimes burned at the stake. As a young man, he attracted the attention of the distinguished lawyer Sir Edward Coke, chief justice of the King's Bench. On a visit back to England in 1652, writing to Coke's daughter, Mrs. Anne Sadleir, Williams recalls that the great man "was often pleased to call me his Son" and speaks of the "honorable and precious remembrance of his person and the Life the Writings the Speeches and Examples of that Glorious Light."[25] (Mrs. Sadleir was unresponsive. A devout Anglican, she refused even to look at Williams's own writings and repudiated his gift of John Milton's *Eikonoklastes*—an indictment of the late Charles I—with the blood-curdling remark "[Y]ou should have taken notice of gods judgment upon him who stroke him with blindness. . . . God has began his Judgment upon him here, his punishment will be here after in hell."[26] We should bear in mind that this was the way in which people routinely thought and spoke about people, however excellent, whose religions differed from their own. That we do not speak this way so often today can be credited to the success of Roger Williams's arguments and to the institutions his arguments helped to create.

Coke arranged for the young man's education at Sutton's Hospital, the future Charterhouse School (an elite "public school" that focused on a classical education), and then at Pembroke Hall in Cambridge University, where Williams received his A.B. in 1627. Williams quickly impressed with his remarkable flair for languages, mastering Latin, Greek, Hebrew, French, and Dutch. In this way he made John Milton's friendship: he taught Milton Dutch in exchange for receiving Hebrew lessons. On graduation, Williams took orders in the Church of England and, in 1629, accepted the post of chaplain at Otes in Essex, the manor house of Sir William Masham—grandfather of the Sir Francis Masham who was Locke's host at Otes in the 1690s.[27] He married Mary Barnard, a member of the Masham household, in 1629.

Unlike Continental philosophers of the seventeenth century (for example, Grotius and Pufendorf), Williams does not cite the Greek and Latin classics often in his works.[28] Nor, indeed, does John Locke. That sort of heavy citation was not the English style; nor, perhaps, would a Puritan dissenter be eager to show reverence for pagan culture. Nonetheless, it is important to bear in mind that Williams received a first-rate classical education, of a sort that emphasized the doctrine of natural law that was becoming increasingly influential in both English and Continental law and philosophy. There is no sign that he knew Grotius's *On the Law of War and Peace* (1625), which derives a system of international morality from the thought of Cicero and Seneca. But he does share Grotius's historical formation: Coke was a strong defender of the idea of "natural law," that is, universally binding moral principles that supply constraints on positive law, and appealed often to the idea that there were binding moral principles behind positive law, to which positive law is answerable.[29] The Catholic natural law tradition built upon Aquinas (and Aquinas's use of Aristotle, though Aristotle himself does not have a doctrine of natural law). The Protestant tradition, by contrast, built primarily on Stoic ideas. Because these ideas were absolutely central to the eighteenth-century framers, we shall discuss them in the following chapter. Here it is sufficient to note that Williams, writing a century and a half before James Madison, nonetheless shared an intellectual heritage with him through the debt of both men to Stoic ideas. The core of the Stoic doctrine on which Williams was raised was the idea that all human beings are of equal worth in virtue of their inner capacity for moral striving and choice, and that all human beings, whoever and wherever they are, are owed equal respect.

In 1630, a leading Puritan reformer was placed in the pillory. One of his ears was cut off, one side of his nose was split, and he was branded on the face with the letters SS, for "Sower of Sedition." Later the other side of his nose was split and his other ear was cut off. For good measure, the man was then imprisoned for the rest of his life. Williams, who witnessed these events, and who was already very critical of the Anglican orthodoxy, decided that he could not live the religious life he wanted in England. He set sail for Massachusetts.

At first, Williams was warmly welcomed by the leaders of Massachusetts Bay Colony.[30] Although Boston found his views about the individual conscience too radical, he was welcomed by the congregation at Salem. He expressed his religious ideas freely. At the same time, he published a pamphlet attacking the colonists' claims to the Indians' property. The officials of Massachusetts Bay called him into court, but took no action when Williams agreed to withdraw the pamphlet. He continued, however, to teach the falsity of the colonists' property claim. He also urged resistance to a proposed oath of loyalty to be taken by all colonists. (He held that a religious oath should not be made mandatory by civil authority, thus anticipating one of the key claims in our Constitution.) During this period Williams spent some peaceful months at Plymouth, where he pursued his study of Indian life and languages.

By 1635/6, the authorities saw that Williams was bent on continuing his divisive teaching. They ordered his arrest. Tipped off in advance, he fled. Looking back on the incident from Providence in 1670, he describes it this way:

> . . . I was unkindly and unchristianly (as I believe) driven from my howse and land, and wife and children (in the midst of N. Engl. Winter now, about 35 years past) . . . I steerd my course from Salem (though in

Winter snow wch I feele yet) untl these parts, whrein I may say as Jacob,

Peniel, that is I have seene the Face of God . . . [31]

So begins the story of Rhode Island. In keeping with his sense of divine deliverance, Williams named the new settlement Providence.

A key part of the life of the new settlement was respectful friendship with the Indians. Williams had always treated them as human beings, not beasts or devils. He respected their dignity. When the great Narragansett chief Canonicus (who spoke no English) broke a stick ten times to demonstrate ten instances of broken English promises, Williams understood his meaning and took his part. When the colonists objected that the Indians could not own land because they were nomadic, Williams described their regular seasonal hunting practices, arguing that these practices were sufficient to establish property claims—a legal argument that strikingly anticipates very recent litigation over Aboriginal land claims in Australia. Linguist that he was, he reports having, at this period, a "Constant Zealous desire to dive into the Natives Language" (C II.750), and he learned several of the languages by actually living with them for long periods of time. "God was pleased to give me a Painfull, Patient spirit, to lodge with them in their filthy, Smoakie holes . . . to gaine their Toung etc." (*Ibid.*).

When Williams arrived as a refugee, then, his dealings with the Indians had long prepared the way for a fruitful relationship. Chiefs Massasoit and Canonicus welcomed him like an old friend, because he had befriended them before he needed them, and had given them lots of gifts for many years. He was already known as a good public debater in the Indian languages, "and there fore with them held as a Sachim" (751). One of the key provisions of the Charter of Rhode Island was that "itt shall not bee lawfull to or For the rest of the Collonies to invade or molest the native Indians . . . ," a provision that Williams particularly sought and, when granted, applauded, noting that hostility to the Indians "hath hietherto bene . . . practiced to our Continuall and great grievance and disturbance."[32]

Throughout his life, Williams continued these friendships. He helped the Narragansetts in their struggle against the aggressions of the Pequot tribe, daring "to put my Life into my hand, and Scarce acquainting my Wife to ship my selfe all alone in a poore Canow, and to Cut through (a stormie Wind 30 mile in great seas, every minute in hazard of Life)" (II.611). One gets the impression that Williams—a physically adventurous man, though also one frequently troubled by pain in his joints and limbs, very likely arthritic—enjoyed joining the Indians in these adventures with the elements. They were in many ways the truest friends he had. Despite his fervent Christian beliefs, there is no record that he ever tried to convert any of them, although he does take a keen interest in the theory of Portuguese-Dutch Jewish thinker Menasseh ben Israel—the same man who had influenced Cromwell to readmit the Jews—that the Indians are the lost tribes of Israel. As he wrote to the governor of Massachusetts Bay, explaining his refusal to return, "I feel safer down here among the Christian savages along Narragansett Bay than I do among the savage Christians of Massachusetts Bay Colony." Williams did not mean that the Indians were converts: indeed, he explains in *Key* that he did not attempt to convert them. The Indians' behavior, for Williams, expressed the Christian spirit of love more truly than did the severities of Massachusetts. He was fond of noting examples of Indian decency and honesty, contrasting their behavior with that of the English, or his Massachusetts neighbors.[33] "It is a strange truth," he wrote in *Key*, "that a man shall generally finde more free entertainment and refreshing amongst these Barbarians, then amongst thousands that call themselves Christians" (CW I.46). Near the end of his life, he recalled that he never denied to Canonicus or (his successor) Miantonomi "[w]hatever they desired of me as to goods or gifts or use of my boats or pinnace, and the travel [i.e. travails] of my own person, day and night, which, though men know not, nor care to know, yet the all-seeing Eye hath seen it, and his all-powerful hand hath helped me" (C II.754). Significantly, then, he imagines God as pleased by his generosity to "Barbarians." In one of his letters from England, he adds at the end: "P.S., My love to all my Indian friends" (C I.387).

Williams's experience of finding integrity, dignity, and goodness outside the parameters of orthodoxy surely shaped his evolving views of conscience. But there was already something antinomian about Williams, something that led him to those "smoakie holes" in the first place, a respectful curiosity about the varieties of humanity that is the archetype of something deep and fine in our traditions as a nation of strangers and immigrants.

Williams immediately provided for religious liberty in the new colony. The majority would make policy, but "only in civil things." Broad liberty of conscience was officially guaranteed. Rhode Island rapidly became a haven for people who were in trouble elsewhere; other settlements were founded.

Baptists, Quakers, and other dissidents joined the Puritan dissenters. In 1658 fifteen Portuguese Jewish families arrived in Newport. Although the Touro Synagogue—America's oldest surviving Jewish synagogue[34] and its first Sephardic synagogue—was not dedicated until 1763 (prior to that time, the Jewish community corresponded with rabbis in Europe), Jews enjoyed the same religious liberty granted to others—a fact that is astonishing when we note that Jews in Britain gained full civil rights only in 1858.

In 1643 Williams set sail for England to secure a charter for the new colony. During the voyage he wrote his book about Indian languages. While in England, he wrote *The Bloudy Tenent of Persecution*, replying to writings of John Cotton. The book, printed in London, was not *sui generis*, but it was a strong and very early statement of principles that we associate with Locke's 1683 work. A democratic charter was obtained, and the colony, uniting the diverse settlements under a single government, again proclaimed liberty of conscience. In 1652, Rhode Island passed the first law in North America making slavery illegal. By this time, Williams had been won over by the Baptists' arguments in favor of adult baptism; he was (re)baptized in 1639 and referred to himself from that time on as a "Seeker." Meanwhile, Cotton's angry reply to *The Bloudy Tenent*, published in 1647, led Williams to produce another work about a hundred pages longer than the first one, refuting all of Cotton's arguments. Published in 1652 in London (during another visit of Williams's to England), it bears the unwieldy title *The bloody Tenent Yet More Bloody: By Mr Cottons endevour to wash it white in the Blood of the Lambe; of whose precious Blood, spilt in the Blood of his Servants; and Of the blood of Millions spilt in former and later Wars for Conscience sake, that Most Bloody Tenent of Persecution for cause of Conscience, upon a second Tryal, is found now more apparently and more notoriously guilty.*

The civil wars and the Restoration made it necessary to renegotiate the charter. Williams again went to England, and found in Charles II a ready ally for his experiment in religious liberty. Williams notes that the Barbados already permitted religious liberty, by omission and policy rather than by explicit royal guarantee. "[B]ut our Graunt . . . is Crowned with the Kings extraordinary favour to this Colony . . . In wch his Matie declar'd himselfe that he would experimnt whether Civill Govrmnt Could consist with such a Libertie of Conscience."[35] With amusement he describes the shocked reaction of the King's ministers when they read the unorthodox document—"but fearing the Lyons roaring, they couch agnst their Wills in Obedience to his Maties pleasure."[36]

The charter was shocking indeed—not only in its odd provision regarding the Indians, but, above all, in its clause regarding religious liberty:

> [N]oe person within the sayd colonye, at any tyme hereafter, shall bee any wise molested, punished, disquieted, or call in question, for any differences in opinione in matters of religion, and doe not actually disturb the civill peace of sayd colony; but that all and everye person and persons may, from tyme to tyme, and at all tymes hereafter, freely and fully have and enjoye his and theire owne judgments and consciences, in matters of religious concernments, throughout the tract of lande hereafter mentioned; they behaving themselves peaceablie and quietlie, and not useinge this libertie to lycentiousnesse and profanenesse, nor to the civill injurye or outward disturbance of others; any lawe, statute, or clause, therein contained, or to be contained, usage or custome of this realme, to the contrary hereof, in any wise, notwithstanding.

What does the clause protect? Belief and the expression of opinion in religious matters, clearly. But Williams throughout his writings was very careful to insist that acts of worship also should enjoy protection. Indeed, in his own writings we rarely encounter the word "belief" without the word "worship" or "practice." In this chapter's epigraph, for example, taken from the introduction of *The Bloudy Tenent*, "consciences and worships" are all permitted. Elsewhere, he uses phrases such as "for either professing doctrine, or practicing worship" (BT 63), "doctrine or practice," "holdeth or practiseth," "doctrines and worships," "to subscribe to doctrines, or practise worships" (BT 63, etc.). It is a bit unfortunate that the charter is less careful, but we can understand the latitude of its protection from the other direction, as stopping where civil disturbance begins. The prohibited forms of disturbance are of two kinds: violations of the rights of others, and breaches of public order and morality. Williams was no John Stuart Mill: he thought that the business of civil government included not only protection of individuals from harm to their rights by others, but also the maintenance of public order and morality. Thus, like virtually everyone at this time, he favored laws against adultery and other so-called morals laws. Not, however, on religious grounds: his conception of public morality keeps it quite distinct from religious norms and justifications.

The final provision in the clause is very interesting: the charter guarantees liberty of religious belief and practice even when a law or custom forbids it. In other words, if law says that you have to swear an oath before God to hold public office, this law is nullified by the charter. Moreover, it appears that the charter nullifies the applicability of laws to individuals when such laws threaten their religious liberty. If a law says that people have to testify on Saturday, and your religion forbids this, then that law is nonapplicable in your case. In other words, it would appear that Williams has forged the concept of accommodation, which soon became widely accepted in the colonies. Laws of general applicability have force only up to the point where they threaten religious liberty (and public order and safety are not at stake).

This was not mere talk. Williams was notoriously skeptical about Sunday as the chosen day for no work. He had considerable sympathy with the theological arguments of the Seventh-Day Baptists. More generally, he saw the burden that comes with imposing a majority practice on all. Rhode Island had no Sunday law during his lifetime.

Williams had already alluded to this idea of religious accommodation in a famous letter to the Town of Providence written in 1654–65.[37] Using the classical trope that compares a society to a ship at sea, Williams imagines that "both Papists and Protestants, Jews, and Turks, may be embarqued into one Ship." His view of liberty of conscience, he now says, turns on two principles: first, that none of these passengers be in any way "compelled from their own particular Prayers or Worship, if they practice any," and, second, that the captain nonetheless has the authority to do all that is needed for the survival and safety of the ship. He can require passengers to pay their way (taxation), he can ask them to obey all orders "concerning their common Peace and Preservation," he can punish mutiny against the ship's civil authority. Williams leaves it unclear whether actual military service in violation of conscience could be required: all he says is that all should "help in Person or Purse, toward the Common Charges, or Defence"—leaving it open that some alternative service, or a cash payment, might suffice in such cases. (At this point he had not yet encountered Quakers, so he may simply not have thought about the issue.) What is important is that, by clearly stating that the captain must allow liberty of conscience up to the point at which the ship's peace and safety are threatened, he lays the foundation for a long tradition that, by the time of the Founding, was exemplified in most of the state constitutions.

Williams lived for almost twenty-five years after the new charter. The disruptive behavior of some Quakers put his principles under severe strain. Writing against their religion, he also objected so strongly to their practices of heckling others that he was sorely tempted to compromise his own doctrines, introducing some restrictions. He contented himself, however, with a book-length attack on George Fox, the Quaker leader (*George Fox Digged out of his Burrowes*, 1676). Williams died in 1684 at the age of eighty-one, and was buried on his own property. His remains are now lodged in the Roger Williams monument on Prospect Terrace in Providence, just at the foot of College Hill, the location of the main campus of Brown University—which, in 1745, became the first university in the colonies that had no religious test for entrance.

Rhode Island did not always stick to Williams's admirable principles. Sunday laws came in after his death, and even, for a short period, some restrictions on office-holding by Jews. Brown University, despite its admirable start, later required a majority of Baptists on the Board of Trustees. Its letterhead, to this day, shows four books emitting radiant light, not exactly an encouraging sign to the non-Christian faculty member. Nonetheless, Rhode Island stood out as ahead of its time. Seen by many pejoratively, as a disreputable and anarchical community, it nonetheless provided a model of religious fairness that the other colonies increasingly adopted, whether they were following Williams or simply learning his truths for themselves.

III. "This Conscience is found in all mankinde":[38] Williams's Defense of Religious Liberty

Behind this political achievement is a body of thought as rich, on these issues, as that of John Locke, and considerably more perceptive concerning the psychology of both persecutor and victim. At its heart is an idea, or image, on which Williams focused with deep emotion and obsessional zeal: the idea of the preciousness and dignity of the individual human conscience. Williams defines conscience as "holy Light," and as "a perswasion fixed in the minde and heart of a man, which inforceth him to judge . . . and to do so and so, with respect to God, his worship, etc."[39] Conscience, for Williams, plays the role that the faculty of moral choice plays in Stoicism, and has basically the same content, although it includes imaginative and emotional elements. Although he emphasizes its religious employment, it is plain that he conceives of it as a general power of choice, the directing capacity of our lives (like the Stoic *hegemonikon*). It is the source of our practical identity: It is "indeed the man."[40] As with the Stoics, this faculty is a source of universal equality among human beings.

Williams has his own very intense religious beliefs, and these beliefs entail that most people around him are in error. Error, however, does not mean that they do not have the precious faculty of conscience: "This Conscience is found in all mankinde . . . , in Jewes, Turkes, Papists, Protestants, Pagans, etc." And even though one thing that is precious about the conscience is its ability, ultimately, to find the truth, that is not what Williams emphasizes: what he reveres is the committed search, the sincere quest for meaning. "I commend that Man whether Jew or Turke, or Papist, or who ever that steeres no otherwise then his Conscience dares . . . For Neighbour you shall find it rare, to meete with Men of Conscience."[41] One can't help thinking of Williams's respect for his Indian friends when one reads passages like this. Furthermore, since he says that "men of conscience" (people who follow their conscience's promptings) are rare, but that conscience itself is in everyone, he clearly holds that the precious faculty of conscience exists even in less virtuous people, and that all deserve equal human respect. (Similarly, the Stoics hold that, although most human beings are "fools," the faculty of choice is present in all and is worthy of respect, though the person be in error.) Conscience, Williams holds (perhaps influenced by the Stoic ideas that were so prominent in his education), is the dignity of the person; it is, indeed, the person himself.

So: everyone has inside something infinitely precious, something that demands respect from us all, and something in regard to which we are all basically equal. That was a common though not universal view in his own day, a view put forward by the prevalent Stoic natural law doctrine in Britain and taught, with a different flavor, in many varieties of Christianity—though Williams gives it unusual emphasis and poignancy. In our time, the view has become even more widespread. Whatever our religious or nonreligious views, we tend to believe that all human beings have moral and spiritual faculties and that these faculties, whether we call them "conscience" or "soul" or "human dignity," deserve respect wherever they are found. This thought supplies, for example, the basis of the modern human rights movement. Catholic philosopher Jacques Maritain, who participated in the framing of the Universal Declaration of Human Rights, reports that it was possible to gain agreement about this basic idea among people from many different nations and religions. He himself found these ideas in the (Catholic branch of the) natural law tradition; people from China, Egypt, and other nations came to it from other sources.[42]

Williams now argues that this precious something needs space to unfold itself, to pursue its own way. To respect human beings is therefore to accord that sort of space to each and every one of them. He expresses indignation that someone "that speakes so tenderly for his owne, hath yet so little respect, mercie, or pitie to the like consciencious perswasions of other Men . . . Are all the Thousands of millions of millions of Consciences, at home and abroad, fuell onely for a prison, for a whip, for a stake, for a Gallowes? Are no Consciences to breath the Aire, but such as suit and sample his?"[43]

These images are revealing. They tell us that Williams thinks of consciences as delicate, vulnerable, living things, things that need to breathe and not to be imprisoned. There are so many of them in prison, all over the world. But all alike should have breathing space. Here, to my mind, Williams makes decisive progress beyond the Stoicism of his classical education. Stoic thinkers (and seventeenth-century thinkers influenced by this aspect of their thought) usually treat the moral core of the person as something rock-hard, something that cannot be damaged by worldly conditions. They therefore have great difficulty drawing any political conclusions at all from their arguments about respect for human dignity. Dignity is so secure within that even slavery and torture cannot affect it: so Stoic writings, beginning from a radical egalitarianism about worth, end up oddly quietistic. Conscience cannot really be coerced: all that power can wrest from it is a kind of insincere assent. Williams, by contrast, sees that the conscience is not invulnerable: it can be damaged and crushed, and it needs space to unfold itself. This insight is necessary for a workable doctrine of political liberty.

Williams has the very keenest sensitivity to any damage to this precious thing, comparing persecution repeatedly to "spirituall and soule rape" (BT 219). And it is "soule rape" when any person is limited with respect to either belief or practice (so long as he is not violating civil laws or harming others): "I acknowledge that to molest any person, Jew or Gentile, for either professing doctrine, or practicing worship merely religious or spirituall, it is to persecute him, and such a person (whatever his doctrine or practice be true or false) suffereth persecution for conscience" (BT 63).

To be more precise, Williams has two distinct images for persecution, rape and imprisonment, corresponding to different types of damage to conscience. Persecution is like imprisonment, in that people whose faculty of conscience is undamaged within still need breathing space to act on their conscience's promptings, searching for meaning through whatever forms of prayer, worship, or writing and speaking they select. But persecution is also like rape, in that it goes inside a person and does terrible damage. Williams clearly thinks that being forced to affirm what you do not believe can harm the soul in its very capacity to strive, deforming and weakening it (though it never destroys the basis of equal respect, because it never extinguishes utterly the capacity for striving).[44] So what is needed is, first, protection for the conscience so that it can grow undefiled, and, second, the creation and protection of a space around it so that it can venture out into the world and conduct its search.

Persecution is therefore a terrible error, one of the worst there can ever be. Williams explicitly says that it is a worse error than being a heretic (C I.348), and that "a Soule or spirituall Rape is more abominable in Gods eye, then to force and ravish the Bodies of all the Women in the World" (BT 182). Indeed, persecution is a doctrine "which no Uncleannes, no Adulterie, Incest, Sodomie, or Beastialitie can equall, this ravishing and forcing (explicitly or implicitly) the very Soules and Consciences of all the Nations and Inhabitants of the World" (BTY 495). Williams does not believe that the offenses to which he compares persecution are trivial—indeed, he is inclined to favor the death penalty for adultery. So we can see how strong his objection to persecution is, if it is worse than these things. Most rulers in all ages, he concludes, have practiced "violence to the Souls of Men" (BTY 12).

One of Williams's reasons for abhorring persecution is instrumental: if you force someone, it hardens their opposition, thus preventing their voluntary conversion, hence their salvation. He makes this point repeatedly when he is in *ad hominem* debate with John Cotton, and it was a common Protestant argument in the period, one that Locke makes central to his own case for toleration. One cannot read Williams's text, however, and doubt that Williams also thinks damage to conscience an intrinsic wrong, a horrible desecration of what is most precious about a human life.

Williams has insisted that this precious something is in us all, and is worthy of *equal* respect. Therefore, he now argued, it is a heinous wrong to give it freedom for some (the orthodox) and to deny this same freedom to others. Again and again, he hammers home the charge of partiality and unfairness. Magistrates "give Libertie with a partiall hand and unequall balance" (BT 401). How "will this appear to be equall in the very eye of Common peace and righteousnesse?" (BT 402). His own marginal summaries of his argument, particularly in the later work, keep recurring to this theme, saying "Unchristian partiality" (BTY 55), "Gross partiality to private interests" (BTY 113), and "Gross partiality the bloody doctrine of persecution" (BTY 290).

Williams has a keen nose for special pleading and unfairness, and he sees it everywhere restrictions on religious liberty are found. He suggests that the error of the persecutor is a kind of anxiety-ridden greed, which is hypocritically disguised as virtue. Each, anxious and insecure, aims to carve out special protections and privileges for himself by attacking in others what he most values in his own life. In his letter to the governors of Massachusetts and Connecticut (my second epigraph) he indicts them for a hypocritical and unfair set of principles—for worshipping, in effect, only the "great God Selfe."

If persecution is the worst of errors, liberty of conscience is, as Williams repeatedly states, a "most precious and invaluable Jewel" (BTY 30). It is for this "one commoditie" that "most of Gods children in N. England have run their mighty hazards" (30). If the psychology of persecution is an anxious selfishness, the psychology of liberty is "meeknesse and gentlenesse toward all men" (BT 92). The proponent of liberty does not indulge in special pleading. Even though he believes that he is right, he doesn't puff himself up, for he knows how difficult his quest is. He remembers God's mercy to him, and he has mercy to those whom he believes in error. He also has an evenhanded spirit of love, gentleness, and civility to all men, a civility that includes respect for their freedom.

In one remarkable passage Williams states that persecution is not only "to take the being of Christianity out of the World, but to take away all civility, and the world out of the world, and to lay all upon heapes of confusion" (BT 201). What does he mean by saying that persecution takes "the world out of the world"? I think he is expressing the view that the spirit of love and gentleness, combined with the spirit of fair play, is at the heart of our worldly lives with one another. Take these things away, and you despoil the world itself. You make it nothing but a heap of confusion.

Williams is an emotional writer. His sense of his own religion is deeply subjective and passionate. Nonetheless, it is not implausible to compare his core ideas to those that will animate the philosophy of Immanuel Kant a century later. (One link lies in the two thinkers' common debt to Stoic thought about human dignity and the importance of impartiality.[45]) At the heart of the thought of both men are two ideas: the duty to respect humanity as an end wherever we find it, and the duty to be fair, not to make an exception for one's own case. Kant's famous "Categorical Imperative" asks people to test the principle of their conduct by asking whether it could without contradiction be made a universal law for all human beings. This test shows us whether we have been partial to our own case. Williams's critique of the leaders of Massachusetts and Connecticut is that their idea cannot pass Kant's test: they love freedom—but only for themselves. They could not will persecution as a universal law, and their selfishness prevents them from willing freedom of conscience (which could pass the Kantian test) as a universal law. Kant's second test for ethical principles is one that he calls the Formula of Humanity: he asks us to test our principles by seeing whether they treat humanity as an end, rather than a mere means; we are to ask whether we are really showing respect to the dignity of human beings, or whether we are just using them as objects in the pursuit of our own selfish ends. This complaint, too, is a constant theme in Williams's writing: the conscience is precious, but people use other people's consciences to serve their own anxious and greedy ends.

Kant's third way of testing principles invokes the idea of autonomy. We are to ask ourselves whether we can view our principle as a law that we could give to ourselves. There is no precise echo of this part of Kant in Williams, but his insistence on the deeply subjective quest of the individual conscience, and the priceless value of freedom in this quest, is in great sympathy with Kant's way of thinking.[46] For both, we are capable of searching and choosing, and that freedom must be respected. For both, doing the right thing because of obedience to a law imposed from outside has no moral worth at all. Finally, Kant speaks of good principles as constituting a "realm of ends," a virtual society of free beings who respect one another as equals. I believe that this idea is very much what Williams is after when he says that persecution takes "the world out of the world": it destroys the basis of human fellowship in respect, free-dom, and civility.

Such ideas of fairness and respect continue to be central to the best work in recent political philosophy in the Western tradition. American philosopher John Rawls, drawing inspiration both from the history of religious strife and from Kant's ideas, has argued that the foundation for a just society must in-volve both impartiality and respect. He advanced a test for political principles that has a close relationship to Kant's thought—and, whether there is influ-ence or not, to the thought of Roger Williams. The thought-experiment that constitutes Rawls's famous "Original Position," in *A Theory of Justice*,[47] imag-ines people who must choose the political principles that shape their common life without knowing where, in the resulting society, any of them is placed. They are thus unable to indulge in selfish partiality. They are forced to choose principles that are fair to all, since any one of them might be anybody. Thus, Rawls argues, they will not design a society that favors only Christian wor-ship, because they might find themselves in the persecuted group. Rawls ex-plicitly says that liberty of conscience is one of the things reasonable people will value most, and that they will therefore not take any risk that they would end up being deprived of it, so they won't agree to allow the issue to be deter-mined by majority vote. It is too central. "[T]o gamble in this way would show that one did not take one's religious or moral convictions seriously, or highly value the liberty to examine one's beliefs."[48] So, if they can't be partial and fa-vor their own liberty, they will have to protect it for everyone. Williams's idea of impartiality is similar: the good colony is one that does not show partiality to majority religious interests, but is fair to all, majority and minority. Williams would have liked the praise of impartiality in the final sentence of Rawls's book: "Purity of heart, if one could attain it, would be to see clearly and to act with grace and self-command from that point of view."[49]

In Rawls's later book *Political Liberalism*,[50] which focuses on religion, he formulates the principle lying behind his doctrine of religious liberty in a very Williams-esque way, stating that equal respect for persons entails respecting their "comprehensive doctrines," the search for the meaning of life in which each person is engaged. Respect thus dictates wide and impartial liberty of conscience (and other liberties as well). Rawls represents himself as drawing from the entirety of the seventeenth- and eighteenth-century tradition of thought about religious difference. There is no sign that he is thinking about Williams, or has read him.[51] Nonetheless, Williams's ideas of conscience and impartiality are well articulated and further developed in Rawls's modern work.

All accounts of religious freedom based on an idea of the strivings of conscience must face the objection that they are themselves sectarian, grounding political principles on a distinctively Protestant set of ideas. There is a grain of truth in this charge in a historical sense: there can be little doubt that Williams came by his ideas because of his immersion in the Protestant tradition. We can, however, defend Williams by pointing out that his conception of conscience taps into intuitive ideas of the person that are very widespread, that are defensible independently of Protestantism, and that turn up, in different forms, in many religions and traditions. They are present in Greek and Roman Stoicism, and they also lie at the heart of the modern human rights tradition, which was crafted by people who came together from China, Egypt, Europe, and North America. By now, moreover, religious traditions that once made less of conscience than did the Protestant tradition have become more focused on the dignity of conscience: certainly contemporary Catholic doctrines lie closer to Protestantism in this regard than do some earlier Catholic doctrines, and Maritain feels free to make this sort of idea the linchpin of a modern nonsectarian human rights tradition that he, a Thomist Catholic, eagerly joins. Williams, moreover, is far more careful than Locke later is to avoid reliance on any doctrine that is distinctively sectarian. Locke relies often on overtly sectarian doctrines, and characterizes religion in a way that would seem very strange to Jews and many others. Williams, perhaps because of his awareness of the radically different religion of the Native Americans, is as careful as one could be not to make this error. Political principles must be based on ideas with a rich moral content. Williams does pretty well in expressing that content in a way that avoids specific theological and metaphysical commitment.

Williams, then, lies at the beginning of a distinctive tradition of thought about religious fairness that resonates to the present day. Compared to Locke, and in some respects Kant, Williams has an extra measure of psychological insight. He helps us see why persecution is so attractive and what emotional attitudes might be required to resist it.

IV. A "Model of Church and Civil Power"[52]

If Williams had offered only an account of conscience and its fair, impartial treatment, he would already have made a large contribution to our understanding of religious liberty. He accomplished much more, however, developing an elaborate account of the proper jurisdictions of religious and civil authority that anticipates Locke's more famous account and that still offers helpful guidance. In this part of his work, Williams is replying to a "model" of church and state proposed by John Cotton. Truth asks Peace what (book) she has there. Peace produces the Cotton manuscript, and reads from it the claim that the church must hold high authority in the civil realm, and should be superior to all civil magistrates, if the peace is to be preserved (BT 221–22). The two hundred pages that follow contain Williams's alternative "model." Notice that if Mark Howe were right, Williams should propose only that the state have no authority over the church; he should not be at all worried about the church having authority in temporal matters. Williams's argument, however, goes in an entirely different direction.

According to Williams, there are two separate sets of ends and activities in human life; corresponding to these are two utterly different sorts of jurisdiction, two sorts of authority. Civil or state authority concerns "the bodies and goods of subjects" (exactly the characterization that Locke later gives). Civil authority must protect people's entitlements to property and bodily security, and it may properly use force to do so (BT 148, BTY 188). (Unlike Locke, Williams has no worked-out theory of what people's entitlements in these areas are. We can see from his writings on Indian property rights that he did have views about the subject, but they were never systematically developed.) The civil law applies to all, including members of the clergy (BT 268). The foundation of civil authority lies in the people, and it is the people who are entitled, democratically, to choose civil magistrates (BT 249).

The other sphere of human life is that of the soul and its safety. Law and force have absolutely no place in this sphere, which must be governed by persuasion only (BT 148). Churches and their officers have this sphere as their jurisdiction (BTY 188), but with the proviso that their only proper means of addressing the soul is persuasion. (Williams has much less to say about churches than Locke does, in keeping with his conviction that the primary responsibility for personal salvation rests with one's own conscience. He is simply rather skeptical of organized attempts to foster spiritual improvement.) The two sorts of authority, civil and spiritual, can coexist peaceably together (BT 223, BTY 40). Peace is in jeopardy only to the extent that churches overstep their boundaries and start making civil law, or interfering with people's property, livelihood, and liberty.

Williams now tells us that there is, of course, a way in which the civil state needs to make laws "respecting religion": namely, it has to make laws protecting it, saying, for example, "that no persons Papists, Jewes, Turkes, or Indians be disturbed at their worship (a thing which the very Indians abhor to practice toward any)" (BT 252). (He thus anticipates an issue that arose at the time of the constitutional framing, when states wanted reassurance that the First Amendment's Establishment Clause would not prevent vigorous legal implementation of the Free Exercise Clause.) Such protective laws are not only permitted, they are extremely important, "the Magna Charta of highest liberties" (BT 220). In this category Williams also places a tax exemption for churches (BT 252), taking a position in a debate about religious establishment that will later become heated. Williams does not even stipulate that the tax exemption would have to be given to all religions on the basis of some fair principle: here he sells his own ideas grievously short.

There is, he continues, another type of law "respecting religion" that is very different from these protective laws: the sort of law that establishes, or forbids, acts of worship, says who can and cannot be a minister, and so on. To say that these should be civil laws "is as far from Reason, as that the Commandments of Paul . . . were civil and earthly constitutions" (BT 253).

Locke later elaborated this distinction further, saying that the state is free to regulate matters concerning property, or health, or safety, even when they bear on religious organizations—so long as it does so impartially.[53] Thus, if the state wants to forbid adult baptism, it had better make sure it does so by an impartial health-related principle that forbids all bathing in water. If it wants to forbid animal sacrifice in a religious context, it can only rightly do so by the use of a neutral and impartial principle forbidding all animal killing of such and such a type. If it is permitted to speak Latin in a marketplace, it must be permitted to speak Latin in a church. In other words, there is an area of church conduct that touches on matters of property and health that the state rightly regulates, but the state must not regulate such matters with partiality toward the dominant religion. In making this explicit, Locke articulates well the spirit of Williams's idea. Locke also grants that there are areas where the jurisdictions of state and church would appear to overlap, for example marriage and the family.[54] Like Williams before him, he says little about how to sort things out in these cases.

Locke diverges from Williams by explicitly insisting that once a generally applicable law has been made by an impartial principle in a sphere the state rightly regulates, people may have no dispensation from that law for religious reasons. If their conscience leads them to disobey, they will just have to pay the price and go to jail.[55] Locke is rather harsh here, and perhaps he speaks too hastily, without thinking of the myriad ways in which generally applicable laws typically favor majorities and disfavor minorities. Were he to consider carefully such cases as forcing Jews to testify on the Sabbath, forcing Quakers to remove their hats in court—cases where there is no compelling state interest that is served by coercion, and a solution could easily be found that would be less burdensome to the minority—it is difficult to believe that someone as attached to fair-mindedness in religious matters as Locke is would not have favored at least some latitude for "accommodation." Whether it would have extended to the refusal of Quakers to perform compulsory military service, and other matters of greater public moment, is unclear. In any case, Williams is not Locke; his chosen wording in the Rhode Island Charter and in his ship-of-state letter suggests that he is sympathetic to the idea of accommodation, where peace and safety interests are not at stake. Generally applicable laws will not be valid, insofar as they infringe religious liberty, except where such momentous interests are in play.

Apart from the issue of accommodation, Williams and Locke have similar pictures of civil and religious jurisdiction. Both make the point that to mingle the two jurisdictions is to harm them both, or as Williams says, to "confoun[d] and "overthro[w] the puritie and strength of both" (BTY 496).

John Cotton makes two claims that Williams must answer, if he is to defend his radical position well. First, he makes a claim about peace and stability: people simply cannot live at peace with one another unless some religious orthodoxy is established. Many people thought this way in the seventeenth and eighteenth centuries. Jean-Jacques Rousseau, for example, says in *The Social Contract* (1762) that "it is impossible to live at peace with those one believes to be damned,"[56] and he makes this claim the foundation of a highly illiberal set of requirements for a compulsory "civil religion" in his model society, enforced by both banishment and harsh, even capital, punishment. Cotton's view, then, remained popular for a long time to come.

In response, Williams invokes both reason and experience on his side. People with false religious views, he says, may be perfectly decent and peaceable citizens. We can see this all the time: that people do live together peacefully, so long as they respect one another's conscience-space. (Once again, life with the Indians provides a handy illustration.) What really breaks the peace is persecution: "Such persons onely breake the Cities or Kingdomes peace, who cry out for prison and swords against such who crosse their judgement or practice in Religion" (BT 79, often repeated). In general, he insists, "there is no other prudent Christian Way of preserving peace in the World but by permission of differing Consciences."

Here again, Williams's thought proves a striking anticipation of a key idea in recent discussions of religious fairness in twentieth-century political philosophy. In *Political Liberalism*, referring to the experience of Europe, Britain, and the colonies in the seventeenth and eighteenth centuries, John Rawls says that we have learned that a society cannot remain stable without the constant use of violence and suppression unless people's "comprehensive doctrines" are respected, and respected impartially, with ample and equal liberty for all. History, he argues, has shown us that any sort of imposed religious orthodoxy that limits liberty leads only to a grudging *modus vivendi*, accepted by the underdog only because he thinks that someday he may be the top dog, able to oppress others.[57] That sort of grudging and temporary allegiance, however, is not a good basis for civil society.

Williams had not seen all the history that Rawls could see, but he understood what he saw keenly and presciently. He refers repeatedly to history, both ancient and recent, using examples of many different sorts that support his case. Williams knew of no example of the other sort: he believed his idea of complete religious liberty, duly protected by law, to be utterly new. (The best he saw elsewhere was an informal regime of toleration, such as apparently existed in the Barbados.) Examples that might have informed the positive side of his argument—for example the tolerant policies of the Indian emperor Ashoka in the second century BCE, or those of Moghul ruler Akbar (1542–1605) shortly before Williams's own time—may have remained unknown to him (although Akbar's achievements were widely recognized in seventeenth-century

England[58]). He reasonably suggests, however, that the old way, Cotton's way, has not worked. People love power and domination too much. Williams's emphasis on people's capacities for political decency does not prevent him from seeing clearly the motives that can deform any decent politics. In his view, the strength of sin is another argument in favor of liberty and nonorthodoxy.

As we have seen, Williams allows some limitation on religious liberty, when peace and safety are at stake. Keen psychologist that he is, however, he repeatedly stresses the danger of hypocrisy in making judgments in this regard.[59] The doctrine of persecution, he says, has all sorts of "Winding Staires and back dores" (BTY 529)—one of which is the constant claim of the would-be persecutor that heretics are threatening peace and stability. Religious liberty must therefore have extremely ample protection, and the threat to stability must be extremely evident, in terms of a manifest breach of *civil* peace, if there is to be any legitimacy to state infringement.

The other argument of Cotton's on which Williams focuses is an argument about competence. Cotton claims that being a good citizen and being a good civil magistrate are inseparable from having the right religion. We simply do not want our public life to be run by sinners, because they are making very important decisions, and if they are sinners they will do so sinfully and badly. Here Williams makes one of his most interesting and novel arguments. God has created different sorts of things in the world, he says, and there are "divers sorts of goodness" corresponding to these different sorts of thing. He illustrates this point at length, talking about the goodness of artifacts, plants, animals, and so on (BT 245). One of the ways God created diversity in the world was to create a type of "civill or morall goodness" that is "commendable and beautifull" in its own right, and that is distinct from spiritual goodness. It can be there in its full form, and be beautiful, even if the person is religiously in error, even "though Godlines which is infinitely more beautifull, be wanting" (BT 245). What is needed to be a good subject in a civil state is the moral sort of goodness, and it is that sort, as well, that we need in our civil magistrates. Later, returning to the point, he insists that the foundation of the magistrate's authority "is not Religious, Christian, &c. but naturall, humane and civill" (BT 398). For many activities in human life, a worldly foundation is sufficient: "a Christian Captaine, Christian Merchant, Physician, Lawyer, Pilot, Father, Master, and (so consequently) Magistrate, &c. is no more a Captaine, Merchant, Physician, Lawyer, Pilot, Father, Master,

Magistrate, &c. then a Captaine, Marchant, &c. of any other Conscience or Religion" (BT 398–99). Particularly surprising is his casual mention of "father" as one of those roles whose duties can be faithfully and fully executed independently of spiritual enlightenment.

What are the duties of a civil magistrate who is also a religious person, when dealing with matters involving religion? Williams says that such a person, toward the religion he believes to be true, owes that religion "a reverent esteeme and honorable Testimonie"; second, he owes it his own personal spiritual submission; third, he owes the officials of that religion protection from violence against their person, and also protection of their "estates from violence and injurie." Toward a religion that he believes false, he does not owe any approbation, but he does owe it "permission . . . for public peace and quiet sake." Second, he owes "protection to the persons of his Subjects (though of a false worship) that no injurie be offered either to the persons or goods of any" (BT 372–73).

There is a good deal in this important passage that is unclear. For example, Williams does not tell us how and in what contexts the magistrate would properly show "approbation" to his own religion; he does not help us to draw the line between a personal statement and an illegitimate public endorsement or establishment. Nonetheless, what is most on Williams's mind is very clear: the magistrate owes the same protection to all citizens, against violence and property crime, whether he likes their religion or not.

In short, for Williams the civil state has a moral foundation, but a moral foundation need not be, and must not be, a religious foundation. The necessary moral virtues (honesty is one to which Williams devotes special emphasis) can be agreed on and practiced by people from all sorts of different religions. To be sure, he adds, a person's religion will connect these moral virtues to higher ends (BT 399), but so far as the moral sphere itself goes, orthodox and dissenter, religious and nonreligious, can agree.

It is not fanciful to see here an adumbration of John Rawls's idea of civil society as involving a set of "freestanding" moral principles concerning which people from different "comprehensive doctrines" can join in an "overlapping consensus."[60] Like Williams, Rawls stresses that political society has a moral foundation. But he holds that this is a "module" that can be linked to different religious doctrines and metaphysical justifications in a variety of different ways. Although people will frequently feel that their religion provides the moral principles with their highest ends or deepest sources (here again he agrees with Williams), they can nonetheless agree about the moral terrain in a way that is, for practical purposes, "freestanding," that is, not requiring the acceptance of a religious orthodoxy or a particular type of metaphysical or religious justification. So we don't have, exactly, a "wall of separation" between people's religions and their political principles. (Recall that Williams used that phrase only once, and in a letter, not at all in his major writings.) We do have separation of jurisdictions between church and state, but where people are concerned, they will rightly see the morality of public life as *one part* of their "comprehensive doctrine"—a part, nonetheless, that they can share with others without converting them to what they take to be the true religion.

This idea is a much more helpful idea to think with than the bare idea of "separation," which might suggest that the state doesn't have anything to do with the deep ethical matters that are so central to the religions. The state needs to be built on moral principles, and it would be weird and tyrannical to ask religious people to accept the idea that moral principles are utterly "separate" from their religious principles. The idea of an overlapping consensus, or, to put it Williams's way, the idea of a moral and natural goodness that we can share while differing on ultimate religious ends, is an idea that helps us think about our common life together much better than the unclear and at times misleading idea of separation. We must respect one another's freedom and equality, the deep sources of conscience that lead us through the wilderness of life. We will only do this if we keep religious orthodoxy out of our common political life. But we can, and must, base that common life on ethical principles that, for many of us, also have a religious meaning and a religious justification. All we need to do, when we join with others in a common political/moral life, is to acknowledge that someone might actually have those ethical virtues, in the way that is relevant for politics, while not sharing our own view of life's ultimate meaning. If we once grant that, then Williams's other argument concerning fairness and impartiality will lead us to want a state that has no religious orthodoxy, that is, just in that sense, "separate" from religion.

Williams's claim about the independence of the moral virtues would have been surprising to the Puritans of Massachusetts Bay. We can find such doctrines in the history of Western religion. They are prominent, for example, in Judaism, where the central moral laws are held to be binding on all human beings, but the ritual commandments only on Jews. The Roman Catholic doctrine of natural law, and of the separation between the moral and the theological virtues, is another relevant source, to which Williams may be alluding by his use of the word "natural goodness." Nonetheless, most of his contemporaries were just not ready to hold such an open and generous view of the moral capacities of heretics and sinners. They simply did not think that someone who was not saved in their way could be a good and trustworthy person. Williams's life with the Indians, and the increasingly diverse and amicable life of his new colony, told him otherwise.

Williams was in the vanguard, but gradually the settlers of the New World were looking around and coming to much the same conclusion, with regard to virtue as with regard to stability. Good people just did seem to come in all colors, so to speak. The initial suspicion with which people always greet a stranger eroded on daily association over the years, until the oddest ways of doing things seemed like things that might be done by a good and honest person. If the Indians can be some of the best people ethically (and at least many Rhode Islanders thought this), what's to prevent us from finding goodness and political capacity in a Baptist, or even a Roman Catholic? The experience of living together gave Williams's radical doctrine strong support.

Looking back at the history we ought to agree with Williams and his fellow colonists. In fact, I believe that we do by and large agree with him. We usually are ready to separate the specificity of a person's religion from the kind of goodness we look for in a doctor, a lawyer, a teacher, even a political leader. Even state adoption agencies do not require religion, or any particular religion, of prospective parents. It is only when we are afraid that we start talking differently—associating Roman Catholics with groveling obedience to Rome, Mormons with wild sex orgies, Muslims with terrorism. One of the greatest dangers in our political life today is that Williams's valuable insight may be lost. It is in danger, certainly, when a person's personal religious beliefs are brought forward as key qualifications for high public office, as happened with the now-withdrawn nomination of Harriet Miers to the U.S. Supreme Court. The inquisitorial spirit of John Cotton lives on in our society. We need Williams's generous and respectful spirit now, as much as people needed it in 1644.

To summarize Williams's ideas, it will be useful to return to the comparison with Locke's later and more famous work. We can now make our philosophical account more precise if we compare Williams's thought to that of three later thinkers who are central to our philosophical tradition on such matters: John Locke, Immanuel Kant, and John Rawls. Locke probably knew Williams's work, and he spent a substantial amount of time working at Otes in Essex, the same noble house where Williams was employed as a chaplain. Kant certainly did not know Williams's work. Rawls probably did not read Williams, but he was a keen student of U.S. history, and understood well the framework that Williams had disseminated through his institutional designs. Despite the extensive similarities between the two works, we may point to six significant differences, all of which, I believe, redound to Williams's favor.

First, Locke never attacks the Anglican establishment; he seems to think that equal liberty is compatible with a religious establishment, so long as that establishment is benign, protecting liberty. Williams is keenly aware of the danger of religious establishments as threats to both liberty and equality: to liberty because a dominant sect will easily slip into curbing the conscience space of minorities; to equality because the very existence of an orthodoxy makes a statement that all citizens are not fully equal. Williams thus anticipates a Madisonian idea that we shall study in the next chapter.

Second, Williams gives us, in his discussions of conscience, an account of the moral basis of the political doctrine, telling us what equal respect is all about and why it is so important. There is nothing like this in Locke, at least not in the *Letter*.

Third, Locke and Williams, as we saw, have subtly different positions on "accommodation," that is, on the question whether laws applicable to all should contain exceptions for people with special religious requirements. Locke is in favor of the exceptionless rule of law, provided that the laws themselves are neutral. Williams is subtly different: he allows exceptions to general laws for conscience's sake, up to the point where the person's conduct would threaten peace and public safety. In so holding, he anticipates a norm that became general by the time of the Founding: all the state constitutions had Free Exercise Clauses with similar "peace and safety" overrides. The difference between Locke and Williams on this point anticipates the difference between Justice Scalia and Justice O'Connor (and others) over the issue of a judicial role in mandating accommodations.

Fourth, Locke argues from Protestant premises most of the time. He seems inattentive to the importance of coming up with arguments for toleration that all citizens can share. He even relies heavily on skepticism about religious truth, a view that many religious citizens could never endorse. Williams does refer to Christian norms at some places in his argument, but he tries hard to develop an independent ethical argument for his political principles, based on the dignity and vulnerability of conscience, the equal worth of all consciences, and the needs of consciences for ample space. His own religious views might have informed some of his ways of thinking, but they do not figure as premises in his arguments. No doubt he was used to talking about important matters to people who were pagan and Christian, Jew and Gentile: there was nobody around who shared Williams's exact beliefs, as he often stressed, and he felt that what politics was about was finding a basis for a common life among people who disagree.

The fifth difference between Locke and Williams lies in the way in which they conceive the space of the political. Locke speaks in terms of separation of jurisdictions. For him, religion and politics don't overlap at all. (As we have seen, he briefly acknowledges that they do in fact overlap in some areas, but he says nothing further on this topic.) For Williams, as we have seen, the different religious doctrines meet, and overlap, in a shared moral space. Each religious person will connect this moral space to his own higher religious goals and ends, but within that space, we are all able to speak a common language and share moral principles. I have argued that this idea of overlap is ultimately more fruitful than the idea of separation, which suggests to religious people that they must give up some ways in which their comprehensive doctrine links the political with the religious.

Sixth and last, Locke is not distinguished as a moral psychologist. He has nothing to say about why people persecute others. Williams does, tracing persecution to anxious fear and the accompanying desire to create security by lording it over others. He has a keen sense both of the inner life of the persecutor and of the inner vulnerability of the persecuted to something that is very like rape, an inner shattering of the soul's integrity and peace. He also understands clearly how people engage in special pleading to favor their own case while appearing to defend morality itself.

V. "Truth and Peace, Their Meetings Seldome and Short" [61]

Roger Williams anticipates many ideas that became current a century later. In effect, he already has hold of the whole family of principles that form what I have called the distinctive American approach to religious fairness. We see the Equality Principle in his relentless attacks on partiality and his insistence that the precious faculty of conscience resides equally in all. We see the Respect-Conscience Principle as an idea that suffuses his entire career: he is committed to the thought that respect for people requires respecting the space within which their conscience searches for meaning. The Liberty Principle, again, is one of the hallmarks of his work, and liberty of religion is that "precious Jewel" that is, for him, at the heart of all people's efforts in the New World. The Accommodation Principle is not yet much developed in his writing, but he understands its general spirit well. The Nonestablishment Principle is a keystone of his political career and is amply demonstrated in his writing, although he says relatively little about its dimensions, and appears not worried enough about matters involving tax benefits that will become central a century later. As Williams's biographer W. Clark Gilpin correctly states, Williams's ideas and principles, once stated, "developed a vitality and independent history of their own," influencing many people who were not at all aware of a debt to Williams, or who even thought they disapproved of him.[62]

Where is the idea of separation in all this, the idea for which Williams is famous? We can see that this is not a key idea in his writing. Instead, such separation as he does recommend between state and church is derived as a consequence of other more central ideas. The ideas of equality, liberty, and respect for conscience, together with the remarkable theory of natural moral goodness, entail the account of separate jurisdictions that does set up a degree of separation between church and state. But Williams clearly does not want separation for separation's sake. Nor, as Howe would have it, does he want it merely, or even primarily, to protect churches. His primary concern is to protect the individual conscience, and this seems to him to require a civil state that is not religious in character and that does not make laws regarding religion, except of the protective sort.

Looking back from our own time to the Founding, we often associate the constitutional idea of freedom of conscience, and the related idea of nonestablishment, more with Enlightenment rationalism and Deism than with their seventeenth-century precursors. But Williams's version of doctrines that later became part of the Enlightenment is distinctive in a number of ways, ways that continued to exert a deep influence on American thought and life, and that are valuable for us today. First of all, Williams speaks as an intensely religious person. Skepticism about religion is no part of his brief for religious liberty—as it is for Jefferson, who often said things about religion that seem dismissive or scoffing. Many Americans who have a hard time identifying with Jefferson's rather smug disdain for religiosity can find their own concerns well represented in Williams's fervent spiritual quest. His arguments show us clearly that one may be a deeply committed religious person while yet believing that fairness, and the worth of the individual conscience, require a wide and equal religious liberty and a ban on religious orthodoxies in state government. Truth and Peace love one another—although their meetings, as he ruefully says at the end of his second treatise, are "seldome and short."

Second, Williams's romantic and deeply emotional picture of the conscience, as a lonely and vulnerable traveler in life's great wilderness, is the source of a distinctively American set of religious attitudes that have deep roots in many of us and that are attractive starting points for political thought. Our tradition is very different from that of France and even England, much more protective of each person's space for both belief and religious practice, and much more skeptical of any kind of public orthodoxy or homogeneity. Williams's idea of conscience explains the roots of this tradition and shows why it is compelling. If we see things Williams's way, we will be strongly inclined to a delicate accommodation of religious needs in all citizens, as well as to scrupulous fairness and constant self-criticism in our pursuit of civil peace and justice.

The thought of Roger Williams is not a complete foundation for good political principles regarding religion. Williams thinks too little about the ways in which taxation can establish an orthodoxy; his doctrine of accommodation is promising, but underdeveloped. And of course, like all thinkers of his time, he has nothing to say about the equality of women. Nonetheless, he has ideas that proved immediately fertile, and deservedly, whether they came to posterity with his name attached or not.

Truth and Peace don't meet often. So often (they comment to each other) they meet up lovingly, only to be parted by the persecutor's sword, by hypocrisy and selfish partiality. But they have a surprise ally. At the end of *The Bloudy Tenent*, a third character makes her appearance.

"But loe!" says Peace. "Who's here?"

Truth replies, "Our Sister Patience, whose desired company is as needful as delightfull" (BT 424).

Patience utters not a single word, but she is clearly there. The year before, in his *A Key into the Language of America*, Williams had written eloquently of the patience of the Indians, who can sit silently for ages, waiting for what they want. "Every man hath his pipe of their Tobacco, and a deepe silence they make, and attention give to him that speaketh. . . ."[63] To his impatient world, Williams commended this example. Now, at the close of his great dialogue, Patience is represented as, in effect, an Indian, silent after the prolixity of her sisters, waiting for a time that may be very long in coming, a time of tender respect for the living conscience. Maybe, just maybe, people in New England will actually study that example and follow it, learning to live respectfully with one another in the howling world. In that silence, at the close of so much speech, rests Williams's hope for the future.

3

PROCLAIMING EQUALITY

Religion in the New Nation

If "all men are by nature equally free and independent," all men are to be considered as entering into Society on equal conditions; as relinquishing no more, and therefore retaining no less, one than another, of their natural rights. Above all are they to be considered as retaining an "equal title to the free exercise of Religion according to the dictates of conscience."

JAMES MADISON, *Memorial and Remonstrance Against Religious Assessments* (1785)

Democratic nations are at all times fond of equality, but there are certain epochs at which the passion they entertain for it swells to the height of fury. This occurs at the moment when the old social system, long menaced, is overthrown after a severe internal struggle, and the barriers of rank are at length thrown down. At such times men pounce upon equality as their booty, and they cling to it as to some precious treasure which they fear to

*lose. The passion for equality penetrates on every
side into men's hearts, expands there, and fills
them entirely.*

ALEXIS DE TOCQUEVILLE,
Democracy in America (1835)

Seventeenth-century thought about religion and the state already focused
on equality. Roger Williams's attack on religious "partiality" emphasized the
equal worth of each human conscience as a source of political principles. In
England, meanwhile, John Locke's influential *A Letter Concerning Toleration*
(1689) made the case for religious liberty in strongly egalitarian terms, concluding: "The sum of all we drive at is, that every man enjoy the same rights
that are granted to others" (69). Locke's doctrines of natural rights and the social contract gave a strong push, in general, to a more egalitarian politics.

During the eighteenth century, however, human equality became the touch-
stone of political life and thought. On the continent, Jean-Jacques Rousseau
argued that inequalities between human beings were social, not natural, in origin; they derived primarily from human greed and envy. Strongly influenced
by Rousseau, Immanuel Kant defended the idea that ethical principles must
be tested by their capacity to treat humanity with respect and impartiality.
Kant supported a thoroughgoing and evenhanded religious liberty, extending
even to atheists, whom Locke had excluded from the scope of his protections.

Meanwhile in Scotland, in work that had a great influence on the American
founding, philosopher Adam Smith used the idea of equality to argue for social
and economic institutions that are now essential parts of our daily life, radical
though they were at the time. In *The Wealth of Nations* (1776), Smith argued
that even a difference as great as that between a philosopher and a "common
street porter" "seems to arise not so much from nature, as from habit, custom,
and education" (WN 28–29).[1] He relied on this idea when he made his radical
arguments in favor of compulsory free public education (already practiced in
Scotland) and an end to laws that impeded the free movement of labor (such
as the requirement that workers register, and remain, in a particular parish).
Using similar arguments, he attacked the evils of British colonialism, both in
America and in India, with its annihilation of local self-government and its

creation of a merchant class at home who hijacked the institutions of government to protect their inefficient monopolies. In England, meanwhile, Mary Wollstonecraft argued in *A Vindication of the Rights of Woman* (1792) that statesmen and thinkers were inconsistent when they proclaimed equal natural rights for all and yet excluded women, confining them to the sphere of the home. Her work, ignored at the time, has by now become a classic statement of principle. Mary Astell (1668–1731) had already made similar arguments in the late seventeenth century, comparing the lot of women to that of slaves.

Especially in America at the time of the Revolution, the idea that human beings are equal—equal in worth and dignity, and more or less equal in basic natural endowment—was a, if not the, key political notion in terms of which all debates were framed. Wollstonecraft's proposal regarding women went on the whole unremarked—although Mercy Otis Warren, first historian of the Revolution and close friend of John Adams, criticized the male framers in similar terms. The equality of African-Americans was also not generally agreed on, and our Constitution notoriously permitted slavery, although opposition to the practice was at least as old as Rhode Island. Nor were the native inhabitants treated with the respect Roger Williams had shown them; here as elsewhere, Williams's radical ideas were centuries ahead of their time.

Despite these culpable inconsistencies, however, the idea of equality had considerable radical force, providing a rationale for rejecting monarchy and creating a republic—and for building a republic that did not contain various baneful types of hierarchy. As historian Gordon Wood puts it, "Equality was in fact the most radical and most powerful ideological force let loose in the Revolution."[2] He shows how this idea was used to dismantle aristocratic hierarchies of privilege that were a holdover, in the colonies, from an English monarchical heritage. On the plane of white male citizenship, at any rate, the idea of equality was a powerful engine for uprooting differences of status and class, where participation in the new republic was concerned. And the acknowledgment of equality as a key value laid the ground for later criticism of hierarchies of race and sex.

Salient among the rejected types of hierarchy was an establishment of religion, by which the framers meant governmental privileges, prominently including money raised through taxation, granted to one church or group of churches. Such establishments were seen as bad because they created a two-tier system of citizenship. Following the idea of equality, the framers of the

Constitution were led to a far more emphatic repudiation of religious establishment than Roger Williams had envisaged, rejecting unequivocally the idea of state financial support for a church or churches. If the seventeenth century was the century that forged our Free Exercise Clause, it was the eighteenth century whose politics forged our Establishment Clause. In the process, the characteristic American notion of religious liberty expressed in Roger Williams's writings was deepened and made more consistent with its motivating insights.

This chapter will trace the connection between thought about human equality and the rejection of religious establishments, prominently including financial subsidy for a church or churches. Focusing in particular on the thought of James Madison, the primary architect of much of the Constitution and certainly of its First Amendment, we will see that opposition to religious establishment was not inspired by disdain for religion or a desire to demote it to a lesser place in human life. For Madison (a devout and curious believer) and for most of his contemporaries, the issue was one of equality: establishments, however benign, create ranks and orders of citizens, defining the status of some as unequal to that of others. After studying the theoretical formulation of these ideas in Madison's famous *Memorial and Remonstrance* (1785), we shall see how these ideas went to work in the formulation of the First Amendment.

Although any constitutional amendment, and certainly this one, is a committee document, involving a plurality of voices and some compromise, and although Madison clearly did not get everything he wanted (for example, the application of his ideas about religious equality to the state governments), two wrongheaded historical views of the "religion clauses" should be rejected. One is the view, recently espoused by Justice Thomas, that the purpose of the Establishment Clause was only to defend state-level establishments from federal encroachment: it had nothing to do with individual rights. This view is false, because the opposition to establishment, throughout the latter half of the eighteenth century and in the thought of the framers, had a great deal to do with individual rights, specifically with the danger that some individuals would be ranked beneath others and would enjoy systematically unequal civil rights. This aspect of establishment was even more clearly understood by the time of the Civil War amendments, which is the relevant time when we consider the "incorporation" of the Establishment Clause, meaning its application to actions of state government (to be discussed in Chapter 4).

The other false view we shall examine is a view known as "nonpreferential-ism." It is associated with the late Chief Justice Rehnquist, who expressed it vigorously in dissent.[3] Nonpreferentialism is the view that the religion clauses only forbid the federal government to prefer one religious sect to another, and that they permit—and deliberately permit—government to foster *and finan-cially support* religion in a general way, giving it preference over nonreligion. Although it cannot be denied that some of the founders (for example, George Washington) supported nonpreferentialism, the history of the framing of the text of the First Amendment makes this view untenable as a view of that text's meaning: the framers explicitly rejected language that clearly stated nonprefer-entialism, and they endorsed language that was associated with the Madisonian tradition of a much more stringent prohibition of state support for religion. I would argue that, once again, equality was the primary reason: despite the so-cial good that could potentially be done by fostering a general religious spirit in society, the framers saw that any such state support itself created ranks and orders of citizens—especially in a nation in which, as we have noted, only be-tween 4 and 17 percent of Americans belonged, at that time, to any church (though most were in some way religious).[4]

These two positions presuppose an originalist or textualist view of consti-tutional interpretation. Thus if one does not endorse such a view, as I do not, one can ponder, instead, the general goals and purposes embodied in the con-stitutional text, as we best understand them today. Since these particular orig-inalist views, however, rest on a very unconvincing reading of the relevant history, it is worth exposing their faulty foundation; for then, it will be clear that even originalists have no reason to endorse them.

The framers did not have clear positions on every important issue. They thought a lot more about tax support for religion, for example, than they did about ceremonial invocations of religion; they treated the latter issue in an off-hand and unreflective manner, to Madison's considerable discomfort in later life. They did, however, lay down wise principles for us to follow and further develop, if the equality of citizens is something we care about.

I. Equal Worth and Dignity: The Stoic Background

Americans in the mid-eighteenth century were steeped in the texts of ancient Greek, and especially Roman, philosophy. Education both in Britain and on the Continent had always been strongly classical, and at this time texts in the Latin language were strongly preferred to those in Greek. Kant, for example, never learned Greek, and Adam Smith's lectures show a detailed familiarity with Roman thought that is absent when he talks in highly general terms of Plato and Aristotle. For the American founders, as for the modern thinkers whom they read (including Rousseau, Smith, and Kant), Roman political philosophy was of enormous importance and, above all, the philosophical ideas of Roman Stoicism, together with the Stoics' eclectic fellow traveler Cicero.[5] As Gordon Wood puts it, "People could not read enough about Cato [the Stoics' stock example of virtue] and Cicero."[6] Not only philosophically inclined writers such as Thomas Paine, but also the general educated public, shared this passion: thus playwright/historian Mercy Otis Warren could expect a warm response for satirical dramas that depicted various British officials as Roman tyrants and expressed Ciceronian ideas about the goodness of republican institutions.[7] The Stoics were never out of fashion. Roger Williams's seventeenth-century classical education clearly acquainted him with their ideas, as did the natural law ideas he absorbed from Coke, his mentor. Williams, however, does not refer to the Stoics or carry on his argument through their ideas, as Americans of the eighteenth century ubiquitously do.

The Roman writers whose works were all the rage included, above all, the Roman republican statesman, orator, and philosopher Marcus Tullius Cicero (106–43 BCE) and the influential politician and philosopher Lucius Annaeus Seneca (c. 4 BCE–65 CE), who ran the Roman Empire as regent during the youth of Nero. To a lesser extent, the founders were also aware of Roman Stoic philosophers Epictetus (first–second centuries CE) and Marcus Aurelius (second century CE) but these authors wrote in Greek, so they were less central. Of particular importance, outside philosophy, were the Roman historian Tacitus (late first–early second centuries CE), who movingly describes instances of Stoic resistance to imperial tyranny during the reign of Nero, and the historian and moralist Plutarch (first–second centuries CE), whose *Lives* of distinguished Greeks and Romans include biographies of Julius Caesar and his assassin, Brutus, that had already become the primary sources for Shakespeare's *Julius Caesar*. Plutarch was a Platonist who argued against many Stoic ideas, but his moral treatises are a major source for Stoic doctrines; moreover, the sort of Platonism he espoused in portraying virtue in his *Lives* had many points of commonality with Stoic ethics, the main difference being a greater activism in the face of social ills.[8]

What did Americans find in these works that so moved and fascinated them? Stoicism in Rome was not just an academic pursuit; it was a widespread social movement. Stoic ideas were diffused into the general culture to a degree unparalleled for a philosophical movement before or perhaps since—though the century we are considering, in America, runs a close second. Roman Stoic philosophers wrote for a general educated public, gracefully and eloquently. In return, they were widely read by that public, so much so that surviving letters of the period show people's earnest efforts to model their human reactions (to political strife, to reputational slights, to grief) on Stoic norms, referring especially to the paradigm of Stoic virtue, Cato. (Marcus Portius Cato was a real historical figure, a politician of the first century BCE, but his role as quasi-fictional character in works of philosophy and poetry[9] is more important here than his historical contribution.) People lived for philosophical ideas, died for them. The conspiracy in the year 44 BCE that led to the assassination of Julius Caesar, strongly supported by Cicero, was highly philosophical in inspiration. Leading conspirator Marcus Junius Brutus even auditioned potential conspirators by asking them some telling philosophical questions.[10] Both Cicero and Seneca, like Brutus, died violent deaths, fighting for republican institutions: Cicero, at the end of the republic, was assassinated by Marc Antony's henchmen after he delivered his famous speeches against the dictator. Seneca, living in the early days of the empire, was forced to commit suicide after an unsuccessful republican conspiracy against Nero in which he and his nephew, the poet Lucan, were both implicated. (Lucan's great epic *Pharsalia* is one of our most important portraits of Stoic heroism, in the person of its hero Cato.)

All this by itself was enough to move well-read and thoughtful Americans who were about to embark upon a perilous political course. Roman Stoicism told them that ideas could change history, and that republican ideas were worth dying for, even should their attempt to change things prove unsuccessful.

Even more gripping, however, was the specific content of the Roman ideas. The Stoics taught that every single human being, just by virtue of being human, contains a portion of the divine. Our ability to perceive ethical distinctions and to make ethical judgments was held to be the "god within," and our capacity for ethical choice makes the inner life of each of us spacious and deep, capable of searching and choosing. Ethical capacity is found in all human beings, male and female, slave and free, highborn and lowborn, rich and poor. And though people differ in ability once they are educated, the Stoics believe that in terms of innate equipment we are all basically equal, and all capable of attaining virtue by our own effort, given suitable education. The very capacity for ethical choice is so significant that its presence eclipses any differences of ability, even ethical ability, that we might encounter. Ethical capacity (often called "conscience" in later followers of Stoicism) is therefore worthy of boundless reverence; it is in effect the person, the core of our humanity. Wherever we find humanity, then, we ought to respect it, and that respect should be equal, treating the artificial distinctions created by society as trivial and insignificant.

More than most, the Stoics meant what they said: they campaigned for the equal education of women, and their ranks included one former slave (Epictetus), one foreigner from the far reaches of the empire (Seneca, born in Spain), and various women (whose writings unfortunately do not survive), not to mention the "new man" Cicero, whose nonaristocratic origins are a constant theme in his writings.

If these Stoic ideas sound familiar, given our discussion in the previous chapter, this is no accident. Stoic ideas played a large role in shaping at least some parts of Christian thought, and they played a major role in educating thinkers of the seventeenth, as well as the eighteenth, century. Dutch thinker Hugo Grotius quotes Cicero and Seneca more often than any other authors; they appear on almost every page of his major work *On the Law of War and Peace*. Stoic/Ciceronian ideas about human dignity and equality were the common currency in which people talked to one another. Although Roger Williams, unlike Grotius, rarely quotes from classical authors, and is obviously a deeply personal and original thinker, we should still read him against that background, which was surely the core of his first-rate English education. Cicero's *On Duties*, known as "Tully's *Offices*," sat on the desk of every English public servant, along with the Bible. Indeed, it was called "the Stateman's Bible." Adam Smith trusts his reader to recognize quotes from it without any footnote, alluding to Cicero the way we would to Shakespeare and the Bible. We should, then, hear Roger Williams's appeals to conscience in a Stoic, as well as a Protestant, context, or, rather, recognize that his Protestant context was steeped in Stoicism. Much later, Kant's appeal to impartiality, which I compared to Williams's, is explicitly patterned on Stoic models. Cicero's *On Duties*, Book III, contains an argument that is a direct antecedent of Kant's request that we test our ethical principles by asking whether they could become a universal law.[11]

The idea of human dignity, and of its boundless and equal worth, is the primary legacy of Roman thought to the world of the American Revolution.[12] What political principles and actions did it suggest? Cicero and the Stoics held that human dignity should never be abused by making it subject to the arbitrary will of another. For contemporary political philosopher Philip Pettit, this idea of "nondomination" is the key to American revolutionary politics, and marks America as the site of a distinctive type of political thought, one based on the idea that one should not be a slave, but a free man in that specific sense.[13] Pettit is correct in observing that the rhetoric of the period is suffused with a hatred of servitude and an intense longing for a politics of free, nondominated, men. I believe, however, that one can understand this emphasis on avoiding servitude more profoundly, and in a way much more pertinent to our thought about religion, if one goes behind nondomination to the notion of human dignity. It is because human beings have a dignity, are not mere objects, that it is bad to treat them like objects, pushing them around without their consent. And it is because human dignity is equal that it is abhorrent to set up ranks and orders of human beings, allowing some to tyrannize over others.

The Romans themselves derived a range of different political lessons from these ideas. Cicero, passionate defender of the Roman Republic in its waning days, believed that human dignity required republican institutions through which people could govern themselves without arbitrary tyranny. He defended the assassination of Julius Caesar in those terms. At the end of his life, when that attempt to salvage the republic had failed and tyranny seemed inevitable, he was deeply depressed, having lost, he said, the two things that he loved most in life: his beloved daughter Tullia (who died in childbirth during her third marriage) and the Roman Republic. He was not consoled by the thought that Augustus was a decent individual (as, in most ways, he proved to be). People were still subjected to the will of another, even should that will prove benign. Many of Cicero's friends fully agreed with him about the republic, whether they were Stoics or not. Some later Stoics, however, thought, or at least said—since freedom of speech cannot be said to be complete under the empire—that a decently accountable monarchy might be acceptable. Some wrote praises of "good" emperors, such as Trajan. One, Marcus Aurelius, agreed to be adopted and to become, himself, the emperor. The experience of empire showed, however, that Cicero was correct: once a monarchy is in place, nothing prevents it from turning in an arbitrary and oppressive direction. Augustus was followed by Tiberius, Caligula, Claudius, and Nero—all of whom were capricious and violent, in different ways and to differing degrees. The lauded principates of later "good emperors" such as Trajan, Hadrian, Antoninus Pius, and Marcus Aurelius were bracketed by the horrible persecutions of Domitian and Commodus. So it came to seem more and more reasonable for Stoic thought to ally itself firmly to the idea of accountable republican institutions. The two anti-imperial conspiracies reported by Tacitus clearly aim at the restoration of such institutions, as well as the termination of Nero's lamentable reign.

Stoicism also contained, however, the seeds of a more quietistic response, the response against which Roger Williams had rebelled. Because the Stoics taught that dignity was all-important and material conditions utterly unimportant, it was possible to maintain that the soul was always free within, whether or not institutions enslaved it on the outside. Seneca's famous letter on slavery (*Moral Epistle* 47) asks masters to show respect to their slaves, and to treat them like full-fledged and equal human beings; but it does not attack the institution of slavery, which Seneca plainly thinks compatible with a dignified free life within, so long as masters do not beat or sexually abuse the slave.

Americans clearly followed Cicero (and later republican conspirators) and, along with Roger Williams, repudiated the quietistic strand in Stoicism, holding that their equal dignity as human beings required an end to the British tyranny. More generally, they agreed that human dignity entails a politics of respect, in which human beings are treated *as equals* and in which they are not subject to "soule rape." Linking the Stoic idea of dignity to the somewhat more emotional and subjective Protestant idea of conscience, they held that in religious matters, people should not be subject to arbitrary whim and interference, on account of their conscience's dignity. Any acceptable account of religious liberty, moreover, would have to be one that guaranteed people *equal* liberty, on the basis of their deep underlying human equality.

Americans understood this politics of respect to require close attention to the symbolic realm, to manifestations of rank and hierarchy that construct unequal groups of citizens. They focused on equality of standing and its symbolic manifestations because they understood the Stoic legacy through the history of the European struggle against feudalism and class distinctions. So great was the American passion for equal respect that the public evidence of class and rank that was still ubiquitous in Europe was hateful to them. Feudalism's legacy could not be overcome simply by giving people equal access to various political privileges. It had to be defeated by a persistent attention to the ways government treats people in the public realm, the messages that government sends. Does it announce by its behavior that some citizens are worth more than others, or more central to the polity? Does it make symbolic statements that marginalize some and elevate others? Americans' attention to these matters, which strikes some Europeans as fussy and excessive, seems crucial in the light of the history of class distinctions, and Americans were determined to create a politics that undid these hierarchies, expressing respect in word as well as in deed.[14]

One more influential Stoic idea that will play a role, ultimately, in constructing our First Amendment is that of human beings as "citizens of the world," or "cosmopolitans." Stoics held that our fundamental kinship is constituted by our common possession of reason and ethical capacity. Political boundaries are superficial, just as wealth and class are. Patriotism is seen as compatible with cosmopolitanism, but cosmopolitanism strongly shaped the content of patriotism, making it more likely that the nation and its unity will be conceived of in ethical terms, rather than in terms of a common soil and heritage.[15] America has always been unusual among the nations of the world in just this way: we do not think that we are fundamentally people of a given race, or soil, or religion. We are held together by ethical commitments (to equal respect and the value of liberty) that transcend particular groups. New immigrants can join us without changing religion or ethnicity, coming to revere those values. Such "cosmopolitan" ideas came to be seen as the mark of the enlightened person.[16] They were not used so much to suggest a style of foreign relations as to suggest a way of thinking about the nation's own unity, in which blood, soil, and ethnoreligious homogeneity are not necessary to hold a nation together: common ethical and political commitments are the right way to cement a republic.

The ideas of human dignity and equality already suggested that a good political community would not establish a single church, tyrannizing over citizens who believed differently. Cosmopolitanism, however, suggested something further: that a religious establishment was not necessary to hold a nation together. The nations of Europe have not thought this way, for the most part. (In Chapter 8 we'll study some consequences of this for the treatment of Muslim immigrants.) Most of them still have established churches. France has a secular establishment that is more intrusive than any of the current European religious establishments, in that it requires a high degree of homogeneity of citizens in the public square. The very fact that the EU constitution almost contained reference to the European Union (EU) as a Christian body shows the extent to which Europeans are still inclined to think of nationhood as a matter of blood, soil, and religious heritage. (In India, which is like the U.S. in fashioning nationhood on the basis of political and ethical aspirations, not common blood and religion, the Hindu right has for years tried to import the European concept of nationhood, tracing their idea of "Hindutva" or "Hinduness" self-consciously to Germany, and arguing that the idea of a single preeminent religion is an essential condition for strong modern nationhood.[17])

The new nation did not think in the European way. Common ethical principles, above all a respect for the equal humanity of all human beings, would, the colonists believed, be sufficient to found a republic. Revolutionary America contained many different strands of thought. Some leading founders (Thomas Paine, Thomas Jefferson) were Deists, rationalistic and highly skeptical of traditional religion. Some (George Washington, Patrick Henry) had inclinations that we might today call "communitarian," seeing shared religious beliefs and practices as a good thing for the social fabric of a young nation. Some, like James Madison and many Baptists, Quakers, and other dissenters—following the lead of Roger Williams—were personally religious but highly skeptical of any association between religion and government. The idea of equal human dignity, however, bound all these diverse strands and people together. Whatever a nation might be, it must find institutional ways to honor the spirit of equal dignity. Eventually, even the communitarians granted that an established religion was not a good way to pursue this goal.

Cosmopolitan ideas also shaped a style of ethical discourse that strongly favored the emerging politics of religious fairness. From Smith and other thinkers of the Scottish Enlightenment Americans drew the idea that good world citizenship required the cultivation of a sympathetic imagination, so that we could see the humanity in one another across sharp divisions, prominently including religious divisions. Something like this is what Roger Williams had already called for in his appeal to the "merciful and compassionate reader." But

Americans who drew on Smith, with his extensive investigations of sympathy, absorbed a distinctive set of attitudes that shaped the developing nation's sense of itself. Once again, this notion was put to work less in thinking about international relations than in the nation's internal grappling with differences of class, region, and especially religion.

II. Attacking Establishment

The idea of equality was associated with religious liberty in virtually all of the colonies. All of the twelve free exercise provisions in state constitutions in 1789 contained language referring to equality or a nondiscriminatory standard, although in two cases this was limited to Christian denominations.[18] In New York and South Carolina, the right of religious free exercise was said to be held by all "without discrimination or preference." Virginia held that "all men are equally entitled to the free exercise of religion." Other states made similar points through words such as "every," "no man can . . . be deprived," and so on.[19] Even states such as Massachusetts, which retained an established church, used the nondiscrimination language. The Massachusetts constitution of 1780 stated: ". . . no subject shall be hurt, molested, or restrained, in his person, liberty, or estate, for worshiping God in the manner and season most agreeable to the dictates of his own conscience, or for his religious profession or sentiments, provided he doth not disturb the public peace or obstruct others in their religious worship."[20] These peace and safety exemptions were common, showing that the colonists agreed in giving religious practice, as well as belief, a broad latitude, on a footing of equality or nondiscrimination.

Rhode Island, Pennsylvania, Delaware, and New Jersey never had any type of establishment. New England very quickly adopted systems of multiple rather than single establishment, favoring Protestant denominations—while guaranteeing (allegedly) nondiscriminatory religious freedom to all. In the South, the Anglican Church was established in all five colonies (Georgia, North and South Carolina, Virginia, and Maryland) at first, but these establishments proved controversial. North Carolina got rid of all establishment in 1776; Virginia, as we shall see, shortly thereafter. Others followed suit. Connecticut was the only colony that had a preferential establishment (establishing a single denomination) at the time of the framing of the U.S. Constitution.

Indeed, establishment of all sorts was on the way out: Connecticut got rid of its own completely in 1818, New Hampshire in 1819; Massachusetts held out until 1833.[21]

Some colonies, then, still clung to the idea of benign establishment. Many colonies also required religious oaths for office holding; some excluded Catholics, some Jews, some only atheists.[22] Even some who had no establishments (Pennsylvania, Delaware) had such oaths.[23] A trend against establishment, however, was under way, the trend that quickly led to the abolition of all state establishments even without the national pressure that Madison wanted to apply.

What were the arguments in favor of this dramatic shift in thinking—arguments that, as we shall see, rather quickly persuaded even the stiff-necked Congregationalists and the hierarchical Anglicans that establishment was a bad idea in the new nation?

First of all, experience showed that establishments talked nicely, but rarely really protected religious liberty with an equal hand. In Massachusetts, a Baptist was jailed for refusing to pay tax to support the established church. Dissenters were frequently excluded from office holding—a significant burden on religious liberty. They were also excluded from many universities: Brown, founded in 1745, was the first university in the colonies to have no religious test for entrance. Dissenters argued that it was a narrow conception of religious liberty indeed that allowed such inequalities of opportunity and social/political voice. Could one really be free to worship in one's own way if choosing the path of freedom meant second-class civil rights? Typical of this line of argument was the argument against South Carolina's established church by Presbyterian William Tennent: the "first, and most capital reason, against all religious establishments is, that *they are an infringement of Religious Liberty.*"[24]

More generally, dissenters simply did not accept the suggestion that an established church, financed by taxpayer money, could treat citizens equally. As they saw it, the minute one church, rather than another, hooked up with state power and state money, members of other religions—or that large group of Americans, at least 85 percent, who had no church membership—were treated as lower in status. This was not simply a likely *consequence* of financial establishment, it was a meaning expressed in the very fact of such an establishment. As Philip Hamburger writes, "Although dissenters often argued in terms of the appealing rhetoric of liberty, they also enunciated their demands in more precise terms—most commonly in terms of some degree of equality."[25] Thus dissenters in Virginia, in 1779, wrote, "We most earnestly desire and Pray that not only an Universal Toleration may take Place, but that all the Subjects of this Free State may be put on the same footing and enjoy equal Liberties and Privileges."[26] Samuel Stillman, a prominent Massachusetts Baptist, asked the governor to grant all peaceable Christians "the uninterrupted enjoyment of equal religious liberty." He emphasized that "equal religious liberty" meant a full equality of all legal and civil rights, without regard to religious differences: "The authority by which he [that is, the 'magistrate'] acts he derives alike from *all the people* [and] consequently he should exercise that authority *equally* for the benefit of *all*, without any respect to their different religious principles."[27] In South Carolina, similarly, William Tennent emphasized that establishments always make invidious distinctions among people, giving some a recognized status and merely tolerating others:

> The law knows and acknowledges the society of the one as a Christian church; the law knows not the other churches. The law knows the clergy of the one as ministers of the gospel; the law knows not the clergy of the other churches, nor will it give them a license to marry their own people . . . The law makes provision for the support of one church; it makes no provision for the others. The law builds superb churches for the one; it leaves the others to build their own churches . . . These are important distinctions indeed, but these are not all. The law vests the officers of the Church of England with power to tax not only her own people but all other denominations within the bounds of each respective parish for the support of the poor—an enormous power which ought to be vested in no denomination more than another.[28]

Even when liberty is not infringed, then, establishment creates asymmetries of respect, voice, and fiscal power. Notice Tennent's cogent objection to turning poverty relief over to a sectarian group, as has happened (in effect) with our predominantly Christian faith-based initiatives. To give this important function to a sectarian group or groups makes citizens fundamentally unequal in status and dignity.

III. Madison and the Virginia Assessment Controversy

James Madison (1751–1836) is commonly called "the Father of the Constitution."[29] His ideas and arguments so consistently dominated discussion of the new republic and its basic structure that, as one historian puts it, "the years 1785 to 1791 belong preeminently to the gentleman from Orange County, Virginia."[30] (With unusual insight, Alley also states that Madison, by issuing his "clarion call for religious liberty," revived the program of commitment to human dignity and fairness that Roger Williams had already inaugurated in the seventeenth century.) Short and unprepossessing, a poor public speaker, Madison influenced others, and influences us until the present day, through the cogency of his ideas and arguments. His biographer, Irving Brant, sounds, however, a warning note: "To know what ultimate position James Madison will hold in his country's history one must know what that country's future will be. If the American people abandon the rights and liberties he worked so hard to establish, he will be forgotten along with them."[31]

Born and raised in Orange County, in western Virginia, Madison grew up on a slaveholding estate. Unusually for a young gentleman from his milieu, however, he chose to come north for college, enrolling in 1769 at Princeton University (then called College of New Jersey). Here he was exposed to a wide-ranging philosophical education that included study of Locke, Montesquieu, Grotius, Hobbes, and the philosophers of the Scottish Enlightenment (Hutcheson, Reid, Adam Smith).[32] Thus he encountered some of the Stoic ideas that were increasingly suffusing his milieu not only directly, through the classical part of his education, but also indirectly, through direct descendants such as Grotius and Smith. He focused on history and government, and especially on a subject that he calls "The Law of Nature and of Nations" (which suggests a particular focus on Grotius, who used the Stoic idea of natural law to justify an account of international law).

From Locke and the Scottish philosophers, meanwhile, the young Madison derived a healthy respect for experience, prominently including history, as a source of political understanding. In *Federalist* 14, he later wrote: "Is it not the glory of the people of America, that, whilst they have paid a decent regard to the opinions of former times and other nations, they have not suffered a blind veneration for antiquity, for custom, or for names to overrule the suggestions of their own good sense, the knowledge of their own situation, and the lessons of their own experience?" Madison was not about to adopt Stoic ideas on the cheap, because they were ancient. He would accept only those that stood the test of his own critical examination in the light of history and his own sense of America's situation. With what he later recalls as the "minimum of sleep and the maximum of application," he finished his degree in three years.[33]

Returning to Virginia, he noticed with the fresh eye of detachment certain differences between Virginia and some of the northern states. Madison's opposition to slavery probably dates from an earlier time, but it becomes more and more pronounced as he often visits friends in Philadelphia. On one such trip he manumitted his personal slave, Billy, who later became an independent merchant, William Gardener, and handled much of the Madison family business.[34] At the Constitutional Convention in 1787 he denounced the entire institution of slavery in very strong terms.

Other differences also prompted critical reflection. Corresponding with a college classmate, William Bradford, who had returned to his home in Philadelphia, he condemns many aspects of Virginia life, including economic inequality and the arrogance of the rich. His rhetoric reaches Williams-esque heights, however, when he addresses the topic of religious liberty: "That diabolical Hell conceived principle of persecution rages among some and to their eternal Infamy the Clergy can furnish their quota of Imps for such business."[35] (Throughout the correspondence, Madison often inveighs against the corruption and malice of the clergy of the established Anglican Church.) Bradford replies: "I am sorry to hear that Persecution has got so much footing among you. The discription [sic] you give of your Country makes me more in love with mine. Indeed I have ever looked on America as the land of freedom when compared with the rest of the world, but compared with the rest of america [sic] Tis Pennsylvania that is so. Persecution is a weed that grows not in our happy soil."[36] Such comparisons nourished Madison's evolving views of religious freedom.

The two friends also discussed the topic of religious establishment. Since Bradford (following Madison's advice) was preparing for a legal career, Madison proposes that he ought to make a study of Pennsylvania's Constitution, focusing on the question, "Is an Ecclesiastical Establishment absolutely necessary to support civil society in a supream Government? & how far is it hurtful to a dependent State."[37] The fact that Madison urges his friend to focus on his own state, which had no establishment and yet was doing quite well, prejudges the answer that was likely to emerge. As Bradford becomes more involved in revolutionary activity against the English, Madison, encouraging him strongly, observes that revolutionary fervor would probably have been dampened had the Northern colonies had Anglican ecclesiastical establishments:

> If the Church of England had been the established and general Religion in all the Northern Colonies as it has been among us here . . . it is clear to me that slavery and Subjection might and would have been gradually insinuated among us. Union of Religious Sentiments begets a surprising confidence and Ecclesiastical Establishments tend to great ignorance and Corruption all of which facilitate the Execution of mischievous Projects.[38]

There are several surprising ideas in this paragraph. First, we see clearly the Stoic inclinations of Madison's analysis: the bad condition is one of "slavery and Subjection," the good condition one in which a people throws off domination. Second, to our surprise Madison does not associate the bad condition (acquiescence in slavery) with the establishment of the Anglican Church (Church of England) alone, although that is how the paragraph starts out. Writing to a friend educated in New Jersey and dwelling in Pennsylvania, neither of which had any establishment, Madison associates passivity and tolerance of servitude with any sort of establishment whatever: they all tend to "great ignorance and corruption." Madison expands on this theme later in the letter, praising the Pennsylvania regime of liberty and nonestablishment: "Religious bondage shackles and debilitates the mind and unfits it for every noble enterprize every expanded prospect."

Third, Madison suggests that establishment is bad not only for reasons of servitude and corruption, but also because plurality of opinion is itself valuable. Diverse opinions undermine ill-earned "confidence" and prevent a complacency that easily leads to passivity. (Throughout his life, Madison showed an unusual degree of interest in a wide range of religions, including Judaism and Islam. He read widely and corresponded with leading Jews in various states. In 1818 he wrote to Mordecai Noah, apropos a speech by the latter consecrating a Synagogue: "Having ever regarded the freedom of religious opinions and worship as equally belonging to every sect . . . I observe with pleasure the view you give of the spirit in which your Sect partake of the blessings offered by our Govt. and Laws."[39])

Not surprisingly, Madison soon became involved in the tangled religious affairs of his own state. In 1776, Virginia was drawing up a Declaration of Rights. George Mason had written a draft, stating "that all men should enjoy the fullest toleration in the exercise of religion, according to the dictates of conscience, . . . unless under color of religion any man disturb the peace, the happiness, or safety of society."[40] In his first major public act, Madison objected to the word "toleration" as too grudging, suggesting legislative grace rather than entitlement, and to the absence of the language of equality. He proposed, successfully, that Mason's language be replaced by the statement that "all men are equally entitled to the full and free exercise of religion according to the dictates of conscience." Toleration suggested hierarchy, as if it were by the blessing of the majority that the minority was not persecuted. That idea was going out, and the idea of human equality was coming in, with Madison in the vanguard. By 1790, even George Washington would write to the Jewish congregation at Newport: "It is now no more that toleration is spoken of, as if it was by the indulgence of one class of people, that another enjoyed the exercise of their inherent natural rights."

Madison also objected that Mason's "peace, happiness, and safety" language was not protective enough: he suggested language that said government could interfere with the free exercise of religion only if equal liberty itself and the very existence of the State were "manifestly endangered." The drafting committee decided not to sort out this dispute; the final draft did not specify the interest that could override a free exercise claim.[41]

The Declaration of Rights established an equality of liberty, but it did not address the issue of establishment, or the requirement of tax contributions for the support of the established church. In 1776 the legislature abolished this tax for non-Anglicans, and for Anglicans in 1779. The issue arose again, however, in 1784, when Patrick Henry, concerned about an alleged decline of virtue, submitted his "bill Establishing a Provision for Teachers of the Christian Religion." Henry began by paying tribute to equality, insisting that his bill did not threaten "the liberal principle . . . abolishing all distinctions of preeminence amongst the different societies or communities of Christians." This, then, was to be a nonpreferential financial establishment, and Henry argued that its nonpreferential character made it compatible with equality. The bill established a tax to support teachers of the Christian religion. Each person could designate the denomination to which he wanted his money to go. If he did not name a church, the money would go "for the encouragement of seminaries of learning." (Thus there is apparently not even a default establishment, although it is obvious that some sects had seminaries and others did not.) Quakers and Mennonites (presumably because they did not have teachers) were permitted to deposit the money in a general fund and use it for any purpose they liked.

The bill attracted widespread opposition. Despite Henry's powerful oratory, it was ultimately defeated, with Madison and Thomas Jefferson leading the opposition. The key document in the defeat was Madison's famous *Memorial and Remonstrance Against Religious Assessments* (1785).

Madison's central argument is that any sort of establishment violates the equality of citizens, "that equality which ought to be the basis of every law." How is this the case here? The bill looks rather fair to the various sects, and Henry had argued that it is utterly nonhierarchical. Madison argues that the very idea that the state has authority to set up some religions over others is wrongheaded and hierarchical, expressing an idea of state power that is inherently opposed to citizen equality. In this case, the state claims the authority to set Christianity above non-Christianity. This result seems fine to most people. But if we grant that the state has this power in the first place, he continues, then we cannot prevent this authority from being used, as well, to set up some particular sect of Christians over other sects. Indeed, the bill already does this, by singling out only Quakers and Mennonites for special exemption, even though there may well be, or come to be, others who think that this state support is inimical to their religion.

More generally, we cannot claim the right of religious liberty without granting it on an equal basis to those who do not follow the religion we believe to be correct:

> If "all men are by nature equally free and independent," all men are to be considered as entering into Society on equal conditions; as relinquishing no more, and therefore retaining no less, one than another, of their natural rights. Above all are they to be considered as retaining an "*equal* title to the free exercise of Religion according to the dictates of conscience."

> Whilst we assert for ourselves a freedom to embrace, to profess and to
> observe the Religion which we believe to be of divine origin, we cannot
> deny an equal freedom to those whose minds have not yet yielded to the
> evidence which has convinced us.[42] . . . [The proposed bill] degrades
> from the equal rank of Citizens all those whose opinions in Religion do
> not bend to those of the Legislative authority.

Madison takes up the radical position of Roger Williams: the very fact that
the state endorses one religion, Christianity, above another is itself a violation
of the equality of citizens. He extends Williams's position to the area of financial support, where Williams had not seen a problem. But what, precisely, is
the equality problem? In the Virginia case, the endorsement is broad, but it is
still exclusionary, "degrading" non-Christians of all sorts, as well as people
who are atheists or without religion. Unlike Williams, Madison does not enumerate these people, presumably out of political prudence: he is waging a legislative campaign against a powerful adversary, so he wants to maximize the
terrain of agreement. He therefore relies on the idea that once the state arro-
gates to itself the authority to back Christianity against non-Christianity, this is
tantamount to giving itself the power, as well, to back one Christian sect
against another. But non-Christians are clearly in the picture when he speaks
of "those whose minds have not yet yielded to the evidence which has convinced us."

Why, though, is mere tax support tantamount to setting up a hierarchy?
Roger Williams did not think so. Madison's position seems to be that the very
fact that the state uses its coercive taxation power to channel money to certain
religions itself makes a statement that these religions are the state's favorites.
Even when it is the entirety of Christianity that gets the benefit, first of all, it
doesn't work well enough (his point about the enumerated exemptions); second, the benefit excludes non-Christians; third, the tax power could always be
abused should the state decide to favor only some sects of Christians; and,
fourth and most important, it makes a statement that the state just should not
be in the business of making. The state just doesn't have any business telling
people that they have to support religion in this, or that, or any way. That very
statement establishes a hierarchy.

Madison's position is easy for us to understand when we focus on the exclusion of Jews, Muslims, and other non-Christians. Henry's bill was not a

truly nonpreferential establishment. Perhaps because of his polemical context, Madison does not talk explicitly about Jews and other non-Christians, but he is probably alluding to their situation, *inter alia*, when he says that the colonies have so far been "an asylum to the persecuted and oppressed," and that the proposed bill would change all that.

What about, though, an imagined revision in which members of non-Christian religions would also be free to support their own churches? Well, the point about the potential danger to liberty involved in the government's declaration of authority over religion still holds. Madison's point about imperfect administration also still holds, and becomes worse once we admit the many religions that don't have clerics in the usual Christian sense. Henry's bill follows a model common in Christianity, in which a congregation has a cleric in charge, who is their teacher. That model does not fit all religions, certainly not Native American religion, Buddhism, Hinduism, Confucianism, but not even all forms of Judaism and Christianity. In Judaism, for example, the rabbi is not an authority figure, he is a learned man, hired by the congregation to think along with the congregation; so it would be inappropriate to give the money to a rabbi (as the bill would seem to recommend), rather than the congregation. Other cases pose even larger problems, and they could not easily be solved in the way Henry tries to solve the problem of the Quakers, since these religions do not always even have organized congregations. If even Henry's list of exemptions doesn't work well enough, we can surely see that a long open-ended laundry list of exemptions, changing every time a new sect or subsect emerged, would be quite impossible to administer, and would give rise to constant political wrangling.

Once we recognize that many religions do not have teachers, we arrive at a deeper understanding of Madison's equality issue. Remember that a vast majority of Americans at this time did not belong to any organized church. Whether they had religious beliefs or not, and most did, they did not choose to become members of, and to support financially, any recognized group. That does not mean that they did not care about virtue, but they chose to pursue virtue, and teach it to their children, outside the confines of organized ecclesiastical authority, mistrustful of orthodoxies and committed to personal seeking. (Recall that even Roger Williams separated himself from all organized churches to pursue his search for God. Many dissenters took this course.) They typically believed, like Williams, that all the organized churches they

knew were corrupt. These people are now being required to support organized churches, so their dissenting and their committed search are being
flouted. Even the default option, in which their money goes to "seminaries of
learning," is a deformation of their conscience. (It's not entirely clear what
"seminaries of learning" means: probably institutions of religious instruction
connected to churches, since there was no state university in Virginia until
1819, so some sort of organized religious bureaucracy.) So we still have exclusion and hierarchy, even in the modified nonpreferential bill. We are telling
such people that, even though they themselves have chosen not to pay into a
church, and not to trust existing ecclesiastical authority, they will have to do
so: in this way the will of the majority (or in many cases a powerful minority)
dominates over people's personal conscientious choices.

Indeed, the more we think about it, the odder the proposed tax system appears, even in its modified nonpreferential form. People who have already
joined a church assume, in so doing, financial obligations to support the
church. In some cases these are conceived as voluntary, but in many cases a
member in good standing of a congregation is required to pay an understood
amount. Tithing is just the practice of setting a fixed amount of expected contribution. Most, if not all, Jewish congregations impose the obligation in an
even more formal way, sending an annual bill, and withdrawing privileges
from people who do not pay their bill. So citizens whose religious membership puts them under such obligations will, in effect, be doubly taxed: they
cannot withdraw the contribution they are already making without losing congregation membership, but they are also required to pay their taxes. The
group of nonmembers will be taxed only once, but that is because they have
(by not joining a church) expressed the choice not to support religious teachers at all. And the tax will force them to offer support that they wish not to offer. Both groups, therefore, are being made to pay one time more than they
have chosen to pay; it seems that both are being wronged. Madison focuses on
the burden to the excluded, but we can add that the church member suffers as
well. And even if churches should all drop compulsory payments once state
subsidies were introduced, this would remove the double-taxation problem,
but it would not remove a deeper problem: some people of faith see government orchestration as itself in violation of their religion.

We should conclude, I believe, that Madison has a strong argument: any
state policy that gives taxpayer money directly to religious institutions and

teachers compromises the equality of citizens. As we shall see, much of our modern Establishment Clause jurisprudence builds on his insight and then asks what precise forms of aid to religion these considerations prohibit. It is generally agreed that direct aid of the Virginia sort is inadmissible, but questions remain. (Are there permissible forms of indirect aid? Can we find neutral principles to support tax support that will be given to both religion and non-religion alike?)

Madison makes some ancillary arguments against Henry's bill that are staples of public debate in this period. Like Adam Smith in *The Wealth of Nations,* he insists that government support for religion harms religion: it makes it into a state bureaucracy, or at least tends in that direction, and this opens the door to corruption and complacency. "During almost fifteen centuries, has the legal establishment of Christianity been on trial. What have been its fruits? More or less in all places, pride and indolence in the Clergy; ignorance and servility in the laity; in both, superstition, bigotry and persecution." If we compare the vigor of religion in today's United States, where every sect must compete for adherents, with the weakness and "indolence" of many of the established churches of Europe, which have lost public support over time, we can easily see the truth of his claim. Knowing you'll get rich no matter what you do is not exactly a recipe for good management or passionate commitment.

My own experience working on religion-state issues in India adds a further point: once a given religion gets hooked up with state power, it becomes much more difficult for its members to innovate, creating new sects or departing from an old one that has lost its vigor. Thus, to take just one example, in America every major religion has heard the demands of women for full inclusion. If a given sect does not respond to those demands, people typically can form a new sect or subsect. All sorts of theological and organizational creativity is unleashed by the fact that no form of any religion has been established as canonical. This is not the case in India, where four major religions have deep connections to state power, and traditional clerics are given power to administer these connections. If you leave the traditional form, you forfeit that power. This entrenchment retards dynamism and creative challenges to the past. Thus, Christian women in India won the right to divorce on grounds of cruelty only in 2001—because male clerics, who didn't care a lot about that issue, represented the religion in governmental contexts, and no change in the religion's official form could take place without them. Bureaucratic entrenchment meant that there was no way for women to get together and effect change. Establishment led to complacency and inertia.

Establishment, Madison continues, also harms government. By setting the churches up in a position of state power, it creates a large force that constantly threatens civil harmony and peace. "What influence in fact have ecclesiastical establishments had on Civil Society? In some instances they have been seen to erect a spiritual tyranny on the ruins of Civil authority; in many instances, they have been seen upholding the thrones of political tyranny; in no instance have they been seen the guardians of the liberties of the people." Moreover, inviting the many churches into the civil sphere introduces a spirit of bickering and factionalism that is very dangerous to political life. (Madison stressed this idea more and more in his later life, depicting an established clergy as unelected leaders who would expect deference and thereby upset the political process.)

Madison's *Memorial and Remonstrance* carried the day. Henry's bill was defeated. The Assembly shortly adopted the Virginia Act for Establishing Religious Freedom, drafted by Thomas Jefferson. Despite its air of eighteenth-century rationalism, its sentiments are fully continuous with Roger Williams's thought. They extend that thought into the area of financial establishment:

> Well aware that almighty God hath created the mind free; that all attempts to influence it by temporal punishments or burdens, or by civil incapacitations, tend only to beget habits of hypocrisy and meanness . . . ; that to compel a man to furnish contributions of money for the propagation of opinions which he disbelieves, is sinful and tyrannical; that even the forcing him to support this or that teacher of his own religious persuasion, is depriving him of the comfortable liberty of giving his contributions to the particular pastor whose morals he would make his pattern . . . ; that our civil rights have no dependence on our religious opinions, any more than our opinions in physics or geometry; . . . that it is time enough for the rightful purposes of civil government, for its officers to interfere when principles break out into overt acts against peace and good order. . . .
>
> Be it therefore enacted by the General Assembly, That no man shall be compelled to frequent or support any religious worship, place, or ministry whatsoever, nor shall be enforced, restrained, molested, or bur-

dened in his body or goods, nor shall otherwise suffer on account of his
religious opinions or belief; but that all men shall be free to profess, and
by argument to maintain, their opinions in matters of religion, and that
the same shall in nowise diminish, enlarge, or affect their civil capacities.

The act concludes by stating of itself that if it is ever repealed, that will be a
violation of the natural rights of human beings.

Jefferson's bill does not use the language of equality in the way that Madison's *Memorial and Remonstrance* so prominently does. It rests, however, on
an account of equal natural rights. Words such as "no man shall" and "all men
shall" make it very clear that the rights in question are given to all without exception, on a basis of equality. No other bill for nonpreferential aid was rein-
troduced—so the public response was not to try to close the loopholes in the
bill, it was to drop entirely the question of aid to religion. A similar tax proposal was rejected the same year in Maryland.

IV. Framing the Constitutional Text

The initial framing of the Constitution already included a radical statement of
religious equality. In Article VI, part 3, after discussing the requirement that
all national and state officials take an oath to support the Constitution, the following clause was inserted: "No religious Test shall ever be required as a
Qualification to any Office or Public Trust under the United States." At the
time, this provision applied only to federal offices, not to the states, many of
which continued to require religious oaths. Like the First Amendment, it became applicable to the states much later, through a reading of the Fourteenth
Amendment, as we shall see in Chapter 4. Even in this restricted form, the
statement is bold and striking, given the prominence of test oaths in Britain.
Nonetheless, when Charles Pinckney introduced it on August 30, 1787, it
passed without demur—the only recorded objection being that it was unnecessary, "the prevailing liberality being a sufficient security against such a
test."[43]

The Constitution in its initial form, famously, contained no explicit Bill of
Rights—once again, because it was thought unnecessary to enumerate rights
about which there was broad consensus. Dissatisfaction arose during the
ratification process, and it became clear that there was wide support for

making things explicit. Madison strongly favored this course. Shortly thereafter, therefore, the first ten amendments were drafted. For the "religion
clauses" we have records of some of the debate in the House, and the textual
proposal of the Senate, though the Senate kept no records of its internal
workings.[44]

Madison had failed to gain election to the Senate because of the influence of
Patrick Henry, his old nemesis, but he did win a closely contested House seat.
From that vantage point, he proposed two amendments relevant to religion:

> The civil rights of none shall be abridged on account of religious belief
> or worship, nor shall any national religion be established, nor shall the
> full and equal rights of conscience be in any manner, or on any pretext,
> infringed.

And:

> No State shall violate the equal rights of conscience, or the freedom of the
> press . . .

As we can see, then, Madison all along wanted at least some provisions of
the Bill of Rights to be binding on the state governments, but he expected opposition, so he broke his proposal into two parts.

Madison's proposals were referred to a committee. (We know nothing
about how they deliberated.) The committee emerged on August 15, 1789,
with the following text, the first to be considered by the entire House:

> No religion shall be established by law, nor shall the equal rights of con-
> science be infringed.

The first House version is even broader than Madison's first proposal, banning not merely a national religion, but all legal establishment of religion. Mr.
Livermore, from New Hampshire, which had a state establishment at the time,
proposed the alternative:

> Congress shall make no laws touching religion, or infringing the rights of
> conscience.

This version apparently protected state establishments, since Congress was denied the power to make any law "touching religion," thus, apparently, any law that would ban such establishments.

Five days later, the House considered another version. There is no record of what happened in the interim:

> Congress shall make no law establishing religion, or to prevent the free exercise thereof, or to infringe the rights of conscience.

One reasonable explanation of the change is that "no laws touching" sweeps too broadly, putting in jeopardy protective laws such as the Free Exercise Clause itself, a point already made by Roger Williams. We notice as well, however, that the new version, unlike Livermore's, seems to allow Congress to make laws disestablishing the established churches in the states; we shall later see that the House, at least, favored extending at least some of the protections of the First Amendment to the states.

Significant, too, is the addition of "free exercise" to "rights of conscience." "Exercise" at the time clearly refers to the practice of worship, whereas "rights of conscience" might be taken to refer only to belief and speech. As we have seen, both Roger Williams and Madison were very clear in their defense of both belief and religious practice, and this was clearly a widespread, and here the dominant, view.

The Senate received the House text with the following small alteration (for which we have no explanation):

> Congress shall make no law establishing Religion, or prohibiting the free exercise thereof, nor shall the rights of conscience be infringed.

Six days later, a very different and far narrower Senate version emerged, as follows:

> Congress shall make no law establishing articles of faith or a mode of worship, or prohibiting the free exercise of religion.

The anti-establishment provision has been drastically narrowed, in a way that seems to permit some types of "benign" and nonintrusive establishment, and even preferential financial support. This version, however, did not prevail. A House-Senate conference committee worked out our final language:

> Congress shall make no law respecting an establishment of religion, or prohibiting the free exercise thereof; . . .

Once this text had passed, Madison turned to the next item on his agenda, proposing:

> No State shall infringe the equal rights of conscience . . .

Because Madison believed that the dangers of oppression and hierarchy were greater at the state level (because there may be more homogeneity at that level), he called this proposal "the most valuable amendment in the whole list."[45] Madison's motion is aimed at free exercise, but it could also be understood to rule out state-level establishments, given Madison's (widely shared) understanding of what equality required. It passed in the House. It was rejected, however, by the more conservative Senate, and was not heard of again.

As we can see, there is no such unitary thing as "the intention of the framers." The text we have is a committee construct. Like any committee construct, it involves compromise among people with different views. Nor should we necessarily believe that the meaning of the text for us today is given simply by what these words meant at the time. That is one theory of constitutional interpretation. In many cases, however, we understand that our understanding of constitutional meaning evolves with new historical experiences. The Free Speech Clause, for example, probably had a relatively narrow meaning at the time of the Founding, protecting only some types of dissident political speech. When Eugene Debs went to jail in 1918 for violation of the Sedition Act (for urging people to resist military induction), there was almost universal agreement that the First Amendment did not protect him. It was only later, as a result of reflection on his case, that the political speech of dissidents in wartime was held to be protected by the First Amendment. And yet, today, such unpopular political speech is understood as a paradigm of what the Amendment protects. Even the most ardent originalists have not proposed reverting to the original understanding in this instance, though they may someday do so.

People generally agree that reflection and experience have deepened our understanding of the abstract terms of the constitutional text.

It is even possible to argue that this change in understanding is, at a more abstract level, precisely what the original text meant: namely, the framers deliberately chose very general terms and did not spell things out in detail, precisely on account of their empiricism: they had decided to leave further specification to history and the processes of public debate.

Thus finding out what the text was taken to mean at the time is by no means the only thing we need to do if we are to think about it well today. We also need to think about history, about precedents, and about our current situation.

Nonetheless, it is still quite interesting to ask what the text meant at the time, and we can say something about this, even with a committee product like this one, by looking at the House journals, together with other documents of the period. We can observe at least the following:

1. **"Free exercise" means practice as well as belief.** Throughout the period, there is a lot of harping on the issue of religious practice. Both Williams and Madison were careful to spell out the fact that the protections they envisaged applied to acts as well as to belief and speech. Most state free exercise clauses did so in one way or another. Here we see that the vaguer idea of "rights of conscience" is ultimately replaced by a word that unequivocally refers to acts as well as belief and speech.

2. **"No law respecting" is broader than "no law establishing."** The vague language "no laws touching religion" was considered too broad, presumably because it would impugn laws protective of religion, and perhaps also because it would allow Congress to disestablish the state established churches. But "no law establishing" was evidently thought too narrow. Why so?

A central idea in Madison's *Memorial and Remonstrance* is that one can establish a state church without any law saying on its face, "the x Church is hereby established." The Virginia Assessment Bill did not say anything about establishment, and yet, in the view of Madison and most of his contemporaries, it effectively did establish a state church. The chosen words are reasonably understood in connection with these familiar arguments: Congress is debarred not only from official declarations of establishment, but also from passing laws that would amount to an establishment, even if that is not stated.

Does the final wording also protect the state establishments from interference? Very likely, and yet there is reason for doubt, since the House went on to pass Madison's proposal binding the states, without (apparently) seeing any inconsistency with their former endorsement of the First Amendment. Perhaps some did not see Madison's connection between equal rights and non-establishment, and voted for his motion binding the states without, therefore, thinking that it threatened state establishments. Here is an area of obscurity: no doubt different people had different reasons for their votes, and we will never know what they were.

3. "Conscience" and "religion": religion is special. As we can see, drafts oscillated between reference to "rights of conscience" and the "free exercise of religion." Possibly the framers saw little difference. "The free exercise of conscience" sounds awkward, and we can at least note that the phrase "free exercise of conscience" simply does not occur in documents of the period. Having decided that "exercise" was what they wanted, in order to protect acts as well as beliefs, they may have slipped over to the word "religion" without any sense of difference. Moreover, they really did not think very much about agnostics or atheists; the many non–church members about whom they clearly did think were typically people like Williams, who searched for religion outside the confines of organized churches.

The words "conscience" and "religion," however, ring very differently in our contemporary ears. As we shall see, it has been a perpetual problem whether conscientious commitments that do not take a religious form receive any protection under the Free Exercise Clause. If they do not, there is an equality problem. If I resist the military draft because I follow the ethical ideas of Henry David Thoreau and you resist the draft because you are an Orthodox Jew, it seems somewhat unfair for your commitment to be honored and mine to be rejected, simply because yours is religious and mine is ethical—and yet this is what our Constitution appears to authorize. Such problems became acute during the Vietnam War, when many people resisted the war for reasons of conscience, only some of which were religious in any traditional sense. We shall turn to that problem in the next chapter. It seems clear, however, that the text the framers chose does make religion (whatever that includes) special for the purposes of the Free Exercise Clause, fair or unfair. Perhaps nonreligious commitments were thought to be sufficiently protected by the Free Speech and Press Clauses. To some extent later interpretations have broadened the understanding of what gets protection, but there are reasons why, in delicate areas such as military service and drug use, such broadening has not gone, and cannot go, very far.

4. **"Prohibiting" and "abridging": weaker protection?** The First Amendment says that Congress shall make no law "prohibiting" the free exercise of religion, but that it may make no law "abridging" the freedoms of speech and press. Does this mean that Congress can "abridge" the free exercise of religion, so long as it does not "prohibit" it? The word "prohibiting" crept into the text after the final House version without recorded debate. Perhaps nothing much is meant by the difference; perhaps "abridging" seems to go well with speech, "prohibiting" with acts. It seems odd to talk of "abridging" an act, as if one could do only part of an act; and we said that the word "exercise," though it includes belief, places an emphasis on the protection of acts. Certainly Madison did not think that he had approved of any differentiation. Ten years later, he wrote, "The liberty of conscience and the freedom of the press were *equally* and *completely* exempted from all authority whatever of the United States." He went on to reject explicitly the reading that Congress is permitted to "abridge" the free exercise of religion so long as it does not "prohibit."[46] We should conclude that the text contains an unfortunate ambiguity that was noticed later on, but that its meaning was very likely what Madison said it was. The fact that no recorded debate touches on this difference strongly suggests that it was not intended as salient, and that the reason for the word "prohibiting" was, as I said, the oddness of the idea of "abridging" an action.

5. **Where is equality?** I have said that the idea of equality is central to the religion clauses. But the word "equal" does not occur in them. We can see that earlier drafts contained this word: why not the final draft? Here, once again, we need to think of the phrases that were actually in use at the time. The word "equal" went naturally with "rights," "natural rights," and "liberty." It did not turn up with "exercise"—thus, when "free exercise" replaced "rights of conscience," the word "equality" dropped out. Surely, however, this omission does not mean that the text does not protect citizens' rights on a basis of equality. If there is anything that all the framers agreed strongly about, and never questioned, it was the idea of equality. "Free exercise" is taken to be grounded in equal natural rights; it is only that the phrase "prohibiting the equal free exercise of religion" would (a) be very odd, and (b) be much too

weak, since Congress is *not* only debarred from partiality in restricting free exercise (restricting it unequally), it is debarred from all sorts and kinds of restrictions on free exercise. Suppose that Congress said, "Nobody may worship God in the United States." That would not offend against equality, but it would clearly be ruled out by the Free Exercise Clause. The text debars Congress from evenhanded restrictions of liberty as well as unfair ones, so the word "equal" could not occur before the words "free exercise."

The idea of equality, it would seem, lies in the entirety of the meaning expressed, particularly in the idea that Congress may not prohibit free exercise—to anyone, is the clear meaning. The "free exercise" means *anyone's* free exercise, and so, like many state constitutions, ours captures the idea of equality by negation.

The prohibition on establishment also carries a clear meaning protective of equal civil rights. The central argument of *Memorial and Remonstrance* was that any establishment makes people's civil rights unequal. In saying this, Madison was echoing decades of debate and stating a widely held position. So, by prohibiting a federal establishment of religion, the text prohibits one very prominent source of pervasive inequality.

Indeed, we might plausibly say that equality is the glue that holds the two clauses together. It is often obscure how they do go together, and their coexistence poses some legal conundrums. For example, if religion gets special breaks under the Free Exercise Clause, isn't this by itself a kind of establishment, of the sort Madison feared? We will try to sort that out later. But we can see that at the time the free exercise of religion was a major expression of human equality, one of the deepest ways in which the equal rights of citizens were to be either protected or infringed. Establishment, meanwhile, is a major threat to equality across a whole range of civil rights. Free exercise alludes to the individual conscience, establishment to institutional arrangements that either set up a hierarchy or fail to do so. But of course hierarchy is bad, ultimately, because of what it does to people, offending against their equality. The focus of the clauses is subtly different, but equal rights are at the bottom of both.

V. Two Misleading Theories

Theories of the religion clauses abound. Many are complementary, offering mutual illumination. When there is genuine conflict, some contenders are plausible and others much less plausible. Two theories that are really not plausible, either as theories of contemporary meaning or as historical theories, have recently become prominent, because in each case an influential Supreme Court justice has stated the false theory. It is worth, then, pausing to show why they are not defensible. Notice that these theories are not offered as modern interpretations or as normative theories of what the clauses should be, but as correct historical readings of the text in its own historical context.

For Justice Thomas, the Establishment Clause does not protect individual rights at all, because it is only a device through which the framers protected the state-level establishments. This theory is important to him because it is generally agreed that the Bill of Rights' protections for individual liberties have been applied to the states through the Fourteenth Amendment—the doctrine known as "incorporation," which we shall discuss in Chapter 4. Most people have held that both the Establishment Clause and the Free Exercise Clause have been incorporated: thus, no state may establish a state religion. While granting that the Free Exercise Clause is "incorporated," Justice Thomas, proposing to overturn decades of precedent, denies that the Establishment Clause is so—on the grounds that it was understood at the time not to protect individual rights at all, but only to insulate the state establishments from congressional interference. Justice Thomas has some prominent academic company, in particular Akhil Amar, in his book *The Bill of Rights*. Amar argues that the Establishment Clause resists incorporation in a unique way, because, as originally drafted, it is concerned not with the protection of individual rights, but only with the insulation of states' power to regulate religion—although Amar concludes that by the time of the Civil War amendments, the understanding of establishment had shifted and this barrier to its incorporation had been removed. Thus his analysis does not ultimately support Justice Thomas's contention.[47]

We can grant that it is plausible that *part* of the force of the Establishment Clause in its final form was this insulation. More precisely, some individuals may have supported the wording partly, or even largely, for that reason. So much, indeed, is true of the First Amendment as a whole, as Amar himself stresses: it was often observed (and explicitly noted by both Madison and Jefferson) that the effect of the free speech and press provisions was to leave to the states the power to regulate both, something that some people liked.[48] It would be most implausible, however, to hold that insulation of state powers was the Establishment Clause's *only* point. The raging debate about state religious establishments, from Roger Williams on through the mid-nineteenth century, focused at all times on individual rights, and not only the free exercise right, which is taken account of in the Free Exercise Clause, but the whole range of civil rights that are rendered unequal by ecclesiastical establishments. As Madison summarized this whole current of thinking, "[A]ll men are to be considered as entering into Society on equal conditions," and ecclesiastical establishments violate that equality, "degrad[ing] from the equal rank of Citizens all those whose opinions in Religion do not bend to those of the Legislative authority." Being regarded as an equal, entering society on equal conditions, is clearly an individual right, something about persons that establishments remove.

As we have seen, Madison's was not an idiosyncratic position, but one widely held, usually by a majority. Even when in a given colony a majority against establishment had not yet emerged, the trend was well under way, and all would shortly disappear. More important, the debate surrounding this trend focused on the idea of equality. State establishments were seen to threaten equal free exercise; they also were seen to threaten political equality, educational equality, employment equality. A wide range of individual rights was understood to be at stake in the question whether Congress might make laws "respecting an establishment of religion."

Now we need to take two steps back, thinking about the question from the point of view of different views of constitutional interpretation. When we ask how to understand the Establishment Clause, we might ask several distinct questions:

1.   What is the most likely meaning of the text at the time of its drafting?
2.   What is the best understanding of the text at the time of incorporation, immediately after the Civil War?
3.   In the light of what we now know about history and human behavior, what is the most plausible and defensible account we can give of the general idea of nonestablishment?

Originalists typically focus on the first question; but even they must, by their own lights, care about the second as well, since they contend that the Establishment Clause was understood to be different from the other clauses at the time when the Privileges and Immunities Clause and the Due Process

Clause putatively incorporated the Bill of Rights. Since Justice Thomas believes that most of the Bill of Rights was incorporated (applied to the states) by the Fourteenth Amendment, but that the Establishment Clause was not, he in particular must care about the second question.

The third question, I believe, is extremely important. The framers left many constitutional ideas highly vague and general, very likely deliberately, so even caring about the original understanding may entail caring about how, in changing circumstances, highly general goals and aims are best specified. Arguably, one key meaning of the constitutional text is that open-ended generality. But if one is not a textualist, one has further reasons to ask oneself, "In the light of what we have learned between the eighteenth century and now, what is the best account of a given constitutional concept?" Thus, as we have observed, the political speech of dissidents in wartime was very likely not part of what the text of the First Amendment protected at the time of its ratification. By now, it is understood to be at the core of what that amendment is all about—because we have learned a lot more about speech and the evils of suppressing it in a pluralistic democracy.

If we pose the third question, we get, I believe, a clear Madisonian answer: establishment, we now know, burdens a wide range of personal liberties, by extending them to citizens on an unequal basis. The Court has repeatedly expressed this same idea, saying that the Establishment Clause is "a coguarantor, with the Free Exercise Clause, of religious liberty. The framers did not entrust the liberty of religious beliefs to either clause alone."[49] If, for the sake of argument, we bracket the historical language and simply think about what the clauses accomplish, we should grant that this analysis is correct.

If we ask the second question, looking for the mid-nineteenth-century understanding of the idea of nonestablishment, we also get a clear result. By that time, as Kurt Lash has argued in an important historical analysis, the discourse about establishment and equality had been widely disseminated, and there was a general shared understanding that establishment burdened the civil rights of individuals.[50] Amar grants that Lash is correct, thus concluding that, at least by the 1860s, establishment was understood to be about "principles of religious liberty and religious equality"[51]

So it is only the first question whose answer might even plausibly be disputed, and we really do not need to reach that question, even if we are originalists, since it is the second question that ought to be dispositive for Justice

Thomas's question about incorporation. Let us, however, return to that question, which we have already begun to address. Lash holds that at the time of the Founding, there was no general understanding that establishments burdened individual liberties: that understanding developed later. In support of this contention he makes an unconvincing argument, pointing to the fact that many people, at that time, still supported establishments.[52] This hardly shows that people did not link establishment to a loss of personal liberty, for they might agree that there was such a loss, but believe that there were good reasons to accept the loss of liberty (reasons of security, reasons of state pride, and so forth). Even John Cotton understood well that establishment curtailed individual liberty: he simply was not a friend of liberty. I think that the evidence shows that from the seventeenth century on, Madison's (and Williams's and Cotton's) point was widely understood: establishment makes liberty unequal.

If we now ask why people (a minority in the Senate, a majority in the House) nonetheless rejected Madison's proposal that the Establishment Clause should apply to the states, we get a wide range of answers. For some, the dominant motive was no doubt a suspicion of centralized government power and a desire to assert state pride and autonomy; in that sense the contention that the Establishment Clause is structural has something going for it. Some no doubt shared at least a part of John Cotton's concern: we need the state establishments to promulgate virtue and ensure security. (Rhode Island was often sarcastically treated as an instance of lawlessness and anarchy.) Some may have thought liberty sufficiently protected by state free exercise clauses and may have seen no good reason for giving yet one more power to the national government.

The question that we are pursuing, however, is not why some people voted against Madison's proposal, but what the meaning is of the language we actually have. That is the question that textualists think important. Whether or not we agree with them, that is the point we are currently considering. So widely disseminated was the connection between establishment and unequal liberty that we should not hesitate to answer the first question in a Madisonian way. Whatever else the framers were worried about, they were very worried that a federal government that allied itself with one particular religion would leave the rights and the standing of citizens unequal in the new nation. Nonestablishment means, at least *inter alia*, protection of individuals against unequal civil rights introduced by national establishments.

The second false doctrine is more superficially plausible, but nonetheless we can confidently rule it out. This is the idea that goes by the name of "non-preferentialism," a theory favored by the late Chief Justice William Rehnquist. Nonpreferentialism is the view that what the Establishment Clause rules out is any *preferential* establishment of religion, that is, one preferring one sect or group of sects to others. It does not rule out a general blanket endorsement of religion, *or general financial aid* to religion. We have already seen that, and why, Madison was against nonpreferentialism. We can now see that this opposition was shared by the group who framed the text.[53] At any rate, as Douglas Laycock argues, "The framers of the religion clauses certainly did not consciously intend to permit nonpreferential aid, and those of them who thought about the question probably intended to forbid it."[54]

To see this clearly, we must go into more detail concerning the rejected drafts. When the Senate received the House version, it first substituted one that clearly states the nonpreferential position:

> Congress shall make no law establishing one religious sect or society in preference to others, nor shall the rights of conscience be infringed.

So the Senate was able to state clearly the nonpreferentialist position. Nonetheless, later the same day (after rejecting several stylistic variants of the nonpreferentialist draft), the Senate abandoned that version, adopting wording close to our final version:

> Congress shall make no law establishing religion, or prohibiting the free exercise thereof.

This version, as we can see, speaks generically of all religion. A week later, the Senate reverted to quite a narrow wording, as we have already seen:

> Congress shall make no law establishing articles of faith or a mode of worship, or prohibiting the free exercise of religion.

This version, narrower still than the first nonpreferential version, and a clear statement of something like nonpreferentialism, was, nonetheless, rejected by the House in favor of our final wording.

Our final version is one of the broadest considered by either house of Congress. Most important, it does not say "a religion," "a national religion," "one sect or society," etc.[55] It says "religion." Establishing "religion" is not the same as establishing "one sect or society" or even "a religion," and these distinctions were before the framers as they argued over the text. As Laycock concludes, "The 'no preference' position requires a premise that the framers were extraordinarily bad drafters—that they believed one thing but adopted language that said something substantially different, and that they did so after repeatedly attending to the choice of language."[56]

Moreover, as we can clearly see from the Virginia controversy, nonpreferential aid had had a good public outing. Henry's bill was as good an attempt at that position as was likely to emerge at the time. It was roundly rejected. Although we cannot use the Virginia debate (and the similar Maryland debate) as direct evidence for the meaning of the religion clauses, it does show us that people understood well the difference between nonpreferential aid and no aid. The various drafts were not being written in a context in which these distinctions had not been worked out and debated. In such a context, it seems clear that the rejection of nonpreferentialist language means something, is not purely inadvertent. Even someone who is skeptical about the use of drafting history as a general tool of interpretation ought to agree that the rejected drafts in this case are one of our best ways of fixing the precise meaning of the words finally chosen.

The late Chief Justice, strangely, neglects the evidence of the rejected drafts, our surest signs of what the accepted draft means, and focuses most of his argument on one stray remark Madison made during the debate: one member of the House objected that the preferred language would disfavor religion, and Madison reassured him that the point of the Establishment Clause was to prevent a "national religion."[57] It is true that Madison said this, but in a political *ad hominem* context in which he was reassuring an individual whose vote he wanted. He was not lying: the draft does have that force, and it also is compatible with state establishments, which was probably the member's primary concern. The fact that the language does more than simply reject a national religion was something Madison did not mention at that particular moment, but, since the final language is very close to his original proposal, and since we know a lot about what he thought and supported, we can infer that this silence doesn't mean that Madison himself held a narrow view of the clause's intention. He himself, along with the majority, voted for broader language against narrower nonpreferentialist language. The Rehnquist argument, then, is singularly unconvincing.[58] More generally, it is a very odd sort of originalism to ignore the text itself (in connection with other rejected texts) and to base one's argument on one remark made during a (partially recorded) debate.

But, say the nonpreferentialists, what about the manifold ways in which religion continued to be supported in the new republic? The first Congress appointed chaplains, a practice that continues to the present day. Presidents Washington, Adams, and Madison issued Thanksgiving proclamations mentioning God, although Jefferson refused, and Madison did so only in time of war and at the request of Congress. In later life, Madison felt that both the chaplains and Thanksgiving Day proclamations had been violations of the Establishment Clause.[59] He said he had never approved of the decision to appoint chaplains. Nonetheless, we are talking not about Madison but about the new nation's general understanding of its Constitution.

We should say, I think, that the framers knew in a general way what they were after, but (hardly surprisingly) had not thought out its implications in all particulars. The area of tax support for religion had received a great deal of scrutiny and debate, and so most people had arrived at a definite position on that. Such things as public displays, public proclamations, and chaplains simply had not been debated, and so people went into them without the sort of guidance that had been offered, in the financial area, by the Virginia debate.[60] It is very interesting that Madison himself changed his view, later, concerning the implications for the chaplaincy of a text that he himself largely authored. It seems that he was clear about the general principles behind nonestablishment, which he had eloquently stated in the *Memorial and Remonstrance,* but less clear about their concrete implications, which would remain to be worked out as history unfolded new problems. This is in keeping with his empiricism. Indeed, the choice of highly general language is a way of giving experience and history time to unfold. Mistakes at the concrete level can be made; the general principles remain, suggesting some key questions to pose of any dubious case. Central among these must be "Does this case create a hierarchy among citizens, so that they do not all enter the polity on equal conditions?" Some specific nonpreferentialist practices apparently seemed benign at first when considered in that light—although hindsight suggested to Madison that in fact they had not been so benign.

In any case, these examples are not very useful to the nonpreferentialist. The chaplaincy is highly preferential: House and Senate chaplains are typically Protestant, and there has never been an organized attempt to represent all the religions from which representatives come.[61] Thanksgiving Day proclamations depend on the judgment of the president in question, and there has never been a guideline suggesting that they ought to be nonpreferential. In fact, they are not nonpreferential. To take two recent proclamations by President Bush (2004 and 2005) as examples, they both refer to God in the singular (thus excluding polytheists and members of nontheistic religions, as well as atheists), call God "Almighty" (thus excluding religions that do not believe in divine omnipotence), refer to God as watching over and guiding America (thus excluding religions that do not ascribe to God this sort of personalized intervention in worldly affairs), and refer to God as "He" (thus offending believers and sects that have worked hard to eliminate gendered language in reference to the deity). If Bush had aimed at true nonpreferentialism, he could have done a lot better—although, as history shows, any way of talking about God or gods very likely excludes someone.

The difficulty of constructing a truly nonpreferential prayer is a major ethical problem with nonpreferentialism. What I am interested in here, however, is that it is also a difficulty for anyone who wants to show that the proclamations made by early (or subsequent) presidents expressed a philosophical commitment to nonpreferentialism. As we can see, the two who had well-worked-out theoretical positions on this issue, Madison and Jefferson, were precisely the ones who either refused to make the proclamation or thought in hindsight that they should have refused. It is possible that George Washington himself was a Henry-like nonpreferentialist. That fact, however, sheds no light on the meaning of the religion clauses, since Washington had nothing to do with framing them, and since it would be utterly unthinkable at the time that the president would be hauled into court (before judicial review even existed!), or even publicly criticized, for such a performance. There is no evidence that even Washington advanced a nonpreferentialist interpretation of the constitutional text.

Moreover, at the time, as the Virginia debate shows, nonpreferentialism typically meant nonpreferential Christianity. And it is amply clear that the framers believed that the new nation had not been founded as a Christian nation. To cite just one example, the Treaty of Tripoli, signed in 1796–1797, enthusiastically endorsed by President John Adams, one of our more cautious thinkers on religious issues, reassures Muslims that the United States is not and never has been a Christian nation.[62] This denial was utterly uncontroversial in discussion of the treaty. In rejecting a nonpreferential Christian understanding of the nation, it is overwhelmingly likely that Adams and others were rejecting nonpreferentialism itself.

In short, the early history shows us something we already know about people: that they often act unreflectively, and that for this reason public debate makes a difference. Before Madison wrote the *Memorial and Remonstrance,* many Virginians no doubt thought Henry's bill very progressive and even-handed. They did not see the subtle equality problem in it until Madison pointed it out—just as we often fail to see what is offensive in some practice or way of speaking until someone points this out to us. After it is pointed out with clear and convincing arguments, things are different. In the case of tax support, things had become clear. In other cases, they became clear, eventually, to some individuals, but their public clarification awaited later work by the Supreme Court. Some issues, such as House and Senate chaplains, have never been given the benefit of full public debate. Most people are not even aware that these (highly sectarian) institutions exist. No doubt future debate and reflection will enrich our understanding. It was wise of Madison and the other framers to specify the constitutional text at a rather high level of generality, since even they themselves (by Madison's own later account) had not thought enough about some of the specifics.

There is good reason to ascribe thoughtlessness and some inconsistency to the framers. There is no reason to saddle them with the false doctrine of nonpreferentialism.

As time went on, and state establishments dropped away, a more radical call for the separation of church and state began to be heard in some quarters. In a famous 1802 letter to the Danbury Baptists, Thomas Jefferson interpreted the First Amendment as "building a wall of separation between Church and State." Such ideas, though they went beyond the ideas of the framers, are defended in terms of an idea of natural rights that they shared. Jefferson's position never became fully mainstream. The ideas of equality and equal liberty continued to be the key ideas in the debate for many years to come.[63] The arguments of the Founding, however, had shown this much: that the mixture of civil with ecclesiastical power involved many dangers—to religion, which would be sapped of its vigor; to the state, which might be undermined by the factionalism of unelected clerical leaders; to liberty, which would be imperiled the minute the state arrogated to itself the right to make decisions in religious matters. Above all, however, the mixture of civil with religious jurisdictions threatened an equality of standing in the public realm that was enormously precious to all Americans. Separation, to the extent that the framers urged it, was not a way of belittling religion, it was a way of respecting human beings.

4

THE STRUGGLE OVER ACCOMMODATION

I assure you very explicitly, that in my opinion the conscientious scruples of all men should be treated with great delicacy and tenderness: and it is my wish and desire, that the laws may always be as extensively accommodated to them, as a due regard for the protection and essential interests of the nation may justify and permit.

GEORGE WASHINGTON,
LETTER TO THE QUAKERS (1789)

It cannot therefore, for a moment be believed, that the mild and just principles of the common Law would place the witness in such a dreadful predicament; in such a horrible dilemma, between perjury and false swearing: If he tells the truth he violates his ecclesiastical oath—If he prevaricates he violates his judicial oath—Whether he lies, or whether he testifies the truth he is wicked, and it is impossible for him to act without acting against the laws of rectitude and the light of conscience.

The only course is, for the court to declare that he shall not testify or act at all.

NEW YORK COURT OF GEN. SESSIONS,
People v. Philips (1813)

I. "Such a horrible dilemma": Minorities in a World of Majority Law

Antigone is placed in an agonizing dilemma. The state, in the person of her uncle Creon, has announced that she may not bury her brother, killed attacking the city. But Antigone's religion and its "unwritten laws" tell her that she must bury her brother, or forfeit all chance of being welcomed by the spirits of her family when she dies. As readers of Sophocles' tragedy, we usually find Creon's rigidity alarming. He has defined public policy in a way that favors the interests of most people in the city. In the process, however, he has imposed a tragic burden on one person. The great Athenian statesman Pericles boasted that fifth-century democratic Athens did things better, refusing on principle to put people in such dreadful predicaments.[1] Athens, he said, pursues the good of the city, but not by requiring its citizens to violate the "unwritten laws" of their religions.

Antigone's dilemma has resonated through the ages, as an example of the terrible damage the state can do when it is insufficiently sensitive to citizens' religious needs. Modern states take this problem very seriously. Hegel, the great nineteenth-century German philosopher, claimed that sensitivity to the *Antigone* problem was a hallmark of the modern liberal state, which is committed to shielding its citizens' religious observances from public burdens. By our own time, however, we can see that liberal-democratic societies have their own special difficulties resolving Antigone's dilemma.

Laws in democracies are made by the majority. Because this is so, democratic legal arrangements are frequently insensitive to the religious needs of minorities. Majorities decree public holidays and days of rest, thinking, as they do so, of the religious needs of the dominant religion. Majority thinking is usually not malevolent, but it is often obtuse, oblivious to the burden such rules impose on religious minorities. Rules about how soldiers should dress (such as bans on headgear other than the military headgear), rules about how people should behave in court (removing their hats), rules about how the military shall be constituted (frequently by conscription of healthy adult males), rules about who shall testify in court (anyone who is subpoenaed, excepting a spouse)—all these and many other common legal requirements reflect majority thinking, which may impose very severe burdens on the religious practices of minorities. The headgear requirements of Jews and Sikhs violate military norms. Quakers believe it idolatrous to remove their hats in court. Quakers, Mennonites, and other religious groups follow requirements of pacifism that preclude ordinary military service. Saturday worshippers cannot testify in court on that day. The list of such clashes is long.

The rule of law is a crucial element of any viable democracy. And yet laws of the sort I've mentioned often put religious minorities in something like Antigone's dilemma: either they have to violate a sacred requirement or they have to break the law and/or forfeit some state-granted privilege. In *People v. Philips*, the case from which my epigraph is taken, Father Kohlmann, a Roman Catholic priest, was required to testify to what the defendant told him in the confessional, thus violating the sacred requirements of his office. If he refused, he would go to jail. As the court says: how could the "mild and just" principles of law put a citizen in "such a horrible dilemma"? Creon could at least argue that the very peace and safety of the state depended on his forbidding the burial of a traitor. New York, however, had no such argument available. The acquittal of one petty thief on account of insufficient evidence was unlikely to shake the foundations of public order, nor was it likely that there would be many criminal cases affected by allowing priests not to testify about confidences in the confessional.

Laws often put law-abiding citizens in a difficult position. The military draft, when it existed, made young adults leave their jobs, their families, their familiar setting, often to risk their lives in foreign lands. A subpoena may force me to testify against my mother, my employer, my best friend, my own child. Sophocles' *Antigone*, however, suggests something that has been widely believed in many times and places: that law-imposed dilemmas involving religion are unusually horrible, because they involve issues that touch on a person's conscience or search for the ultimate meaning and purpose of life. (Because we think marriage is similarly central, we have favored accommodation here too: we don't require spouses to testify in court against one another.) Some such burdens to religion may have to be borne, if the peace and safety of the state are really at stake, or if there is some other extremely strong state interest. But it seems deeply wrong for the state to put citizens in such a tragic position needlessly, or in matters of less weight. And often matters lying behind laws of general applicability are not so weighty; sometimes they come down to the mere desire for homogeneity and an unexamined reluctance to delve into the details of a little-known or unpopular religion.

The issue of accommodation has several dimensions. One of these is leg-islative: when is it appropriate and permissible for legislatures to enact laws that grant accommodations to religious minorities? Another is judicial: when, if ever, does the Constitution itself require granting accommodation to an in-dividual plaintiff or plaintiffs, as a requirement of the free exercise of religion itself, even when democratically enacted laws do not give a plaintiff such an accommodation? The role of the judiciary is very likely to be linked closely to the interests of religious minorities, who would be unable to prevail through the legislative process.

In both cases we have to look over our shoulder for an Establishment Clause problem. Laws that carve out a special place for some or all religious believers can seem to favor religion in a way that may be impermissible under the Establishment Clause. Judicially required accommodations may also ap-pear to pose a problem, especially if similarly situated nonreligious people are denied a similar dispensation. Sometimes this apparent unfairness looms large, as when religious conscientious objectors in wartime can get out of mili-tary service, while people with weighty secular reasons are denied. In general, the issue of accommodation forces us to look hard at the special place given religion under our Constitution: is it fair, and should the apparent unfairness be mitigated by taking a tough line against accommodations from laws appli-cable to all?

Although accommodation seems in some cases to pose a problem of fair-ness, considerations of both fairness and liberty strongly support the practice of granting accommodations, in at least some form and in at least some cases. When Christians may observe the day of rest that their religion requires, with-out loss of job or unemployment benefits, but those who observe a different day of rest may not, there is a burden on the liberty of these minorities to prac-tice their religion, and the burden seems unfair. They are being penalized for their non-Sunday day of worship, an intrinsic part of their religion. When the majority may testify on all the days when courts are actually in session—be-cause the days of court sessions are structured around the calendar of the ma-jority religion—and other people have to choose between a religious violation and a civil penalty for refusing to appear in court, here again, there seems to be both unfairness and a burden on liberty, the liberty to observe one's chosen day of rest undisturbed. When the majority may wear whatever their religion requires them to wear when appearing in court, or when serving in the police or the military, but Jews, or Sikhs, or Quakers are penalized for following their religion's instructions (by wearing yarmulkes or turbans, or keeping their hats on in court), there is a burden on these minorities' religious observance, and the burden is unequal, unfair. The majority is permitted to act with due religious scruples, and the minority is not. When Christian prisoners are permitted to light votive candles and Jewish prisoners are denied the right to light Hanukkah candles (together with a whole host of other minority-disfavoring practices that are one of the most unpleasant features of our troubled prison systems),[2] we find, once again, both burden and unfairness. (The rejoinder that prison is not a place of liberty anyway is undermined by the alacrity with which a sphere of liberty, in such important matters, is given to the majority.)

How can our democracy be fair to religious minorities in matters of the greatest significance? This is the key question underlying our tradition of accommodation. This chapter will trace our attempts to grapple with this urgent question, arguing that a substantial degree of accommodation, including at least some judicial dispensations from laws of general applicability, is probably required by the First Amendment, and that other forms of (legislative) accommodation are permitted. I shall argue that the colonial period already saw a consensus favoring accommodation in many matters, some trivial and some quite weighty (military service, the incest laws). Although we cannot say for certain that the First Amendment's text, as understood at the time, compels accommodation from generally applicable laws, it is clear that such accommodations were strongly favored at the time and were features of many state constitutions. At least as important, the underlying values embodied in the text of the First Amendment, considered in the light of experience, strongly favor at least some judicially compelled accommodations. More recently, as the rise of the modern state makes law a more and more ubiquitous and intrusive part of citizens' lives, the question of accommodation has taken on a new urgency and breadth—giving rise to a widely shared public understanding, articulated by the Court in the so-called *Sherbert* test, that at least some accommodations are constitutionally required.

This consensus was upset by the Court's 1990 decision in *Employment Division v. Smith*,[3] a case that set off widespread public outrage, especially for its contention (in Justice Scalia's majority opinion) that minorities will always do worse in a democracy and that there is nothing to be done about this. A vast majority of Americans thought that there was indeed something to be done about it, and supported the corrective Religious Freedom Restoration Act of 1993, which the Court promptly struck down, saying that it exceeded Congress's authority. Nonetheless, over time Congress and the Court have ironed out their differences to at least some extent, converging on a regime that protects at least some judicial accommodations and allows others to be introduced legislatively, at both the federal and the state level. This part of our tradition, at least right now, is in a reasonably healthy state.[4]

II. Accommodation at the Founding

How was the issue of accommodation understood at the time of the Founding? And what approach to the issue is likely to be embedded in the text of the First Amendment, as it was understood at that time? These are two separate questions, though not utterly unrelated. Showing how the issue was generally understood does not establish the meaning of the terms chosen by the framers, although it may possibly shed light on that meaning. Nor does either question exhaust the interpretive questions that confront courts today—even for people generally sympathetic to textualism. The great social changes that have intervened between 1789 and the present—including, prominently, the assumption of more and more administrative functions by the modern state— may lead wise judges to lean one way or another, especially when the intrinsic meaning of the religion clauses is so unclear. Indeed, one very likely understanding of the text of the religious clauses is that their key concepts are deliberately left abstract and general, with lots of room for further deliberation and specification. The founders wisely did not attempt to nail down every detail for all time.

Michael McConnell, judge on the U.S. Court of Appeals for the Tenth Circuit and one of the leading scholarly writers about the religion clauses, maintains that at the time of the Founding there was a general understanding that the "free exercise of religion" included a limited right to accommodation, meaning exemption from laws of general applicability, and that the Free Exercise Clause should be understood to imply such a right.[5] In other words, he uses historical context (the meaning commonly attached to the relevant terms in other contemporary documents) to argue for a specific interpretation of the constitutional text, one that, in his view, we should also accept as binding courts today. A leading U.S. constitutional historian, Philip Hamburger, has

argued against McConnell's historical claim.[6] Hamburger concedes to Mc-
Connell that accommodations were granted in specific types of cases during
the colonial period, but he argues that there was no understanding, at the state
or federal level, that they were constitutionally required.

McConnell's argument draws on three types of evidence: the beliefs of
some influential figures at the time of the Founding, the language of state constitutions, and actual practices in a range of cases. He points, first, to the evidence that both Washington and Madison had considerable sympathy for
religion-based accommodation. Washington, addressing the weighty issue of
military service, assures the Quakers that people's "conscientious scruples"
should be treated with "delicacy and tenderness," and that laws should be "as
extensively accommodated to them, as a due regard for the protection and essential interests of the nation may justify and permit." He meant, of course,
that Quakers would be allowed to refuse military service without legal penalty.
Similarly, Madison's understanding of "duties of conscience" was very broad,
embracing both belief and worship, and many associated areas of practice.
Thus his repeated insistence that we must protect the ability of people to obey
duties of conscience entails some types of accommodation from laws of general applicability, in cases involving oaths, military service, and so forth. A nation cannot simply avoid this issue by refusing to make laws that give rise to it:
for any nation must have a military, some practice of oath taking in court, and
so forth. So Madison's considerations could only be addressed by some degree of accommodation, some exemptions from generally applicable laws,
whether by legislative or judicial action. It is plausible to believe that Madison
understood this and made this a part of his concept of "rights of conscience"
and "the free exercise of religion."

The beliefs of individuals are always tricky as evidence for the meaning of a
group document; we have seen that Madison often had to compromise to get
the best result he could. Nor do these views give evidence about the question
of judicially compelled accommodation: they might be read as saying only
that legislatures ought to craft such exemptions. More probative evidence,
however, comes from the use of "free exercise" and related language in state
constitutions. All the state constitutions had Free Exercise Clauses (five omitted
atheists, two were limited to Christians), and all included at least some conduct as well as belief, although in some cases the protected conduct was limited to worship. All expressed Roger Williams's idea that the protected belief

and conduct had limits, supplied by the "peace and safety" of the state (the most common limiting expression). Indeed, these clauses look very like the Rhode Island charter: although they do not expressly state that laws are invalid insofar as they burden conscience, they do say that the only limit to the free exercise of religion is one supplied by peace and safety. How could they have said that, McConnell argues, if all that the protection of "free exercise" meant was that all generally applicable laws were to be upheld in all cases, even when they burdened minorities? What would have been the point of this override clause? The limitations make sense only if there was already an understanding (as in the Rhode Island Charter) that there was at least some latitude for accommodation against laws of general applicability. Otherwise, why not just say that people have religious freedom but they have to obey all the generally applicable laws?

A further argument not made by McConnell may be added to his. The no-accommodation position was well-known at the time, since it is John Locke's position. Locke thinks that government may not play favorites: thus, if it is legal to use water for bathing, it cannot be illegal to use it for baptism; if it is legal to use Latin in a school, it cannot be illegal to use it in a church. But once that issue of neutrality is dispensed with, people must obey any laws that are applicable to all. If for reasons of conscience they cannot obey, they ought to disobey the law and take the civil penalty. This position (which is in essence the position of Justice Antonin Scalia today) was much discussed, and could easily have been stated without circumlocution. Why, then, did the state constitutions not say straightforwardly what they meant, if what they meant was that people have to obey all generally applicable laws?

Discussing "peace and safety" further, McConnell draws attention to James Madison's attempt, in arguing against George Mason, to insert into Virginia's constitution an even more protective view of religious liberty. For Mason, recall, religious liberty was protected "unless under color of religion any man disturb the peace, the happiness, or safety of society." For Madison, this was not protection enough; he urged that government could interfere with the free exercise of religion only if equal liberty itself and the very existence of the state were "manifestly endangered." Surely, McConnell plausibly argues, this controversy would not have mattered had the shared notion of the "full and free exercise of religion" not included some right of exemption from generally applicable laws that conflict with conscience. (The actual language of most state constitutions, mentioning peace and safety but not happiness, seems more protective than Mason's proposal and less protective than Madison's.)

Next, McConnell points to actual practices in the preconstitutional period. Three areas of controversy were oaths, military conscription, and religious assessments. In all, the resolution of the conflict "suggests that exemptions were seen as a natural and legitimate response to the tension between law and religious convictions."[7] Witnesses in trials typically had to take a religious oath. (Because perjury prosecutions were uncommon, fear of divine punishment was seen as crucial to reliability.) Quakers and several other sects refused to take oaths on conscientious grounds. States might have responded by insisting on oaths for everyone, or by dropping the oath requirement for everyone. Instead, however, religious exemptions were created, allowing affirmation in cases of conscientious scruples. By 1789, virtually all states had legislated such exemptions. As for military conscription, Quakers, Mennonites, and Moravians were typically exempted from conscription. This practice was formalized by the Continental Congress in the following words:

> As there are some people, who, from religious principles, cannot bear
> arms in any case, this Congress intend no violence to their consciences,
> but earnestly recommend it to them, to contribute liberally in this time of
> universal calamity, to the relief of their distressed brethren in the several
> colonies, and to do all other services to their oppressed Country, which
> they can consistently with their religious principles.[8]

Note the Williams-like language: to conscript conscientious objectors is conceived as an act of wrongful violence against the conscience. Once again, the solution is neither to abandon conscription nor to force conscience: it is to carve out areas of exemption, in this case by legislative action. Finally, even when religious assessments were introduced or contemplated, their proponents always carved out space for conscientious objection. Thus, Massachusetts and Connecticut exempted Quakers and Baptists, expressly alluding to their "alleged scruple of conscience."[9]

These three areas were the most conspicuous, but many other exemptions can be found. North Carolina and Maryland exempted Quakers from the requirement to remove their hats in court. William Penn was actually imprisoned in England for his refusal to remove his hat, and the scandal created by

this incident redoubled the determination of the colonists to do things differently: other states soon added the same exemption. One of the most surprising exemptions of all can be found in Rhode Island, where, in 1764, the state
legislature passed a law allowing Jews to govern their own marriages "according to their own usages and rites." And in 1798, the state legislature explicitly
exempted Jews from the operations of the state incest law, "within the degrees
of affinity or consanguinity allowed by their religion." (Jews were understood
to encourage marriages between uncle and niece, which are not required but
are favored under Jewish law; they were illegal under Rhode Island law.)[10] Because history shows that people are unusually squeamish about any deviation
from generally applicable laws involving sex, this was a large concession, even
for the state of Rhode Island. (Interestingly enough, such marriages are legal
in Rhode Island to the present day, although they are illegal in most other
states.[11]) Notice that all these cases involve conduct, not just belief: they offer
yet further evidence that free exercise was generally understood to protect religiously motivated actions.

Once again, all these are cases of legislative accommodation, so they supply
no direct evidence for what was understood to be judicially compelled as a
reading of constitutional requirements; probably there was no such shared
understanding. These statutes, however, do provide useful background about
the general idea of religious free exercise, and thus serve indirectly to illuminate the constitutional text and its intellectual context.

With McConnell, we may add a general observation: if generally applicable
laws are understood to have no exemptions, what really becomes of religious
liberty? Religious liberty, from the seventeenth century onward, has been understood as liberty for minorities against the incursions of the majority. A (duly
limited) right of accommodation/exemption seems necessary to make sense of
the very idea of liberty of conscience, and, in particular, of equal religious liberty. One reply (Locke's, and, today, Justice Scalia's) will be that if we have laws
that are truly neutral, not targeting religion as such, or a particular religion, that
is sufficient for fairness. McConnell, however, makes a powerful case that our
traditional understanding of religious liberty involved at least some individual
rights of conscience against generally applicable laws. We may add that considerations of fairness and equality (not stressed by McConnell) bolster this argument: religious liberty is not a very significant constitutional value in a
democracy if it is the sort of thing that can be granted hierarchically, rather than

being granted to all on terms of equality. Notice that this line of argument is independent of originalist textual interpretation, and makes sense even if one thinks that the right approach to the text is not originalist.

Hamburger begins his rejoinder with an argument from silence: nobody said that there was a general right to accommodation, or that it was implicit in the constitutional language. On the second point he is probably correct, although the widespread support for accommodation as entailed by rights of conscience must be taken into account when pondering this point. Concerning the peace and safety issues, he argues that they are not a positive characterization of religious liberty, but just an account of when religious liberty can be denied. Of course this is correct, but it hardly reaches McConnell's point, which is that there would be no need to mention these exceptions unless religious liberty was taken to include at least some rights to accommodation. If it weren't, we would expect something like, "provided that they do not breach any law duly enacted." Finally, though he grants, as he must, that accommodations were granted in the cases to which McConnell points, he argues that these practices do not suffice to establish a general right of exemption. This seems plausible enough, though certainly the pattern of exemptions is a strong and consistent one, encompassing most of the contentious issues of the time. Preconstitutional practice cannot conclusively demonstrate a constitutional requirement; it can, however, show how key concepts were generally understood.

McConnell has shown that a widespread understanding of the ideas of liberty of conscience and the free exercise of religion involved the idea of accommodation. What we can plausibly say is that these accommodations were seen as a good thing, and perhaps in many cases, by many people, as implicit in the notion of religious liberty. Most people, then, would have thought it a good thing if legislatures created escape hatches for people whose consciences were burdened by laws of general applicability (at least if the escape hatches didn't create serious harms), and such exemptions would not have been seen as creating an impermissible establishment of religion. Whether accommodations are implicit in the constitutional language is less clear, and Hamburger is correct in suggesting that uncertainty remains on that question. We simply have no evidence that the chosen language was best interpreted, at the time, to entail the invalidation of any (federal) law that did impose substantial burdens on minority religion.[12] There is too little clarity about how the framers understood the allocation of authority between Congress and the courts on this question. Clearly many people did attach McConnell's meaning to the idea of free exercise, but McConnell takes a further step that may not be warranted. On the other hand, the absence of an open-and-shut case for original textual meaning does not entail that our constitutional language is not best read in hindsight—given our long experience with majority law and minority disability—as entailing such a right. As I've repeatedly said, the text has an abstractness that seems to invite interpretation in the light of new learning. Modern judicial opinions that ground accommodation in the language of the First Amendment do not become illicit if we accept, to a limited extent, Hamburger's contention that the issue was not fully resolved at the time of the amendment's framing.

For a long time little happened to test the issue of accommodation at the federal level. The federal government simply did not play a very pervasive role in people's daily lives. Apart from the question of military conscription (already settled at the level of policy in favor of accommodation for conscientious objectors) there were, apparently, no laws that burdened the religious freedom of minorities. Things were different at the state level, where some early cases show an understanding of the issue that supports McConnell's general picture—although, obviously, these people were not interpreting the federal Constitution, and although other cases rejected the accommodationist claim.

In 1793, Jonas Phillips, a Pennsylvania Jew, was subpoenaed to testify on a Saturday in a civil case.[13] He refused, citing Jewish law and claiming that he was entitled to a special exemption that would allow him to avoid testifying on his Sabbath. The court, however, imposed a fine. He appealed. The defendant eventually waived the benefit of Phillips's testimony, and he was discharged from the fine. Phillips's legal claim therefore was never resolved by the Pennsylvania Supreme Court, which simply recorded that the case had been resolved. Thus the case only shows disagreement about the issue of accommodation, Phillips alleging that he had such a legal right and the trial court denying this. On the other hand, the legal claim itself, the waiver granted by the defendant, and the court's withdrawal of the fine show a climate of sensitivity to the issue.

The case of Father Kohlmann, the first religion case whose written opinion has come down to us, goes much further, articulating an expansive accommodation right as the correct interpretation of the "free exercise" clause of the

New York State constitution. What was Father Kohlmann's horrible dilemma? James Cating, a New York City Roman Catholic, was robbed. A short time after, he received his stolen property back from his priest, Father Kohlmann. When questioned by the police, Father Kohlmann refused to say anything about how he received the stolen property, explaining that the information reached him through the confessional. Other evidence led to the indictment of Daniel Philips. Called to testify, Father Kohlmann refused, saying this:

> [I]f called upon to testify in quality of a minister of a sacrament, in which my God himself has enjoined on me a perpetual and inviolable secrecy, I must declare to this honorable Court, that I cannot, I must not answer any question that has a bearing on the restitution in question; and that it would be my duty to prefer instantaneous death or any temporal misfortune, rather than disclose the name of the penitent in question. For, were I to act otherwise, I should become a traitor to my church, to my sacred ministry and to my God. In fine, I should render myself guilty of eternal damnation.[14]

So Father Kohlmann, like Antigone, feels compelled to refuse obedience to the general law for the weightiest reasons of conscience. He might, like Antigone, have persisted in his refusal and suffered the penalty of civil disobedience. But if he had been sent to prison for his refusal, in a matter so central to a minority religion (he was pastor of the only Roman Catholic church in New York), what would we think of the society that imposed that burden upon him?

The district attorney's answer was clear: we would think this a fair society, dedicated to the equal treatment of all citizens. Indeed, far from trying to avoid the issue of equality in framing his critique of Father Kohlmann, Mr. Gardinier chose to showcase it, claiming that what equality means is that we all obey the laws, and nobody gets any special rights. Equality is just that, impartiality: all laws apply alike to all. Religious freedom has been granted to all on a basis of equality. But this freedom does not extend to "exemption from previous legal duties."

Mr. Gardinier's position keeps on returning in the history of this topic, so we should pay close attention to his argument. On the surface it is plausible enough. It is indeed important that laws apply impartially, not giving some citizens special favors over others. But the problem is that this description does not quite fit the case, because it does not acknowledge that laws passed by the majority can create unequal and asymmetrical burdens for minorities. Jonas Phillips's situation, when subpoenaed on a Saturday, is not equal, but strikingly unequal, to that of the Christian: he faces a burden that no Christian has to face—because the law has already established Sunday as a legal day of rest. So too with Father Kohlmann. Law is set up so that sacraments of the majority religion may be observed without legal burden. For example, all states, then and, for the most part, now, exempt spouses from being forced to testify against one another, on grounds that derive from the general Christian understanding of the sacrament of marriage. Protestants, the majority, do not have the sacrament of confession, so nobody had thought about the issue Father Kohlmann faced. When thought is given to this issue, one can immediately see that Father Kohlmann is being treated not as an equal, but as an unequal, since he, unlike Protestants, is being forced to violate a sacred requirement. Although it is theoretically possible for the majority religion to impose such disabilities on itself, it is highly unlikely.

In an important opinion, speaking for a unanimous court, Mayor De Witt Clinton argued that the very reasons of equal and impartial concern cited by the district attorney actually compel the law to offer Father Kohlmann an exemption. With vivid imagination, Clinton describes the horrible dilemma, arguing that the principles of the law are, as Roger Williams would have said, mild and gentle: they do not put people in such a bind. He then argues that the New York constitution itself, conceived in the spirit of "the most exalted charity," should be interpreted to require such an exemption. "It is essential to the free exercise of religion, that its ordinances should be administered—that its ceremonies as well as its essentials should be protected . . . To decide that the minister shall promulgate what he receives in confession, is to declare that there shall be no penance; and this important branch of the Roman catholic [*sic*] religion would be thus annihilated." (We might say that McConnell's interpretation of the First Amendment, while perhaps not the only legitimate reading of the text, is, similarly, the one that "exalted charity" would dictate.) Notice that the opinion rests, correctly, on the issue of the sacraments. Ministers in other faiths receive confidential communications and do not wish to divulge them; what makes Roman Catholic confession special is its sacramental character and the centrality of that sacrament to the religion. (If a Protestant minister wanted to make a case for a similar exemption, he would have to do much more than to say that he doesn't like being made to reveal what has been told him in confidence.)

Clinton turns to the "peace and safety" language of the New York constitution, arguing that the exemption of priests from testifying about what they learn in the confessional does not threaten the peace and safety of the state. He grants, then, that accommodation has a consequential override; he simply denies that this case rises to that level of risk. This case is different, he tells us, from others we can imagine, where peace and safety really are threatened:

> If a religious sect should rise up and violate the decencies of life, by practicing their religious rites, in a state of nakedness; by following incest, and a community of wives. If the Hindoo should attempt to introduce the burning of widows on the funeral piles [*sic*] of their deceased husbands, or the Mahometan his plurality of wives, or the Pagan his bacchanalian orgies or human sacrifices . . . the hand of the magistrate would be rightfully raised to chastise the guilty agents.[15]

This language should raise a red flag for us, showing us how ready even liberal defenders of religious liberty are to demonize what they do not know, and, especially, how ready people are to be horrified by unfamiliar sexual practices, even when they involve no harm to nonconsenting parties. Surely, it should strike us as odd that nudity, "orgies," and even polygamy are treated as similar to murder of women and children. Nonetheless, these scare images are in the service of a positive point: the Roman Catholic confessional does not violate people's rights and it does not threaten public order.

Father Kohlmann prevailed. The principle of religious accommodation, and the idea that constitutional language entails it, had received a major theoretical development.

Sometimes decisions went the other way. In 1831, in another case very like that of Jonas Phillips, another Jew, confusingly named Levi Philips, was called to testify in a case involving an estate of which he was the executor. The plaintiffs were not asking for his testimony to be bypassed altogether; they only asked a brief continuance so that he would not have to testify on Saturday, arguing that the Pennsylvania constitution's free exercise provision compelled it. They cited Father Kohlmann's case in their support. The Pennsylvania Supreme Court turned them down, arguing that legal obligations always take precedence over all other duties. Respectfully disagreeing with the recent New York case, the court expresses its own view: "That every obligation shall yield to that of the laws, as to a superior moral force, is a tacit condition of membership in every society. . . ."[16]

There was, then, a good deal of disagreement about how far accommodations are constitutionally compelled. We can see how the battle lines are drawn: on the one side, the ideas of Roger Williams, favoring an ample space for conscience to unfold itself and a spirit of mercy and gentleness in the law; on the other side, a fear that disorder and bias will plague any system in which laws applicable to all have minority exceptions. These same two positions contend today. (The former had the support of Justice O'Connor—until her recent retirement—and at least a substantial minority of the current Supreme Court, as well as the overwhelming support of the Congress and the American people. The latter has the support of Justice Scalia and several other members of the Court, as well as that of liberal religious scholars who hold that religious accommodations are unfair to the nonreligious.) We cannot say that one side or the other represents the "true" position of early Americans. What we can say is that the understanding of equality used by the early anti-accommodationists is harsh and in a sense superficial, underrating or denying the damage done to conscience by majority laws that place asymmetrical burdens on minorities. (The much weightier point against such accommodations, that they are unfair to the consciences of the nonreligious, had not yet surfaced.)

III. A Note on Incorporation

When the First Amendment was drafted, it applied only to acts of the national government. As we've seen, Madison and many others wanted to bind state governments, as well, to uphold the list of rights. Madison made a particular effort with the religion clauses, and it almost succeeded. In a climate of suspicion about national power, however, his motion ultimately failed in the House after passing in the Senate. All state constitutions had free exercise clauses, and most had, or shortly came to have, some type of anti-establishment provision. There was, however, no mechanism, at the national level, for protecting religious liberty and equality against a careless or malevolent state or local government.

Before very long, this need was felt. In 1845, a Roman Catholic priest, Father Permoli, was fined fifty dollars for saying prayers over the body of one of his parishioners in St. Augustin's Catholic Church in the city of New Orleans. Public health laws made it illegal to expose a corpse in any place other than the city's own obituary chapel—clearly a great burden for Roman Catholic funeral practices.[17] Father Permoli ultimately appealed to the U.S. Supreme Court. The Court, however, insisted that it had no jurisdiction in his case: "The Constitution makes no provision for protecting the citizens of the respective states in their religious liberties; this is left to the state constitution and law: nor is there any inhibition imposed by the Constitution of the United States in this respect on the states."[18]

As time went on and the role of government in citizens' lives became more and more all-encompassing, it seemed more and more anomalous that no standardization in basic liberties existed and that fundamental rights could be abridged unequally by the states.

The Civil War was, of course, in many ways about just this issue, and its outcome meant a victory for standardization and national power in at least some central areas of citizens' lives. Slavery was abolished by an assertion of national power, and the Fourteenth Amendment was added to the Constitution in order to create rights against state governments:

> No State shall make or enforce any law which shall abridge the privileges or immunities of citizens of the United States; nor shall any State deprive any person of life, liberty, or property, without due process of law; nor deny to any person within its jurisdiction the equal protection of the laws.

These words were drafted in the wake of the Civil War experience. But they are highly general, and by now it is widely agreed that all three of the amendment's components—the Privileges and Immunities Clause, the Due Process Clause, and the Equal Protection Clause—protect some fundamental rights of citizens against state governments. The exact parameters of these protections, however, remain to some extent disputed.

For our purposes, the most urgent question is whether the Fourteenth Amendment means that all the rights enumerated in the Constitution's Bill of Rights are henceforth "incorporated," meaning that they are now rights of citizens against state as well as federal government. Many scholars believe that the Privileges and Immunities Clause originally had this purpose, and there is some evidence that the drafters of the Fourteenth Amendment intended to include the first eight amendments as "privileges and immunities." The evidence is not, however, conclusive, and there are some dissonant facts.

In particular, there was an unsuccessful effort in 1875 to amend the Constitution so as to "incorporate" the religion clauses, which some think could not have happened if there was a shared understanding that "incorporation" had already taken place. The political force of the Blaine Amendment, however, lay in what it added to the existing religion clauses: an explicit prohibition of government funding of parochial schools:

> No State shall make any law respecting an establishment of religion or prohibiting the free exercise thereof; and no money raised by taxation in any State for the support of public schools, or derived from any public fund therefore, nor any public lands devoted thereto, shall ever be under the control of any religious sect, nor shall any money so raised or lands so devoted be divided between religious sects or denominations.

As we shall see further in Chapter 5, the Blaine Amendment was part of the Republican Party's anti-Catholic agenda, and what it was really doing was inserting nativist ideas of separation of church and state into the Constitution. (Nativism was an anti-immigrant movement that particularly opposed the immigration of Catholics from southern and eastern Europe.) The fact that the amendment opened with the high-minded words of the existing First Amendment may well have been a political strategy: Blaine is trying to wrap his anti-Catholic nativism in the mantle of the Constitution. So his use of these words does not imply that he thought the First Amendment, as it then existed, had not already been incorporated. As to the failure of Blaine's proposal, which is supposed by some to show that incorporation was not at the time a settled issue, it may show, instead, that anti-Catholic nativism was not a settled issue, and that non-nativists thought that the admirable parts of Blaine's proposal (the existing First Amendment) had already been incorporated.

We should probably conclude that at the time of the Fourteenth Amendment different people thought different things about its implications for the Bill of Rights, and the whole matter was not resolved with clarity. We should not forget, however, that the nation had fought a painful war over just the issue of limiting states' rights. The nation was now a true union, for better or worse. The idea that in matters of fundamental rights and liberties some citizens would be unequal to others, just on account of the accident of residing in one state rather than another, had become odious to Americans, however much the exact list of the protected rights awaited later clarification.

Most of the personal liberty protections in the Bill of Rights were explicitly incorporated during the first half of the twentieth century—though through the Due Process Clause of the Fourteenth Amendment, rather than the Privileges and Immunities Clause. The Free Exercise Clause of the First Amendment was held to apply to the states in 1940, when the Supreme Court declared unconstitutional the conviction of a Jehovah's Witness (for breach of the peace) after he played a proselytizing record (which included anti-Catholic material) to passersby on the streets of New Haven, Connecticut. The Court found that his liberty interest was constitutionally protected, given that he had engaged in no threatening or personally abusive behavior, and thus had posed no "clear and present menace to public peace and order."[19]

The Establishment Clause was incorporated shortly thereafter, in a case dealing with state government support for transportation to parochial schools.[20] At the time of incorporation, as I argued in Chapter 3, the Establishment Clause was securely and generally understood to involve protection of individual liberties. So the Court reasoned in 1963, declaring the clause a "coguarantor, with the Free Exercise Clause, of religious liberty."[21]

Incorporation raises, today, two distinct questions: first, has most of the Bill of Rights been incorporated? Second, is there a special issue about the Establishment Clause, such that it has not (rightly) been incorporated, although the Free Exercise Clause and other provisions of the Bill of Rights have? Nobody can doubt that under precedents of long standing, the Establishment Clause has been incorporated. What this second question means, then, is, "If we should discard decades of precedent and decide to return to the original understanding of the constitutional text, is there a special impediment to regarding the Establishment Clause as incorporated?" We should not disregard decades of precedent, so in a sense the matter could end right there. I have argued, however, that the alleged asymmetry between the Establishment Clause and other parts of the Bill of Rights rests on historical misunderstanding and philosophical error. There is no convincing argument, either originalist or nonoriginalist, against treating the Establishment Clause just the way the Court has treated it, as a coguarantor of individual liberties.

Incorporation remains intellectually controversial. Scholars continue to debate the merits of the Court's theories and arguments. But by now incorporation is settled law, enshrined in a host of precedents that command widespread approval. Thus Justice Thomas's proposal that we reject it is very radical, as he stresses: it would require us to reject at least sixty years of precedent. At the political level, incorporation continues to generate challenges. A lower court ruling on school prayer in the 1980s declared that it was all right for Alabama to establish a state religion.[22] Very recently, the Republican Party of the state of Texas has declared that America is a "Christian nation."[23] People who could say this could easily declare Texas a Christian state, announce that it will fund only Christian schools, and set up conspicuous Christian monuments in all state buildings. That is what is at stake in the denial of incorporation, and we should strongly reject that assault on equal liberty.

These examples remain anomalies. On the whole, there is really no controversy about what sort of nation, and what kind of state governments, Americans want. We are not back in the 1780s, when fearful antifederalists wished to limit severely the power of the central government, and southern states wanted to shore up their right to hold slaves. We are now a union, a large complex nation with a huge federal government, and we have come to think of ourselves as Americans first, Texans or Alabamans or Rhode Islanders second. We are not in favor of creating regimes of unequal basic liberty at the state level; we have taken a stand in favor of equal liberty.

In some matters it may be very good for different states to experiment with different ways of doing things. In new and highly controversial areas such as physician-assisted suicide, medical marijuana, and same-sex marriage, a limited degree of state autonomy is probably a good way of testing the implications of social changes. But when a provision has been enshrined in our Constitution since 1789 as a basic right of all Americans, we simply don't want states to play around with it. The Civil War is over, and the Confederacy lost. The incorporation of the Bill of Rights is a way of expressing the idea that all Americans are equal in their enjoyment of the fundamental rights and liberties that our Constitution protects.

IV. Mrs. Sherbert's Job, the Yoder Children's Schooling

As time went on, government assumed more and more roles in people's lives. It was now the primary educator, the primary provider of social welfare benefits, and a major employer itself. This multiplication of functions created more and more friction with people's religious requirements. At the same time, the religious diversity of America was rapidly on the rise, as new immigrants brought new religions, and new splinter groups developed domestically. Jehovah's Witnesses, Seventh-Day Adventists, Mormons, the Amish, and small numbers of Hindus, Buddhists, and Muslims[24] joined the familiar "others": Jews, Roman Catholics, Quakers, Moravians, and Mennonites. Some of the new groups inspired particular fear. (My next chapter will follow the inglorious record of America's treatment of Mormons, Jehovah's Witnesses, and Roman Catholics.) More generally, however, the need for some principle to help us understand how and when religious belief and practice should be "accommodated" against generally applicable laws needed to be found. The Court's jolting alternation between a generous spirit of accommodation and a defense of exceptionless rules fueled the demand for clarity. As it became clearer that rock-bottom issues of fairness hinged on the result, a formula was created. Adell Sherbert was the plaintiff who provoked this helpful clarification.

Seventh-Day Adventists (hereafter SDAs) belong to a homegrown American religious movement started by William Miller (1782–1849). Miller believed that the Bible included coded references to the end of the world and the Second Coming of Jesus, which (in the early 1830s) he dated to 1843–1844. When this prediction failed to materialize (the "Great Disappointment"), many believers left the church, but others remained, including leader Ellen Harmon White; they formally organized the church in 1863. By now it has over 13 million members in over 150 countries. Adventists focus on both spiritual and temporal concerns. Strict about diet and health, they have been in the forefront of antismoking and anti-alcohol movements. The founder of Kellogg's cereals was an Adventist who had studied nutrition and intestinal health. The promotion of religious liberty for all faiths has been a cherished political cause of the church, which participates in international movements on this question. Its egalitarian ethos denounces all social hierarchies created by distinctions of race, class, and gender. Many SDA members have been conscientious objectors, although they have volunteered in noncombat roles. In

Germany during World War II, Seventh-Day Adventists were among the persecuted religious groups; many members were sent to concentration camps or mental institutions.

Spiritually, Adventists focus on praise of God's goodness, consecrating their Sabbath as a day of worship and devotion. They believe that Saturday, not Sunday, is the proper day for worship, pointing to the claim in *Genesis* that "on the seventh day" God rested from his labors. Saturday worship is required of all members. Typical Saturday observances include classes for both adults and children, and a worship service, often involving praise music.

Adell Sherbert, born in 1902, lived and worked in the textile mill area of South Carolina, near Spartanburg. She had worked at the Spartan Mill in Beaumont for over thirty years when, in 1957, she joined a local branch of the SDA church. For a time her religious affiliation caused her no problems. Five days a week she worked with her fellow workers, most of whom celebrated the Sabbath on Sunday. On Saturday she and her husband worshipped with their SDA congregation. In 1959, however, economic constraint led all the mill owners in the area to shift to a six-day workweek. Naturally enough, the added day was Saturday, innocuous to the vast majority. Adell Sherbert refused to go to work on Saturday and was fired from her job. Other mills in the area offered her work, but all had six-day schedules, including Saturday, and none was willing to accommodate her religious schedule. She always insisted that she was willing to accept any employment, whether in a mill or in another industry, that did not require Saturday work. Because she refused other jobs, she was turned down by the state when she applied for unemployment compensation, on the grounds that she had declined "available suitable work."

Mrs. Sherbert went to court, complaining that her ability to practice her religion had been unfairly burdened. The state denied this, saying that they were simply treating everyone the same. In 1963, the U.S. Supreme Court found in Mrs. Sherbert's favor, in a landmark opinion by Justice Brennan that still shapes legal analysis today. Mrs. Sherbert and her husband continued to live in the same area. I have not been able to find out whether she ever returned to work. (She was sixty-one by the time her case was decided.) She died at the age of eighty-seven, in 1989.

The opinions in the case stress the fact that important religious requirements of minority religions can easily be "trod upon" by majority practices.[25] The First Amendment clearly protects both religious belief and, to some extent, religious conduct. Mrs. Sherbert's conduct is clearly conduct prompted by religious scruples. A principle is needed, however, to determine when law may restrict such conscientious conduct. The majority opinion articulates this standard in the form of a balancing test. First, it must be determined whether government's conduct imposes a "substantial burden" on the person's free exercise of religion. If it does, then we must ask whether that interference can be justified by a "compelling state interest." In other words, no ordinary state interest will do to override a conscientious claim. It must be an unusually weighty interest. And the law must be narrowly tailored to achieve this interest in the least burdensome manner possible: "no alternative forms of regulation" could be envisaged that would advance that interest "without infringing First Amendment rights."

Mrs. Sherbert had clearly suffered a burden: unlike adherents of mainstream Christianity, she was forced to make a choice between violating her religion and forfeiting her benefits. To make a religious violation a condition of receiving a benefit, the Court argued, is like fining someone for Saturday worship. The Court observes that adherents of the majority religion have been spared such horrible dilemmas: when Sunday work was authorized during the war, South Carolina explicitly stated that employees might refuse such work for reasons of conscience, with no penalty at all, not even to seniority or promotion.

Notice, then, that the equality issue is prominent in this influential opinion; indeed, it can be said to be what drives the entire argument. Equality is not advanced as an extra consideration, over and above the idea of substantial burden; it is one constituent of the idea of substantial burden. Clearly, it would not be constitutional to restrict religious liberty for all: so, as we argued in Chapter 1, the issue of liberty is to that extent distinct from the issue of equality. But the particular feature of this burden that stands out in the Court's analysis is that it is an unfair burden, a burden that "fines" Mrs. Sherbert for her religious convictions.[26] The state, it is clear, would have been free to deny everyone unemployment compensation: that by itself would not have infringed religious liberty. What infringes religious liberty here is the unfairness with which the benefit is applied.

Does the state have a compelling interest in its exclusionary policy? There might have been such an interest: the Court mentions *Braunfeld v. Brown*, an earlier decision upholding Sunday closing laws.[27] Here, they argue (I'm not

convinced), the financial loss to Jewish merchants (and other Saturday Sabbath observers) was outweighed by the strong state interest in having only one
legal day of rest. But Mrs. Sherbert's case, they conclude, is not like that. The
history of waivers of Sunday work during the war suggests that the administrative difficulty of processing conscientious claims was not overwhelming
and that no "compelling interest," therefore, exists.

The "Sherbert test" quickly became the lens through which the Court
looked at all comparable claims for accommodation. It looks like a pretty good
way of balancing the state's need for at least some uniformity with the rights of
minorities to be free from burdens on their religious practice. The central
concepts in this "test" need further delineation. For example, should "substantial burden" be limited to cases in which the religion absolutely *requires*
the conduct that has been impeded, or should there be a somewhat looser
standard? Clearly the mere fact that someone feels like doing something as an
expression of religious attachment should not be recognized as constituting a
substantial burden; and yet to recognize a burden only when the conduct in
question is absolutely required by religion seems too prohibitive, ruling out
cases of religiously central conduct that has not been authoritatively ordained.
Such a standard, besides being too strict, would unduly burden religions that
do not issue commandments, but leave much to the conscience of the individual. Not surprisingly, a standard looser than that of command, but still requiring some religious centrality, has on the whole prevailed.

Another unclear question is whether the burden must be one that is clearly
discriminatory, such that the majority is able to do comparable things without
burden. Burdens on Sabbath observance look clearly discriminatory, since
Mrs. Sherbert's neighbors could observe their sacred day without penalty.
Similarly, penalties for peyote use look discriminatory, since alcohol has always been protected in sacramental contexts, even during Prohibition. But
there are other cases of putative accommodation—exemptions from the draft,
religiously grounded educational dispensations—where the idea of discrimination does not apply so neatly, and yet one still may judge that, at a more general level, there is unfairness in being prevented from abiding by the dictates
of one's conscience when others are not so burdened. In such cases, as we
shall see, courts have still found grounds for accommodation, interpreting the
fairness issue less narrowly and at a higher level of generality.[28]

A third difficult question concerns the notion of a "compelling state inter-est." This category has been notoriously difficult to specify. Surely it would not be wise to try to offer an exhaustive *ex ante* list of such interests, given the changing functions of the modern state. The evolving case law, proceeding in-crementally, has helped a good deal to clarify the interests that may be admit-ted into that category. Nonetheless, the extreme vagueness of the concept has also caused problems, giving rise, for example, to premature denials of accom-modation when courts don't like or don't understand a particular religion, or fear its practices.[29]

Thus *Sherbert* left many difficult problems to resolve. Nonetheless, it was a major achievement, suggesting a test that shaped legal reasoning for decades, and that still seems wise today. Subsequent developments show that the *Sher-bert* approach currently has the overwhelming support of the American people.

The Supreme Court did not grant many religious accommodations, even under the *Sherbert* test. In a group of unemployment cases similar to Adell Sherbert's, they did grant similar accommodations.[30] A Florida Seventh-Day Adventist won unemployment compensation after she refused Saturday work A Jehovah's Witness in Indiana won compensation after he asked to be laid off from his work in an armaments factory, citing religious opposition to work of this sort. An Illinois man who cited religious reasons when he refused tempo-rary employment in a jewelry store that would have required Sunday work won compensation even though his religious objections did not stem from membership in any organized sect.

Outside the unemployment sphere, however, the Court often either failed to find a substantial burden or did find a compelling state interest. In *U.S. v. Lee* (1982), an Amish employer, citing religious reasons, refused to pay Social Security tax for his employees.[31] The Court found that there was a burden, but there was also a compelling state interest, since "it would be difficult to ac-commodate the comprehensive social security system with myriad exceptions flowing from a wide variety of religious beliefs." In *Goldman v. Weinberger* (1986), Jewish soldiers who sought the right to wear the yarmulke in the mili-tary were told that the military is different from other areas of U.S. life: for the military, no compelling interest is required, and a mere "rational basis" for the rule (a very weak standard) is sufficient.[32] In *Bob Jones University v. United*

States (1983), an evangelical university that forbade interracial dating on religious grounds lost its tax exemption.[33] That was a burden to their religious exercise, the Court held, but it was outweighed by the "fundamental, overriding interest in eradicating racial discrimination in education." In two cases involving Native American religion, which the Court does not try very hard to understand, the required use of a Social Security number for a child (in *Bowen v. Roy*) was found not to be a substantial burden, despite parents' belief that it would steal her spirit, and the government's plan to build a road through sacred lands (in *Lyng*) was also found not to create a substantial burden.[34] In both of these cases it might have been reasonable to find a compelling state interest; to deny the existence of a burden seems a bit cavalier. *Lyng*, in particular, shows a certain degree of obtuseness about the communal religious practices of Native Americans, which cannot very easily be fit into the individualistic framework of Free Exercise jurisprudence.

It is important to notice, however, that in all of these unsuccessful cases the *Sherbert* test is asserted and taken as foundational. Even in *Goldman*, where the *Sherbert* framework is not actually applied, the rationale for not applying it is that the military is *sui generis*.

In 1972, however, in a landmark case, the Court once again found both a substantial burden and the absence of a compelling state interest—this time in a context far from that of unemployment compensation. One of the most cherished legal uniformities in American life is that of compulsory public education. Compulsory schooling is such a routine part of our daily life that we forget that it once was highly controversial. Both industry and parents, in both the U.S. and Europe, during the eighteenth and much of the nineteenth centuries, strongly resisted the idea that all children would attend primary school, and the addition of secondary school gave rise to even more complaint. Lots of parents wanted to be able to use their children for agricultural and other types of labor. The British Liberal Party, in the late nineteenth century, split over the issue of compulsory education. Free-market Liberals argued that parents should be able to contract freely for the labor of their children. On the other side, Aristotelian philosopher T. H. Green argued that no person can be truly free without education, and that the freedoms of parents and the market must be limited to make room for the development of children's mental powers and social opportunities.[35] (A century earlier, Scottish philosopher Adam Smith had commended the Scottish practice of compulsory primary schooling, complaining that in England, where there were no such laws, children's faculties were "mutilated and deformed" by being sent to long hours of monotonous factory labor.)[36] So the question where parents' rights leave off and the state's legitimate interest in the education of its children for both personal opportunity and public citizenship begins is one with a long and contentious history. For a long time, however, the T. H. Green/Adam Smith argument has been virtually universally accepted, and there has been no serious challenge to the idea that all children should in general be required to attend primary and secondary school until the age of sixteen. The only question remaining was whether this is a case in which religious commitments might give rise to an exception.

The Old Order Amish are a small sect that grew out of the Anabaptist movement in Switzerland and Germany. (Although they are often confused in the public mind with Mennonites, they split from the Mennonites in the eighteenth century, seeing them as too worldly.) Persecuted in Europe, they took refuge in Pennsylvania, where William Penn promised them a haven from bigotry. Since then they have established communities in other states, including Wisconsin and Ohio. The Amish lead a simple agricultural life, keeping their distance from the modern world. Of the approximately 180,000 Amish in the United States, fewer than half belong to the Old Order Amish Church, one of the strictest of the four Amish sects. The Old Order Amish do not participate in Social Security or Medicare, and they avoid all voluntary participation in politics and the legal system. They own no cars, have no electricity or telephones. And yet they are prosperous and productive citizens, frequently quite wealthy. They believe in allowing children a chance to understand the temptations of worldly society and to leave the sect, if they so choose: indeed children are turned loose at age seventeen to explore the outside world in a regular ritualized practice of adolescent exploration called *rumspringa* (from German *herumspringen*, meaning "to jump around"). The Amish also believe, however, that the sect's very survival depends on their ability, prior to that experiment in difference, to teach their children the skills of farmwork, carpentry, and housekeeping, and the values of communal solidarity and pacifism that go with them. Crucial to this teaching is actual practice, especially in early adolescence.

Wisconsin, like most states, requires children to be in school (either public school or an accredited private school) until age sixteen. (An eighth grade education sufficed until 1933.) Homeschooling is permitted, but the hours of instruction and the basic curriculum have to be approved as "substantially equivalent to instruction given to children of like ages in the public or private schools where such children reside." Frieda Yoder, age fifteen, Barbara Miller, age fifteen, and Vernon Yutzy, fifteen, left school after the eighth grade and did not reenroll. (The Yutzys were Mennonites, but they joined the case and made similar arguments.) The three children were not approved for any home-schooling or other exemption. The state of Wisconsin charged the parents with violating the law. They were convicted and fined five dollars each. Because the Amish will not defend themselves, believing that "turn the other cheek" is the right philosophy, their legal defense was paid for by public dona-tions through an interfaith forum called National Committee for Amish Reli-gious Freedom.

The parents—Jonas Yoder, Wallace Miller, and Adin Yutzy[37]—never chal-lenged the state's right to require education for all children up through the eighth grade. They focused on the high school years, holding that sending their children to school those two remaining required years was contrary to their religious beliefs. Children would be exposed to the temptations of worldly society at an age when they would be particularly vulnerable to peer pressure. They would also fail to have a crucial Amish type of education, a kind of "learning by doing" that is at the core of Amish life. The brief for the parents states that "the Amish are emphatically in favor of education—but an 'education for life' as seen in the terms of their religious view . . . Amish edu-cation has followed in the pattern of classical *wisdom* rather than *technos* [*sic*]." Amish education is said to focus on moral wisdom and communal life, including skills required for sustaining the community. The Amish parents simply deny that all education must conform to the pattern imposed by the state, including its values of "consumption and competition."

The legal claim was brought on behalf of the parents, not the children, and the actions of the state were held to impede the religious freedom of the par-ents. So what is at stake is not, directly, the children's freedom of religion; rather, it is the freedom of the parents, including the freedom to perpetuate their own way of life and their freedom to direct the religious education of their children. Indeed, it was an odd feature of the case, remarked on in Justice Douglas's dissenting opinion, that little was heard either about or from the children. Only one of the children, Frieda Yoder, testified. She monosyllabi-cally endorsed the view that the reason she did not go to school was because of her religion. Justice Douglas's proposal that the children be asked for their opinions about their parents' views seems quite naïve: how can minor children, living at home with their parents in a conservative community that "shuns" dissidents, freely express a view in such a delicate matter? Nonetheless, it would have been good to have heard more about how to balance the religious freedom of the parents (seen as encompassing certain rights to direct their children's education) against the children's interest in choice and opportunity, including the opportunity to exit from the community if they so chose. The fact that the community protects exit options through *rumspringa* (oddly, not discussed in the opinions) helps assuage at least some worries about exit options (although this tends to be a time of wild indulgence, associated with drug problems, rather than a time of learning further employment-related skills). The case also had a troubling gender aspect that was never mentioned. While Amish boys, withdrawn from school, were at least learning marketable skills of carpentry and farming, girls were typically performing domestic tasks, which do not give them ordinary "exit options" for financial independence. This entire issue needed more discussion.

The case followed the *Sherbert* guidelines closely. First of all, the Court argues that the interests at stake for the parents in the case are "fundamental rights and interests," including the free exercise of religion and also the "traditional interest of parents with respect to the religious upbringing of their children." Although it appears in this initial statement that two separate interests are mentioned, the subsequent analysis treats them as a single interest, in the free exercise of religion. No constitutional basis for the parental right is ever identified, *other than* the Free Exercise Clause of the First Amendment. Indeed, the Court makes it clear that no parent with a purely secular claim of a similar sort would have prevailed. It looks quite clear, then, that the parental right is being held to flow from the right of religious free exercise.

The parents' claim that the educational requirement "interferes with the practice of a legitimate religious belief" is now examined. The Court begins by insisting that religion is special. "A way of life, however virtuous and admirable, may not be interposed as a barrier to reasonable state regulation of education if it is based on purely secular considerations; to have the protection of the religion clauses, the claims must be rooted in religious belief." Belief, however, is not the only thing the Constitution protects: the Court insists that substantial areas of religious conduct also enjoy the protection of the Free

Exercise Clause, and thus are "beyond the power of the State to control, even under regulations of general applicability." The fact that Wisconsin applies the same rule to everyone does not show that there is no substantial burden to religious free exercise: "A regulation neutral on its face may, in its application, nonetheless offend the constitutional requirement for governmental neutrality if it unduly burdens the free exercise of religion." The Court concludes that Yoder and the other parents have made their case to this extent: there is a substantial burden.

Does Wisconsin, on the other side, have a compelling interest that could override this claim? Education, admittedly, is a state interest of great importance, but it is not "totally free from a balancing process." In this case, Wisconsin's claim that the two further years of school attendance are necessary to prepare the children "to be self-reliant and self-sufficient participants in society" is without merit. The Amish community has shown that it can be highly self-reliant and productive; indeed, the fact that they reject public welfare shows that the children could not possibly be a drag on state funds. (Here the Court interprets self-reliance with unfortunate narrowness, in terms of the ability to earn an income rather than in terms of the child's own development of capacities and skills relevant to citizenship and the conduct of life in general.)

Wisconsin also claims that the two years in question (called a "brief period" by the Court) are "imperative to enable the Amish to participate effectively and intelligently in our democratic process." This claim, too, is rejected: the Amish can "function effectively and intelligently" within their own self-imposed restrictions. Indeed, in many ways, says the Court, they resemble the self-sufficient farmers admired by Thomas Jefferson—a rather implausible claim, since Jefferson surely did not admire those who shunned all participation in public life.

Was *Wisconsin v. Yoder* rightly decided? The case continues to generate controversy today. The case is less clear-cut than *Sherbert*, because the fairness issue arises at a more abstract level. In *Sherbert*, the majority gets to observe their holy day without penalty; Mrs. Sherbert doesn't. In *Yoder* there is no comparable educational exemption for the majority, so the way the fairness issue figures is at a higher level of generality: the majority gets to abide by and preserve their religious ways of life and the Amish (arguably) don't. Should the Court make an accommodation in such a case? Several aspects of the Court's analysis are disturbing. The Court never considers the possibility that the children may choose to leave the community, and thus might need an education that enables them to participate knowledgeably and respectfully in democratic politics, rather than simply to avoid it. Nor do they ask what actually becomes of children who leave: do they prosper, or do they end up on welfare, or otherwise unhappy? One can't help feeling, too, that the status of the Amish as a kind of "model minority"—wealthy, orderly, no problem to anyone—influences the reasoning more than it really should, given that what we're dealing with is the education of children for a life in which they may be part of that community, but also may not. Given the Court's uneven record in dealing with strange minority religions, which we'll see more fully in our next chapter, the favorable treatment meted out to the Amish seems a little unfair: they get a break in part because they are wealthy and established, and don't pose any big challenge to majority Protestant values of thrift and virtue.

People have also disagreed about how crucial the two years in question are to the interests mentioned by Wisconsin (personal well-being and democratic citizenship): do children in the first two years of high school learn skills of autonomy and democracy that they would be unable to learn at a younger age? Or are these years primarily taken up with dating and peer pressure?

On balance, the case was probably rightly decided, because the burden involved was an extremely severe one, and the State certainly did not show a compelling interest that would be served by denying the exemption and that could not be served in some other non-burden-inflicting way. One may differ about the application of the *Sherbert* test to this case, however, while agreeing that the Court's clear legal analysis articulates a very workable and clear-edged doctrine of accommodation. The Free Exercise Clause can supply individuals with reasons of conscience that prevail against all state interests but the very highest—only, however, if the grounds for accommodation are religious in nature. Accommodation has its limits: it is pretty clear that the parents could not have won the right to take their children out of school at age ten, or perhaps even age twelve. At the margins, however, even an extremely strong public interest such as the interest in education must yield before the overwhelming importance of religious free exercise.

Yoder was an important deepening and extension of *Sherbert*. It confirmed that *Sherbert* was the law of the land, and it clarified some of *Sherbert*'s implications. Equally important, the *Sherbert* framework was widely employed at the lower court level, in cases that were never reviewed by the Supreme Court, and it did result in a modest success rate for minorities pressing religious claims. Scholars often say that religious plaintiffs almost never received accommodations, even after *Sherbert*. This claim, however, is seriously in error. The Supreme Court reviews only a small minority of the cases that are appealed to it. Typically it accepts a case only if it presents a novel or unresolved legal issue, or if the Court is inclined to go against what the lower court has done, or needs to clarify an issue on which different circuits have decided things differently. This being the case, we should hardly be surprised that the cases in which religious plaintiffs had received accommodations under the *Sherbert* test did not get to the Supreme Court: the Court was pleased with the legal framework that it had established, and lower courts were correctly applying that framework, without major differences between circuits. A recent thorough study of all Free Exercise cases after *Sherbert* shows clearly that minorities (particularly small sects and denominations) are the standard plaintiffs in such cases and that, while they lose more than half the time, they do much better under the *Sherbert* framework, and under the Religious Freedom Restoration Act, which restored the *Sherbert* framework, than they did under the more restrictive framework established by the *Smith* decision in 1990.[38]

Even when lower courts eventually denied religious accommodations, the *Sherbert* regime led to a keen sensitivity to minority interests that had often been absent earlier. Consider the story of the Tennessee snake handlers.[39] The Holiness Church of God in Jesus' Name directs its members to handle poisonous snakes and to drink strychnine. The church was founded in 1909 by George Went Hensley, following the injunction of *Mark* 16:17–18 to "take up serpents, and if they drink any deadly thing it shall not hurt them." It had continued to practice charismatic healing at the fringes of rural Tennessee society until the state decided to get involved, passing a law against "Handling Snakes so as to Endanger Life." Pastor Pack and other church elders were enjoined to cease and desist their practice with snakes (although the strychnine was allowed to continue).

Here is a minority religion that the majority is bound to find alarming. Court proceedings showed a predictable measure of panic: for example, a thirty-year-old consenting adult who was bitten (nonfatally) in the arm was referred to as an "Indian boy." Nonetheless, the appellate court tried everything in its power to limit the law so as to make it more friendly to the sect. In particular, they suggested that the law might be restricted so as to apply only to situations in which nonconsenting parties were in danger. The Tennessee Supreme Court ultimately sided with the original injunction and against the appellate court—but in the meantime it showed a careful sensitivity to the history and practices of the cult. The opinion gives a long and sympathetic history of the movement, showing clearly why snake handling was thought important, and documenting the spiritual effect of this practice on believers. Instead of scoffing or demonizing, the court really tries to understand, and to figure out whether there was some way to give the sect its most central practices without endangering nonconsenting parties. The court now announces that "the scales are always weighted in favor of free exercise and the state's interest must be compelling; it must be substantial; the danger must be clear and present and so grave as to endanger paramount public interests."

In the end, they found such an interest, saying that "the handling of snakes in a crowded church sanctuary, with virtually no safeguards, with children roaming about unattended, with the handlers so enraptured and entranced that they are in a virtual state of hysteria and acting under the compulsion of 'anointment,'" posed a danger to public safety, and in particular a danger to children and families. The injunction is compared to the requirement of polio vaccination. This result is plausible, and what we might have expected. What is interesting, however, is the length of the route the court took to get there. *Sherbert* produced a climate of heightened sympathy to religious interests, particularly those of small and odd minorities. To deny a request for accommodation becomes a difficult matter, requiring a showing of knowledge and sensitivity, and a very serious public interest. When we see, in our next chapter, how the claims of Mormons and Jehovah's Witnesses were treated in the pre-*Sherbert* era, we will have even stronger reasons to applaud the *Sherbert* framework. It alerted all Americans to the dangers faced by minority religion in a majority society.

V. The Demise of Accommodation: Employment Division v. Smith [40]

Native Americans have perhaps suffered more than any other U.S. religious minority from majority disdain and majority tyranny. This tyranny has included theft, violence, forced removal of children from parents, and the forced "reeducation" of these children so as to Christianize them and remove traces of their tribal religious beliefs and practices. Not least of the problems in the troubled relationship of majority Americans with Native Americans is a failure to respect Native American religions as religion. Roger Williams's respect for the dignity of his Indian friends was the exception; disdain for "pagan" and "heathen" practices has been the rule.

Native American religions are diverse; to some extent the contemporary sense of unity in belief and practice results from deliberate reconstruction. Nonetheless, one can generalize, to at least some extent, concerning what is currently accepted as the common core of Native American traditions. Native American religion is communal. It has no Bibles, no creeds, no sanctuaries. Nature and land play central roles in Native concepts of sacredness. Divinity is sought in a multifaceted relationship to the sacred in nature and in the universe, rather than in a relationship to a singular quasi-paternal God. For such reasons it was easy for many of the founders to assume that Native religion was hardly religion at all. Jefferson, great defender of religious freedom that he was, spoke with strong denigration of the customary practices of the Indians.[41] Madison was in some respects a true follower of Roger Williams; he defended the land rights of the Indians and favored a strong system of federal jurisdiction, holding that states were more likely than the nation to seize lands and take other unjust actions.[42] Like Williams, he understood that nomadic peoples could establish land rights. Even he, however, favored assimilation and a degree of Europeanization as being in the Indians' best interest. He focuses on culture, not religion; but he certainly does not express respect for Native Americans' religious practices.

Over the years, as we now can see with regret and collective guilt, majority attitudes and majority greed ended up depriving the Native Americans of many precious liberties, of property, and, through the forced conversion and "reeducation" of children, of much in the practice of their own religious traditions, which often have to be reconstructed and even reinvented today. For these and other reasons, the economic and psychological condition of the Native inhabitants is perilous, and alcoholism is but one of the ills endemic to a people persistently subordinated. The search for psychological health and, in particular, for the treatment of alcohol abuse has often been associated with the renewal of Native American religious practices. This is the context for one of the twentieth century's most significant religious freedom cases, *Employment Division v. Smith*.

Al Smith, known to the white world as Red Coyote (a name he still goes by today, to live up to his appearance), is a full-blood member of the Klamath tribe of southern Oregon. His family once had a name in the Klamath language, but, like so much in any Native American life, it has been lost, ever since federal Indian agents in the nineteenth century gave all the Indians "American" names in a mass renaming process. Al Smith sometimes imagines arriving in the spirit world, only to find that nobody knows him: "We never heard of any Al Smith," he imagines his people saying.[43] In 2001, at the age of eighty, however, Smith looked defiantly unassimilated: "His hair (black when he was young, iron-gray now) hangs nearly to his waist, thick and straight . . . His eyes have a distant look, as if he is seeing something others cannot."[44]

As a small child, Smith lived with his tribe, who owned and logged a large stretch of prime forest near the Williamson River in Oregon. He remembers happy times fishing, or gathering berries for jam. At the age of seven, however, like so many other Indian children, Al was taken from his family and sent to a Catholic boarding school to learn to be "American." The school made sure that he did not learn his Native language, his tribe's history, or anything about traditional religion. A local Catholic historian explained the mission of these schools: to "take the child away from the barbaric surroundings of the teepee and . . . mold him in the ways of civilization."[45] The school had high walls to discourage escape.

Al Smith kept resisting. He avoided Christian baptism by lying that he had already been baptized. He ran away often, trying to get back to the forest. The state police always caught up with him. Once he was beaten by a priest with a leather strap.[46] After yet one more runaway attempt at the age of twelve, Al was transferred to the Stewart Indian School, run by the Bureau of Indian Affairs. This school was still bent on Americanizing, but it treated its students better. Al excelled at football and track, and did well in math. But when he reached adolescence he also began drinking heavily. After he left school he drank more and more heavily, panhandling and rolling drunks. His drinking problems continued in the army. Sentenced to prison after a court-martial for drinking on duty, he was diagnosed by an army doctor as an alcoholic. He also got tuberculosis and spent a long period in a sanitarium.

Meanwhile, Smith received a notice from the federal government that his tribe was officially "terminated": considered ready for assimilation, the Klamath had been dropped from federal tribal rolls. Each member got a check for his or her share of tribal lands, which had been sold off to private developers.[47] (There was widespread suspicion that the termination program was primarily a way of putting valuable land, coveted by private developers, onto the market.) So, Al Smith was officially not even an Indian anymore.

By the time Al Smith was in his late thirties, his alcoholism had become debilitating. On January 15, 1957, he went to Alcoholics Anonymous, determined to begin a new life. Forty years later, he still celebrateed that date as a solemn anniversary. AA, like other twelve-step programs, asks people to entrust their lives to a "higher power." Smith had no religion of his own, so, he recalled, he decided to turn to the Indian god, present to him only as a distant memory of a time when his life had seemed whole. He began to pray to "[a] God that I didn't even understand."[48]

Over the years Smith became a highly effective alcohol counselor, working with Native people, first in Denver and then back in Oregon. By 1975 he was back in the part of Oregon where he had grown up, working as an alcohol counselor for a new group in Portland. A compelling public speaker, he addressed AA meetings all over the West Coast.[49] Meanwhile, his own personal search for his Native religion deepened. He became convinced that Native American religion, especially when combined with AA's twelve steps, was a great source of strength to Native people struggling with alcoholism.[50] He was introduced to the Sun Dance, one of the most sacred ceremonies in Native spirituality. Soon after, he linked up with the Native American Church, which uses the drug peyote in its (reconstructed) traditional rituals. Peyote rituals can be documented going back thousands of years, although the church's version is a nineteenth-century construct that borrows elements from Christianity.[51]

Peyote is a hallucinogen, but participants who have eaten the plant in these nightlong ceremonies describe an effect that is quite unlike the wild hallucinations frequently associated with LSD:[52] one of increased concentration, inward focus, and fascination with the fire. (Epps notes that the drug also helps users cope with the physical rigor of sitting cross-legged, with no back support, for twelve to fifteen hours.)[53] Actual hallucinations are rare, and are not regarded as auspicious. Al Smith was hesitant about peyote: according to the AA philosophy, an alcoholic cannot take any mind-altering drug. Eventually, however, as part of his personal spiritual search, he tried it on several occasions in the late 1970s. He found that it did not lead him to fall off the wagon.[54] In fact, he found it beneficial: "I have been assisted to a place where I have a better understanding, or led to an understanding, which helps me become a good person," he later said.[55]

Al married, had a daughter at the age of sixty-two, and got a new job to be close to his family, as counselor at ADAPT, the Douglas County Council on Alcohol and Drug Abuse Prevention and Treatment. He began work there in September 1982. Smith was praised by all as an outstanding counselor, measured, serene, and with a Native religious consciousness that could "elevate a discussion to a different plane."[56] Although Smith continued to use peyote from time to time in the sacred ceremony, the topic of peyote never came up at work—until, in 1983, a new employee, Galen Black, asked Al questions about the peyote ceremony, and eventually tried the drug himself on his first visit. Black talked enthusiastically about his experience. As a result, in 1983 he was suspended from his job. Smith was then questioned about his peyote use. He admitted it, and was fired in March 1983. The state denied him unemployment compensation because he had committed "a willful violation of the standards of behavior that an employer has the right to expect of an employee."[57] The case was all the easier to make in that peyote use was illegal under Oregon state law. (Although for many years peyote was not illegal, in the 1960s and 1970s an increase in hallucinogen abuse led to new laws classifying it with LSD as an illegal drug.)[58]

The Smith case is undoubtedly a difficult one. Everyone involved was acting in good faith. The superiors at the treatment program who fired Smith and Black were sincere practitioners of the AA philosophy. They were convinced that any use of any drug would compromise sobriety and that a drug-user could not counsel alcoholics. Research casts doubt on this idea, showing that Native Americans who get involved in Native American religion, including its use of peyote, have a better recovery rate than those who do not.[59] On the other hand, all such research is preliminary and inconclusive, and the AA philosophy has a long track record of success. As for the state, the Oregon state constitution has an unusually strong neutrality requirement: the state cannot give any religion a benefit that it does not give to other religions.[60] Given this requirement, state officials were concerned not only about peyote, which might prove harmless enough when used only in the sacred ceremony, but about a flood of claims from other religions and quasi-religions what would wish to use drugs. For example, a group calling itself the "Universal Industrial

Church of the New World Comforter," basing its teachings on alleged revelations from space aliens, urged its ministers, called Boo Hoos, to cultivate "the herbs of the field," and interpreted this to urge the private cultivation of marijuana.[61] As Garrett Epps remarks, "Any second-year law student could find important distinctions between peyote religion and the Universal Industrial Church. Peyotists used only small amounts of peyote, and only during ceremonies. The sacrament was usually not available to strangers and newcomers . . . ."[62] Nonetheless, one can see why sincere state officials, acting in good faith, would worry about creating an exemption for peyote and imagine a slippery slope.

The case eventually reached the Supreme Court. Suppose the Court had applied the *Sherbert* test. The case would have been a difficult one. On the one hand, the religious interest represented by Smith (and perhaps Black, though he was merely curious and not yet a member) is serious, authentic, and weighty. Even if his dismissal from that particular job could be given a plausible justification, the denial of unemployment compensation seems as punitive in his case as it was in Adell Sherbert's. On the other hand, the state is generally thought to have a strong interest in stopping the use of dangerous drugs. If one thinks antidrug laws are at all appropriate, one is also likely to think that they supply the state with a very strong interest. This issue is complicated by the fact that alcohol, the majority's drug of choice, is legal in general and therefore legal for religious purposes. No celebrant of the Mass will pay a legal penalty for using wine in the process—although surely, in terms of actual human damage to both users and others who encounter them, alcohol ranks extremely high and peyote extremely low. Alcohol, moreover, in addition to its destructive effect on individual lives, is strongly linked to crimes such as assault and domestic violence; peyote, especially in its ceremonial use, is not linked to any increase in crime. So the claim of a compelling interest, to be convincing, ought to take cognizance of these facts.

Justice O'Connor's concurring opinion in the *Smith* case applies the *Sherbert* framework, endorses it, and finds that state law had placed a severe burden on the ability of Smith and Black to exercise their religion freely. She finds, however, a compelling state interest on the other side: the interest "in enforcing laws that control the possession and use of controlled substances by its citizens."[63] Insisting that "drug abuse" is "one of the most serious problems confronting our society today,"[64] she makes no distinction between general use and sacramental use, but speaks only of Oregon's interest "in prohibiting the possession of peyote by its citizens."[65] This reasoning is a little peculiar, rather as if the Court in *Yoder* had spoken of Wisconsin's interest in making sure that "its citizens" get a high school education, rather than asking about its interest in denying an exemption to a very small religiously motivated group. Just as Wisconsin teenagers would not all abruptly leave school as a result of the Amish exemption, there is no reason to think that all Oregonians would start using peyote as the result of a narrow, religiously circumscribed, exception. (Indeed, now that the sacramental use of peyote has been legalized under federal law, we can see firsthand that such a result has not followed. Even Justice Scalia has emphasized this fact in a 2006 case that we shall later discuss.) Nonetheless, at least Justice O'Connor's reasoning follows and upholds the guidelines laid down by years of First Amendment jurisprudence, insisting, as had previous cases, that the Free Exercise Clause protects religiously motivated conduct as well as belief, and that it requires at least some exemptions from laws of general applicability.

Not so the majority opinion, written by Justice Scalia. This opinion is one of the most widely criticized in all of the Court's recent jurisprudence. Its legal reasoning, its treatment of precedent, and its attitude to the place of religious minorities in majority society have all come in for strenuous criticism, not only from liberals but from religious conservatives such as Michael McConnell, a leading authority on Free Exercise.[66] Scalia not only refuses to apply the *Sherbert* framework, he insists that it never has been settled law. Sweeping away years of jurisprudence with breathtaking confidence, Scalia makes six claims—each of which Justice O'Connor, in her concurrence, carefully rebuts.

1. **Conduct is not protected.** Scalia argues that the First Amendment protects belief, but permits states to regulate religious conduct, so long as it does so in a way that does not single out one religion over another for bad treatment. Here he invokes an 1874 case involving Mormons, *Reynolds*, that does say this; but, as we shall see in our next chapter, that case is an anomaly, motivated by panic about deviant sexual practices.

2. **Law is supreme.** "We have never held that an individual's religious beliefs excuse him from compliance with an otherwise valid law prohibiting conduct that the state is free to regulate."[67] Here, in a most extraordinary fashion, he cites *Minersville v. Gobitis*,[68] a case that concerned Jehovah's Witnesses' refusal to

salute the flag. Besides being a free speech case, not a religion clause case, this case is one of the most notorious errors in the Supreme Court's history, and was almost immediately overruled. Citing *Gobitis* in a religious freedom case is like citing *Plessy v. Ferguson* (the notorious case in which the Court defended the "separate but equal" principle) in a case involving racial discrimination.

3. Accommodation means anarchy. "Any society adopting such a system will be courting anarchy." This is the heart of the matter: Justice Scalia in all sincerity does believe that exceptions to generally applicable laws create an unworkable system. But he offers no evidence that anarchy has ensued during the many years when accommodations have been granted, even in weighty matters such as military conscription.

4. The apparent precedents are not real precedents. Justice Scalia argues that *Sherbert* (and its relatives) were unemployment cases, and that such cases are different because their context "lent itself to individualized governmental assessment of the reasons for the relevant conduct."[69] The unemployment cases he allows to stand untouched, and the *Sherbert* test, as applied to them, remains good law. Most oddly, however, Justice Scalia does not acknowledge that *Smith* itself is at least in part an unemployment compensation case. He does mention a relevant difference: Mrs. Sherbert's conduct in going to worship on a Saturday was not illegal under South Carolina law, as Smith's and Black's use of peyote was under Oregon law.[70] But to conclude from this that there is no right to use peyote sacramentally is circular, prejudging exactly what the case asked the Court to resolve.

Yoder is clearly not an unemployment case, and it is clearly a relevant precedent. In order to deny its precedential value, however, Justice Scalia argues that it is a "hybrid" case, relying not only on the First Amendment but also on the right of parents to educate their children.[71] This reasoning is also highly peculiar, since *Yoder* grounded that parental right in the religious clauses of the First Amendment, insisting that a claim of a similar type with a secular basis would not have prevailed. Repeatedly the case insists on a specific reading of the Free Exercise Clause as justifying the result.

As for the many other cases in which the *Sherbert* test was applied, all Justice Scalia has to say about them is that the plaintiffs lost.[72] But how is this relevant, given that in the process the constitutional standard was repeatedly affirmed? As Justice O'Connor says, "Indeed, it is surely unusual to judge the vitality of a constitutional doctrine by looking to the win-loss record of the plaintiffs who happen to come before us."[73] To her protest we can add the new data about the efficacy of the *Sherbert* framework in defending minority rights at the lower court level—in cases that the Supreme Court did not review, but allowed to stand.

5. The "compelling interest" test would be a "constitutional anomaly."[74] This point is closely related to the anarchy point, as the "anomaly" is described as a "private right to ignore generally applicable laws."[75] (Scalia's point would seem to be that such a balancing test is not used, or not explicitly used, in the free speech area. Nonetheless, in this area the standard is not mere rational basis review either, so it may be that there is an undeveloped and implicit notion comparable to the notion of compelling interest.)

6. Leaving protection of minority religious conduct to the political process will "place at a relative disadvantage those religious practices that are not widely engaged in; but that unavoidable consequence of democratic government must be preferred to a system in which each conscience is a law unto itself or in which judges weigh the social importance of all laws against the centrality of all religious beliefs." One can only say that disadvantages to minority religion are not, in fact, "inevitable"; *Sherbert* and *Yoder* had shown another way. Nor is the alternative the anarchic one that Justice Scalia somewhat phobically depicts: it is a system of careful balancing and judicial oversight.

This opinion is somewhat shocking for its lordly way with precedent. At its heart, however, is a passionate commitment to an understanding of the rule of law according to which any exception for an individual threatens the workability of the entire system. This concern for uniformity goes all the way back to John Locke, as we have seen, and there is nothing disreputable about it. Notice that Justice Scalia does not hold that states may not pass laws giving religious exemptions: indeed, he points to the fact that some states, for example Arizona, have already given a legislative exemption for the religious use of peyote. But an exemption that is democratically enacted into law is very different, in his view, from one created by judges. Scalia has consistently held that the competence of the judiciary does not extend to the granting of individualized exemptions from laws that have been duly and properly enacted. This position is a coherent and respectable one.

What cannot be respectably asserted, however, is that the traditions and precedents of the Court never endorsed the *Sherbert* framework. They clearly did. As Justice O'Connor insists, *Yoder* rejected just the interpretation of the Free Exercise Clause that Scalia now adopts, saying that generally valid laws may produce unfair and unconstitutional burdens on the religious freedom of individuals. The tradition insists on highlighting the harsh impact of majority rule on minorities, as Justice Jackson insisted in *Barnette*, overruling *Gobitis*.[76] Nor do the precedents focus on belief, neglecting burdens on religiously motivated conduct: indeed, the central cases concern conduct, and conduct that was burdened as the incidental effect of laws that were neutral, not unfairly targeting a particular religion. Far from being a "constitutional anomaly," accommodation, and the use of the compelling interest test, were a constitutional norm, and religion is a favored activity, triggering heightened scrutiny.[77] The mandate of the First Amendment, as Justice O'Connor convincingly summarizes it, is "preserving religious liberty to the fullest extent possible in a pluralistic society."[78]

Justices Blackmun, Brennan, and Marshall dissent. They join Justice O'Connor in declaring support for the *Sherbert* framework, as a "settled and inviolate principle of this Court's First Amendment jurisprudence."[79] (They reject her finding of a compelling state interest.) As for the contention that minority liberty is always at risk in a majoritarian democracy, the dissenters write, "I do not believe the Founders thought their dearly bought freedom from religious persecution a 'luxury,' but an essential element of liberty—and they could not have thought religious intolerance 'unavoidable,' for they drafted the religion clauses precisely in order to avoid that intolerance."[80]

Americans of good faith can disagree about whether religiously grounded accommodations are best handled legislatively or by a mixed legislative-judicial system under which at least some accommodations are constitutionally compelled and judicially enforced. Justice Scalia's legislation-only doctrine is impossible to assail simply by looking back to the colonial period, since there was obviously no track record of judicial review, and accommodation, generally favored, was secured legislatively. It is certainly not crystal clear what the text of the First Amendment itself protects. Although the framers surely thought that accommodation was a part of religious fairness in general, it cannot be proven conclusively that the meaning to be attached to the Free Exercise Clause, as originally drafted, was that accommodations should be seen as constitutionally compelled. (What we probably can rule out with certainty, however, is the belief-conduct distinction on which some of Justice Scalia's arguments rely.) The framers drafted a text of abstract generality, leaving a good deal to be pinned down by later interpreters. What cannot be plausibly disputed, however, is that the more recent traditions of the Court acknowledge the central importance of protecting minority rights in a majority culture and take on, as a proper function of the judiciary, the job of protecting certain religious freedoms of individuals that are burdened by otherwise valid laws. We may debate whether this tradition has been good or bad. There are many reasons to think it good, seeing how state power has repeatedly burdened minorities heedlessly and obtusely, and seeing that legislatures are not typically reliable guardians of minority rights. Surely the protection of individuals in their fundamental rights, against such legislative obtuseness, is a paradigmatic function of the judiciary. What we should not debate, however, is that such has been the judicial tradition since *Sherbert*. Thus *Smith*, throwing out the *Sherbert* test except in a narrow range of cases, changed our legal regime in fundamental ways.

The U.S. public was outraged by *Smith*. Citizens of many sorts, and groups of many sorts, rose up to protest it. (In retrospect, one might even say that *Smith* performed a useful public service by generating public awareness of the need to protect minority religion and of the relevant legal history.) The liberal American Civil Liberties Union (ACLU) was joined by the Christian Legal Society, the American Jewish Congress by the National Association of Evangelicals. In 1993, Congress passed, by overwhelming majorities in both House and Senate, the Religious Freedom Restoration Act (RFRA). President Clinton signed the bill into law. RFRA was a deliberate end run around *Smith*. It observed that *Smith* had virtually removed the compelling interest test in religious freedom matters, and announced the intention to restore it. From now on, the *Sherbert* regime would be federal law and courts would be bound to apply it. Where did Congress get the authority so to limit the jurisdiction of the Supreme Court? So it was claimed, from section 5 of the Fourteenth Amendment, which grants Congress the "power to enforce, by appropriate legislation, the provisions of this article." Since the Free Exercise Clause was incorporated under the Fourteenth Amendment's guarantee of due process, this textual appeal was at least reasonable.

For four years, RFRA was the law of the land. At the state court and lower federal level, religious plaintiffs began winning again, approximately as they did in the *Sherbert* years, and much more often than from 1990 to 1993, when *Smith* prevailed.[81] The Supreme Court, however, was not amused.[82] In 1997 in a case, *City of Boerne v. Flores*, involving the claim of a Catholic church to be free from a city's historic landmark law, so as to carry out proposed renovations on its building, the Supreme Court declared RFRA unconstitutional as applied to the states, on grounds of federalism: Congress lacks the power to regulate the states in this way.[83] The argument also, and perhaps more deeply, concerns the separation of powers: the Court was plainly disturbed by this legislative attempt to evade its decisions. Interestingly, the significant ruling came in a case whose plaintiff was a religious group, a case that only indirectly and marginally involved individual liberties. This probably made it easier for the majority to deny that unfair burdens on individuals followed from the upholding of laws of general applicability, and for Justice Stevens even to insist on an Establishment Clause problem: RFRA favors religion over nonreligion, by giving the Catholic Church a break that a public landmark owned by an atheist would not get. Most of the Justices agreed up to a point on the federalism issue. It was left to Justice O'Connor (joined by Justice Breyer) to insist, once again, that *Smith* was wrongly decided, and that the Court should first "put our First Amendment jurisprudence back on course" before deciding the federalism issue raised by RFRA.

Al Smith never again found full-time work as an alcohol counselor. He went to work for Goodwill Industries; meanwhile his wife, Janet Farrell, got a degree in special education and currently works as a special ed professional. At the age of seventy, Al retired and became the primary caretaker of his two young children. On November 6, 1999, he celebrated his eightieth birthday, with a celebration on the grounds of the University of Oregon Law School (where Dave Frohnmayer, who prosecuted *Smith* as Oregon's attorney general, has been university president since 1994). After a feast organized by Janet, people sat in a circle singing peyote songs, and took turns holding the sacred eagle feather while they talked about the contributions Smith had made to their lives.[84] Still healthy and vigorous—although he needs the support of a low metal lawn chair to sit around the fire all night—Smith continues to play a major role in Native American religious functions in Oregon and to use peyote occasionally in sacred ceremonies.[85] Federal law decriminalized the ceremonial use of peyote in 1994.

VI. Accommodation After Smith and Boerne: Restoring the Balance?

Smith and Boerne seemed to many to put a dagger into the heart of minority religious freedom. Much, however, was left standing. Although it took a while for this to become clear, RFRA remained valid law as applied to the federal government, a fact that would have important implications for minority rights. Where the states were concerned, the unemployment cases remained good law—wherever, as in Sherbert and not Smith, the religious conduct on the basis of which compensation was ultimately denied was legal under applicable state laws. Such cases continued to come forward, and the Sherbert framework remains in force to decide them. Justice Scalia also allowed the Sherbert framework to remain in force in "hybrid" cases. This category has proven both controversial and difficult to interpret, but it has led to some minority victories, particularly in areas that link free speech to religious freedom issues.[86]

Equally important was Smith's insistence that a statute would not be upheld if it unfairly targeted one religion as against another. Smith understood the requirement of fairness rather narrowly: one might argue that the drug laws of Oregon precisely did target Native American religion for special burdens, by requiring only Native Americans to forgo an essential sacrament, and thus were discriminatory in effect. That argument gains plausibility from the lack of restriction on alcohol, an essential element of sacramental life in some Christian denominations. The fact that the drug laws were not passed with discriminatory intent was apparently sufficient, in Justice Scalia's view, to save them from invalidation. On the other hand, the fairness requirement was not without teeth.

Santeria, an Afro-Cuban religion, is alarming to the majority, particularly because of its practice of animal sacrifice. Animals are killed by slitting the carotid artery of the neck; the animal is then cooked and eaten. When the Church of the Lukumi Babalu Aye announced its plan to open a branch in the city of Hialeah, Florida, city government was alarmed. In an emergency public session, they passed a law making it illegal to kill an animal in a "public or private ritual or ceremony not for the primary purpose of food consumption."[87] Here is a type of unfairness with which John Locke was already familiar in the seventeenth century, when it was criminal to speak Latin in a worship service, but not in a university classroom, and criminal to use water for sacramental purposes of immersion, but not criminal to use it to take a bath. Locke, though rather like Scalia in his defense of laws of general applicability, objected strenuously to this sort of discriminatory special pleading. If there was a health reason not to immerse people in water, then that reason ought to apply to all bathers, not just to full-immersion baptism.

Hialeah claimed that its aims were to protect the public health and prevent cruelty to animals. Obviously enough, however, the law was ill fitted to those ends: for the same sorts of animal killing, or even more painful sorts, were permitted for food consumption. "[T]he ordinances are drafted with care to forbid few killings but those occasioned by religious sacrifice." So the laws are clearly a result of "government hostility," which is just as objectionable when masked as when overt. The law was invalidated.

Other cases followed the same pattern. In one of particular contemporary interest, policemen in Newark, New Jersey, had been forbidden to wear beards, but an exemption was offered for certain skin conditions. Two Sunni Muslim officers objected, citing their religious belief that they were obliged to grow their beards and producing evidence from the Quran. In an opinion written by Justice Samuel Alito when he was a federal appellate judge—and a relatively rare victory for minorities in the Alito canon—the officers won their case, on the grounds that a secular exemption from the policy had already been granted.[88] This case follows the pattern of *Lukumi*, but Alito goes further toward protection of minorities than *Lukumi* was willing to go: there was no evidence that the police policy was crafted with a discriminatory intent, and yet it was invalidated. Alito thus seemed to be quietly moving back to something close to a pre-*Smith* understanding of minority religious rights.

Meanwhile, states were quick to enact RFRA into state law. By 2005, twelve states had enacted RFRA-like language: Alabama, Arizona, Connecticut, Florida, Idaho, Illinois, Missouri, New Mexico, Oklahoma, Rhode Island, South Carolina, and Texas. (One can see here the broad bipartisan reach of RFRA, since the enumerated states include some with very liberal traditions and also some of the nation's most conservative.) Still other states have interpreted their state constitutions to require an RFRA-like regime (for example, Massachusetts, Michigan, Minnesota, Ohio, Washington, Wisconsin).[89] The enduring appeal of RFRA and its widespread popular support will doubtless lead to the expansion of this list.

The other remaining avenue of redress, after *Smith*, remained federal law. *Boerne* left it (temporarily) unclear whether RFRA was still constitutional as applied to the actions of the federal government itself—an area that Congress might have greater power to regulate. Moreover, there were certain areas of state action that Congress apparently had been given power to regulate: interstate commerce, and state actions that involve federal spending. Responding to this open door, Congress promptly began to introduce RFRA protections into these areas of state action. Eventually the project was narrowed to two specific areas: burdens imposed on individual free exercise by "land use regulations" and burdens imposed on people who are inmates in prisons or mental institutions. The result was the Religious Land Use and Institutionalized Persons Act of 2000 (RLUIPA).

In May 2005, in an important opinion, the Supreme Court upheld RLUIPA against a challenge based on the Establishment Clause. The case was brought by prisoners in the Ohio penal system, members of a variety of minority sects, who alleged that prison officials denied them "the same opportunities for group worship that are granted to adherents of mainstream religions, forbidding them to adhere to the dress and appearance mandates of their religions, withholding religious ceremonial items that are substantially identical to those that the adherents of mainstream religions are permitted, and failing to provide a chaplain trained in their faith."[90] Since every state, including Ohio, accepts federal funding for its prisons, the case raised issues under the federal law.

Hearings held in Congress prior to the passage of RLUIPA, and cited in the case, showed a distressing pattern of unequal and capricious burdens on inmates' religious freedom. One prison in Ohio allowed Jewish prisoners kosher food, but denied Muslim prisoners halal food. Jewish prisoners across the country complained that prisons routinely refuse to provide sack lunches for fast days, which would allow inmates to break their fast after sundown. (Presumably Muslim prisoners had a similar problem.) The Michigan Department of Corrections forbade the lighting of Hanukkah candles, although it permitted Christian votive candles. Sacramental wine for Roman Catholic prisoners always posed problems. Religious articles of various sorts

were routinely treated with contempt. (The U.S. public is outraged over alleged mutilations of the Quran in U.S. prisons in Iraq, but we should also be
outraged by our practices toward our own citizens.)

The Sixth Circuit Court of Appeals held that the way in which religion is
singled out for special treatment by RLUIPA violates the Establishment
Clause. The Supreme Court agreed to hear the case precisely in order to address that issue. While granting that some ways of favoring religion might "de-
volve into 'an unlawful fostering of religion,'" the Court insisted that "'there is
room for play in the joints between' the Free Exercise and Establishment
Clauses, allowing the government to accommodate religion beyond free exercise requirements, without offense to the Establishment Clause." (Note that
the accommodation goes "beyond free exercise requirements" in the post-
Smith era, but not before *Smith*, when precisely whether the accommodation
is required by the Free Exercise Clause would have been the first issue before
the Court.) RLUIPA does not violate the Establishment Clause, because it "al-
leviates exceptional government-created burdens on private religious exercise." In other words, it is because of government policy that some prisoners
cannot exercise their religion freely, and RLUIPA is simply redressing that inequality. (We could plausibly say, although the Court did not, that not to grant
the prisoners' plea would raise a far weightier Establishment Clause issue, that
of establishing mainstream Christianity in the prisons.) Moreover, the Court
argues, there seems to be no plausible government claim of a compelling interest in peace and safety, since Ohio already extensively accommodates mainstream religions. Whatever prisons need to do for peace and safety they may
still do, but they have not made a convincing case that the minority cases are
of this sort.

Cutter v. Wilkinson was a unanimous decision. Only Justice Thomas even
wrote a separate (concurring) opinion, and this only because he had held that
the Establishment Clause protects states from federal action, and thus he had
to do extra work to show how he would reach the same result. Even he, however, did reach it. Whatever divides our Court in the area of religious accommodation, there is great, and welcome, unanimity in upholding this limited
legislative attempt to give strong RFRA-like protections to some of America's
most vulnerable people.

Meanwhile, the Court has committed itself, again unanimously, to enforcing the original RFRA at the federal level. Congress legalized the sacramental

use of peyote in 1994, creating an exception to the Controlled Substances Act. Nonetheless, the U.S. government continued to go after another hallucinogen with similar sacramental uses. The Centro Espirita Beneficenta União do Vegetal is a small sect in New Mexico with Brazilian origins. It sought legal permission to use sacramentally a tea called "hoasca," which contains the hallucinogen dimethyltryptamine, which is illegal under federal drug law. The case was argued presupposing the constitutionality of RFRA as applied to the federal government, and therefore presupposing a framework under which the government had to show a "compelling interest" in order to justify its burden to religious exercise.[91] The opinion does not even spend any time asserting RFRA's continued validity. Moreover, the classic RFRA cases from the pre-*Smith* era, *Sherbert* and *Yoder*, are used as precedents, on the understanding that the purpose of RFRA was to reestablish the pre-*Smith* standard.

In a unanimous opinion authored by Chief Justice Roberts, the Court rejects the government's claim of a compelling state interest: (a) evidence fails to show significant health dangers from the merely sacramental use of the drug; and (b) the government does not have a compelling interest in the uniform and exceptionless application of the Controlled Substances Act, as has been shown by the example of peyote, whose sacramental legality has caused no big problems.

The government had also argued that, although the law is clearly amenable to *legislative* exemptions, it does not follow that it is also amenable to judicially crafted exceptions. Justice Roberts replies with a strong defense of the role of the judiciary under federal RFRA:

> RFRA . . . plainly contemplates that *courts* would recognize exceptions—that is how the law works [citing the provisions of the law] . . . Congress' role in the peyote exemption—and the Executive's—confirms that the findings in the Controlled Substances Act do not preclude exceptions altogether. RFRA makes clear that it is the obligation of the courts to consider whether exceptions are required. . . .

It is significant that Justice Scalia signed on to this opinion. It does not really reject his *Smith* analysis, since it is plainly a neutrality case: the government is treating the sect that uses hoasca differently from the way in which it treats the sect that uses peyote. Nonetheless, the argumentation seems to have undergone a subtle shift, as no worries are expressed about the danger of anarchy created by an exception to generally applicable laws, and the role of the judiciary in crafting such exceptions is strongly affirmed. At oral argument, Justice Scalia observed that the success of the peyote exemption is a "demonstration you can make an exception without the sky falling."[92] That exception was legislative. His willingness to join the majority opinion in *Gonzalez* indicates that he is no longer convinced that a regime of judicially crafted exceptions need lead to anarchy.

VII. Should Religion Be Special?

Under our Constitution, religion is special. The framers rejected wording that spoke in general of "rights of conscience" and chose wording that singled out religion for free exercise protection. Currently, the prevailing legal norm is that free exercise accommodations given on the basis of religion do not always cause an Establishment Clause problem. But understanding what the law is today is not our only task. Especially since the law of accommodation is murky and has undergone some dramatic shifts in recent years, we need to think about the underlying principles embedded in our Constitution, and to try, at least, to figure out where they lead in this difficult matter.

One of the most central commitments in our constitutional tradition is a commitment to fairness, to treating citizens as equals, where that means that no hierarchies should exist under law in our nation. Religious membership and nonmembership should not be special sources of advantage or disadvantage under law. And yet this chapter has related, sympathetically, a tradition of accommodation that does give religion preference over nonreligion, at least in some matters. The tradition's reason for favoring accommodation was itself a reason of fairness: the majority makes laws that suit itself, and minority believers often encounter special, unequal burdens as a result. What, though, of the nonreligious citizen who has some other reason for seeking an exemption to the law in question?

For example, what if Mrs. Sherbert had refused to work on Saturday because she had five small children and no husband, and felt that they badly needed her attention on the day when school is not in session? What if she had an elderly mother at home and could not find a weekend caregiver? What if someone wanted an exemption from the drug laws because she was convinced that discovering the meaning of existence, for her, required listening to the symphonies of Mahler while using marijuana? And, most urgent of all, what about those exemptions from military conscription that we have doled out to Quakers and Mennonites since the beginning of our nation? Aren't there citizens who have nonreligious but very weighty reasons for being opposed to military service, for example ethical convictions that forbid them to engage in violence? Aren't they being treated unfairly when they are denied exemptions just because their reasons are not religious in nature?

We can easily see a practical reason for the status quo: religious reasons are typically reasons that pertain to a group of people, and the genuineness of the claim is therefore relatively easy to assess. Even when a person has a somewhat divergent interpretation of his or her religion (as was the case with the Jehovah's Witness who refused work in the armaments plant), we can at least study the tradition, understand its debates, and see how the person fits in. Nonreligious reasons are more likely to be personal and individualistic, thus far more difficult to assess for sincerity and significance. In the Vietnam War, we know well that people were prepared to say more or less anything to avoid the draft, so there had to be some way of limiting conscientious objector status. Doing so with reference to religion seems at least as fair, from a practical point of view, as any other way. But a practical reason of this kind does not dispense with the question of fairness, so we really want to know whether there is anything more to be said in favor of the current regime.

A practical argument that seems weightier is the argument that religion, being a matter of group affiliation and identification, is more likely to be a ground of persecution than various individualistic commitments; so, more care needs to be taken to protect religious free exercise than to protect nonreligious commitments. Historically, that may well be one of the reasons why the framers wrote the clause as they did: the ill of religion-based persecution was at the forefront of their awareness, and other types of persecution didn't loom so large.

That reply runs into difficulty in the modern era, when we can look back and see that one of the groups that has suffered most in our history is the group of atheists and nonbelievers. Atheists have suffered disabilities of many kinds, prominently in England, where many forms of employment and political participation were utterly closed to them until the end of the nineteenth century. Well-known atheist Charles Bradlaugh was elected three times to Parliament, and each time ejected; only in 1886, elected for the fourth time, was he permitted to take his seat. The U.S. has been a little better, but the story of disabilities attached to atheism, including many under state laws, is still very long. So, we can't maintain that the favoring of religion simply rights a wrong that religious minorities suffer, or might suffer, and that nonreligious people do not suffer. We should at least be alert to areas, such as military conscription, in which an atheist can have systematic reasons for conscientious objection that are ethically, rather than religiously, based.

A somewhat better argument for the preference is structural: under the Establishment Clause religion suffers disadvantages, and this compensates for the advantages it has under the Free Exercise Clause, creating a total regime that is fair.[93] For example, if a public library wants to erect a public display honoring Immanuel Kant, or John Stuart Mill, or Henry David Thoreau, the Establishment Clause poses no obstacle, and the display can go forward. Should it, however, want to honor Jesus, or Mohammed, or Krishna, Establishment Clause problems immediately loom, and the display may or may not be able to go forward. On the other side, so the argument goes, if I say that I won't serve in the army because I'm a Kantian, or a follower of Thoreau,[94] that cuts no ice, whereas the follower of a pacifist religion will get an exemption. Thus, the argument goes, my overall situation as a Kantian or Thoreauvian citizen is roughly fair: I have space in one place, to compensate for a lack of space in another.

This argument says much that is true, and no doubt doctrine has evolved as it has, allowing "play at the joints," precisely because there is an overall sense of fairness about the balance between the clauses. And yet such a formalistic reason seems a bit *ad hoc*. Certainly it does not explain why *religion* should be special, what it is about *religion* that marks it out for special free exercise treatment.

At this point, scholars typically take one of two courses. Some simply say there is no good reason for religion to be preferred, for accommodation purposes, over weighty secular commitments. These people typically embrace the result in *Smith,* though for reasons very different from Justice Scalia's reasons.[95] Cutting back on Free Exercise accommodation seems just the way to go for such people, since it evens up the playing field.

The other common course is to propose some account of what might be thought special about religion. If that or those characteristics are present in at least some secular commitments, perhaps accommodation should be cautiously extended to those cases.

What should the account be? Typically, analysis proceeds along two fronts: on the one hand, by identifying features that seem plausible criteria of religion; on the other hand, by enumerating the recognized religions of the world. Through a dialogue between these two approaches, the hope is, we can come up with at least a set of plausible criteria that are not too narrow and exclusionary.[96]

That religion concerns a person's relationship to God is not a particularly helpful criterion, since it is just not true of many of the recognized religions of the world, such as Buddhism, Confucianism, and Taoism. Nobody seems to want to exclude these religions, so the requirement of theism has long been dropped, at least as a necessary condition.

The idea that religion involves a group and some organized structure of authority is, again, true part of the time, but far from all of the time. From the early colonial days on, many religious Americans have been, like Roger Williams, solitary seekers, affiliated with no official structure, and our tradition has shown a great deal of skepticism about organized structure.

Some accounts then propose that religion involves very strongly felt commitments, commitments central to a person's life. This is, of course, often true, and yet that subjective account of religion's specialness is both underinclusive—failing to cover many cases of religious membership that are habitual and not particularly emotional, or that involve religions based on ritual practice rather than strong feeling—and overinclusive, surely taking in many people's relationship to their family, their local region, even, in many cases, their house, their money, their car, their sports team. Nobody wants to give a draft exemption to someone who is intensely attached to his car, however sincere the attachment may be. Nor—should I discover that my employer will not let me attend an afternoon White Sox game without penalty—ought I to have grounds for litigation under the First Amendment when I am fired and denied unemployment compensation.

What about the idea that religious requirements are experienced as obligatory and nonoptional? That gets closer, perhaps, but again, it's both underinclusive and overinclusive. It fails to include people who don't experience their religion this way, a serious problem when we include religions that have no structure of authority and no textual source. Buddhism, Reform Judaism, Unitarianism, and quite a few other religions have no category of the nonoptional: everything is to be judged by the conscience of the individual. The other side of this problem is that the category would include people who feel a sense of nonoptional commitment to trivial things, things we don't want to dignify by the protection of religion. (One man claimed he felt a nonoptional commitment to dress like a chicken, and sought religious protection for this behavior.[97]) We don't want to get too deeply into the question of assessing people's beliefs for silliness, but we also don't want to dignify frivolous claims.[98]

A more promising approach focuses on subject matter: religion concerns what one might call ultimate questions, questions of life and death, the meaning of life, life's ethical foundation, and so forth.[99] This goes in the right direction, proposing at least one of the central criteria we ought to consider; my own approach will follow this line.

Now we must turn to the question why religion might be singled out for special protection. In an important recent paper, Andrew Koppelman argues that the defects in inadequate subjectivistic accounts of religion's value mean that we ought to declare forthrightly that finding the ultimate meaning of life has intrinsic value; it is because of the objective value of success, so to speak, that the search for meaning has value.[100] Since the state cannot take any position on the nature of the ultimate meaning of life, the best it can do is to support the search for it, in all its forms, without discriminating among them. Koppelman argues, in this way, for a broad category of accommodation, which would include theistic and nontheistic searches.

I think that this account makes progress, but, to me, it is just a bit too dogmatic. We live in a country in which many people are skeptics, doubting that there is such a thing as the ultimate meaning of life, and where many others have dogmatic anti-meaning views. For the government to declare what Koppelman declares goes just a bit too far for true fairness to such skeptical and/or anti-metaphysical views.

We may get some help, I think, by returning to Roger Williams's idea of conscience. For Williams, the faculty with which each person searches for the ultimate meaning of life is of intrinsic worth and value, and is worthy of respect whether the person is using it well or badly. The faculty is identified in part by what it does—it reasons, searches, and experiences emotions of longing connected to that search—and in part by its subject matter—it deals with ultimate questions, questions of ultimate meaning. It is the faculty, not its goal, that is the basis of political respect, and thus we can agree to respect the faculty without prejudging the question whether there is a meaning to be found, or what it might be like. From the respect we have for the person's conscience, that faculty of inquiring and searching, it follows that we ought to respect the space required by any activity that has the general shape of searching for the ultimate meaning of life, except when that search violates the rights of others or comes up against some compelling state interest. Political respect is addressed, in the first instance, to a "capability" of people, one that demands both development and exercise; it is not addressed, except derivatively, to the functions such a faculty performs.[101] We may arrive at a political consensus concerning the need to respect human faculties, without at all agreeing concerning the value of the specific activities that these faculties perform. This account seems to me an improvement on Koppelman's, since it shows more respect to skeptics and anti-metaphysical dogmatists—who can still agree with other citizens about the respect due to human powers of searching.

Something like this Williams-based account is probably the best we can do in trying to make sense of our feeling that there really is something about religion or quasi-religion that calls for special protection and delicacy. It will help us distinguish the faculty that we respect when we respect "religion" from the faculties used by my car lover, who isn't engaged in a search for meaning, or the person who feels called to dress like a chicken when going to work, which is (probably) just too silly to count as a genuine search for meaning. Much though I love the White Sox, it will probably distinguish quasi-religious searches from that one too, since, even though subjectively the fate of one's team may seem to bear on the ultimate meaning of life, it seems unlikely that this content would survive the inspection of a reasonable observer, and our Williams-based standard is not a subjectivistic standard.

This account will also distinguish the case of religion from the case of the person who simply loves her family. Family attachments should certainly receive more legal attention and social support than they currently do, and we should probably conclude that the woman who is fired because she can't find a sitter is suffering an injustice—but not an injustice of the same sort, pertinent to this particular part of our constitutional tradition. They should be dealt with in another department of law.

Not all searches for meaning are good or carried out by good people; the southern slaveholder's search for meaning (invoking God, as Lincoln noted, to defend the institution of slavery) will pass this first part of the test, and the state should not get involved in saying that a given religion is evil or racist. However, claims based on such religious beliefs will be defeated at the next stage, by considerations of harm to others and by a whole host of compelling state interests.

The Williams account requires us to extend the category of religion somewhat further than we typically do, when we include Buddhism, Taoism, and other nontheistic religions. For we now need to include many idiosyncratic and highly individual searches, searches that Williams himself would surely want to respect, antinomian and unaffiliated "seeker" that he was. Group membership is surely helpful, if what we want to know is how important Saturday worship, or pacifism, is to the relevant belief system. There is at least a track record to go on here. Nonetheless, we cannot in good conscience exclude many good-faith seekers whose account of meaning finds no communal home.[102]

Obviously there is always a problem about insincere or manipulative religious claims in this area, and these are a little easier to deal with when we have a record of group membership to go on. We then need not assess each individual's personal beliefs; we need only consult the overall doctrines of the group. In the individual case, we obviously have to determine whether the claim is sincere or pretextual, and this is not an inquiry that judges are well equipped to undertake. Such inquiries will typically privilege articulate people and disadvantage the inarticulate; so there is a good case for granting such accommodations rather stingily. Nonetheless, there is no principled way to exclude individualistic searches, and our nation has long been familiar with heterodox religious expression.[103]

Theory rarely dovetails with good legal and judicial practice, but in this case the convergence is reasonably robust. During the Vietnam War, the courts had to grapple with a host of conscientious demands for exemption. They adopted the limiting view that a person's opposition to war had to be general, not just an opposition to the Vietnam War. One might not approve of that limit: after all, one can think of forms of ethical searching that have the consequence that the Second World War is ethically permissible and the Vietnam War is not ethically permissible. Indeed, many Americans hold beliefs of that sort, and standard just war theory in both the Protestant and Roman Catholic traditions probably would support such a distinction. In any case, having made that questionable but pragmatically helpful move, the courts then had to figure out how far, and on what basis, to extend the category of religion. They did so in a way that has some rough similarity to my Williams-based proposal, giving draft exemptions, in two famous cases, to forms of committed searching for meaning that had no group affiliation.

A draft resister named Daniel Andrew Seeger was denied conscientious objector status under the Selective Service Act, which defined religious views as views involving a belief "in a relation to a Supreme Being."[104] Seeger supported his views, which he called "religious," by reference to Plato, Aristotle, and Spinoza. He had evidently thought long and hard about questions of meaning and obligation. He was, however, agnostic about belief in a Supreme Being, and he said so. The Supreme Court, noting the presence of nontheistic religions in the U.S., insisted that belief in a Supreme Being could not be necessary for a religion-based exemption, if that really meant belief in a traditional God. But, they argued, the standard could, and should, be interpreted more broadly. Citing the doctrines of Paul Tillich and testimony from a leader in the ethical culture movement, they said that the idea of a Supreme Being could include a moral ideal for humanity, or "the power of being." They proposed that the standard in the act should be interpreted as that of "[a] sincere and meaningful belief which occupies in the life of its possessor a place parallel to that filled by the God of those admittedly qualifying for the exemption."[105]

This test would not meet with Roger Williams's full approval. The standard invoked is perhaps a bit too vague and general, since the place such ideas fill in people's lives can vary greatly. Moreover, it focuses on the content of Seeger's beliefs, rather than on the fact that the faculty of searching is involved. It does, however, emphasize the organizing and meaning-involving nature of religious searching, and it extends the exemption to someone whose search concerns similar ultimate matters. Seeger later said, "I appear to be the beneficiary of the American justice system in its most pristine and beautiful form, the way we *expect* it to perform. I am not deluded into thinking that this is the way the American justice system *always* works, but I experienced it as it *should* work, administered by people who were conscious of doing something important and who were at their best throughout."[106]

Seeger's case, decided in 1965, preceded the war. As war, and resistance to it, heated up, the problem of demarcating religion had to be faced once again. In 1970, the Court extended the idea of religion still further, to a man named Elliott Ashton Welsh II, who explicitly denied that his beliefs were religious, crossed out "religious" on his application for conscientious objector status, and insisted that the duty not to kill another human being is not superior to human relations but, rather, "essential to every human relation."[107] The plurality said that conscientious objector (C.O.) status extended to "all those whose consciences, spurred by deeply held moral, ethical, or religious beliefs, would give them no rest or peace if they allowed themselves to become a part of an instrument of war."[108] This formulation arguably does worse than *Seeger*, for reasons we articulated in discussing subjectivistic accounts: it focuses on a mental state that may vary greatly among people who are sincere seekers in Williams's sense. It may also be underinclusive, omitting people who belong to organized religions that teach pacifism, but who are not particularly emotional about it. The content-based formulation in *Seeger* seems preferable, and *Seeger* was also more carefully reasoned, using Tillich and ethical culture for guidance. Nonetheless, the basic idea of extending accommodation to a number of serious good-faith searchers after meaning whose views fail to fit into any organized sect is a good one. Justice Harlan, who was not impressed by the specific legal formulation of the plurality, nonetheless thought the result at least rectified the injustice that dissident and lonely seekers suffered previously under our constitutional regime.

Where accommodation is concerned, and particularly when we are concerned with a weighty matter such as killing other human beings,[109] it seems reasonable to stretch the account of religion as the Courts did in these two statutory cases, including lonely seekers who belong to no recognized group if they can give a good enough account of themselves. This stretch, even if not justified by an airtight philosophical argument, does at least remedy the unfairness that might be done to such people had we not stretched the definition. Welsh and Seeger seem like people who should not be put into Antigone's terrible position, however flawed any generalization we offer is likely to seem. A different sort of unfairness no doubt remains: such formulations reward articulate people and penalize those, equally sincere, who cannot give a good account of themselves. Many such people will be protected anyway, if they belong to a religious group that has a clear record on such issues.

But the seeker who is both solitary and inarticulate will remain at a disadvantage. The Vietnam War had such a pronounced class aspect—virtually nobody I ever met had to serve—that we should be troubled by this result.

I like the modern view inspired by Williams, but I can certainly understand that not everyone will be persuaded by it. Many principled people will prefer the Lockean view articulated in *Smith*, for reasons of fairness to nonreligious seekers. At this point, what sways me are the pragmatic and historical arguments for giving religion a special place. Religious minorities have suffered greatly all over the world from laws made by and for the majority. But, in practical terms, only two courses are open to us: either deny accommodations altogether or allow them, on some basis that we can reasonably restrict and administer. If we allow them, as fairness to religious minorities over the years might seem to require, then we need to have some account of how and why we do it, and this account had better be as fair and decent a one as we can give. Otherwise, in the process of pursuing fairness, we will be committing a deep sort of unfairness. So I'm inclined to say that we should forge ahead with something like the Williams account of reasons of conscience, whatever problems it involves, using it to defend at least some accommodations as constitutionally required, and many other legislative accommodations as permissible. We mitigate the unfairness to nonreligious searchers as much as we possibly can, by extending the account of religion as far as we can, compatibly with administrability.

One can see why some people, including Justice Scalia and, for different reasons, the recent scholars who defend *Smith* on fairness grounds, are reluctant to get involved in this complicated and messy business; and yet the claim of the latter to be pursuing fairness needs critical scrutiny. Without the protection of free exercise accommodation, minority religion will suffer unfairness, as it always has in the past; so by stripping that protection away William Marshall and other related scholars are not exactly standing up for fairness across the board, much though they might be pursuing it for nonreligious people. The messy way seems the best way, all things considered, although we should grant that it is a pragmatic solution and not ideal theory. That way should include at least some constitutionally compelled accommodations, as even *Smith* allows. With Justice O'Connor, I believe that *Smith* was wrongly decided and that a return to the *Sherbert* regime would be even more adequate. The messy but decent way should also include a further open area free for legislative accommodation, as protected by *Cutter v. Wilkinson*. Finally, it should include a capacious definition of religion that does as much justice as possible to good-faith lonely seekers.

Much disagreement remains in this area, as is natural with issues this complicated and this important. Justice Scalia and Michael McConnell, two conservative Republicans, remain miles apart on the question. McConnell thinks that *Sherbert* was correct and that many accommodations are constitutionally compelled. Scalia has made clear his support for some legislative accommodations. Nonetheless, he prefers a constitutional regime of exceptionless rules, and a judiciary who never stand up for the religious rights of minority citizens, even in egregious cases (outside the areas we have discussed). In another way, McConnell is miles apart from a scholar such as William Marshall, who defends an end to accommodation on fairness grounds, thinking about the wrong done to nonreligious people. So there are deep divisions and intense conflicts. At one time, in the upheaval occasioned by *Smith*, many Americans feared that our admirable tradition of protecting minorities was coming to an end.

By this time, however, we can see the tradition's remarkable powers of self-adjustment, even in the midst of disagreement: legislative accommodations have been upheld, even, it seems, in the divisive case of peyote and mescaline. At least some judicially mandated exemptions remain, though far fewer than Justice O'Connor, Michael McConnell, and I would want. And the definition of religion has been adjusted to be as fair as possible to people who are not theists and who don't belong to any group. Americans, and their courts, will continue to disagree on all these issues, but we should all admire the seriousness, and the subtlety, of our tradition's wrestling with the fundamental issue, Antigone's issue: how to respect the individual conscience when it seems to butt up against the rule of law.

By now we can understand what Roger Williams and John Rawls were after when they asked for political principles that are ethically rich, not ethically neutral, but are nonetheless principles that we can all share, although we differ in our ultimate religious and secular commitments. The ideas of our Free Exercise tradition are such ideas: ideas of equal respect for all citizens' consciences, "delicate" accommodation of conscientious scruples, and fairness to minorities who live in a majority world.

5

FEARING STRANGERS

Polygamy has always been odious among the northern and western nations of Europe, and, until the establishment of the Mormon Church, was almost exclusively a feature of the life of Asiatic and of African people.

Reynolds v. U.S. (1878)

The Catholic worshiper is not to think, but to believe and obey; . . . the voter is not to inquire and examine, but to deposit his ballot as the ecclesiastical authority directs. . . . The Catholic clergy are on the side of slavery. . . . They love slavery itself; it is an institution thoroughly congenial to them, consistent with the first principles of their Church.

THEODORE PARKER,
"Rights of Man in America" (1854)

I. Principles and Anxieties

On March 7, 1859, ten-year-old Roman Catholic Thomas Whall, a student at Boston's Eliot School, a public school, refused to recite the Protestant version of the Ten Commandments, as required by Massachusetts law. Previously, pupils had chanted the commandments as a group, and Catholic pupils were able to mutter their own version (which omits the Protestant second commandment against the worship of any "graven image") in a way that escaped notice. On this day, however, teacher Sophia Shepard had asked each student to recite individually. When Whall refused a second time, a week later, an assistant to the principal said, "Here's a boy that refuses to repeat the Ten Commandments, and I will whip him till he yields if it takes the whole forenoon." Whall's hands were beaten with a rattan stick "for half an hour until they were cut and bleeding."[1]

Principles lose their grip in times of fear. Ever since the founding of the first colonies, our country has known an uneasy oscillation between a commitment to equal respect and a fear of strangers that at times undermines that commitment. In Roger Williams's New England and James Madison's Virginia, the "bloudy tenent of persecution" sometimes got the upper hand, subordinating people who believed and worshipped in a way that the majority found unsettling. Our constitutional founding marked a striking victory for Williams's Respect-Conscience Principle, as the religion clauses protected a regime of equal liberty—at least at the federal level. After the Civil War, incorporation eventually extended these principles to the states.

A constitutional tradition, however, is only as robust as are the judges and legislators who interpret and implement it. Our own has known many backslidings, when confronted with people whom the majority found more threatening than minorities with whom they had already learned to live. Perhaps the high-water mark of fearful religious discrimination was the period between 1850 and 1945, when our country received floods of immigrants from many nations. Their diverse ethnic and religious traditions inspired anxiety: were our American traditions about to be subverted by aliens with different, and possibly antidemocratic, values? America was also spawning homegrown sects that seemed weird and potentially subversive.

People fear new things most of the time, but what they fear most, perhaps, is anything new that seems to undermine cherished traditions and loyalties. Particularly ominous are new views of political authority and new attitudes to sexuality and family. When challenges of these types appear on the scene—particularly when combined with lower-class or unfamiliar ethnic origins—people can easily feel that civilization itself is coming to an end.[2] Such crises of anxiety are exacerbated by background fears about changes in the economy, or the structure of the family, or the nation's security.[3]

This chapter will study three such panics, times during which admirable principles of equal respect and equal liberty seemed to fly out the window, and politics was driven by fear and hate. We have seen the key ideas that form our admirable tradition of accommodation for reasons of conscience, a tradition that, I've argued, goes all the way back to the Founding, although it took some time for its principles to become firmly established. Now we are ready to understand why this solidification took so long, as we confront some emotional roadblocks that slowed the progress of our tradition of equal liberty.

In the burgeoning new Mormon religion, the majority saw a threat to its political authority, its control over valuable property, and, in general, the hegemony of Protestant Christian belief and practice. Polygamy was the hot-button issue that drove people into a true panic, until cherished norms of religious respect and free speech were, for a time, deeply compromised.

Jehovah's Witnesses were not as numerous, but their custom of public preaching made them conspicuous. Another group of homegrown "heretics," their denial of the divinity of Jesus, their refusal of military service and voting, their upsetting custom of proselytizing from door to door, and, above all, their refusal, on religious grounds, to pledge allegiance to the flag made them, and especially their children, a handy target for a more general fear of a subversive "fifth column" that might destroy American life from within.

No group in our midst, however, has suffered as much from fear and loathing as Roman Catholics, today the largest single religious denomination in our nation. As floods of new Catholic immigrants from Ireland, Italy, and Eastern Europe entered the country, people became terrified that the whole character of America was about to change and that democratic values would shortly be replaced by subservience to papal authority. The horrendous treatment of young Thomas Whall, which violated our Founding's deepest principles, was a typical example of the virulence of anti-Catholic prejudice. As Roger Williams would have said: the "bloudy tenent" became "yet more bloudy" by Protestant attempts to "wash it clean in the blood of the Lamb," i.e., to find a morally virtuous pretext for horrible persecution. To understand this panic we must move from the Free Exercise Clause to the Establishment

Clause, tracing the fate of the Madisonian idea of equal citizenship in the public square, as it interacted with fear and hate.

We need to understand these panics for several reasons. First, they show us the ultimate resilience of our constitutional values, but also their temporary fragility. They thus prompt us to look around us today and ask whether there may not be other groups in our society who are being ill treated in much the way that the Mormons, Jehovah's Witnesses, and Roman Catholics were treated in the period between 1850 and 1945. We have to learn to look beneath the attractive moral language in which persecution often clothes itself, asking whether the conduct involved actually amounts to persecution, even when its proponents may sincerely believe that they are defending moral values, and even civilization itself.

Second, these three cases show us how some of our contemporary debates arose, and what forces, sometimes not very nice, have shaped some of our modern political rhetoric in the area of religion. In particular, we'll see that the call for a "separation of church and state" has not always been the decent equality-protective slogan that people who respect equality might like it to be. It actually gained currency as part of an anti-Catholic political movement, and its underlying meaning, at least at first, was "Don't let the Pope take over our government and our schools."[4] This historical understanding helps us untangle the strands of our current debate, as we try to keep our eyes on the really good values—equality and equal liberty. We need to ask very carefully to what extent "separation" protects these values, and to what extent it might on occasion even undermine them. We need to ask ourselves whether we like talk of "separation"—insofar as we do—because we are following the prejudices of earlier eras or because we have engaged in serious reflection about fairness, asking what it really means to have public schools, and a public culture, that really treat people as equals.

Finally, we need to understand these three cases because they are still with us, despite the progress made by law and public debate. Jehovah's Witnesses encounter relatively little direct discrimination today, but the whole issue of pledging allegiance to the flag is intensely current—and, with it, the threat that the pledge has always posed to those whose consciences dictate a refusal to pledge. Anti-Mormon sentiment is still rife in our society. As a Mormon, Mitt Romney, campaigns for the presidency, the lower-class origins of Mormonism remain a target of ridicule, and the religion's beliefs about the polygamous family, despite having been abandoned long ago, still inspire widespread fear. Journalist Jon Krakauer's recent book about Mormon polygamy, for example, is a direct descendant of the sensationalistic anti-Mormon novels of the 1850s. It manages to meld contemporary instances of highly unusual dissident behavior with the history and traditions of the mainstream religion itself, thus whipping up panic about what the book's own subtitle calls "A Story of Violent Faith."[5] Catholics, finally, still suffer acutely from suspicion that they may be pawns in a foreign takeover bid. Although we have by now had a Catholic president as well as several other candidates for national office, and although our nation has not for some time been run by the WASP elite that used to sneer at Irish and Italian immigrants, there is no doubt that anti-Catholicism remains a force in our political life, and is at least one part of what we must confront when we think about funding for religious schools and public displays of the Ten Commandments. We can approach today's difficult Establishment Clause issues with a better mental balance if we know, first, this sad history of fear and bad behavior.

II. Mormon Polygamy: "Always . . . Odious"?

Majority Americans have difficulty talking about Mormonism.[6] Condescension, outright ridicule, and scare stories all abound. Hinduism, Buddhism, and other religions much further than Mormonism from the American mainstream are typically treated with respect. Mormonism usually isn't, even though by many criteria Mormons count (even more than the Amish) as a "model minority": hardworking, frugal, economically productive. Unlike the Amish, moreover, Mormons have made enormous contributions to education and the arts in America. Brigham Young University is the largest private university in the nation, educating some 30,000 undergraduates and many graduate students. The Mormon Tabernacle Choir is one of America's most glorious musical groups, and the high level of music and dance in Utah generally can be credited chiefly to the artistic creativity of Utah's Mormon population, and this, in turn, to a religion that (unlike many forms of dissident American religion) strongly supports the arts as vehicles for the glorification of God.

Still, people can't stop sounding what historian David Brion Davis calls the "themes of counter-subversion," portraying Mormons as unthinking pawns of a machine-like organization with an outlandish ideology that is at one and the same time both repressive and subversive. Part of the problem is that Mormons are different—but not *very* different. They revere both the Old and the New Testaments and affirm the divinity of Jesus. Their own sacred scripture, *The Book of Mormon*, continues the Judaeo-Christian tradition, adding a chapter to its history, but focusing centrally on Jesus and his role as Savior. Mormons recognize the major Christian sacraments, including communion. As Seth Perry shrewdly observes, the fact that all these continuities are combined with some startling discontinuities—a new sacred book, a new doctrine of salvation, a new tradition of revelation and prophecy—"often leads popular pundits and even otherwise detached scholars of religion to talk about Mormons the way one might talk about that kid in class with mittens pinned to his jacket—bless their hearts, they try, but they just don't quite get it."[7] Christians who find many different ways to deal with the existence of miracles in the recognized Bible find it difficult not to scoff at the story of Joseph Smith's revelation from the Angel Moroni. Miraculous events that allegedly occurred thousands of years ago can be ignored, or read allegorically or mythically, or historicized as an example of the thought categories of an ancient people. A miracle that allegedly took place in upstate New York in the early nineteenth century is very difficult to circumnavigate.

Many Americans find it easy to stereotype Mormons because they have little contact with the Mormon tradition. During the writing of my book on higher education, *Cultivating Humanity*, I studied Brigham Young University as one of the small core group of universities whose curricula I examined, asking how they prepare young people for democratic citizenship in a complex nation and world.[8] I therefore got to know a good deal about the university and the religion, including its liberal and rationalist wings.[9] Persuaded by the arguments of these Mormon liberals, I expressed strong concern with the treatment of dissident faculty members at BYU, contrasting BYU with the major Catholic universities, where a strong religious identity has proven compatible with a commitment to academic freedom. In the process, I learned a good deal about different aspects of the Mormon religious tradition, and I continue to learn more from the numerous Mormon students who attend our law school.[10]

We can't understand what the uproar was all about without talking about the religion's basic claims and the personality of its founder. The narrative that lies at the heart of Mormonism is that a "lost tribe of Israel," leaving the Near East, made its way ultimately to the New World. *The Book of Mormon* recounts that history, together with extensive ethical teachings. Its style is close to that of the King James Bible, and it has particularly close affinities with the Old Testament (cross-references are typically signaled by notes at the foot of the page). The historical books and the prophets are the most important sources of parallels—although the divinity of Jesus is strongly affirmed and celebrated, and the sacraments are revealed.

The Old Testament affinities of *The Book of Mormon* are strengthened by the fact that Jews are characteristically treated with friendly respect, as fellow outsiders in a Gentile world. Indeed, the text chastises the Gentiles for thinking that the Bible is all theirs and that nobody else can possibly possess a sacred book:

> And what thank they the Jews for the Bible which they receive from them? Yea, what do the Gentiles mean? Do they remember the travails, and the labors, and the pains of the Jews, and their diligence unto me, in bringing forth salvation unto the Gentiles? O ye Gentiles, have ye remembered the Jews, mine ancient covenant people? Nay; but ye have cursed them, and have hated them, and have not sought to recover them. . . . Thou fool, that shall say: A Bible, we have got a Bible, and we need no more Bible. Have ye obtained a Bible save it were by the Jews. Know ye not that there are more nations than one? (2 *Nephi* 29:4–7)

This is an appropriate rebuke to mainstream Christianity, which typically does think of itself as European and Caucasian, forgetting its Semitic and thus Asiatic origins. Notice how Justice Waite, in my epigraph, thinks of American values as those of Northern and Western Europe, contrasting them with Asian values. (Even today, classes in "the classical tradition" or "the Western tradition" typically read the Bible along with Homer and Sophocles, forgetting its Near Eastern origins.) The spirit of *The Book of Mormon* is that of return to an authentic biblical religion, away from the Gentiles' pseudo-religion. Joseph Smith saw himself, and was seen by others, as a "prophet-restorer."[11]

On the most skeptical account, Joseph Smith was a charlatan who simply invented the entire 531-page text, dictating it to his friend Oliver Cowdery (who sat nearby, probably in the same room, though separated from the plates by a blanket, while Smith put his head deep into the black hat and dictated), as if it were a translation of writings on the tablets given by the Angel Moroni. (The original tablets were seen by a few people, but were lost soon after the translation. Smith maintained that the angel took them back to keep them safe from the world.) Smith's early career does give some grounds for concern about fraud, since he was accused of bilking people out of their money by claiming to have a magic stone that could locate hidden treasure.[12] His biographer Richard Bushman, however, makes a strong argument against such a reading of the origin of the scriptural text. Smith, Bushman argues, was not a highly educated man, and his letters do not show the kind of mastery of English style that would make a deliberate literary creation of this scope and density thinkable.[13] When he sat down to write consciously and deliberately, he produced nothing like this. Bushman is a believing Mormon, and his own alternative explanation is that Smith had a series of visions that genuinely transmitted information from the angel.

A further alternative is also available, consonant with the way in which many religious rationalists approach visionary experience: namely, that Smith's voracious reading and his deep love of the Old Testament had put the biblical text deeply into his mind, so that, when his mind was freed of constraint, in a trancelike or visionary state, he had experiences in which a text came cascading out that drew on his extensive reading.[14] Whatever we believe, Bushman seems correct in suggesting that deliberate fraud is not the best explanation for the text as we have it.

Smith was an extraordinary religious entrepreneur. A man of charismatic attractiveness and intense energy, he made a deep impression even on those who set out to scorn him. Josiah Quincy, son of John Quincy Adams, visiting Smith at Nauvoo, Illinois, in 1844 (shortly before Smith was murdered), called him a "man of commanding appearance . . . a hearty, athletic fellow, with blue eyes standing prominently out upon his light complexion, a long nose, and a retreating forehead." Quincy could not forbear a certain class-based disdain—he mentions that Smith was "clad in the costume of a journeyman carpenter when about his work" and that his clothes "had not lately seen the washroom." His summary, however, is that "'a fine-looking man' is what the passer-by would instinctively have murmured."[15]

Despite Smith's persuasive powers—or perhaps in a sense because of them, since they made the religion successful and thus more threatening—Mormons were seen as troublemakers everywhere they went: first New York, then Ohio, Missouri, Illinois. Each state found new ways to harass the growing group of believers, usually by assailing Smith with frivolous criminal and civil complaints, and his followers with mob violence.[16] What was the uproar all about? It certainly was not about polygamy, which was probably being secretly practiced from around 1835, but was not publicly commanded until shortly before Smith's death. The salient issues seem to have been class, religious strangeness, and control over property and the political process. Mormons were a large and energetic group. When they moved into a new state *en bloc*, they threatened entrenched power interests. The fact that they were at the same time low-class (they are typically described pejoratively as "rough," like workmen, and so on), that they had a new strange orthodoxy, and that they hung together, forming a distinct interest group, made local politicians feel insecure.[17] So the harassment continued, each state using its own distinctive legal apparatus to make life difficult. Mormons believed that America's constitutional tradition was on their side, and they frequently spoke of the free exercise of religion. They saw all too clearly, however, that the Bill of Rights did not apply to the states and that the current fervor for states' rights was their enemy. For this reason, as well as for ethical reasons, Mormons became firm opponents of slavery and favored an expansive role for the federal sphere. Joseph Smith had embarked on a run for the presidency when he was imprisoned in Nauvoo, Illinois, on a frivolous charge and then murdered in the jail, along with his brother, Hyrum. The jail was stormed by a hundred men. Smith died fighting: he somehow got hold of a gun and fired six times into the crowd, then tried to escape through the window. He was struck by four bullets.[18]

The Mormons quickly left Illinois. Led by Brigham Young, they tried a different strategy, seeking freedom in a territory that as yet had no state government and was directly under federal control.

In Utah, Mormons quickly took control. They had the numbers to dominate local politics and to make sure that juries and judges had sympathy to their cause. Industrious and ambitious, they soon amassed large amounts of property and became an influential force in the territory's economic life. All this did not make them more popular. Indeed, opposition to them intensified, if anything, and pro-slavery inhabitants of the territory had keen resentment at being outnumbered by a group of antislavery people whom they thought they had reason to despise. Still, the Mormons' calculation that consolidation of power outside the recognized apparatus of the states would prove the wisest course proved correct; Mormon life, and power, moved on from strength to strength, with no successful opposition.

It is difficult to determine precisely when the practice of polygamy began, but it is clear that it was Smith who began it. *The Book of Mormon* consistently opposes the practice, but in an interesting way, which suggests that Smith was wrestling with the idea. Five passages denounce it, calling it "whoredom" and threatening divine punishment to groups who are accused of practicing it (*Jacob* 1:15, 2:23–27, 3:5; *Mosiah* 11:2–4; *Esther* 10:5). The passages, however, portray the polygamists as imitating the practice of Old Testament patriarchs, and the message is typically, don't think that it is all right for you just because it was the practice of David and Solomon. Particularly interesting is *Jacob* 2:22 ff.:

> But the word of God burdens me because of your grosser crimes. This people begin to wax in iniquity; they understand not the scriptures, for they seek to excuse themselves in committing whoredoms, because of the things which were written concerning David, and Solomon his son. Behold, David and Solomon truly had many wives and concubines, which thing was abominable before me, saith the Lord . . . For I, the Lord God, delight in the chastity of women. And whoredoms are an abomination before me; thus saith the Lord of Hosts. Wherefore, this people shall keep my commandments, saith the Lord of Hosts, or cursed be the land for their sakes. For if I will, saith the Lord of Hosts, raise up seed unto me, I will command my people; otherwise they shall hearken unto these things. (2:22–24, 28–30)

The text is unequivocally emphatic—and yet, it contains an escape clause. God states that He will issue a command if polygamy is what He wants; in the absence of that command, polygamy is an abomination.

During the time of the translation project with Cowdery, the practice of polygamy by the Old Testament patriarchs troubled Smith. He was trying to figure out why such a practice was permitted to the patriarchs. And after all, despite mainstream Christianity's proud pretense that monogamy is the true and only virtuous way, this same people accepts a sacred text in which polygamy is ubiquitous, and is nowhere divinely condemned. Abraham had both Sarah and Hagar; Jacob had two wives and two concubines (*Genesis* 29–30); Elkanah had two wives (1 *Samuel* 1:2); Rehoboam had eighteen wives and sixty concubines (2 *Chronicles* 11:21); Abijah had fourteen wives (2 *Chronicles* 13:21); David had a large harem (1 *Chronicles* 14:3); Solomon had seven hundred wives and more than three hundred concubines (1 *Kings* 11:3).[19] The passage from *The Book of Mormon* records these facts with (if we were to read it psychologically) a deep ambivalence: this Old Testament example must not be followed, and yet it is not very surprising that people want to imitate it. God condemns it, and yet He reserves the right to make a new commandment.

At some point in the 1830s, it seems that Smith had a revelation that polygamy had in fact been commanded by God. He called it "the most holy and important doctrine ever revealed to man on earth."[20] Apostle Orson Pratt recalled, in 1869, that Smith told selected individuals in 1832 that he "had inquired of the Lord concerning the principle of plurality of wives, and he received for answer that the principle of taking more wives than one is a true principle, but the time had not yet come for it to be practiced."[21] In 1843 he revealed publicly that he had had, considerably earlier, a revelation that the time had in fact come to practice polygamy, but he allows the date of the revelation to remain unclear. It seems likely that Smith began the practice himself, in secrecy, by the early 1830s.[22] From 1830 on there were rumors about allegedly improper conduct by Smith with women other than his wife. It appears that a woman named Fanny Alger, a maidservant in the Smith home, became a polygamous spouse of Smith in 1835, although his friends, shocked at the rumors, understood the relationship as adulterous.[23] Meanwhile, Smith publicly reaffirmed the principle of monogamy in 1835, and again in 1838 and 1842. By this time he had probably contracted a relatively large number of plural marriages, including marriages with women previously married to other men,[24] and had urged his associates to do so—as many as twenty-nine other men by the early 1840s.[25] At first, Smith's associates were shocked and revolted by the idea, as were the women in question, both first and second wives. (Smith's first wife, Emma, found the idea particularly difficult.) Typically, these people were won over in the end by their confidence in Smith's vision and their consequent conviction that polygamy had indeed been commanded by God. It was not until 1852, in Utah, however, that the practice was officially recognized and urged on all Mormon men. Even then, many Mormon men and women were deeply reluctant, and polygamy was never practiced by more than 20 to 40 percent of Mormon males.[26]

Polygamy was typically defended with arguments both theological and practical. Theologically, it was closely linked to the idea of the eternity of marriage, which was revealed at the same time as part of the same doctrine, which had the theological effect of raising the status of women to full eternal equality.[27] Practically, the practice was represented as a good way of raising large families quickly and thus populating the territory with a strong Mormon majority. Mormons also insisted that male sexuality was better controlled by polygamy than by monogamy. The polygamist had no need to sneak around and commit adultery, or visit prostitutes. Thus women would ultimately do better, and were less likely to be abandoned.[28] Indeed, the doctrine was part of a movement to give women greater equality within the religion, and Mormon women got the vote in 1870, during the high tide of polygamy.

As typically practiced, polygamy did not mean a harem: wives typically lived in separate households, and the husband visited a non–first wife relatively rarely. Defenders of the practice insisted that it must be practiced in an orderly way, under the close supervision of church leadership. Mormons did insist, however, that these marriages were consummated and were not purely spiritual.[29]

Mormon women had many complaints about the custom, and first wives had particular difficulty.[30] Consent of both first and subsequent wives was required, but the concept of consent could be hazy, when women were told that consenting was a spiritual requirement, or publicly condemned for failure to "follow counsel."[31] Typically, therefore, women kept their complaints private. Complaints typically did not focus on exorbitant sexual demands. The standard complaint was loneliness and lack of understanding. "He cannot know the craving of my nature," wrote one young polygamous wife in 1874. "He is surrounded with love on every side, and I am cast out."[32] Such complaints, however, are hardly unknown in monogamous relationships. (Leading feminist Elizabeth Cady Stanton had just such a lonely marriage, as did, and do, many women whose husbands work and leave them the care of home and children.)

The same circumstance of distance and absence seemed advantageous to some women. "If her husband has four wives," one wife commented, "she has three weeks of freedom every month." Another concluded that there was "more independence on both sides in polygamy," although she rated monogamous marriages as more successful because they gave "security and confidence."[33] Perhaps they do, to some, but "the grass is always greener" is a maxim to consider here. Certainly women in monogamy had no financial or legal security and could be abandoned at any time, a fact much stressed in nineteenth-century feminism. Mormon sociologist Kimball Young, in a study of 175 polygamous marriages published in 1954, rated 53 percent as "highly" or "reasonably successful," 25 percent as "moderately successful," 23 percent as burdened by "considerable" or "severe conflict."[34] We don't have comparable studies of monogamous marriages at that time, but we do have a large amount of anecdotal evidence of adultery, conflict, cruelty, and neglect.

On balance, polygamy does not seem to have been particularly bad, and it had at least some advantages. In addition, many of the problems it did have were associated with reversals of expectation, and could therefore have been expected to lessen over the generations. When one looks at these relationships, it is crucial to compare them not with some idealized picture of monogamous marriage, or even with monogamous marriage today, but with the reality of that time. Monogamous married women lost all independent legal rights upon marriage, becoming one legal "person" with their husbands.[35] Divorce was virtually impossible for an unhappy or even an abused woman to obtain—adultery was the only ground recognized by many states, and the "guilty party" had no right to remarry. By 1900 there were only four divorces per thousand marriages.[36] Elizabeth Cady Stanton's efforts to liberalize divorce shocked even many feminists and won little support. No laws against nonconsensual intercourse in marriage existed—a fact that led philosopher John Stuart Mill (thinking of both Britain and America) to complain that the lot of a wife in monogamous marriage was even worse than that of a slave.[37] Domestic violence was nowhere punished by law. Nor did any women in the U.S. have the vote—except for Mormon women, after 1870. In 1873, the year before *Reynolds*, an Illinois law forbidding women to practice law had been upheld by the U.S. Supreme Court, on the grounds that "[t]he natural and proper timidity and delicacy which belongs to the female sex evidently unfits it for many of the occupations of civil life. The constitution of the family organization, which is founded in the divine ordinance, as well as in the nature of things, indicates the domestic sphere as that which properly belongs to the domain and functions of womanhood."[38] These soi-disant friends of women— often the very same ones who were publicly inveighing against Mormon polygamy on the grounds that it enslaved women—had no intention of opening to them any of the opportunities through which they might have been able to escape from abusive or violent marriages.

All in all, then, it is difficult to see Mormon marriage as worse than monogamous marriage as then practiced. Perhaps it was somewhat better, to the extent that women of the working class, as most Mormon women were, had fewer obstacles of propriety and nicety standing between them and independent action or useful work. From the point of view of some religious doctrines, polygamy is undoubtedly worse than monogamy. From the point of view of the Mormon religion at that time, monogamy is worse than polygamy. From the point of view of legitimate state interests, it is not so easy to find compelling arguments against polygamy that are not also arguments against key elements of the dominant form of monogamous marriage.

The public debate about polygamy, however, did not look at these facts soberly and clearly. Never, for example, was women's position in monogamous marriage subjected to critical scrutiny when polygamy was attacked. Indeed, the whole episode is one of our history's most shocking instances of that common human vice of neglecting the beam in your own eye. Cries of "slavery" and "torture" were raised even while the legitimate complaints of monogamist feminists (demanding divorce on grounds of cruelty, access to the professions, and other reasonable things) were utterly scorned. Nor were the serious arguments of polygamists about the decline in adultery and prostitution addressed.

Instead, there was an outbreak of what can only be called public hysteria around the issue. Popular novels depicted polygamy as a hotbed of sensual lust, rape, physical brutality, and incest.[39] These novels were little better than a kind of prejudice-filled pornography. ("'Will you go with me?'" asks the polygamist to his runaway wife. "'No,'" answers the woman, who is about to give birth. "'Then you are done for,' said Yale; and deliberately, before my very eyes, in spite of my wild screams for his mercy, he fired at her, and scattered her brains over the floor. I fell down in a deathlike swoon.")[40] They also have a marked class element: illustrations depict Mormon men as rough and crude, linking their brutality to women with their lower-class origins.[41] People also asserted with no scrap of evidence that polygamy would lead to hereditary abnormalities, signaled by "the yellow, sunken, cadaverous visage; the greenish-colored eye; the thick, protuberant lips, the low forehead; the light, yellowish hair, and the lank, angular person."[42] Note how the common tropes of anti-

African racism (thick lips, low forehead) are combined with features that had to be acknowledged as common among Mormons, such as light hair, light eyes, and an "angular" physique—all described in such a way as to suggest that they are quite diseased and revolting.

What was the public furor about? The era was a time of profound insecurity in the nation as a whole. At such times, the idea that civilization itself is crumbling, an idea often linked to fears of a new or unpopular form of sexuality, commonly surface. (In this sense, the panic over polygamy has much in common with today's inflamed climate of opinion concerning same-sex marriage, although there had been no pressure to legalize polygamy outside Utah.) Even before they began the practice of polygamy, Mormons had already been targeted as subversives and repeatedly subjected to physical violence. Their growing political power and their control over property made them seem even more threatening than other new and dissident groups. Given this history, it is not surprising that sexualized attacks on the religion found a receptive audience.

Politics was not slow to respond to the public furor. The new Republican Party adopted, in 1856, a platform that explicitly linked polygamy with slavery, calling for the abolition of these "twin relics of barbarism."[43] (It would surely have been more accurate to say that the "twin relics" were slavery and traditional marriage with coverture, the point made by John Stuart Mill and other feminists—and yet American politicians neglected this comparison.) The tumult leading up to the Civil War temporarily put opposition to polygamy on the back burner. Once one of the "relics" had been confronted, however, politicians turned to the other. In 1862, Congress passed the Morrill Anti-Bigamy Act.[44] Once in a while, in the debates leading up to the passage of this law, someone raised the issue that polygamy might count as protected religious expression, but the following comment, from Representative Roger A. Pryor of Virginia, was typical:

> It is not true that polygamy pretends to any religious sanction. It is not true that the Mormons practice it as a pious observance.
>
> I have looked through the Mormon Bible—a disgusting farrago of nonsense and blasphemy, written in ribald parody of the more obvious characteristics of Scripture phraseology—I have examined this only dogmatic exposition of the Mormon faith, and nowhere do I find a word of recognition of the practice of polygamy.[45]

The congressman's contempt for the new religion clearly antecedes any acquaintance he may have with *The Book of Mormon* (and that acquaintance cannot have been thorough, or else he would surely have pointed out that polygamy is frequently condemned). It is difficult to see what in the text would give rise to words such as "ribald parody" and "disgusting farrago," since the style of *The Book of Mormon* is throughout deeply serious, elevated, and morally earnest. If one takes exception to its style and content, it would be difficult not to fault the Old Testament in similar terms. It's one thing to say, "That religion is not my own, and I do not believe it." It is quite another to pillory and ridicule someone else's sacred text. In any case, the congressman has not bothered to study Mormon doctrine, or he would have discovered that there is a central doctrine of continuing revelation: God intervenes in history, making new commandments known. The text I cited earlier makes reference to just such a possibility in the case of polygamy. Clearly Mormons, who on balance did not love the idea of polygamy, took it up only because they were convinced that it was a new sacred commandment. Repeatedly, they expressed their allegiance to the Constitution and their belief that the First Amendment protected them in their religious expression. The dismissive attitude of majority Christians to this constitutional issue is most unfortunate.

The Morrill Act proved unenforceable, because Mormons controlled political offices, including judgeships, in the territory. So an assault had to be made on the group's political power. In 1869, the Cullom Bill was proposed, giving the territory's governor power to appoint all judges, sheriffs, and notaries. In 1870, while the law was being debated, a large gathering of Mormon women in the Salt Lake Tabernacle protested the bill. No doubt the meeting was organized by the Mormon hierarchy, but the women showed great independence and zeal. A reporter for the *New York Herald* wrote that it was "perhaps one of the grandest female assemblages in all history," and added that "whatever may be the individual reader's opinion of the merits or demerits of Mormon institutions it will not be denied that Mormon women have both brains and tongues. Some of the speeches give evidence that in general knowledge in logic and in rhetoric the so-called degraded ladies of Mormondom are quite equal to the Women's Rights women of the East."[46] One month later, Mormon women in Utah were granted the right to vote. No doubt this was also a political move, doubling the number of Mormon votes in the territory. How reluctant, however, monogamists were, and long remained, when confronted with similar opportunities to increase their voting strength!

The Cullom Bill passed the House in March 1870, but failed to reach the Senate floor. (Many senators favored a less confrontational approach, believing that the "civilizing" influence of the railroads would take care of the problem over time.[47]) At this point, President Grant, publicly committed to controlling "the Mormon menace" and to "the ultimate extinguishment of polygamy," got to work crafting a substitute bill. In 1874, the Poland Law gave U.S. district courts in Utah exclusive civil and criminal jurisdiction, limiting local courts to estate and divorce settlement.[48]

Mormon leaders firmly believed that they would win a constitutional case under the First Amendment, so they looked for a suitable plaintiff. They found one in George Reynolds, bookkeeper and private secretary to a succession of church presidents. A "mild and obedient" man,[49] Reynolds had been a polygamist only for a few months and had only two wives. Young and appealing, he did not fit the scare image of the "grizzled tyrant" abusing women much younger than he.[50] Nonetheless, the strategy of legal confrontation was a risky one, given that proof of polygamous marriage was exceedingly difficult in a faith in which no public marriage records were kept. Arrested and charged, Reynolds was on the verge of acquittal due to lack of evidence when his second wife, Amelia Jane Schofield, subpoenaed, testified against him. (Note the remarkable catch-22: she is denied the spousal exemption from testimony on the grounds that the marriage is not a real marriage, polygamy being a legal impossibility; but he is facing conviction precisely on the grounds that it was *marriage* he was attempting to contract, not simply an affair.) The defense conceded that a plural marriage had been proven, but argued for accommodation on grounds of conscience. The judge summarily dismissed the appeal to conscience, on the grounds that "external acts" were not protected. On appeal, however, Reynolds's conviction was thrown out because the grand jury had been improperly impaneled (in a way that evidently excluded Mormons).[51]

The federal government indicted Reynolds again almost immediately. At the second trial, Amelia Jane Schofield Reynolds was nowhere to be found. The government went looking for her, but none too shrewdly, since the subpoena had the name of "Mary Jane Schobold." Moreover, when the marshal went to Reynolds to try to serve the subpoena, he blundered further, asking for the whereabouts of "Mary Jane Schofield." Reynolds replied, "You will have to find out." The marshal later admitted that he had not announced the nature of his business or that he was a marshal. The next day the court issued a new subpoena with the correct name. He went to the Reynolds home. The woman there, Mrs. Reynolds (the first), said that she had not seen Amelia Schofield for weeks. The prosecution then succeeded, despite strenuous objections from the defense, in having Schofield's testimony from the previous trial read into the record. Convicted, Reynolds appealed to the U.S. Supreme Court.[52] In addition to raising a number of legal issues, Reynolds argued that his conviction should be thrown out because he believed polygamy to be his religious duty.

Reynolds's case presented a number of apparently weighty legal anomalies.[53] First was the (apparently) improper impaneling of the grand jury. Second was the process of selection for actual trial jurors: the prosecution asked each potential juror whether he practiced polygamy, and, if the person refused to reply on the grounds of self-incrimination, immediately excluded him for cause. As the defense noted, it is not at all usual to question jurors about crimes they may have committed, nor is the Fifth Amendment worth much if refusal to answer is understood to be tantamount to an admission of guilt. Even if there is no technical violation of the privilege in this situation (since it prevents you from being convicted on your own evidence, not from being excused from jury service), there is a clear violation of usual standards of juror selection. Even worse was the trial judge's attitude to defense challenges. Repeatedly jurors admitted that they had already formed definite views about the case, and the judge repeatedly refused to allow the defense to exclude these jurors for cause.

A further issue raised at the time was the admission of Amelia Reynolds's testimony from the first trial. The right of a defendant to cross-examine witnesses called against him is a very basic right. The "confrontation clause" of the Sixth Amendment has undergone a complicated interpretive history. At the time of *Reynolds*, the clause would not have been understood to exclude Amelia's testimony. More recently, in *Crawford v. Washington* (majority opinion by Justice Scalia),[54] a more defendant-protective standard has prevailed, under which Amelia's testimony would not be admissible. So, the trial judge did not commit legal error at the time, but an evolving understanding of problems with the then-prevailing interpretation of the confrontation clause has led to recognition of a different standard.

Another weighty problem, possibly the worst, was the behavior of the trial judge when he summarized the case to the jury, saying:

> I think it not improper, in the discharge of your duties in this case, that you should consider what are to be the consequences to the innocent victims of this delusion. As this contest goes on, they multiply, and there are pure-minded women and there are innocent children,—innocent in a sense even beyond the degree of the innocence of childhood itself. These are to be the sufferers; and as jurors fail to do their duty, and as these cases come up in the Territory of Utah, just so do these victims multiply and spread themselves over the land.[55]

I think it is fair to say that an unbiased court would not have needed to adjudicate the divisive and difficult constitutional issue, because it would have found grounds to overturn the conviction in one or more of the other areas. The inclusion of obviously biased jurors and, especially, the judge's egregious summary are clear examples of justice perverted by malice. A focus on these issues would only have postponed the constitutional confrontation, but it might have postponed it for quite some time. A stern reproof to public officials on these other matters, so central to the rule of law, might also have served as notice that the rule of law applies even, and especially, when one doesn't like a person or group; and that very commitment to fair play might have made officials less zealous in going after new prosecutions.

Instead, however, the Supreme Court rushed to decide the constitutional issue, devoting only the most casual, and careless, attention to the weighty legal challenges. (On the judge's charge, Justice Waite observes that the judge was simply repeating what speeches in Congress had been saying: ergo, "There was no appeal to the passions, no instigation of prejudice"[56]—an argument that rests on the extraordinary premise that speeches made in Congress never appeal to the passions or instigate prejudice!) Now admittedly, the Court was in uncharted territory when it faced the issue of religious accommodation in 1874. It did not have the wide range of interesting cases and approaches that form the substance of our current Free Exercise jurisprudence.

The U.S. Constitution clearly applied because the case was a federal case, Utah being a territory; but, because the Free Exercise Clause had not yet been securely incorporated, there was no range of precedents at the Supreme Court level evaluating state laws for possible unconstitutionality. The only relevant cases were the decisions of state courts, as such not binding on the U.S. Supreme Court. These cases did tend in an accommodationist direction, as we have seen: Jews (sometimes) did not have to testify on Saturday; the Catholic priest did not have to divulge what he learned in the confessional. But we are dealing with tendency, not unanimity; nor did the Court have to pay any attention to these state cases, if it didn't want to. We cannot say, then, that the Court was wildly out of control when it treated Reynolds's First Amendment claim dismissively. We can, however, say that to treat any minority religion this way goes profoundly against the entire spirit of respect that animates the First Amendment.

Chief Justice Waite makes, first, a claim about beliefs and acts—namely, that the First Amendment protects only belief—and offers no protection at all to actions. His tortuous and unconvincing historical argument utterly neglects the debates surrounding the drafting of the amendment and the evidence of early drafts—all of which, as we've seen, tells strongly in favor of reading the word "exercise" as offering protection to acts as well as belief. Nor does Justice Waite confront the evidence of the state constitutions at the time of the Founding, which also typically protect acts—up to the point at which they threaten peace and safety. And, as we have said, he doesn't look at earlier cases. Instead, he alludes to several statements by Jefferson—not a framer of the First Amendment—that don't really prove what Waite needs to prove anyway, since Jefferson says only that we should not protect acts that threaten peace and safety. Nobody doubts that Congress has the power to protect peace and safety. What is at issue is the standard of proof: do we have to show that peace and safety are really at issue or do we only need to show that the act was illegal under some duly authorized law? The peace and safety standard has never been exhaustively interpreted: since colonial times, however, it has been understood to be a tough standard, not simply meaning that some law has been broken, but meaning that there is some imminent danger of mob violence or civil strife. Waite does not attempt to apply that standard to the case: he concludes that the mere violation of a duly enacted law is the standard: religious belief cannot "be accepted as a justification of an overt act made criminal by the law of the land."[57] His argument, however, does not support this conclusion.

Given the weak standard of protection Waite has set up, he doesn't really need to attack polygamy or to show that it threatens peace and safety, as that standard has been traditionally understood. Nonetheless, he is eager to do so, summoning up an orgy of violent crime, and the deterioration of democracy itself, as the likely outcomes of polygamous marriage. In the passage that is my epigraph, he summons racism to his aid, connecting monogamy with Northern and Western Europe (that is, the old immigrants), polygamy with all those places from which suspect new immigrants were pouring in, as well as with the scare images of Asia and Africa. What did the people who wrote and read this paragraph think about their own religion? They probably thought the Jews dangerously "Asiatic," but what about the Old Testament itself? It is both Asiatic and polygamist, and yet it was then, and is now, a sacred text for the vast majority of the nation's inhabitants. What did they really think about Abraham, Elkanah, David, Solomon, and so many other heroes and patriarchs? At least we'd expect some acknowledgment from the Court that polygamy has in fact not "always" been "odious" in the majority tradition.

Having linked polygamy to Asia and Africa, Justice Waite goes on to consider two religiously motivated crimes that no decent society would permit. His examples: human sacrifice, and the immolation of a wife on her husband's "funeral pile [sic]."[58] The inappropriateness of these analogies is remarkable. The first clearly involves harm to a nonconsenting party. The second has long been illegal in India precisely because, though represented as suicide, sati typically involves force and is in effect a murder. Polygamy, to begin with, doesn't cause death: indeed, as I have argued, it is hard to show that it had any bad consequences that monogamous marriage, as then practiced, did not have. Second, it does involve consent. If one were to say that we should redouble our vigilance lest women be pressured into any marriage, monogamous or polygamous, to which they had not fully consented, that would be a sensible policy statement that would give rise to at least some criticism of polygamy as practiced, though perhaps such a statement would not be one for courts to make. Its natural consequence would be policies expanding educational and employment opportunities for women, since a woman can hardly consent freely when the alternative is destitution. But all of this is quite far from Justice Waite's universe of discourse. He seems eager, simply, to tar polygamy by association with the bad practices of allegedly primitive races.

Having advanced his racial views, Justice Waite turns to political theory, and to the writings of influential German-American political scientist Francis Lieber, who had written widely used textbooks on self-government and political ethics.[59] Lieber had also written extensively about marriage, arguing that monogamy is connected to democracy and self-government, polygamy to "the patriarchal principle," and thence to authoritarian government.[60] Justice Waite affirms these connections, holding polygamy to be a danger to democratic self-government. How were these connections supposed to work, one might well wonder, seeing that monogamous marriage was itself thoroughly patriarchal? It turns out that Lieber's answer makes essential reference to his own racial theories. In an article attacking the idea of statehood for Utah, he wrote:

> Monogamy does not only go with the western Caucasian race, the Europeans and their descendants, beyond Christianity, it goes beyond Common Law . . . It is one of the elementary distinctions—historical and actual—between European and Asiatic humanity . . . It is one of the pre-existing conditions of our existence as civilized white men . . . Strike it out, and you destroy our very being; and when we say *our* we mean our race—a race which has its great and broad destiny a solemn aim in the great career of civilization.[61]

In the same article, he worries whether Utah might be the first "*bona fide* Africanized*" state in the Union.[62] Whether Lieber got these ideas from his old life in increasingly racist Germany or from his more recent life as a slaveholder in South Carolina,[63] his writings seem to have been the source of Justice Waite's connection between polygamy and African peoples, as well as of the ideas about patriarchy and autocracy that Waite explicitly credits to him.

Polygamy did not get a fair hearing in *Reynolds*, because it did not get a hearing. What, in retrospect, should an unbiased Court have said? Or, better, what should it have said had it the established legal framework for First Amendment adjudication that *Sherbert* and *Yoder* later provided? If we ask ourselves what the Supreme Court of the post-*Sherbert* and pre-*Smith* era would actually have said, it is clear enough that the Court would have found a compelling state interest against the practice, because that is the way the Court typically proceeded even then, if the practices in question were shocking or unfamiliar.

What, though, might a convincing such argument have been? Is there, in fact, a compelling state interest in prohibiting polygamy? Today, the most convincing such argument seems to be a sex-equality argument: men are permitted plural marriages, and women are not. The case could be analyzed in much the way that *Bob Jones*, the case concerning a religious university's ban on interracial dating, was analyzed: although there is a substantial burden to Mormons' free exercise of religion, the state's overwhelming interest in eradicating sex discrimination (racial discrimination in *Bob Jones*) provides a compelling interest. Notice, however, that this same compelling interest could have been used, as well, to throw out laws, in those days, that denied women divorce on grounds of cruelty, physical or mental; that denied women the vote; that denied that rape within marriage was genuine rape; that denied women access to the professions—all of these being the trappings of conventional monogamy. Nor has sex discrimination ever been recognized as a compelling state interest on a par with race: laws that discriminate on grounds of sex receive only intermediate, not strict, scrutiny.

The other issue that seems serious is one of administrative complexity: once plural marriages are permitted for both men and women, a bewildering network of relationships can be envisaged, and *U.S. v. Lee* (1982), the case of the Amish employer who refused to pay Social Security tax, held that a compelling state interest can be constituted by the state's reluctance to see a dramatic increase in its administrative burdens. These seem reasonable issues on which to focus. They are not the issues at stake in *Reynolds*. On the whole, if there were a sex-equal polygamy practiced on genuine religious grounds, there is no very strong argument for its invalidation under the *Sherbert* compelling-interest standard.

After *Reynolds*, prosecutions for polygamy became commonplace.[64] Given that Mormon women refused the assigned role of passive victim pleading for rescue and did not cooperate with prosecutors, women, too, began to be prosecuted, charged with fornication.[65] Meanwhile, the legal assault on the church broadened. The territory of Idaho passed a law requiring all who registered to vote to take the following oath:

> I do swear . . . that I am not a bigamist or polygamist; that I am not a
> member of any order, organization or association which teaches, advises,
> counsels or encourages its members . . . to commit the crime of bigamy
> or polygamy, . . . or which practices . . . celestial marriage as a doctrinal
> rite of such organization; that I do not, and will not, . . . teach, advise,
> counsel, or encourage any person to commit the crime of bigamy or
> polygamy, . . . either as a religious duty or otherwise.[66]

In *Davis v. Beason*, the Supreme Court upheld the constitutionality of this
test oath. Whatever one thinks of *Reynolds*, *Davis v. Beason* is deeply shocking. The ban on membership in a church that teaches certain beliefs is clearly
a violation of the Free Exercise Clause, even as narrowly interpreted in
Reynolds; the ban on pro-polygamy speech raises severe problems under the
Free Speech Clause. Moving from egregious to more egregious, in 1890 the
Court upheld Congress's seizure of Mormon lands and property and its dis-
solution of the corporate structure of the church—on the ground that allowing
the Mormons their property rights promoted polygamy, hence "a return to
barbarism." These words were written by the same Justice Bradley who denied Myra Bradwell the right to practice law in the state of Illinois.[67]

This is a sorry episode in our nation's history. We seem to be good at dealing with small unobtrusive minorities, very bad at dealing with large powerful
ones or, as we'll see, small noisy ones, particularly when the religion is both
new and linked to working-class origins. I've suggested that the legal regime
we had between *Sherbert* and *Smith* (which, I believe, plausibly realizes the
goals embodied in the Free Exercise Clause) would have done some good
work in restraining prejudice and suggesting that only certain sorts of arguments will get a hearing. Justice Waite could ride roughshod over fairness in
part because he was inventing the legal framework as he went along. Nonetheless, *Reynolds* shows us that courts are often no better than the climate of public opinion around them. If we want a fair nation, we must try to make it fair
pervasively, and not just trust that a few people will set us right when we have
gone terribly wrong. That means, always, not pointing out the mote in our
neighbor's eye without attending to the beam in our own. "Unchristian partiality" and "the Great God Selfe" is what Roger Williams would have said.
Those sins are still very much with us.

III. "I Pledge Allegiance": Jehovah's Witnesses and the Crisis Over Loyalty

In times of uncertainty, Americans rally around the flag. It's not that people don't love their nation in times of prosperity and safety. But, just as family members may omit daily expressions of love when things are going along in an ordinary way, so too, in good times Americans typically have felt less need to express their love of America through public rituals. We all recall how, in the wake of 9/11, the flag popped up everywhere: on houses, cars, lapel pins. So we can see that danger and the flag are close companions. What we may not know is that before the 1890s the flag played a very small part in our public life together. Schools typically did not fly the flag. There was no Pledge of Allegiance. There was no code about how the flag should be treated. All these things came with the advent of an era of unprecedented tumult and uncertainty.

The 1890s saw a rapid swell of immigration, much of it from nations (Ireland, Italy, Eastern Europe) that had not been a large part of our previous ethnic mix. Many of the new immigrants were Roman Catholics, thus creating a dramatic shift in America's religious composition. Meanwhile, the economy was also undergoing rapid changes, and these changes, while they created new wealth (for example, the railroad empires that built much of Chicago), also created new inequalities and a class of impoverished factory workers who were aware of not enjoying the fruits of the nation's general prosperity. Economic unrest made for social instability. At the one end of things, there was the proud gleaming surface of American life, as the nation welcomed the world to the Columbian Exposition in Chicago in 1892 that celebrated the four hundredth anniversary of Columbus's "discovery" of America. The pristine classical pavilions, the formal French-style gardens—all suggested a sedate elite America that novelist Eric Larson evocatively names the "White City."[68] Just down the road, however (as Larson's novel effectively shows) were the parts of America that nobody wanted to notice: poor, hungry, crime-ridden.

So what was America? What values held it all together? If we can't figure that out, people thought, we haven't a prayer of remaining a unified successful nation, while waves of immigrants, with their different customs and ideas, sweep over us. (Something like this anxiety is now hitting Europe, as immigration alters the composition of once-homogeneous populations.)

Into this anxious climate stepped a popular magazine, *The Youth's Companion*, and two of its most innovative recruits, James Upham and Francis Bellamy.[69] Upham, nephew of the magazine's owner and founder, headed the Premium Department. Bellamy, hired in 1891, quickly developed a close working relationship with the more experienced Upham. Both men were strong Baptists and sons of Baptist ministers. Both were convinced that young people needed a moral education grounded in religion. Bellamy had been active in the temperance movement, but by 1890 had become passionate about the egalitarian movement known as Christian socialism.[70] Both men agreed that the nation was drifting toward consumerism, greed, and a loss of moral values. Upham's initial response was to begin a movement to encourage public displays of the flag, particularly in schools, through the creative use of prizes and contests. He sponsored an essay contest on the topic "The Patriotic Influence of the American Flag When Raised over the Public Schools," giving a giant flag to each state's winning essay. Later, along with offering low-cost flags for purchase, the magazine concocted a scheme to help students raise money to purchase flags for their schools, by sending free packages of "flag certificates" to any student who asked; these certificates (which made the purchaser a shareholder "in the patriotic influences of the School Flag") were then to be sold at ten cents apiece. "Follow this plan, and any school can raise $10.00 for a beautiful Flag sixteen feet long in a day's notice."[71] The scheme proved hugely popular.

Enter Bellamy. Since he has now been conclusively proven the sole author of the Pledge of Allegiance,[72] it is worth pausing to ask who he was. In today's America, socialism and fervent nationalism do not sit easily together. In the 1890s, they did. Concern for economic justice was frequently coupled with a type of moral fervor that sought expression in strong professions of patriotic sentiment. Bellamy favored programs that promoted economic justice for the poor. But countering the tendency to greed and immorality also required Americans to think what America is really all about, and to say publicly and daily that it is about moral values, not just about greed. The need to teach young people that money and competition were not everything was intensified by the upcoming Columbian Exposition, where the whole world would see the acquisitive greedy America on display. Bellamy thought that this major event should be marked by something deeper, a public statement of rededication to the values ("liberty and justice for all") for which the nation stood at its Founding.

But there was something else that motivated Bellamy, something disquietingly familiar in this era: suspicion and fear of foreigners. Today we tend to associate fear of immigrants with right-wing politics, not with socialism. In the economic populism of the 1890s, however, xenophobia loomed large—not illogically, since new immigrants were a threat to the indigenous poor, more than to the rich. Bellamy's concern about immigration was, however, more moral than economic: he reasoned that they could easily subvert the fabric of democracy that America had taken so long to build. Nor was his argument based simply on a reasonable concern that large numbers of people not raised with habits of democratic participation could not be easily assimilated. Like most such arguments in the period, Bellamy's was both anti-Catholic (decrying "the fanatical immigrant" who was assumed to be slavish in politics because slavish in religion[73]) and, above all, racist:

> A democracy like ours cannot afford to throw itself open to the world. . . .
> Where all classes of society merge insensibly into one another every alien
> immigrant of inferior race may bring corruption to the stock. There are
> races, more or less akin to our own, whom we may admit freely, and get
> nothing but advantage from the infusion of their wholesome blood. But
> there are other races which we cannot assimilate without a lowering of
> our racial standard, which should be as sacred to us as the sanctity of our
> homes.[74]

For Bellamy, the Pledge of Allegiance was crucial both because it affirmed a moral basis for nationhood in a world of greed and also—and inseparably—because it affirmed the values of a Protestant, Northern and Western European America against the subversive values vaguely associated with new immigrants from Southern and Eastern Europe, and their Catholic faith. For that reason it is not altogether surprising that the pledge itself expresses liberal ideals, while the ritual of compulsory school recitation that Bellamy associated with it expresses a less lofty set of values, creating an imposed order into which all newcomers would be inserted at their peril.[75]

After a few preliminary drafts, the pledge emerged in the form it kept until 1954: "I pledge allegiance to the flag of the United States of America, and to the republic for which it stands, one nation, indivisible, with liberty and justice for all." Written originally for the Columbian Exposition, where it was recited by the huge assembled crowd, under the leadership of President Benjamin Harrison (whom Bellamy had converted to the flag movement), the pledge began to be made compulsory in the public school systems of many states. At first there were numerous alternative patriotic rituals, and even a variety of distinct pledges, but Bellamy's version quickly caught on, with the powerful support of the American Legion, the Veterans of Foreign Wars, the Daughters of the American Revolution (DAR) and other patriotic women's groups, and, finally, the Ku Klux Klan—which at the time was as intensely anti-Catholic as it was anti-black.[76]

There were public criticisms of the enforced recitation of the pledge. Some said only that the connection between the ritual and real patriotism had not been demonstrated; others insisted that the ritual would be positively deleterious, a quick slapdash nostrum that would positively distract teachers from the patient reflective process of civic education that was really needed.[77] On the whole, however, people were so eager to think that the perceived patriotism problem could be readily solved that they ignored these plausible arguments. The pledge became mandatory in state after state, as did the ritual then associated with it, pupils standing at attention and extending their right arm straight out toward the flag, palm up. (This salute was modified only much later, when its similarity to the Nazi "Heil Hitler" salute became embarrassing and the hand-on-heart salute was substituted.)

Some families did not want to go along with this ritual. The first documented resistance came from foreign nationals attending the public schools: a British girl in New Jersey, and, the following year, a Canadian boy in the same state. Both children of lifelong legal U.S. residents, they told their teachers that their parents had explained to them that they ought to stand respectfully during the ceremony, but that they had already sworn allegiance to another flag, so they should not swear allegiance to the American flag. The school boards in question decreed that the children could not attend the public schools if they would not say the pledge. One member said, "[I]f he is not an American, he should go to a private school and pay his tuition or go back to Canada or England."[78] (One student told the *New York Times* that she knew an American girl who asked not to sing "God Save the King" in Canada and was told, "That is the proper spirit. It is right for you to maintain your love for the land that you were born in."[79]) Eventually, after widespread public criticism of the school board, the Canadian boy was quietly reinstated.

Religious objections also began to be heard. Mennonites standardly refused to say the pledge, which they believed to be incompatible with their religion.[80] Interestingly, this refusal led to no public controversy until World War I, when Mennonites were already unpopular for their pacifism.[81] In 1918, a Mennonite girl went to school every day and was sent home every day for her refusal. In what soon became a common catch-22, the father, a conscientious objector, was then prosecuted and sent to jail for not keeping his child in school. He appealed his conviction, showing that it was not he who had prevented his daughter from attending school. The judge rejected his appeal, condemning him for poisoning his daughter's mind.[82] Such cases multiplied. In one town in Delaware, in the single year of 1928, thirty-eight Mennonite children were expelled from school.[83] Because Mennonites believe that it is wrong on religious grounds to initiate litigation, their predicament led to no public test of the pledge's constitutionality.

Other small Christian sects encountered the same difficulty. One of the most remarkable cases was that of nine-year-old Russell Tremain in Bellingham, Washington, in 1925. The Tremains were members of a pacifist sect called the Elijah Voice Society, which rejected the pledge on grounds that displays of patriotic sentiment are connected with militarism and war.[84] Because he refused to say the pledge, Russell was not permitted to attend school. His father was then jailed for contributing to the delinquency of a minor. Russell was placed in a state children's home, where he was compelled to salute the flag. Nine months later, Russell's parents had not relented—so the judge granted the state permanent custody of the boy, for the purpose of putting him up for adoption with "Christian, patriotic parents." Judge Brown argued that by advising their son not to salute the flag the parents were endangering him by inculcating "a feeling to disregard all law." Moreover, he reasoned, the parents' religious objections could not be taken seriously, because it was impossible to imagine that the "millions of fine men and women of America who salute the flag are violating a law of God." (In other words, because majority religion permits X, it is unthinkable that any religion could prohibit X.) Because the parents were no longer Russell's legal parents, they were forbidden to visit him at the children's home.[85] The American Civil Liberties Union tried to give the family legal assistance, but the Tremains, like the Mennonites before them, refused to sue. Only in 1927, when a new judge took over on the juvenile court, was Russell returned to his home, with the understanding that the parents would send him to a private school.[86]

The compulsory flag-salute issue was languishing for want of willing plaintiffs. Enter the Jehovah's Witnesses, whose combination of unusual views with willingness to litigate gave them a formative role in American law throughout the twentieth century. The Witnesses are an indigenous American sect that quickly spread to many other parts of the world. In 1940, the church had approximately 40,000 U.S. members.[87] By now it has around 6 million members worldwide.[88] Descendants of the Millerites who founded the Seventh-Day Adventist Church, Witnesses believe that the true Christianity has been lost through apostasy and must be restored. Originally called "Bible Students," they follow the example of their first leader, Charles Taze Russell, who closely studied scripture to determine the nature of authentic Christianity. Witnesses are particularly well-known for their belief that Jesus was created by God and is not one with God; that the Holy Spirit is God's active force, not a third person in the Trinity; that the end of the world will come at some point in the relatively near future, when a small group of righteous believers will be saved. Witnesses believe that the injunction to the apostles in *Acts* 5.42 means that all good Christians should go from house to house preaching the gospel, and they do this, to many people's annoyance. They also preach in the streets and sell *The Watchtower*, their magazine; they believe that parents should involve their children in public preaching. Witnesses refuse military service and most forms of participation in politics. Beginning in 1931, when the movement's leadership was assumed by Joseph Francis Rutherford, a lawyer and briefly a judge, they do not, however, refuse to litigate.

The Witnesses' refusal to recite the pledge stems not (as with the Mennonites) from their views about military service, but from their analysis of the Old Testament's prohibition of idolatry. They believe that the injunction not to worship idols or graven images applies to the pledge. Thus, they are extremely happy to stand at respectful attention while others say the pledge. They even created an alternative pledge that they were willing to say:

> I have pledged my unqualified allegiance and devotion to Jehovah the Almighty God and to his Kingdom for which Jesus commands all Chris-

tians to pray. I respect the flag of the United States and acknowledge it as
a symbol of freedom and justice for all. I pledge allegiance and obedience
to all the laws of the United States that are consistent with God's law as
set forth in the Bible.[89]

None of this helped them, however, and trouble of the familiar sort began.

Many Americans didn't like the Witnesses. They found their public proselytizing irritating, and they didn't like their vehement denunciations of other
religions. (In something of an irony, given the way in which anti-Catholicism
lies behind so many of the persecutions of this period, Witnesses were vehe-
mently anti-Catholic, often rudely and upsettingly so. In fact, the case that established that the Free Exercise Clause was incorporated concerned a
Jehovah's Witness whose public anti-Catholic hectoring upset the citizens of
Connecticut, with its substantial Catholic population.[90] This early victory established the Witnesses' right to preach unpopular doctrines in the streets.)

The pledge, however, was not so straightforward a matter. In the 1930s and
early 1940s, America was anxious not only about its economic and social crisis, but also about the increasingly likely prospect of war with Germany. They
saw any group who refused the pledge as a "fifth column" of subversives, who
were likely to be working for the enemy. The Witnesses, as the most conspicuous such group, began to be hated and feared.

This fear is all the more peculiar in that it was known—and, like all matters
connected with the Holocaust, should have been known more widely than it
was—that the Witnesses were being persecuted in Germany because of their
conscientious stance toward "idolatrous" public observances. Already unpopular because they refused military service during World War I, they began
to be persecuted in earnest when they refused to say "Heil Hitler" and to give
the associated salute. A recent study of religion in the Third Reich concludes
that 97 percent of Witnesses in Germany encountered some form of persecution; about 10,000 were sent to concentration camps, and a full third of the
whole sect, an estimated 2,500 to 5,000, lost their lives.[91] The sect was officially banned in 1935, and the Watchtower Society's printing operation was
closed down. In concentration camps, Witnesses were made to wear a purple
triangle.[92] Witnesses in the U.S. sometimes mentioned the overt similarity between the U.S. flag-salute ritual, with its straight-arm salute, and the German
ritual that their co-religionists courageously refused.

The Witnesses began to challenge the compulsory flag salute in the courts. In early cases in various states, they had little success, although once in a while a dissent, at least, sympathized with their concerns.[93] By 1936, there were mass expulsions—often attended by the usual concomitant punishment of the parents for not sending their children to school.

Lillian and William Gobitas (the correct spelling of the name, misspelled in later court documents) grew up in Minersville, Pennsylvania, a town in the coal belt that was hard hit by the Depression. Their father, Walter, ran the Economy Grocery. He worked long hours to make the business a success, but he also extended credit to poorer families who experienced financial hardship. All six of the Gobitas children helped in the store, and all received a serious religious education that included proselytizing—but, as Lillian Gobitas Klose stressed in a 1998 interview, their parents made sure that they had fun too, riding the family bicycle, listening to the radio, taking family trips. Lillian didn't like it when she occasionally had to proselytize in her own hometown, because she was embarrassed to stand out from her peers, but it obviously did her little harm, because, when trouble began, she was president of the seventh grade class and an A student. "It was a pleasant time," she told scholar Shawn Peters.[94]

In 1935, Joseph Rutherford laid out the arguments for refusing the pledge. The Gobitas family studied the biblical texts he invoked. Lillian and her brother Billy were asked to ponder the issue as an individual issue of conscience. Lillian had a hard time with the decision. She kept having the thought, "Oh, if I stop saluting the flag, I will blow all this!"[95] After a few months of embarrassed conformity, Billy came home one day smiling proudly: he had finally found the courage to say no. Lillian was inspired. "I really felt that it was the right thing to do—I just didn't have the courage to go ahead. So that spurred me." She explained her biblical arguments to her teacher, and the teacher hugged her, praising her courage. Her classmates were not so kind. A few tried to understand her position, but most shunned her.[96]

Neither the state of Pennsylvania nor the local school district had a compulsory flag-salute law, but the superintendent of schools, Charles Roudabush, was determined not to tolerate such insubordination. He sought an opinion from the state and was told that he could punish the children if the district had a formal flag-salute requirement.[97] He then called a meeting of the school board and summoned the Gobitas family. Walter met privately with

several board members before the meeting, pleading for tolerance of their un-
conventional religious views. These men were unsympathetic, saying, "Come
on, Wally. . . . We're under a lot of pressure. If you could just forget this flag
thing, it would save us all a lot of trouble."[98] At the meeting, Walter stressed
that the children were showing no disrespect to the flag. The children each
submitted letters—thoughtful, each distinctive in style and content,[99] obviously written by them—spelling out their religious reasons for refusing the
salute and the pledge. Roudabush insisted that the children were guilty of insubordination. The board unanimously passed a formal pledge-and-flag-
salute rule, stating explicitly that refusal was equivalent to insubordination.
The children were expelled.

Walter Gobitas immediately took matters into his own hands, filing a complaint against the school board; he made his own constitutional arguments.
Although the school board tried to get the U.S. district court to dismiss the
complaint, the presiding judge, Albert Maris, refused. A Quaker, Maris
showed keen sympathy with the situation of a small religious minority. In his
opinion refusing to dismiss the complaint, he criticized with particular strin-
gency the school board's contention that the objections of the children were
not religious. "Liberty of conscience," he wrote, "means liberty for each individual to decide for himself what is to him religious." To permit public officials to decide that other people's reasons, which they think religious, are not
religious "would be to sound the death knell of religious liberty. . . . To such a
pernicious and alien doctrine this court cannot subscribe."[100] He suggested
that the school board's policy seemed to violate the Gobitas children's rights
under both the Pennsylvania and the U.S. constitutions.

The case then went to trial. Walter and the two children testified about
their religion at length. Lillian described Maris as "a very agreeable person,
not formidable at all." Though very nervous, she was able to outline her beliefs and to give chapter and verse from the Bible—despite objections from
the school board's lawyer that the case was turning into "a bible study session."[101] Roudabush was the only witness for the defense. An angry and in-
temperate man, he insisted that the children had "perverted views" about the
flag salute because they had been "misled" and "indoctrinated" by their parents. He insisted that the flag salute "is not a religious exercise in any way
and has nothing to do with anybody's religion."[102] In finding for the plaintiffs,
Maris wrote at length about the nature of their religious beliefs, concluding,

"I think it is . . . clear from the evidence that the refusal of these two earnest Christian children to salute the flag cannot even remotely prejudice or imperil the safety, health, morals, property or personal rights of their fellows."[103] Interestingly, then, he understood the relevant legal standard in much the way that I have argued the framers understood it, and in the way that state constitutions had typically construed it: religious freedom is to be accommodated unless public peace and safety are jeopardized. While the case was under appeal, the children attended a private school thirty miles from Minersville.

At the next stage, the family sought, and received, legal assistance from both the ACLU and lawyers within the Witness hierarchy. In November 1939, the Third Circuit of the U.S. Court of Appeals upheld Maris's ruling.[104] Judge Clark, writing for a unanimous court, noted that William Penn had been expelled from Oxford in circumstances that resembled those of the Gobitas children.[105] In March 1940, the U.S. Supreme Court agreed to hear the case.

Minersville v. Gobitis is one of the low-water marks of twentieth-century Supreme Court jurisprudence. Along with cases such as *Dred Scott* and *Korematsu*, it is widely regarded (and was regarded already at the time) as a huge blunder, in which a climate of public anxiety got the better of constitutional liberty. Things are, however, a bit more complicated. First of all, the case was badly argued at the Supreme Court level. Joseph Rutherford, head of the Witnesses, insisted on arguing it himself, and he did not do a good job.[106] Digressive, stuffed with irrelevant material about the religion, and highly polemical in character, his brief did not do a good job of delineating the legal issues. *Amicus* briefs from the ACLU and the American Bar Association did better, but Rutherford took the main role at oral argument, and botched things again.

A second crucial element in the case was Justice Felix Frankfurter, who wrote its majority opinion, persuaded other justices to join it, and, when it was reversed later in *Barnette*, led the minority in a stinging dissent. Frankfurter, the lone Jew on the Court, and a judge deeply respected by his peers, might have been expected to side with the victims of religious persecution. As he himself noted, in his *Barnette* dissent, "One who belongs to the most vilified and persecuted minority in history is not likely to be insensible to the freedoms guaranteed by our Constitution."[107] He stressed that his own personal sympathies lay strongly with the Gobitas children. Nonetheless, Frankfurter had strict views concerning the limits of judicial power. He believed, more fervently than many on the Court in those days, that judges should not be legislators, but should defer to the legislature in all but the most extraordinary cases. Frankfurter was also a fervent patriot, who liked to whistle "The Stars and Stripes Forever" as he walked in the halls of the Court, and who told his biographer, on his deathbed, "Let people see . . . how much I loved my country."[108] His intense love of his adopted country and his fear for its safety in time of war led him to attach great importance to the pledge and to the flag salute. In 1944, in a speech for the District of Columbia's "I am an American Day" celebration, he compared love of country to romantic love, saying that it was too intimate an emotion to be publicly expressed except in poetry. He then read a rather sentimental ode to the flag by Franklin K. Lane, which included the lines "I am not the flag, not at all. I am but its shadow."[109]

Frankfurter's majority opinion, although it cites *Reynolds* as a precedent, does not rest on the belief-conduct distinction. Indeed, Frankfurter states that the First Amendment both puts "the affirmative pursuit of one's convictions about the ultimate meaning of the universe and man's relation to it . . . beyond the reach of law"[110] and also entails that restriction on conduct expressive of religious conviction can only be justified by "specific powers of government deemed by the legislature essential to secure and maintain that orderly, tranquil, and free society without which religious toleration itself is unattainable."[111] And despite his usual deference to the legislative branch in making such determinations, on which he vigorously insists here, he does not rest his entire argument on deference, since he also insists that national unity and cohesion supply the state with "an interest inferior to none in the hierarchy of values."[112] "National unity is the basis of national security." (It would appear, then, that even if Frankfurter had had the job of applying the stringent *Sherbert* test, he would still have found for the school board, since a substantial burden can be justified by a compelling state interest.) Frankfurter is also at pains to insist that the legislature's judgment about what promotes that interest is at the very least plausible. The flag, he writes, is "the symbol of our national unity, transcending all internal differences, however large."[113]

The entire Court joined Frankfurter (Justice Murphy did so after initially planning to dissent, being brought round by Chief Justice Hughes)—with one exception. Justice Stone wrote a strong and eloquent dissent. The law in question, he argues, "seeks to coerce these children to express a sentiment which, as they interpret it, they do not entertain, and which violates their deepest religious convictions."[114] What the First Amendment's protection of liberty is all about is its protection against government power. If it means anything at all, it means that the state cannot compel people to violate their conscience. Most such infringements of conscience have been justified in the name of the public good. "The framers were not unaware that under the system which they created most governmental curtailments of personal liberty would have the support of a legislative judgment that the public interest would be better served by its curtailment than by its constitutional protection."[115] So, if these guarantees of liberty of religion and speech are to have any meaning at all, they must mean that these liberties are upheld against legislative judgments, at least in some instances. A searching judicial inquiry is particularly important when we are dealing with the interests of minorities, who are often targets of prejudice and misunderstanding.[116]

Although the specific doctrine that an individual's religious liberty can be substantially burdened only in the presence of a "compelling state interest" would not be formally articulated for another fifteen years, Stone maps it out here, with particular reference to the vulnerability of minorities, insisting that the judiciary has the responsibility of scrutinizing legislative judgments in such cases. "With such scrutiny," he concludes, "I cannot say that the inconveniences which may attend some sensible adjustment of school discipline in order that the religious convictions of these children may be spared, presents a problem so momentous or pressing as to outweigh the freedom from compulsory violation of religious faith which has been thought worthy of constitutional protection."[117]

Thus Stone's dissent was on the track of the principle that has guided constitutional interpretation during much of the recent era, a principle that goes all the way back to Roger Williams. He was probably wrong to suggest that a searching judicial inquiry is warranted only when minority religion is at stake. The broader principle later articulated in *Sherbert* and *Yoder* seems fairer and more satisfactory. He is surely correct, however, in seeing that the liberties of minorities are more at risk, in democracy, than those of the majority. Stone failed to articulate the other important part of the *Sherbert* test, namely that the law not only must serve a compelling state interest but also must be narrowly tailored to serve that interest in the least burdensome manner possible. He thus left a significant loophole that would need addressing. Nonetheless, his opinion adumbrated an important principle.

Minersville v. Gobitis is not base, or even legally shocking. (It is far less legally shocking, certainly, than *Smith*, which unwrote a substantial legal tradition; nor is it full of objectionable prejudice, like *Reynolds*.) We must remember that at this time, with the Free Exercise Clause so recently incorporated, and with very few precedents at the federal level, the Court had few legal guidelines, and one of the primary ones that it did have, *Reynolds*, gave very poor guidance. Frankfurter wrote an opinion that was not marred by prejudice, and he had strong arguments on his side. He surely, however, overestimated the strength of the state's interest in the compulsory flag salute—he thought about the general danger that beset the nation in 1940, rather than about the conscientious acts of two respectful teenagers who would certainly not be imitated by their scoffing peers. Stone has a better understanding of the weakness of the state's interest; he also shows insight into the values central to the religion clauses when he places emphasis on the likely fate of minorities, especially unpopular minorities, in a majoritarian world. Frankfurter reasoned plausibly, but somehow managed, in his pursuit of judicial restraint, to miss the gravity of the conscience issue and tradition of accommodation that lies behind it—thus missing, in effect, the core value inherent in the Free Exercise Clause.

Everyone was worried about chaos, but they were looking for it in the wrong place. National security was almost certainly not at risk in the behavior of Lillian and Billy. The safety of the Jehovah's Witnesses, as it emerged, was profoundly at risk. In the wake of the decision, widespread violence against Jehovah's Witnesses broke out all over the nation.[118] Sometimes people referred to the Court's decision as if it had said that Witnesses were disloyal. More generally, the decision was taken by many to mean open season on this alleged "fifth column." Vigilantes waylaid Witnesses who were proselytizing, killed and injured large numbers, and burned down Witness meeting places, often with the passive support of the police and the active participation of the American Legion. In Texas, the ACLU implored the governor to call out the Texas Rangers to protect Witnesses, in default of the usual protection from officers of the law.[119] In Maine, anti-Witness rioting brought chaos to four towns, as mobs broke into Witness homes, forced them to salute the flag, and beat them for refusing.[120] The governor intervened only when it seemed likely that Maine's summer tourist season would suffer from the chaos.[121] The *New York Herald Tribune* reported that the mob read out the *Gobitis* opinion as a call to arms. The ACLU, which made the most serious effort to publicize the Witnesses' plight, estimated that 1,488 Witnesses in 335 communities had been attacked by vigilantes from May to October 1940. Only four states were free of such disturbances.[122] The situation was compounded by widespread workplace harassment and discrimination.[123] Many children were sent to reformatories. Eleanor Roosevelt expressed deep concern for the Witnesses' plight in her column. As the tide began to turn, a police chief in Virginia was convicted for depriving a group of Witnesses of their civil rights under the "color of law." (They had been tied together, forced to drink castor oil, and marched through the streets of Richwood.)[124]

Meanwhile, the journalistic and scholarly response to the Supreme Court's decision was almost uniformly hostile.[125] Particularly stinging was an extensive critique in *The New Republic*, a journal that Frankfurter had cofounded.[126] The editorial inveighed against the curtailment of civil liberties in response to wartime "hysteria," saying, "we are in great danger of adopting Hitler's philosophy in the effort to oppose Hitler's legions." Surely, it reasoned, the children's nonobservance was not a large security problem, and there were other ways of securing the desired patriotic end, without compelling them to salute against their conscience. The magazine also mentioned that a Nazi court had recently handed down a very similar decision.

Pondering these critiques, as well as the violence the decision seemed to have unleashed, several members of the Court began to reconsider their votes. Justices Murphy, Black, and Douglas gave indications that they would now vote to overturn *Gobitis*. (Murphy had always been on the fence. Douglas and Black both said later that they had been persuaded by their great respect for Frankfurter and the "mesmeriz[ing]" effect of his intense patriotism.[127]) Meanwhile, two Justices (Charles Evans Hughes and James McReynolds) retired, and their places were taken by newcomers James Byrnes and Robert Jackson. The latter had already published a critique of *Gobitis*. Thus, it appeared that there remained only three solid votes to uphold the decision: those of Justices Frankfurter, Reed, and Roberts.[128]

The next case on the issue to reach the Court was *West Virginia v. Barnette*, in 1943. The issues were very similar to those in *Gobitis*. The state flag-salute requirement had been adopted in 1942, in a way that suggested that the Witnesses were its specific target. A group of Witness children in the Charleston area were expelled; their families brought suit. This time the Witnesses were represented by a competent Witness lawyer, Hayden Covington. As before, the ACLU and the ABA submitted briefs. After oral arguments and discussion of the issues, Stone, by then Chief Justice, assigned the majority opinion to Jackson, rather than, as had been expected, to himself.

Jackson's legal analysis took a very different path from that mapped out in Stone's *Gobitis* dissent. Stone had treated the case as one of religious liberty, arguing that the right reading of the Free Exercise Clause protects a space for minority religious expression even against generally applicable laws, in the absence of a compelling state interest. Jackson virtually ignored the issue of religion, treating the case as one of compelled speech, and referring to the First Amendment in a general way. Confronting head-on Frankfurter's argument about deference to the legislature, he insists that the whole purpose of the First Amendment is "to withdraw certain subjects from the vicissitudes of political controversy, to place them beyond the reach of majorities and officials and to establish them as legal principles to be applied by the courts."[129] He then argues that a major purpose of the First Amendment has always been to protect citizens from compelled uniformity of belief:

> If there is any fixed star in our constitutional constellation, it is that no official, high or petty, can prescribe what shall be orthodox in politics, nationalism, religion, or other matters of opinion or force citizens to confess by word or act their faith therein. If there are any circumstances which permit an exception, they do not now occur to us.[130]

In a subsidiary argument, he claims that compulsory unity does not work in any case. "Those who begin coercive elimination of dissent soon find themselves exterminating dissenters. Compulsory unification of opinion achieves only the unanimity of the graveyard."[131]

Jackson's opinion is justly admired, and it is surely one of the most eloquent articulations of the general idea of liberty of conscience in our tradition. The opinion has been very important in general First Amendment jurisprudence. To those who are looking for specific guidance in interpreting the religion clauses, however, it has few implications. Religion is classified with a range of other topics, and the case is treated as a compelled-speech case. The key issue on which Jackson focuses is not religious liberty, or even liberty of conscience in a more general sense: it is the freedom from being compelled by government to utter words and ideas with which one disagrees. Jackson speaks majestically, but ultimately narrowly, about this specific situation, without giving any suggestion about broader exemptions from government regulation on the basis of religion. Both because of its narrowness (it pertains only to compelled speech) and because of its breadth (it pertains to all speech, not to religious speech in particular), the opinion gives little guidance for later interpretation of the religion clauses.

Admirable though Jackson's opinion is, it seems unfortunate, at least for the history of the religion clauses, that Jackson failed to develop Stone's interesting suggestion about levels of scrutiny, which promised to make a creative contribution to the interpretation of these clauses in particular, adumbrating the *Sherbert* test and also linking such an approach to evolving standards of equal-protection law in the areas of race and gender. Had Stone reserved the *Barnette* opinion for himself, we might have understood the specific values inherent in the religion clauses better and sooner. As it was, however, the outcome was right, an important principle was ringingly defended, and Jackson's powerful reply to Frankfurter developed the Court's role in protecting First Amendment freedoms.

Lillian Gobitas married and moved to Atlanta. Her children were granted an exemption from the flag salute in school. One day some girls ambushed her daughter Judith in the rest room and tried to beat her up, both for her flag-salute refusal and for her refusal to wear fashionable miniskirts. The school counselor said, "I will not have that in my school." He called the other girls' parents, and the girls apologized to Judith.[132]

IV. Anti-Catholicism and the Separation of Church and State

Violence and discrimination against Mormons and Jehovah's Witnesses were blots on our tradition of religious peace. These problems, however, were, for the most part, temporary and small-scale, simply because the numbers of "subversives" in these two religions were small. By contrast, anti-Catholicism virtually took over America's political life for a long period, beginning in 1830 and ending who knows where, since some of it is still around, but diminishing, at least, by 1960, when the first Roman Catholic was elected president of the United States. The fact that five out of the current nine Supreme Court Justices are Roman Catholics (Justices Roberts, Scalia, Thomas, Kennedy, and Alito), and that their religion has only occasionally been a significant factor in public debate about their views, shows the distance America has traveled. The journey, however, had not even begun in the days when Thomas Whall was beaten at the Eliot School.

What were anti-Catholics worried about? Class was one obvious issue, since the new Catholic immigrants were, largely, from working-class backgrounds.[133] Then as now, people tend to accept middle-class immigrants more easily than working-class immigrants, seeing the latter as a potentially subversive force. Economic competition was another issue, since these new workers threatened the job security of native-born workers. Both the Irish and the Italians, moreover, were unpopular ethnic groups, stigmatized as indolent and soft by contrast to the hardworking Protestants from Northern and Western Europe. The sheer number of new Catholic immigrants compounded the perceived problem, for it really did look as if the U.S. was being invaded by hordes of strangers.

Doctrinal and institutional objections to Catholicism often served as masks for these highly general insecurities. Nonetheless, these worries were also genuine, expressing a long Protestant tradition of anti-Catholicism that had caused centuries of bloody strife in Europe. Common tropes of the old strife—the Pope as the Antichrist, the church as a scarlet whore—took center stage in the new American debate, fueled by scurrilous propaganda about sexual excess and corruption.[134] The best-selling book of the nineteenth century before the publication of *Uncle Tom's Cabin* was Maria Monk's *Awful Disclosures of Hotel Dieu Nunnery* (1836), a fictional exposé of lurid sexual doings in a Canadian convent.[135]

The central doctrinal objection Protestants made to Roman Catholicism was to the hierarchical character of the church. For the Protestant, each conscience is free to seek God on its own, and also to read scripture on its own; the relationship between person and God is direct, free, and immediate. For the Catholic, a weighty hierarchy of prelates, and indeed the entire political structure of the church, mediates between person and God. Protestants felt that Catholics didn't rightly appreciate the inviolability of the individual conscience. Their tendency to think this way was exacerbated by the rise, in Europe and to some extent in the U.S., of a conservative ultramontane brand of Catholicism that refused the sort of reformist attitude that much later brought Catholicism somewhat closer to Protestantism in its attitude to the conscience. Ultramontanists even began to take back some types of autonomy traditionally granted to worshippers and their local parish trustees, thus fueling the idea that Catholics are antireform, antiprogress, and pro-tyranny.[136]

One might buy these religious arguments without drawing any political consequences from them. Religious movements can live together in political harmony even though they differ greatly about individual spiritual autonomy. Reform Jews, for example, agree with Protestants in their strong defense of the individual conscience, whereas Orthodox Jews ascribe far more weight to the authority of text and tradition. Reform and Orthodox Jews have never, however, had a major falling-out about political issues, and I am not aware of any Reform Jew who has maintained that Orthodox Jews should not or could not be good American citizens. As Roger Williams said, it seems possible to differ greatly about ultimate spiritual authority while agreeing about the characteristics of a good citizen and a good magistrate.

Nativist Protestants, however, did not rest content with the religious argument. They linked to it a political argument.[137] Catholicism, they held, simply doesn't believe in autonomy as an important value at all, not even as a political value. Catholics favor hierarchy in political life just as in the spiritual life. Protestant respect for the spiritual life of the conscience is, by contrast, associated with the democratic value of respect for each individual citizen. So what on earth will happen to democracy when hordes of people who don't really believe in democracy arrive on our shores?

Unlike some of the ideas we have discussed in this chapter (the idea that Mormon women are beaten and raped far more often than other women, the idea that Jehovah's Witnesses are a fifth column subverting national unity), this idea was not absurd. Even though today we easily separate the citizen from the believer, understanding that John Kennedy, John Kerry, and today's Catholic Supreme Court Justices will respect and implement the U.S. Constitution as their oath of office requires, it was not so implausible to have real worries in the mid-nineteenth century. The Roman Catholic hierarchy, in Europe, had played a powerful and, on the whole, a reactionary role in the struggles for political liberty in 1848 and after.[138] Ultramontanists also took positions that seemed to undermine a search for greater economic equality, stressing the moral value of the sufferings of the poor, as if it might even be morally bad to introduce changes to make that lot better.[139] Some of the leaders of the new Catholic hierarchy in the U.S. were themselves ultramontanists, and announced that they did want to dominate American politics.[140] Moreover, the fact that the Catholic hierarchy on the whole supported the pro-slavery cause during the Civil War, citing Aristotle and St. Paul on their side, increased the suspicion that this religion was linked to political, as well as spiritual, tyranny.[141]

There were, then, some real issues to worry about. The real issues, however, quickly got magnified and sensationalized: people talked as if all Catholics are in favor of "slavery" and the overturn of democratic values. They said that (all) Catholics want to impose on America a "union of church and state," meaning that America would no longer be either democratic or pluralist, but ruled by the Vatican.[142] As so commonly happens, the voices of the many Catholics, both priests and laypeople, who strongly supported democracy and took issue with the far-out claims of European ultramontanists[143] were either ignored or taken to be hypocrisy, concealing the real mission of the church. Behind ordinary Catholics, non-Catholic Americans all too quickly thought they glimpsed fiends, plotting to destroy the social order, or, pliant dupes, who "followed orders like professional soldiers and labored unknowingly to abolish free society. . . ."[144] The long tradition of Catholic rationalism and the consistent commitment of the church to critical argument as an educational value were completely ignored.

In earlier times, the phrase "separation of church and state" had been used but rarely, the central focus being where it belonged, on issues of liberty and equality. Now, however, the phrase conveniently supplied a counterweight to the rhetoric of "union of church and state." If Catholics were thought to stand for the latter, right-thinking Americans would rally round the former.

We associate the Republican Party with the abolition movement, Lincoln, and high-minded democratic values. But the Republican Party was also the party of rabid anti-Catholicism and anti-Mormonism. In the populism of those times, indeed, opposition to slavery seemed to entail anti-Catholicism and anti-Mormonism.[145] The anti-Catholic movement created strange bedfellows: the Republic Party on the one hand, the Ku Klux Klan on the other.[146] The point of overlap was called "nativism," or zealous protection of cherished American traditions that were thought to be under threat.

The flashpoint of these controversies was the future of the public schools. When America's tradition of religious fairness got going, there were no public schools, and so the framers, not surprisingly, had nothing to say about how public education could shape young citizens for a society in which all are

treated with equal respect. By the 1840s, however, the idea of public education had taken hold, and great importance was attached to the public schools
as cradles of democracy.[147] If they were to be cradles of democracy—it was
generally agreed—they had to have a moral character. Disregarding Roger
Williams's distinction, most people at the time thought that they also had to
have a religious character. Horace Mann, who was about as nonsectarian as
any leading educator at the time, thought that worries about pluralism would
be taken care of if students simply did Bible reading with no commentary.
Protestants easily thought that such classic Protestant exercises were neutral
and individualistic, not Protestant. Even Mann's program, however, was far
from neutral, since the whole idea of reading the Bible for oneself (in English
translation, and indeed in a particular Protestant King James English translation) and deciding for oneself what to make of it was just the idea on the basis
of which Luther created the Reformation. It's rather extraordinary that people
had so little sense of history that they didn't notice this, or perhaps they simply didn't care. At any rate, most educational practice was much more sectarian than what Mann proposed, including, as in the Thomas Whall case,
compulsory reading of the Ten Commandments in their Protestant version.

Predictably and rightly, Catholics protested such practices, pointing out
how sectarian and how unfair they were. The brutal treatment of Whall and
other Catholic children added anguish to their anger. Many Catholic parents
consequently rallied round the emerging Catholic schools, where their children would not be abused. Others continued to stick it out in the public
schools, trying to make them genuinely fair.

Nativists, meanwhile, tried in the first instance to make public schooling
compulsory and religious schooling illegal. The rhetoric surrounding such
campaigns left no doubt as to their target. A 1923 campaign song in Michigan,
for example, went as follows:

> Our boys and girls must go to school,
> In Michigan, my Michigan,
> And learn to live the golden rule,
> In Michigan, my Michigan.
> Each boy to be a gallant knight,
> Each girl to help make laws that's right,
> And save us from the papast [sic] blight,

In Michigan, my Michigan.
An Amendment comes before our folks,
In Michigan, my Michigan;
To rid our state of all paroks,
In Michigan, my Michigan;
So awake ye freemen, sleep no more,
Until our Public Schools are sure,
Let's keep them free forevermore,
In Michigan, my Michigan.

When the movement to ban religious schooling failed, as a result of the Supreme Court's decision in *Pierce v. Society of Sisters* (1925),[148] attention turned to two further issues, which would become the substance of twentieth-century Establishment Clause jurisprudence: financial aid to sectarian schools, and school religious observances.

The issue of funding had been on the table since the colonial period, when Madison argued that the use of taxpayer money for religious purposes, even if plural and to some extent voluntary, created an establishment problem by conveying the message that citizens were not all equal in the public square. The new debate was different, however, since what was contemplated was not giving funds to the majority religion, but allowing minorities who preferred private schooling to receive certain sorts of aid. It was all very well to talk of "separation of church and state" as a constitutional value—and people often acknowledged that doing so required supplementing and repairing the actual constitutional tradition—but the fact was that at the time when these debates began, there was no separation in the public schools, which were not just de facto Protestant, but often aggressively so. One might have thought that equal respect entailed a certain measure of separation, as Madison had argued, simply because any religious statement made by the state is bound to be unfair to someone, and sectarian in some way. But in the case where the majority had already taken over the schools, the shoe seemed to be on the other foot: equal respect might plausibly be seen as requiring what Protestants saw as a breach in the "wall of separation," so that Catholic children would have a safe place to study where they would not be persecuted. At any rate, the issue was complex, and it is not surprising that it has taken roughly a century to thrash it out—still very incompletely, as we shall see in Chapter 7.

Meanwhile, President Grant and his Republican allies made various attempts to prevent aid to religious schools, introducing a series of constitutional amendments (none ultimately successful) that explicitly extended First Amendment rights to the states and that emphasized separation in a way that the existing constitutional text does not.[149] Grant kept pushing on the issue, holding in one public speech in 1875 that "if we are to have another contest in the near future of our national existence, I predict that the dividing line will not be Mason and Dixon's but between patriotism and intelligence on the one side, and superstition, ambition, and ignorance on the other."[150] Nobody was in the dark about what he really meant.

The issue of religious observance in the schools was closely tied to the issue of funding, for the only plausible argument against funding for sectarian schools was that the public schools were genuinely public and nonsectarian. Since they clearly weren't, concerned and fair-minded people began to ask how the schools themselves could promote values of equal respect. It was at this point that separation, long a mantra of rabid nativists, began to be turned around into something of a positive value, in connection with ideas of equality. Self-styled "liberals" and many other thoughtful people began to discuss the issue. Fighting against the nativist conception of separation,[151] they nonetheless endorsed separation as an ideal in connection with the notion of fairness. They understood that separation could be a positive value only if it constrained all religions, including majority religion, opening the public square, and the public schools, for genuinely equal access.

Thus the liberal debate about establishment returned, in effect, to its Madisonian origins, asking Madison's questions about civic equality. To this company many Jews, particularly Reform Jews, were drawn. They saw in the idea of separation of church and state a vision of equality for themselves: only if Christianity were to be thoroughly separated from government would Jews truly enjoy equal citizenship.[152] Isaac Meyer Wise, one of the great intellectual leaders of Reform Judaism in America, called at one and the same time for separation of church and state and for an end to the persecution of Catholics, and he actively campaigned along with Catholics for the removal of the Bible from the public schools. "We are citizens of this country, not by the tolerance of any sect," he wrote in 1855, "but by right and justice, hence we must always stand on the side of justice."[153]

Separation was beginning to be seen, then, not as a weapon of persecution, but as an element of justice. It is important to see, however, that it could be a part of justice only in connection with other values. If we ask in the abstract, "Should the police protect the campus of a religious university from violence and theft?" and "Should the fire department come to the aid of a religious school?" the bare concept of "separation" might appear to dictate the answer "no." After all, the police and the fire department are parts of the state, and the religious schools are parts of the church. Only rabid anti-Catholics, however, would really answer "no" to this question, since most people would see in the refusal of police and fire protection a terrible assault on the equality of Catholic citizens going about their legal daily business. Surely they, too, deserve the equal protection of the laws. On the other end of the spectrum, there are clearly some types of aid to sectarian schools that would compromise the equality of citizens for Madison's reasons, because they would make the statement that some citizens count more than others. Where the boundary falls is a matter requiring complex thought. In such deliberations, the idea of equality will have to do most of the work, and separation must follow in its train. Our next two chapters will follow these difficult arguments.

V. Fear and Constitutional Principles

These three distressing episodes show the vulnerability of America's social and political tradition of toleration, a tradition that goes back to the colonial period. Securely though Americans seemed at times to grasp the Respect-Conscience Principle and the associated ideas of equal religious liberty and nonestablishment, that grasp was not stable in times of fear and social unrest. Unpopular minorities became the victims of a hysteria that looks to us, in retrospect, shocking, a betrayal of some of our deepest values.

It is not difficult to understand how such things could happen. Americans are human and vulnerable. Regrettably and culpably, like people in many other times and places, they can surrender even their best commitments in times of fear. Fortunately, the respect-conscience tradition triumphed, over time, over fear and violence. Today, for the most part, we live on terms of civil peace with one another, Protestants, Catholics, Mormons, and Jehovah's Witnesses. People rarely face physical violence for their conscientious religious commitments. Even after 9/11, there was so little anti-Muslim violence that inhabitants of nations that see a lot of this sort of violence (India, for example) expressed surprise.

How might these episodes have been prevented, or their violence mitigated? And how might we prevent similar things in the future? Law is only one force in any democratic society, and constitutional law is only one, sometimes small, part of the legal order. Nonetheless, we can see clearly how the fluid and ill-defined character of fundamental constitutional principles made this mess worse, and how their gradual clarification, through a growing tradition of precedent, began to make it better. Constitutional rights stand up for minorities when they are powerless to stand up for themselves. The Bill of Rights was needed in the first place not because of the majority, but because of the vulnerability of minorities. Because incorporation came so late, however, and because there were few precedents at the federal level, the legal tradition that would slowly, over time, make the religion clauses a working reality in American life was only in its infancy in this period. When we look at *Reynolds* and *Gobitis* from the perspective of the philosophical ideas I have drawn from the tradition, and also when we look at them from the perspective of a later tradition of interpretation, they look like shockingly bad decisions. Even if polygamy would almost certainly not be protected by the Supreme Court today, the callous and inflammatory argumentation in *Reynolds*, and its misleading insistence that the First Amendment is best understood to protect belief only, and not conduct, are relics of the past. Nonetheless, at the time Justice Waite wrote it, *Reynolds* was perfectly plausible, because there really was no firm guidance in the precedents.

Today's Americans are not better people. We are still vulnerable to panic and hysteria. Nor, very likely, are our Supreme Court Justices better people than Justice Waite and, certainly, the great Justice Frankfurter. What, then, has changed? Changing social norms have certainly played some part in creating a climate that makes some of the incidents described in this chapter unthinkable today. But legal argument has also played a creative role. What makes cases such as *Reynolds* and *Gobitis* unthinkable today is not just social change; it is also a tradition of legal argument that has gradually refined, deepened, and extended our idea of what free exercise requires. Just as our understanding of free speech has progressed and deepened—from the time in 1918, for example, when Eugene Debs went to prison for his speech urging Americans not to serve in World War I—so that we now see that the protection of dissidents in dangerous times lies at its very heart, so too with the religion clauses. We now see what we didn't see so clearly before: that protection of vulnerable minorities from hysteria and "soule rape" is at the heart of what they protect. And because these insights are not just in philosophical books and articles, but are embedded in a tradition of precedent, it is unlikely that we will lose them utterly. The constitutional tradition is in that sense like a set of railroad tracks that keep a train moving in a certain direction. A car cruising along the road can easily veer off course. It's less likely, at least, that a train car running on tracks will go wildly off course. In the period examined in this chapter, the religion clauses were cruising along the road; in the aftermath of *Gobitis, Barnette,* and the subsequent cases that built on their insights, there is, at least, if not one set of tracks, an intersecting system of tracks that keeps things on a course compatible with equal respect. In *Smith,* Justice Scalia certainly flipped a switch sending the train off onto an adjacent track. But it didn't leap the rails altogether. The tradition was too strong for that. Constitutional principles protect the deepest values of the tradition from heedless tampering at the hands of hysterical majorities. The Bill of Rights, in particular, protects minorities from imposition from a strong and distant central government swayed by majority interests.

The period we have examined built the basis for a solid understanding of the Free Exercise Clause. For the Establishment Clause, however, the struggle over understanding was only beginning. Anti-Catholicism and reactions against it showed people that the problem of religious establishment was much larger and more ramified than the old problem of religious assessments. That problem remained, in the form of an ongoing debate about the use of taxpayer money for religious purposes. New aspects to the question, however, had surfaced. How could the public schools remain centers of moral education, while being newly fair to the claims of religious minorities? How could America construct a public culture that expressed due respect for citizens of all religious and secular backgrounds? The fact that America had in key respects been a de facto Protestant establishment had now been acknowledged. The legal consequences of that acknowledgment had yet to be measured.

6

THE ESTABLISHMENT CLAUSE

School Prayer, Public Displays

The Establishment Clause prohibits government from making adherence to a religion relevant in any way to a person's standing in the political community. . . . Endorsement sends a message to non-adherents that they are outsiders, not full members of the political community, and an accompanying message to adherents that they are insiders, favored members of the political community. Disapproval sends the opposite message.

JUSTICE O'CONNOR,
Lynch v. Donnelly (1984)

I knew that some people would not agree. But my answer was always, what is fair to everyone? What does the Constitution mean?

ELLERY SCHEMPP, PLAINTIFF IN
Abington v. Schempp (1963),
IN A 2004 SERMON

I. Establishment and Equality

What is wrong with religious establishment? The tradition we have been examining identifies a number of distinct yet interconnected dangers. One is a danger of factionalism, as religions might jockey in the public square to get a larger share of the political pie. Another is a danger of government intrusion into citizens' religious lives, as government might tell churches how to manage their internal affairs. Yet another is the related danger of coercion, as an official religion or religions might curtail the conscience space of those who don't join in. But above all, the tradition sees in establishment a threat to equality. By throwing its support behind an orthodoxy, government makes a statement: this is the official doctrine of our nation. Such a statement, as Madison saw, suggests that nonadherents are not fully equal members of the political community, and they don't enter the public square "on equal conditions." Even if they are not coerced, the implication is that they exist at the sufferance of the dominant group, not as citizens of equal worth in their own right. This danger is just as great if the establishment singles out a group of religions as if it singles out just one. Even an establishment of all religion over nonreligion, as we've seen, does not solve the equality problem.

Britain, and most of continental Europe, chose the path of establishment, eventually protecting many liberties for religious minorities, but adopting a public orthodoxy. Even today Europeans of the majority religion feel no problem when a crucifix hangs at the front of all public school classrooms in Italy, or when public money is used for support of the established Anglican Church. France, only an apparent exception, has adopted a public orthodoxy, indeed a legal establishment, of secularism, curtailing the equal expressive liberty of religious citizens. The U.S., obsessed with equality, refused both of these courses from a very early date. Experience had shown the colonists that establishment was never fully equal or equally free.

Equality, as we've seen, was a central theme at the Founding, when religious establishments were criticized, and also in the nineteenth century, when state establishments were gradually rejected. It is also a key theme in recent Establishment Clause jurisprudence. *Everson v. Board of Education* (1946), the case in which the Establishment Clause was incorporated (applied to the states), stressed the Madisonian connections of the clause, and its link with ideas of nondiscrimination, as well as equal liberty.[1] In another important case, Justice Brennan insisted that the key issue is that government "may not place its prestige, coercive authority, or resources behind a single religious faith or behind religious belief in general. . . ."[2] Similar statements abound. Justice O'Connor was especially persistent in emphasizing this theme. She used it, over the years, to elaborate a set of standards with which to think about the constitutionality of various public policies.

Once more, we need to pause to ask what this idea of equality is all about. There are quite a few different ways in which citizens may be said to be equal or unequal. They may be equal or unequal in wealth and income, in subjective happiness, in one or more specific dimensions of valuable functioning (for example, health, or educational attainment). The equality we are discussing here is something different and very basic, closely correlated with the idea of equal respect. It is the idea that people are of equal worth as citizens, and are therefore to be treated *as equals* by laws and institutions. Citizens may have different views about the basis or ground of that equal worth. Christians will ground equality in our equality before God; others will ground it in some related conception of the soul; others will find other accounts. I have argued in Chapter 2 that the political realm should avoid a comprehensive religious or metaphysical account of human equality, precisely in order to leave room for, and to show respect for, the many different ways in which citizens interpret this idea.

Nonetheless, as I also argue in Chapter 2, we may use for political purposes a rather general idea of conscience, as the capacity to search for meaning in life. This capacity is one aspect, as we said, of a more general notion of human dignity, a notion that has guided American political thinking since the time of the Founding, and one that has become increasingly prominent worldwide, in constitutions of many nations and in the documents of the international human rights movement. So, at the most general level, we are saying that our political principles include a commitment to the idea that all citizens are equal in dignity, and, because of that dignity, are to be treated with equal respect by laws and institutions. (Dignity and respect are a pair, to be understood together; dignity probably cannot be defined altogether independently of respect.)[3]

Using this thin and inclusive idea of human dignity, we can then argue that dignity entitles all citizens to be treated with equal respect by laws and institutions. What this means is that politics may not create tiers or levels of citizenship, may not make citizenship hierarchical. That is what Madison meant by asserting that all citizens must be able to enter the public square *on equal conditions*. Equal standing requires not just noninterference; it requires, as Madison saw, a symbolic politics that acknowledges equality and does not create ranks and orders of citizens. One might think that the symbolic domain is unimportant. So thought many defenders of the Virginia assessment, who said that, after all, nobody is really made to pay the established church if he does not want to. What Madison saw, however, is that a failure of respect in the symbolic domain is like an insult, a slap in the face, and, moreover, it is the sort of slap in the face that a noble gives to a vassal, one that both expresses and constitutes a hierarchy of ranks.

The American tradition has long been preoccupied with the symbolic domain, for good reason. For Americans came from a Europe in which distinctions of hereditary privilege pervasively determined the course of every life, and in which the trappings of nobility and monarchy were ubiquitous. Their obsession with equality was an obsession with ending the legacy of feudal hierarchy, and this required a sensitive focus on public symbolism as well as on interference with liberty. Government must not make statements (through explicit utterance, or through monetary policy, or through public ceremonies and displays) that a reasonable observer could construe as saying that a given group of citizens is ranked above another group. That equality in rank is of the essence of the particular way in which American democracy respects human dignity, and it is a very good way, one that is of value to any society that contains, as all modern societies do, a plurality of religious groups, and nonreligious people, and which, at the same time, claims to have equal respect for human dignity.

Recent Establishment Clause cases look like a mess. The proliferation of standards and distinctions is perplexing even to scholars. The orderly three-prong "*Lemon* test," which attempted to organize earlier standards, was never really applied as a complete defining norm; it was often supplemented with other ideas and standards. Today, though it is still used, it has been so often questioned that other related ideas assume a larger and larger place in the Court's decisions. One might expect to find this unclarity at the margins in any area, and the fact that the Court persistently takes marginal cases in this area may conduce to the feeling that things are unclear. The unclarity, however, seems not simply an unclarity in application; it seems to extend, as well, to the choice of principles by which to justify a policy about unclear cases. Is there any order at all in this (apparent) chaos?

To the general public, moreover, there is something very bizarre about the Court's obsessive focusing on seemingly trivial details of the cases: how far one monument is from another, what the sight lines look like from monument to capital, whether a crèche is next to a magic wishing well or not, whether a school prayer is introduced by a teacher or not.

To some extent unease about the legal tradition is justified. The multiplicity of principles, the changes of direction, and the different approaches of the different Justices show that interpretation of the Establishment Clause has not fully found its feet, has not arrived at a solid consensus on the salient principles of the sort we have in the Free Exercise area, however much individuals differ concerning specifics. The fact that the tradition seems to be groping for an account is, all by itself, neither surprising nor bad, given that the issues it must face are evolving social issues, many not envisaged by the founders. How the abstract principles and goals embodied in the constitutional text should be applied to a changing social reality is a question that seems to require flexibility. Indeed, one major trouble has been a premature search for rules that can be mechanically applied. As Justice Burger said in *Lemon v. Kurtzman*[4] (the case that has sometimes been taken to hand down such a set of rules), the line between church and state, "far from being a 'wall,' is a blurred, indistinct, and variable barrier depending on all the circumstances of a particular relationship."[5] As Aristotle said about justice, so here: it is crucial not to have standards that are mechanically applied to a convoluted and changing subject matter.

Recognizing complexity in the application of principles and standards is not, then, in itself problematic. It is to the credit of the tradition, on the whole, that it has allowed itself to get so baroque and contextual that it takes surprisingly many particular circumstances into account in deciding particular cases. A wise recognition of complexity, however, does not mean forgoing the search for an orienting account. Aristotle, while recognizing complexity in application, nonetheless thought that the lawgiver, and people in general, need a general account of relevant goals and principles that, while not regarded as either fixed or complete, would still guide the approach to concrete cases, helping us to identify features of salience. Too often, the modern Establishment Clause tradition has lacked that sort of overall orientation, or has been a scene of contention, as different Justices supply different orientations.

With Madison and Justice O'Connor (and the main lines of Establishment Clause jurisprudence in the latter half of the twentieth century), I shall suggest that a good guide is the idea of equality. We make progress when we ask, in each case, "How does the policy in question affect the equality of citizens in the public realm?" "What statement does it make concerning the equality of citizens who differ in religion and/or nonreligion?" This idea runs like a thread through the cases, on the whole explaining them well, and at least picking out one salient theme in them. It certainly does much better than the bare idea of separation, relied on excessively by some Justices during the recent period, in helping us see why some interactions between government and religion are deeply objectionable, others less problematic. On the whole, the recent correction of balance in the religious school funding area represents, I'll argue, a convergence back to the equality norm from an excessive reliance on the norm of separation, as if it were an end in its own right. An equality-based reconstruction of the tradition, while not exhaustive, will at least prove useful in framing public debate about the issues, which often goes askew when the idea of separation is used, as it so often is, as a dominant and self-explanatory value. Equality provides an orienting account, which a variety of more specific principles can help to structure in useful ways. Wise practical reason, grappling with all the circumstances of the case, will then be necessary to apply these principles to particulars.

The Madisonian idea of equality is closely linked to the idea of "neutrality"—which typically means that the state does not take sides—between one religion and another, or between religion and nonreligion. There are, however, subtle conceptual differences that need to be borne in mind. First of all, neutrality is sometimes linked to a formalistic conception of equality, as sameness of treatment. The Madisonian conception of equality is richer and more substantive: it means that the public realm respects and treats citizens as people of equal worth and entitlement. Sameness of treatment is not always enough for substantive equality. We know, for example, that bans on interracial marriage were unconstitutional even though they affected both blacks and whites symmetrically, because they upheld an underlying hierarchy, which the Supreme Court called "White Supremacy."[6] In asking about religious equality, we need to keep our eye on the more substantive idea of equality, as an absence of hierarchy, of domination on one side and subordination on the other. The Madisonian conception of equality is also not ethically neutral, and using "neutrality" as our dominant concept might mislead us, by suggesting that we want principles without any definite ethical content. The idea that citizens should be equally respected and that hierarchies should not exist among them is a substantive, antimonarchical, and antifeudal ethical/political idea, albeit one that, in today's United States, people who disagree about many other matters can agree to endorse.

The framers thought about establishment, but they did not analyze every pertinent issue.[7] The use of tax money for the support of religious activities was a prominent topic of debate since before the Founding. This issue continues to be salient until the present day. By contrast, the framers had little sustained theoretical interest in the equality issues involved in public ceremonies and displays. Although both Jefferson and Madison worried about Thanksgiving Day proclamations, there was no body of public thought, addressed to this issue, comparable in detail and depth to Madison's analysis of the funding question. Principles that were brought to bear on the latter issue were not carefully applied to the former. As to religious observances in the public schools, that issue was utterly off the table because there were no public schools in the modern sense. As Chapter 5 has shown, once public schools were widespread, in the nineteenth century, people took a very long time to recognize that the prevalence of Protestant observances in them might pose an Establishment Clause problem.

The public schools badly needed reform to bring them into line with the idea of equal respect for conscience. They needed to be pruned of their sectarian Protestantism and made truly hospitable to, and respectful of, children from a wide range of religions, or of no religion. Because children are particularly vulnerable both to authority and to peer pressure, reconstructing the schools as a space of true equality has been no easy matter. It is not surprising that this issue still generates sharp disagreements. It is important to see, however, that it is the search for equality that has driven such changes as the ban on school prayer and Bible reading—not an arrogant conviction that religion is unimportant or marginal. Religious people often felt, and feel, aggrieved at such changes, but they should not: such changes respect each person's equal conscience space, a value that religious people can join Roger Williams in enthusiastically endorsing.

The issue of public monuments and displays has been, and remains today, difficult and divisive. Religious people plausibly feel slighted when they are told that they may not express their deepest convictions by erecting a monument to them in the public square. Why does everything else get to go on in the public square, they want to know, and not the most important thing of all? How come a monument to Elvis, or an auto show, or a parade of new fashions would all be totally fine in a city park, but a crèche or a display of the Ten Commandments might not? Is the Court saying that commercial values are superior to religious values? No, I would argue: it is saying, instead, that in such matters the equality of citizens is always deeply at risk. Therefore special care needs to be taken to figure out whether the display in question violates this equality. Unfortunately there is no simple rule for this: the answer must come from the details of the particular case.

Finally, in Chapter 7, we shall confront the perennial problem of financial aid to sectarian institutions, focusing on school aid, which has been the most divisive and prominent such issue. In this area the same considerations Madison confronted are still with us, but the problem has ramified, given the burgeoning role of the modern state in people's lives. Nonetheless, I shall argue, Madison's guidance still proves valuable. We should ask: does the aid in question show an endorsement of one religion or several religions over others, or of religion over nonreligion? We must also ask, however, whether a refusal of aid is an illicit form of discrimination against religion. For example, if churches were the only buildings in a town that the fire department did not protect, this would look like antireligion discrimination. It is in this area that the bare idea of separation is the most misleading, since it might suggest that it would be good to tell the fire trucks to stay away from the burning church. Following the twistings and turnings of the Court's confrontation with this nest of problems, we shall see that equality, supplemented with other principles, helps sort things out.

The equality tradition I shall trace has deep roots and a long history in the Court's decisions, which used to be consensus decisions. In recent years, the changing membership of the Court, combined with zealous Court-focused activity by conservative legal scholars, has managed to create dissensus concerning some core guiding principles of Establishment Clause interpretation, where little existed from the 1940s to the 1980s. By now the idea that the Establishment Clause means that the public realm needs to be fair to citizens of all different religions, and to citizens of none, is under attack. Justice Scalia believes that the government may favor monotheism and disfavor polytheism, nontheistic religion, nonreligion, and even versions of monotheism that think of God as "unconcerned." Justice Kennedy, while not accepting that radical proposal, seems to support the idea that the Establishment Clause prohibits only coercive support for religion, not support that consists in giving endorsements of religion, or even a particular type of religion. The late Chief Justice Rehnquist, while agreeing with tradition that government may not show favor to one religion as against another, argued that the government may generically favor religion over nonreligion. Most radical of all, Justice Thomas denies that the Establishment Clause applies to the states at all, so any state may establish a church if it so chooses, show favor to its chosen religion in the public schools, put up public displays that indicate government's favor for a particular religious tradition, or fund only religious schools, or only schools of some particular religion. All these positions were once radical, situated on the fringes of academic scholarship. Today they are all lodged at the heart of the Court's debates. All seem deeply problematic, no matter what theory of constitutional interpretation we accept, and all are at work eroding an earlier salutary consensus, particularly in the areas of school prayer and public displays. The concluding section of this chapter will examine this new set of threats to equality as a guiding Establishment Clause norm.

II. School Prayer: Equality, Coercion, and Peer Pressure

The public schools have long held a special place in Americans' conception of their democracy. By bringing together citizens from diverse backgrounds and educating them in an atmosphere of respect for persons and civic purposefulness, the schools are thought to supply essential ingredients for the health of our political life. More than any other set of institutions, a long and widespread tradition holds, public schools make it possible for people with widely divergent religions and views of life to work together for common political purposes. So Americans have long been unusually sensitive to the ways in which religion might enter divisively into public education. Although in 1925 religious minorities won the right to educate their children in sectarian schools, this right came with the proviso that the state might still impose on those schools reasonable curricular requirements connected with shared citizenship.[8] And it was widely hoped that a large proportion of children who might be eligible to attend sectarian schools would prefer the public schools, thus choosing a deeper integration into American norms and values.

It is widely agreed today that the mission of the public schools involves building character and imparting values, especially those essential for good democratic citizenship. A long tradition, starting with Roger Williams at least, has argued that such ethical/political values could be imparted without religious content, in such a way that people from many different religions, and nonreligious people too, could share a common moral education for citizenship and learn to live together on terms of mutual respect. Many Americans, however, cannot accept the idea that the ethical instruction children need to have in the public schools can really work unless it has a devotional aspect. They feel that children who pray together at the start of the school day are far more likely to care deeply about the moral and civic values that the rest of the day imparts (along with its intellectual lessons). Because prayer, in their own personal religious lives, is so intimately bound up with virtue and moral choice, they have a hard time imagining a civic morality without prayer. Removing prayer from the schools seems to eviscerate morality, making it a tepid sort of "religion of secularism" that may even undermine what religious parents attempt to teach their children.

These are legitimate concerns. Separating morality from religion does leave it lacking in support, from the point of view of many Americans' religious conceptions. Even a nonreligious person can see that religious concerns often supply motivations to act morally, without which morality all on its own might seem less urgent to many people. No less a rationalist than Immanuel Kant came to the conclusion that the power of selfishness and the tendency to dominate others were so strong in human psychology that they could be counteracted only by joining a group of people who could bolster each other's determination to fight against temptation. He argued, further, that this group would not be efficacious morally unless it was united by the idea of a higher being: so it would have to be a religious group. Kant thought that most existing churches did not perform their job well, since they encouraged people to vie for superiority with members of other religions and to establish hierarchies and inequalities. But he still maintained that religion in some form is essential for shared moral endeavor.

For many people, Kant's diagnosis is probably correct. Even the most hardened skeptic should grant that much energy for good in American life, including virtually the entirety of the abolition movement and the civil rights movement, has religious roots. So there are strong reasons why Americans concerned about their children's morality would want their children to pray, and at least plausible reasons why they think that prayer has to have a place in the public schools, as well as in the home and in the sectarian schools. Thinking in this way, the early founders of the public schools made sure that some form of religious observance was prominently included in them: Bible reading, or the Lord's Prayer, or some other type of prayer.

Here's where the fairness issue rears its head, however. We want the schools to impart civic morality. But we also want them to be fair to children (and parents) who come from different backgrounds, both religious and non-religious. Two distinct, though related, sorts of fairness are at issue: fairness among the religions, and fairness between religion and nonreligion. It's relatively easy to see that any observance that is even generically religious makes the statement that ours is a religious nation, and that nonreligious children and their parents, insofar as they remain nonreligious, are not quite fully equal Americans. If children from nonreligious families join their peers in such observances, it may alienate them from their parents, whom they may come to see as not quite fully American. If they don't join in, they may become alienated from their teachers and classmates. These problems were particularly keen during the Cold War, when religiosity was closely associated with patriotism and atheism with communism; but it is with us still today.

It is more complicated, but extremely important, to see that no religious observance that even the most thoughtful school board could design could be truly fair among the diverse religions that America by now contains. Any Bible is either the version preferred by Protestants or the version preferred by Roman Catholics, and it either contains the New Testament, which Jews cannot accept, or it does not, thus offending believing Christians. Any statement of religious belief that has any content at all uses concepts that are controversial among the religions. Mentioning the divinity of Jesus alienates non-Christians; not alluding to Jesus alienates most Christians. The idea that God is the Creator and Supreme Judge is common in Christianity, Judaism, and Islam. Such ideas are rejected, however, by some Christians, by Deists, by most Unitarians, and by many Reform Jews, who have long debated whether God should be understood as a person-like entity or rather as the rational force in nature. The very word "God," while acceptable to monotheists, is not acceptable to polytheists, nor would a reference to "gods," or even "God or gods," be acceptable to monotheists. Some religions, moreover, do not recognize a deity: Buddhism, Taoism, and Confucianism, all growing in the U.S. today, are among them. To young Buddhists, a prayer to "God" would be a jolting request to abandon the metaphysical tenets of their own religion for those of someone else's.

The debate over school prayer is all too often cast, as it was at the height of the Cold War, as a debate between believers and "godless atheists." Atheists deserve equal treatment, and they have not always received it. One of the things Americans can be proud of is that we have not excluded atheists from our public life to the extent that the British did, denying atheist Charles Brad-laugh the right to assume his seat in Parliament (to which he was repeatedly elected) five times, because he would not swear an oath to God. (The sixth time he was elected, in 1885, he was seated, and the law regarding the oath was changed.) America rejected such test oaths in the Constitution itself, though fully equal respect for atheists has been a long time in coming, and is not yet fully here. It is, however, vitally important to see that the equal rights of atheists are not the only, or perhaps even the primary, issue at stake in the debate over school prayer. Any specific choice of a devotional religious language is also unfair to many believers, and this problem is more and more evident in an America of rapidly increasing religious diversity. Bearing this problem in mind is helpful, in case one is inclined to think that restriction on school prayer is a way of denigrating religion.

School prayer is not exactly like other issues involving public religious observances, because children are involved. Children, our tradition wisely recognizes, are different from adults in several ways. They are under the guardianship of their parents, whose views about what doctrine they want to impart to their children deserve respect. They are also highly malleable, easily swayed by both authority and peer pressure. All human beings have tendencies to conform, but young people are particularly vulnerable. Their future lies in the control of the adults who teach them, so they rightly fear alienating those adults by standing out as "different." Even more, perhaps, they fear being stigmatized and ostracized by other children, who all too easily behave badly to children who stand out as different, or who hold values that look "un-American" or "unpatriotic." Edward Schempp, father of the plaintiffs in *Abington School District* v. *Schempp*, testified that he decided not to have his children apply to be excused from the mandatory Bible reading and Lord's Prayer recitation, because he "thought his children would be 'labeled as odd balls'" before their teachers and classmates every school day; that children were liable "to lump all particular religious difference[s] or religious objections [together] as 'atheism' and that today the word 'atheism' is often connected with 'atheistic communism,' and has 'very bad' connotations, such as 'un-American' . . . with overtones of possible immorality."[9] His fears are reasonable. We recall the way in which the friendly and high-achieving Lillian and Billy Gobitas were pilloried for their refusal, on conscientious grounds, to recite the Pledge of Allegiance. Children are always on the lookout for nonconformity, and the pressure they put on other children not to stand out as "weirdos" is extreme. Nor are teachers immune from these vices, as the behavior of the high school principals in both the *Gobitis* and the *Schempp* cases shows. For these reasons our tradition has wisely acknowledged that a ceremony that might possibly be acceptable if only adults were involved can be constitutionally problematic when it involves children.

Such cases often involve coercion, or something that looks like coercion, as well as government endorsement of a particular religious message. For that reason they are often seen to raise issues under both the Free Exercise Clause and the Establishment Clause. The tradition has repeatedly insisted, however, that, while coercion may be an essential element of a free exercise violation, there can be an Establishment Clause problem even when no coercion is involved.[10] It is helpful to focus on the equality issue when thinking about this further problem. And the tradition has repeatedly done so, with increasing emphasis, in the cases that define the Court's position on school religious observances.

The history of school prayer began, it would seem, with a period, in the mid-nineteenth century, during which the people involved sincerely believed that certain generically Protestant religious exercises were inoffensive. They saw no reason to require them, because they were ubiquitous. But they also saw no reason to limit them, since they thought them neutral. Once Catholics and other objectors had made it clear that they were not so neutral, some such people backed off, concluding that any imposition of a religious orthodoxy would involve unfairness. Unfortunately, a different reaction was all too common: mandatory statutory imposition of religious observances. At the turn of the twentieth century, only one state, Massachusetts, had a law making morning prayer or Bible reading mandatory.[11] After 1910, eleven more states passed such laws, perhaps in response to the rapid upsurge of immigration from Catholic Europe. A smaller number of states and local communities, reacting to these trends, passed laws saying that such observances shall *not* be required, or even that the school board must supply the type of Bible preferred by the student.[12] President Theodore Roosevelt declared that the public schools ought to be "absolutely nonsectarian," and that it was therefore "not our business to have the Protestant Bible or the Catholic Vulgate or the Talmud read in those schools."[13] The contours of the modern debate were basically set.

The issue remained dormant for some time; at least, no litigation reached the Supreme Court. During the Cold War, however, widespread uncertainty about the future, combined with a desire to distinguish the U.S. from "godless communism," led to a keen interest in mandatory prayer. The Supreme Court's controversial involvement in the issue began in 1961, when the New York State Regents recommended that local school boards require the following prayer every day: "Almighty God, we acknowledge our dependence upon Thee, and we beg Thy blessings upon us, our parents, our teachers, and our Country."[14] The local school board of a district in Hyde Park, New York, complied, like others, requiring that every morning, after recitation of the Pledge of Allegiance (to which the words "under God" had recently been added), students should recite the regents' prayer aloud, in the presence of a teacher, who would either lead the recitation or select a student to do so.[15] No student was compelled to participate: any student could be excused on written request by a parent or guardian; the child could stay in the room but not participate, or leave the room, all "without fear of reprisal or even comment by the teacher or any other school official."[16] The school board had learned the lessons of *Barnette* well.

The school board never denied that the prayer was a religious observance. The board of regents argued that the prayer, though religious, did not create an Establishment Clause problem because it is "based on our spiritual heritage."[17] Ten parents challenged the practice on Establishment Clause grounds, challenging both the particular prayer and the authority of the state board of regents to direct prayer.

Several problems with the regents' prayer should be fairly obvious. First, the prayer, though acceptable to many Christians and Jews, is not acceptable to all, since it involves the theologically contentious idea of a personal God who cares for mortals like a parent, who grants blessings in response to intercession, and who will grant the prayers of the good and not those of the bad. (As Ellery Schempp, plaintiff in the landmark school prayer case of 1963, argued in a sermon he gave in 2004, "The prayer of the 9/11 hijackers is a chilling reminder that prayer does not insure goodness."[18])

Not all Christians and Jews accept this conception of prayer. (Several prominent Jewish organizations, including the American Jewish Committee and the Synagogue Council of America, filed amicus briefs opposing the regents' prayer.) Still less will such a prayer be acceptable to Unitarians, polytheists, nontheistic believers (such as Buddhists and Taoists), agnostics, and atheists. To be sure, a student could leave the room, stand in silence, or refuse to stand. Consider, however, that the prayer is placed just after the Pledge of Allegiance, and contains a request for blessings on "our Country," thought to be gravely imperiled at the time. A nonparticipating student would surely risk being stigmatized not only as antireligious but also as antipatriotic.

The case was decided by a lopsided majority, with but a single dissenter. Writing for the Court, Justice Black stressed that imposed prayer was one of the odious practices of England from which the colonists had fled. That, he continued, did not always stop them from setting up their own establishments and enforcing their own conceptions of prayer; but opposition to the whole idea of establishment grew rapidly, and eventually, by the time of the Constitution, prevailed.[19] Justice Black identifies several distinct dangers in the imposition of prayer by the state; he mentions a danger to public peace and a danger to liberty.[20] He insists that the union of government and religion "tends to destroy government and to degrade religion."[21] The theme of equality, however, receives significant emphasis. Virginia's debate over establishment in the eighteenth century, he argues, focused on placing all groups "on an equal footing so far as the State was concerned."[22] And the great danger in prescribed prayer is seen as that of "the Government's placing its official stamp of approval upon one particular kind of prayer or one particular form of religious services." Despite the noncoercive nature of the prayer, it looks unlikely that any policy will be found "which treats with equality both participants and nonparticipants."[23]

The regents' prayer at least appeared to be noncoercive. Distinguishing the two religion clauses, Justice Black insists that coercion need not be shown for an Establishment Clause violation, since that clause "is violated by the enactment of laws which establish an official religion whether those laws operate directly to coerce nonobserving individuals or not."

Justice Black insists vigorously that opposition to governmentally prescribed religious observances does not indicate "a hostility toward religion or toward prayer."[24] Instead, it grows out of a well-justified fear of what happens when government allies its authority to a specific religious message. "It is neither sacrilegious nor antireligious to say that each separate government in this country should stay out of the business of writing or sanctioning official prayers and leave that purely religious function to the people themselves. . . ."[25]

After *Engel*, states did not try to impose a specific prayer on all schoolchildren. Some states, however, continued to seek a neutral and acceptable way of opening the day with something like religious devotion. Pennsylvania required that "[a]t least ten verses from the Holy Bible shall be read, without comment, at the opening of each public school on each school day. Any child shall be excused from such Bible reading, or attending such Bible reading, upon the written request of his parent or guardian."[26]

Ever since the nineteenth century, Bible reading, without comment, had been taken by many Americans to be a neutral and nondenominational practice. It is not. To begin with, there is the difficulty about which version of the Bible should be used: different groups of Christians have different authorized versions. More obvious still, and important to the argument of the case, Jews will not accept a Bible that includes the New Testament, and reading from the New Testament without comment could be confusing and harmful to Jewish children, as a scholar testified.[27] To Christians, however, a Bible without the New Testament would not be authoritative, as another scholar testified.[28] Further, the practice of not commenting, while apparently the most neutral way of doing things, is actually a Protestant custom, unacceptable to Catholics: Protestants believe that each person should interpret the Bible using his or her own thought, whereas Catholics think that acceptable interpretation must be guided by church authority and tradition. So even within the familiar Judaeo-Christian traditions, problems of fairness and favoritism immediately crop up, and these problems were much emphasized in the case.

Those problems are greatly magnified when we consider the non-Judaeo-Christian religions, whose sacred texts the Pennsylvania authorities did not even attempt to respect. It is one of the oddities of the case, and a sign of how parochial Americans tend to be in religious matters, even when they are trying to think broadly, that Islam was a central feature of the story behind the case, but it was not mentioned once in any of the opinions. The Schempps were Unitarian/Universalists, a non-Christian religion that encourages free seeking and an absence of dogmatism. The case did not, however, begin with objections on the part of the Unitarian parents, Edward and Sidney. This is one of the rare such cases that begins with a child's own initiative and curiosity. Ellory Schempp (who later changed his name to Ellery[29]) was a high school student when the requirement came into force. His school accompanied the mandatory Bible reading at the start of the day with a group recitation of the Lord's Prayer, and both were immediately followed by the flag salute and a series of important announcements. (Thus students who were given permission to miss the religious observances were also very likely to miss the important announcements.) Students took turns doing the readings, going to the school's radio-television studio so that their voices could be broadcast throughout the school on the communications system. Teachers in each classroom would then supervise the children, who were asked to stand and join in the recitation of the Lord's Prayer.

Ellory Schempp, sixteen, was a gifted and unusually thoughtful young man. He recalls that he used to cherish his long walk to school as a time when he could think about issues. He had studied the Constitution, and he did not like the new Bible and prayer requirements. He thought that they were unconstitutional. He decided to protest, in a way that focused on the issue of fairness. One day, when his turn to go to the studio and read came up, Ellory read from a copy of the Quran that he had brought with him. He recalls:

> It was a little scary when I made this protest. I mean, I knew I wasn't doing anything really bad—I wasn't hurting anybody. But I did not know what would happen when the Principal learned about this. I felt confident that the ideas I had were shared by some of my friends, and quite likely by . . . thoughtful people, like at the Unitarian Church and the ACLU. I had my thoughts prepared to answer criticisms. And I knew that some people would not agree. But my answer was always, what is fair to everyone? What does the Constitution mean?

It didn't take long for Ellory to find out what the principal thought: immediately he was packed off to the principal's office and given a lecture about respect for school rules. The principal then sent him to the guidance counselor, who "inquired about my family health."

We can see, then, that the alleged inclusiveness and nondenominationality of the school prayer practices were bogus. The authorities had no intention of being fair to everybody. They wanted Judaeo-Christian piety. They did not want even to hear about Muslim piety, and the idea of students hearing verses from that book led not to applause and "What a good idea," but to disciplinary authority. The fact that none of the nine Justices mentions this fact, or Islam, is really strange, but it does show how hard it is to think respectfully about religions that are not at a given time practiced by large numbers of Americans. Even if the authorities had had the most zealous attachment to equal respect, it would seemingly be impossible to construct a devotional exercise with prescribed readings that truly expressed it. The Abington school authorities, however, were not even trying to observe this fundamental norm.

Ellory, with his parents' support, decided to pursue the issue. Borrowing his father's typewriter, he wrote a letter to the ACLU that he now describes as "rather pretentious":

> Gentlemen:
>
> As a student in my junior year at Abington Senior High School, I would very greatly appreciate any information that you might send regarding possible Union action and/or aid in testing the constitutionality of Pennsylvania law which arbitrarily (and seemingly unrighteously and unconstitutionally) compels the Bible to be read in our public school system. I thank you for any help you might offer in freeing American youth in Pennsylvania from this gross violation of their religious rights as guaranteed in the first and foremost Amendment in our United States' Constitution.
>
> Sincerely yours,
>
> Ellory F. Schempp

Enclosing ten dollars as a "retainer," he mailed the letter. The ACLU was not eager to take the case, because they felt that the main threat to civil liberties at the time was McCarthyism, but they sent Bernard Wolfman, a distinguished authority on tax law then in private practice, now Fessenden Professor of Law at Harvard Law School, to interview the family. Wolfman was astonished that the parents said, "Talk to the kids," and left the room. When Wolfman asked the three children whom they prayed to, Ellory's sister, Donna, said, "You are Jewish, aren't you? Well, Unitarians are like Jews and they are individualistic." Wolfman, impressed, recommended that the ACLU take the case. After failing to find more mainstream families to join the case, they decided to go ahead with the oddball Schempps.

Meanwhile, Ellory was applying to college. He later learned from the admissions director at Tufts that his high school principal had a letter of disrecommendation to every college he applied to. When Tufts accepted him, the principal even telephoned the Tufts admissions office to ask them to rescind their decision.[30] Meanwhile, his brother, Roger, was "roughed up" by other kids on the school bus, and some of Donna's friends were told not to speak to her. Donna's parents gave her a letter to give to her friends explaining that the family was not anti-god, but just pro-Constitution. She says passing out the letter to her friends was at least as bad as being ignored by them. As the school bus passed their home, kids would call out, "Here is the Commie camp."

Ellory, meanwhile, graduated from Tufts, Phi Beta Kappa and Sigma Xi, the year his case was decided; he went on to earn a PhD in physics at Brown University in 1967. Today he is a noted physicist (at first in the academy, later in private industry) who has focused on the development of magnetic resonance imaging (MRI). He has thirty-three publications in peer-reviewed journals. An avid and highly skilled mountain climber, he has remained active in the Unitarian/Universalist Church, and also in the American Civil Liberties Union. In a 2004 sermon about democracy, he stresses that "a core concept is how the rights of the majority are to be exercised with respect to the minority. . . . We have a duty to respect others. . . . Americans always believe in fairness. Sometimes even to minorities."

Because Ellery (by now with the new spelling of his name) was in college by the time the case got to court, he was not, officially, a plaintiff. His parents, Edward and Sidney, however, had long taken up his cause, and the eventual plaintiffs were the parents and the two younger children, who were still in school.[31] Once again, the Court was not divided: the case was decided with but a single dissent, that of Justice Stewart, who had dissented in *Engel*. Justice Clark wrote the majority opinion, which was supplemented by concurrences by Justices Brennan, Douglas, and Goldberg. Justice Clark's opinion develops some of the subordinate themes of *Engel*, such as civil peace and co-ercion, but draws particular attention to the equality issue.

The Bible reading, it is quickly established, is a religious exercise, and it is not entirely neutral, as expert testimony had argued.[32] Americans are and long have been a "religious people" (213), but we also have a tradition of respecting liberty of conscience. (Significantly, Justice Clark refers at this point to Roger Williams, whose image of religiously diverse people embarked on a single ship at sea he quotes at length.[33]) This tradition mandates "absolute equality before the law, of all religious opinions and sects . . . The government is neutral, and, while protecting all, it prefers none, and it *disparages* none."[34] The whole tradi-tion of interpretation on this question supports that idea of "wholesome 'neu-trality,'" recognizing "that powerful sects or groups might bring about a fusion of governmental and religious functions or a concert of dependency of one upon the other to the end that official support of the State or Federal Govern-ment would be placed behind the tenets of one or of all orthodoxies."[35] It is no defense to insist that the issue is minor: "The breach of neutrality that is today a trickling stream may all too soon become a raging torrent. . . ."[36] As in *Engel*, the Court insists that coercion, while necessary for a Free Exercise violation, is not necessary for an Establishment Clause problem.[37]

In an analysis that subsequently took on great importance in the tradition, Justice Clark suggests a test for constitutionality in Establishment Clause cases:

> The test may be stated as follows: what are the purpose and the primary effect of the enactment? If either is the advancement or inhibition of reli-gion then the enactment exceeds the scope of legislative power as circum-scribed by the Constitution. That is to say that to withstand the strictures of the Establishment Clause there must be a secular legislative purpose and a primary effect that neither advances nor inhibits religion.[38]

These sentences are the source of the famous *Lemon* test, which we shall discuss further in Chapter 7. We understand the import of the proposed test better when we read it in context, seeing how it picks up on the theme of "wholesome neutrality," "absolute equality before the law," and "prefer[ring] none and disparag[ing] none." The test is proposed as a way of getting at fairness, and its language makes it crystal clear that the relevant neutrality is not only among the religions but also between religion and nonreligion.

Like Justice Black, Justice Clark is aware that the Court's decision may be construed as expressing hostility to religion; like Justice Black, he rebuts the charge. The state may not show hostility to religion, nor may it establish a "religion of secularism." Moreover, nothing has been said to prevent the comparative study of the Bible in courses on the history of religion or on literature. What is unconstitutional is the fact that government mandates a devotional religious exercise; this violates the norm of "strict equality."

At the time, during the anxiety of the Cold War, the *Schempp* decision aroused great hostility. Many Americans wanted to pray publicly. Only "commies," many suggested, could object to that wish. Today, in hindsight, I believe that we can see how wise the decision was. The mandated religious exercise was not fair to all, and even the provision for excused absence still left minority children vulnerable to stigmatization. This vulnerability was made all too real in the scapegoating of the Schempp children by their peers and the astonishingly aggressive behavior of the principal to a child whose disobedience consisted in trying to show respect for another major world religion, Islam. High school students and even high school principals are not paradigms of fair conduct, and it doesn't take much knowledge of human nature to predict that violations of equal respect will be ubiquitous in any regime in which the state puts its muscle behind an orthodoxy of religious observance.

III. Moments of Silence, Graduation Prayer

Ishmael Jaffree was a public defense attorney in Mobile, Alabama.[39] Early in his legal education he decided that he would work without self-enrichment, for the good of poor defendants. Raised as a Baptist, he became an agnostic in college. His wife, Mozelle, belonged to the Baha'i faith, a sect that teaches tolerance, universalism, and peace, and that has been cruelly persecuted by both Christians and Muslims, most notably in today's Iran, where the property of all Baha'is has recently been seized by the government. Parents of three young children, the Jaffrees agreed that their children should learn about different religions and should ultimately choose their own, or none. They were also determined to raise them to have a robust sense of their dignity and equality, not always easy for African-American families in the Mobile of the 1980s.

Five-year-old Chioke Jaffree came home upset one day in 1982. His teacher had led the class in singing grace before lunch: "God is great, God is good, Let us thank Him for our food." His sister, Makeba, had a similar experience, except that her teacher, Pixie Alexander, also had the class recite the Lord's Prayer.[40] These observances were at odds with the teachings of the Jaffree home, and the children were not told that the observance was strictly optional. (Even if they had been, five-year-olds probably would not have understood the whole issue.) The teacher simply led them in the recitations.

Already in 1978, the state of Alabama had passed a law authorizing a one-minute period of silence in all public schools "for meditation." It is important that this law was never challenged. It remains good law, and the Supreme Court has explicitly said that similar "moment of silence" laws are constitutional. In 1981, however, a new additional law was passed, authorizing a period of silence "for meditation or voluntary prayer." Its prime sponsor, State Senator Holmes, said that the bill's explicit mention of prayer was an "effort to return voluntary prayer to our public schools . . . it is a beginning and a step in the right direction."[41] Senator Holmes said that he had no other purpose in view. A year later, in 1982, a further law was passed, authorizing teachers to lead "willing students" in a specific prescribed prayer referring to God as "the Creator and Supreme Judge of the world."[42] Because Jaffree brought his complaint before the passage of the 1982 law, and because the state quickly stopped trying to defend that law, legal argument focused throughout on the 1981 law.

Ishmael Jaffree tried to take the matter up with his children's teachers, but he made no headway. Eventually he brought a lawsuit. He later testified that he brought the suit because he saw the prescribed prayer as indoctrination, and he preferred inquisitiveness and tolerance: "I want my children . . . to be free to examine, to explore, to ponder, to think about, to be exposed to different philosophies."[43] He and his children ultimately paid a heavy price:

> My children have experienced all types of abuse from neighbors. Some of the children in our neighborhood, which is mostly white, have stopped playing with my children, and other children laugh at them . . . How are my children going to handle this? I don't know. I have suffered emotionally myself and it has drained me . . . I'm perceived as an outsider . . . disrupting Mobile's quiet tranquility.[44]

The case was heard by District Court Judge Brevard Hand. Hand wrote a 20,000-word opinion in the state's favor. His argument was, for its time, novel: Alabama is not bound by the Establishment Clause, because the Establishment Clause has never been incorporated. "Alabama has the power to establish a state religion if it chooses to do so."[45]

Not surprisingly, since lower courts are bound by decisions of the Supreme Court, the appeals court overruled the district court. The case was ultimately appealed to the Supreme Court, which found in Jaffree's favor by a margin of 7–2. Jaffree did not argue the case himself, but he worked closely with the lawyers who did. After he won, Jaffree notes, teachers were still praying in many schools. "But they are very careful not to pray in *my* children's schools."[46]

The *Jaffree* case seems more difficult to resolve than *Schempp*, because there seems to be nothing wrong with asking students to observe a moment of silence. Indeed, in this noisy fast-moving society, a moment of silence seems like a very good thing, and much more than a "moment" might be still better. Nothing in the Court's decision objected to the idea of a mandatory moment of silence, and of course it would always have been fine for any student to use that moment for prayer. However, the 1981 law—which, notice, supplemented the "moment of silence" law that was already on the books—explicitly authorized teachers to lead students in prayer, and the purpose of the new law, officially announced, was to return prayer to the schools. Moreover, as the experience of the Jaffree children showed, teachers did not simply say, "You may now meditate or pray." They chose specific prayers and graces, and led the children in those particular prayers. The only difference between this situation and the *Schempp* case, then, was that different classrooms were praying in different ways. There was nothing optional about the prayers on the part of the students, and the law was not even careful enough to insist that anyone who did not want to join the teacher could be excused. (How could a five-year-old be excused from grace before meals without missing the meals or standing out conspicuously as a weirdo?)

The Court focuses on the fact that the 1981 law added "prayer" to the existing 1978 law, and that the legislative history made it very clear that the primary purpose of the new law was to advance religion. The 1978 law already protected students' right to engage in voluntary prayer if they chose to do so. The new law conveys "a message of state endorsement and promotion of prayer." By now the *Schempp* test, further elaborated as the *Lemon* test, is guiding interpretation. Thus, showing that the law's primary purpose is to advance religion is sufficient to show it is unconstitutional.[47] But the way in which the Court makes this argument highlights the equality issue. Referring to Justice O'Connor's opinion in a public display case that we shall analyze in the next section, the Court says that, when asking whether a law has a secular purpose, the question to be posed is "whether the government intends to convey a message of endorsement or disapproval of religion."[48] In her separate concurring opinion, Justice O'Connor further elaborates her own "endorsement test":

> [T]he religious liberty protected by the Establishment clause is infringed when the government makes adherence to religion relevant to a person's standing in the political community. Direct government action endorsing religion or a particular religious practice is invalid under this approach because it "sends a message to nonadherents that they are outsiders, not full members of the political community, and an accompanying message to adherents that they are insiders, favored members of the political community." . . . [T]his view . . . requires courts to examine whether government's purpose is to endorse religion and whether the statute actually conveys a message of endorsement.[49]

Observing that twenty-five states have some type of moment-of-silence law, she reasons that such laws can be constitutional if they do not contain any message of endorsement suggesting that prayer is the favored activity. "The crucial question is whether the State has conveyed or attempted to convey the message that children should use the moment of silence for prayer."[50] This question can only be answered by a searching inquiry into the history of a statute. Of course people may differ in their account of what constitutes an endorsement, but "the relevant issue is whether an objective observer, acquainted with the text, legislative history, and implementation of the statute, would perceive it as a state endorsement of prayer in public schools. . . . A moment of silence law that is clearly drafted and implemented so as to permit prayer, meditation, and reflection within the prescribed period, without endorsing one alternative over the others, should pass this test."

The "objective observer" standard is a helpful elaboration of the endorsement test. Obviously litigants will differ in their subjective perceptions, especially when their personal interests are at stake. O'Connor's insistence on objectivity (in the sense of freedom from bias and favor), and her further requirement of historical knowledge, flesh out the standard in a way that gives it bite and clarity—although wise practical reason will still be required to apply it in a particular case.

Justice O'Connor's worry about standing in the community is not merely academic. Again and again, the cases testify to the painful exclusion of nonconforming children. Being stamped as an "oddball" is already to be not fully equal in the political community; this inequality becomes more problematic still when, as so often happens, religious conformity is linked to moral health, to patriotism, and to other key civic values. Kids who are seen to be living in "the Commie camp" are surely not fully equal citizens. The Jaffree children also suffered great distress, which apparently compounded the racial tensions that were already present in their lives.

Alabama's less directive moment-of-silence law remains constitutional. In 2000, the state of Virginia passed a law that required a daily moment of silence in the public schools, to enable students to "meditate, pray, or engage in any other silent activity." The U.S. Court of Appeals for the Fourth Circuit upheld the constitutionality of this law, arguing that the reference to prayer "introduced at most a minor and nonintrusive accommodation of religion," and that the law served, in a neutral way, the interests of both religious and nonreligious students.[51] In October 2001, the Supreme Court declined to review the case. This case was probably rightly decided because the wording of the law is genuinely neutral and the record does not show that the state's purpose was to promote religion. Clearly, however, vigilance about its actual implementation in the classroom remains important.

The dispute over religion in the public schools continues. In our final chapter we shall discuss the words "under God" in the Pledge of Allegiance, its latest chapter. There remains one important case to discuss, which brings the series begun in *Engel* to a confusing turning point. It took up the issue of prayer at graduation ceremonies.

Deborah Weisman was a student at Nathan Bishop Middle School in Providence, Rhode Island.[52] School principals in the city were authorized by the

Providence School Committee to invite members of the clergy to deliver prayers at graduation ceremonies, so her principal, Robert E. Lee, invited a local rabbi. As was customary in the school district, Lee gave the rabbi a pamphlet called "Guidelines for Civic Occasions," prepared by the National Conference of Christians and Jews. The pamphlet recommended that public prayers at civic ceremonies be composed with "inclusiveness and sensitivity," though it also acknowledged that "[p]rayer of any kind may be inappropriate on some civic occasions." The principal advised the rabbi that his prayer should be nonsectarian.[53] The actual prayer delivered by the rabbi was quite sensitive and appealing. It focused on America's protection of minority rights and civil liberties. But it was hardly nonsectarian, since it attributed the good aspects of American life to the agency of God, referred to God repeatedly in the singular, and stated that the families present at the graduation offer thanks to God for this important milestone.[54] It's not surprising that such a prayer emerged after consultation of a pamphlet written by Christians and Jews. It would be acceptable to most, though not all, of them, and to many Muslims. It would not be acceptable to Hindus, Buddhists, other nontheistic believers, or to agnostics and atheists. And yet, the prayer claimed to speak on behalf of those present. The actions of the principal, who not only gave the rabbi specific instructions about the type of prayer to compose, but also gave a Christian-Jewish pamphlet to help him, suggest an unpleasant degree of state control over religious choices.

Deborah Weisman's father, Daniel, a professor of social work, had already been at odds with the school district over graduation prayer: in 1986, his older daughter's high school graduation involved a prayer addressed to "Jesus Christ." He and his wife, Vivian, sent a letter of complaint to the principal, but received no reply. As his daughter Deborah prepared to graduate from middle school, he reminded the school of the Establishment Clause problem, and was informed that the school had selected a rabbi to give the prayer. (Apparently they believed that this should satisfy the worries of a Jewish family.) Weisman tried to get a restraining order stopping the school district from including prayer in the ceremony; he failed, and the prayer was recited, with Deborah and her family in attendance. He continued his litigation. The school argued that the prayer was nonsectarian; moreover, participation was voluntary in two ways: a child could simply not join in, but simply stand and remain silent in a show of respect. Any child could also choose not to attend the graduation ceremony, which is not required for official graduation. The district court found that the prayer violated the Establishment Clause, and the appellate court affirmed.

When the case was appealed to the Supreme Court, it became politicized, with the participation of prominent groups on both sides. The U.S. government entered the case on the side of Lee, and Solicitor General Kenneth Starr helped the petitioners to argue it. Other groups arrayed on the Lee side included Focus on the Family, the Southern Baptist Convention Christian Life Commission, the United States Catholic Conference, and the Christian Legal Society. Many legal scholars helped to write the various amicus briefs. On the Weisman side, briefs were filed by, among others, the National School Boards Association, the state of Delaware, the Council on Religious Freedom, the National Coalition for Public Education and Religious Liberty, Americans for Religious Liberty, and the American Jewish Congress. The brief for the last was authored by distinguished legal scholar Douglas Laycock.[55]

On the one side, proponents of upholding the constitutionality of the prayer could point to its (relatively) nonsectarian character, to the fact that no action was required on the part of those attending, apart from standing in respectful silence (and they were already standing at that point in the ceremony), and to the fact that the entire occasion was a voluntary event. On the other side, the argument was that the prayer was actually not at all neutral, that standing in silence during the prayer could easily be construed as a type of participation, given that believers were doing exactly the same thing, and that a high school graduation ceremony is not a voluntary event, but one that centrally raises issues of standing in the community, of inclusion and exclusion.

Given the changed composition of the Court, the outcome was very much in doubt, since four Justices (Scalia, Thomas, White, and Rehnquist) seemed willing to uphold the constitutionality of the prayer, while four (O'Connor, Stevens, Souter, and Blackmun) seemed likely to find it unconstitutional. Justice Kennedy's vote was in doubt; indeed, he changed his mind after beginning to draft an opinion on the other side. In the end, he wrote a strong majority opinion finding the practice unconstitutional, which was joined by the other four, but he significantly altered the argumentative playing field, insisting on the coerciveness of the practice as the primary reason for his finding.

So far as it goes, the opinion gives a clear victory to the opponents of the practice. It insists that the principal "directed and controlled the content of the prayers," and that "it is a cornerstone principle of our Establishment Clause jurisprudence that it is no part of the business of government to compose official prayers for any group of the American people to recite as a part of a religious program carried on by government."[56] Even though students can graduate without attending the graduation ceremony, the immense importance of such ceremonies in American life puts great pressure on students to attend. It is claimed that a student can simply not participate, but it is not clear what that freedom amounts to. Standing in respectful silence would mean doing the same thing that the participants are doing, and would give no room for the dissenter to differentiate her own view; as for walking out or protesting, that is not a real option for young people, given the nature of peer pressure and public pressure, which supply a coercion that "can be as real as an overt compulsion."[57] Nor is the issue one of such small importance that it can easily be overlooked: to say this would be to insult and trivialize the beliefs of the participants.

The opinion, then, finds the exercise coercive and therefore unconstitutional. Justice Kennedy does not say that coercion is a necessary element of an Establishment Clause violation, but he does not deny this either, as had our three previous cases. For this reason, Justices Blackmun and Souter (joined by Stevens and O'Connor) each wrote concurring opinions, both of which reaffirm the earlier line of reasoning. Justice Souter's opinion gives a detailed refutation of both the "nonpreferentialist" interpretation of the Establishment Clause and also of the theory, much stressed by the plaintiffs, that the Clause does not forbid the state to sponsor noncoercive religious observances. The coercion test, Justice Souter plausibly insists, would render the Establishment Clause a "virtual nullity," adding nothing that is not already covered by the Free Exercise Clause.[58] The opinion, talking a lot about Madison's and Jefferson's views, emphasizes the equality theory: noncoercive state practices may "demean religious dissenters 'in public opinion.'"[59] Although the Establishment Clause's conception of neutrality is "not self-revealing," it has by now been endowed with a specific content: "the State may not favor or endorse either religion generally or one religion over others."[60]

The equality-based endorsement test is alive, then, but it is not clear that it can still command majority support. The case was an unusually difficult one.

So perhaps Justice Kennedy's narrow opinion does not represent what he would now say about the less ambiguous cases, such as *Engel* and *Schempp*. Nonetheless, the tradition that bases analysis of school prayer on a fundamental concern for fairness is now seriously at risk.

IV. Public Displays: Equality in Context

Governments like monuments and displays. They like them all year round, and they are particularly fond of them at holiday seasons. Some displays obviously express government's intent to favor one religion over others. Others may be pluralistic enough to avoid that problem, although it is difficult to imagine a display that could honor all the many religions that America by now contains. There remains, further, the danger of expressing a generic favoritism for religion as against nonreligion. A display put up by government is like a message. It says, "This is what we like and think important. This is what we have arranged for you to look at with our sponsorship."

The issues that arise in assessing public monuments and displays are, then, similar to those that arise in the school prayer context. There are also some important differences. Public displays involve both adults and children, and the children are not required to be in any specific public place, as they are required to be in school. Public displays, then, look more voluntary than school prayer: someone who doesn't like a given display is free to avoid it, without the sort of special excuse or message of nonconformity that leads to stigmatizing behavior.

On the other hand, there's a way in which public displays can also look nonvoluntary: anyone who has business at a given state house will be bound to walk past what is on display there. Anyone who uses a public park will inevitably see some big monument or display erected there. Since public displays are typically on land that is open to the public for use, the voluntariness of viewing the display is not, after all, so obvious. The person who chooses not to view a given display (short of walking around with her eyes closed) is unable to use a given piece of public property that others are free to use. Moreover—since coercion is not our only concern—even the bare knowledge that the state has expressed a message that demeans a given class of citizens can reasonably be thought to affect those people's standing in the community, whether they view the message or not. African-Americans could avoid the overt signs of segregation as much as they liked, but if a public drinking fountain carries the message "Whites only," that demeans all blacks in the community, whether or not they come to look at the sign.

Displays, then, are highly sensitive places where government makes statements that have importance for the equality of citizens in the community. It seems quite unreasonable, however, to suggest that no state may erect any display at the holiday season that has any religious reference at all. If the Establishment Clause meant that Santa and Rudolph and Barbie would be the only acceptable symbols at the holiday season, and that nothing with religious content could even accompany them, that would suggest to most Americans the "relentless and all-pervasive attempt to exclude religion from every aspect of public life" that could itself pose a constitutional problem, establishing secularism as France has chosen to do.[61] It would also be unfortunate, giving commercial and nonethical values priority over ethical and spiritual values. In this area, then, the Justices are aware not only of an equality issue on the other side, but also of a danger to civil peace, since it is likely that Americans would rise up, in some manner, against such an attempt, were one made. This sensitivity has meant that the Court typically bends over backward to give a monument the most generous possible construal, approving some displays that a strict academic analysis might find problematic on equality grounds.

Every year the city of Pawtucket, Rhode Island, erects a holiday display in a park owned by a nonprofit organization and located in the middle of the city's shopping district. The display includes many traditional secular symbols of the holiday season, "including, among other things, a Santa Claus house, reindeer pulling Santa's sleigh, candy-striped poles, a Christmas tree, carolers, cutout figures representing such characters as a clown, an elephant, and a teddy bear, hundreds of colored lights, a large banner that reads 'SEASONS GREETINGS.'" For over forty years, it has also included a Nativity scene. The figures at issue in the case, purchased by the city in 1973 for $1,365, are over five feet tall. No money had been spent on maintenance of the crèche in recent years. Individuals and the ACLU challenged the constitutionality of including the Nativity scene in the display. By a 5–4 margin, in 1983, the Supreme Court upheld its constitutionality.

The Pawtucket case is not an easy one. The Nativity scene is large and conspicuous; it is clearly a sectarian religious symbol, indeed a very central and very holy one; and there were no symbols associated with other American religions.

It seems clear that the largely Italian-American political establishment of Paw-tucket strongly desired a sectarian symbol. On the other hand, the crèche was part of a colorful diverse display that sent the message of holiday celebration. Reasonably, the Court's analysis turned on particular circumstances.[62]

Justice Burger, who wrote the majority opinion, makes two important points. First, he insists, correctly, that the tradition has never been one of "rigid, absolutist" insistence on separation of church and state; the metaphor of separation is not a wholly accurate characterization of what the Establishment Clause forbids, since no institution in American society can exist in total isolation from government. The cases have consistently rejected such a rigid reading of the clause, in favor of an approach that recognizes a "blurred, indistinct, and variable barrier depending on all the circumstances of a particular relationship."[63] The second point, closely related, is that, this being the case, no sharp-edged rules are likely to be helpful. The clause supplies a general orientation, but careful consideration of each case and contextual line drawing will be required.

It is Justice O'Connor's concurring opinion, however, that helps move analysis along, supplying the often confusing tradition with an orienting account. She begins with the ringing affirmation about people's equal standing in the political community that is the epigraph to this chapter and that has already appeared in our analysis of *Wallace v. Jaffree*.[64] A focus on equality is nothing new. In her concurrence, however, Justice O'Connor makes it into a helpful set of questions for judges to ask. Acknowledging the "*Lemon* test," she then notes that its two most important prongs, "secular purpose" and "secular effect," are not by themselves easy to apply. It is hard to know what question we ought to be asking when we ask whether a display's purpose, or effect, is secular. She proposes that a focus on the idea of government endorsement helps in both areas. When asking whether the purpose of a display is secular, we should ask "whether government's actual purpose is to endorse religion."[65] The requirement of "secular purpose" is not satisfied by any minor secular purpose that might be found (an area of confusion in earlier cases). "The proper inquiry under the purpose prong of *Lemon*, I submit, is whether the government intends to convey a message of endorsement or disapproval of religion."[66] As for "effect," we ought to ask, regardless of what government meant to convey, what did it actually convey? Here we should not ask whether the display has some incidental effect that constitutes a benefit to religion (another area of confusion in earlier cases). Instead, "What is crucial is that a government practice not have the effect of communicating a message of government endorsement or disapproval of religion. It is only practices having that effect . . . that make religion relevant . . . to status in the political community."[67] (As we have seen, *Wallace v. Jaffree* elaborated this standard further, in terms of the perceptions of an informed and objective observer.)

Justice O'Connor now applies her own test—and of course one could agree with her analysis and disagree with its application. (That is basically what happens in Justice Brennan's dissent—so a majority of the Court supported the O'Connor analytical framework.) Pawtucket, she reasons, did not intend to communicate endorsement of Christianity or disapproval of non-Christian religions in setting up its display; it intended to celebrate "the public holiday through its traditional symbols."[68] As for effect, "the overall holiday setting changes what viewers may fairly understand to be the purpose of the display" to one of holiday celebration.

The next application of the O'Connor framework came in the Pittsburgh case that we introduced in Chapter 1.[69] The Allegheny County Courthouse erected two holiday displays. One, outside the courthouse, consisted of a Christmas tree forty-five feet tall, a menorah eighteen feet tall, and a message from the mayor of Pittsburgh declaring the city's "salute to liberty." The other, inside the courthouse, on its grand staircase, was a crèche bearing a sign that it was donated by a local Roman Catholic organization. Over the manger was an angel bearing a banner proclaiming "Gloria in Excelsis Deo, Glory to God in the Highest." By a 5–4 vote, the Court found the first display constitutional and the second unconstitutional.

So far as orienting theory goes, *Allegheny* contains nothing new. The majority opinion draws attention to the "endorsement" framework and traces it back to *Engel*, finding that a core meaning of the Establishment Clause is that government may not make religious adherence "relevant to a person's standing in the political community." It vigorously protests against Justice Kennedy's attempted weakening of "endorsement" to "proselytization," which asks for "unmistakable" clarity concerning government's intent to favor specific sects.[70] In her concurrence, Justice O'Connor repeats and elaborates her framework.

On the side of practical reason, the case makes progress by showing how crucial context is to the judgment about the state's message, intended and received.

The fact that the two displays are at a building associated with government's central functions counts against them. Everything that happens at city hall is "implicitly marked with the stamp of government approval."[71] From this point on, however, significant differences between the two displays may be found. The crèche stands alone, in a prominent place; no secular message is attached. It therefore "inevitably creates a clear and strong impression that the local government tacitly endorses Christianity."[72] The outside display is not exactly the same. First of all, the display's one religious symbol, the menorah, is not a sacred symbol, and it is not even necessarily a religious symbol. The Court correctly notes that the Hanukkah lamp commemorates the revolt of the Maccabees against imperial power, and that for many Jews the meaning of the holiday is a secular one, the celebration of freedom.[73] The menorah is next to the huge Christmas tree, not, today, a religious symbol. This placement contextualizes it, creating a Pawtucket-like impression that the city is celebrating the holiday season. Finally, the mayor has supplied a secular message, that of liberty, to link the elements in the display together and indicate their overall purpose. The message is a plausible link, and it does without too much strain give the display a secular purpose.

Allegheny is a confusing case, even with respect to the majority, because different Justices join different parts of the Court's opinion. Those who uphold the outside display do so on subtly different grounds: Justice O'Connor, for example, does not think that we need to say that the menorah is partly a secular symbol. Justice Brennan's dissenting view of the outside display makes things more complicated still, since he accepts the traditional analytical framework while applying it with an opposite result. This sort of complexity makes it look like a mess. And yet, we would expect just this, if we follow the orienting equality-based theory: for indeed, as Justice O'Connor has repeatedly insisted, and not she alone, what message a display intends to convey and does convey is a complicated contextual matter. Wise practical reason will focus on details, and disagreement about how to understand details of context does not mean that the overall analytical framework is defective.

V. Public Displays: The Ten Commandments

One of the most divisive public issues to come before the Court in recent years is that of the constitutionality of various public displays of the Ten Commandments. The Ten Commandments are a symbol of deep meaning to Christians and Jews in America. They can be found in many places throughout our public landscape—not least (as the Justices frequently mention) on the Supreme Court building itself, where Moses holding the commandments figures alongside many other lawgivers, religious and secular. One thing that all nine Justices agree about is that this display on their own building is constitutional. But that is an easy case, since the theme of the display is clearly "law," and the display is not endorsing either religion over nonreligion or any particular religion.

An easy case at the other end of the spectrum was the huge monument bearing the Ten Commandments that Judge Roy Moore, chief justice of the Alabama Supreme Court, set up in the rotunda of the Alabama Judicial Building. The four-foot-tall, two-ton granite display was set up without permission of the other justices, in the middle of the night. Ordered by the U.S. district court to remove the monument, Moore refused to obey the order, but was overruled by his eight colleagues. The U.S. Supreme Court refused to hear his appeal of their decision. Alabama's judicial ethics panel then removed Moore from office. More recently, Moore has unsuccessfully run for governor, losing a Republican primary in June 2006.

The Moore case, I said, is an easy case. And yet, in a Gallup/CNN poll, 7 percent of Americans disapproved of the federal court order to remove the monument.[74] This widespread endorsement of the commandments is connected to people's perception that a Godless elite is trying to "separate" church from state in a ruthless and mechanical way, removing cherished symbols of America's Judaeo-Christian heritage. Separationist rhetoric has indeed confused the issue, obscuring the all-important issue of fairness. We make progress, I believe, if we emphasize that issue.

The Ten Commandments are not secular. Although six of them command ethical conduct, and their content might be shared by people from many religions, or of no religion, even in these cases it is evident that it is the Judaeo-Christian God who is doing the commanding, since the whole list is introduced by "I am the Lord Thy God: Thou shalt have no other gods before me." That fact might make even "Thou shalt not steal," etc., problematic for a person who does not recognize the Judaeo-Christian God. Such a person could accept that it is important not to steal and not to kill, but could not accept those propositions *as statements handed down by the authority of the*

Judaeo-Christian God.[75] That is a subtle point, however, which might be disputed. What cannot be disputed is that the first four commandments are overtly religious. They express the importance of not recognizing any God or gods other than this one, of not making graven images, of not taking God's name in vain, of keeping God's Sabbath holy. These commandments are not only sectarian; they offer a rebuke to polytheists and to all worshippers who do not recognize this particular God. The biblical occasion for Moses' ascent of Mount Sinai was the apostasy of the Hebrew people, who had begun to worship other gods. It is no accident that attack on other modes of worship is central to the sacred text he received.

Even among Jews and Christians, the commandments are sectarian, in the sense that any particular version of them is a sectarian version. Catholics do not accept the same list of ten that Protestants standardly accept. The Catholic version (based on the second enumeration, in the book of *Deuteronomy*) omits the prohibition of graven images: so, the Protestant third commandment (about taking the Lord's name in vain) is the Catholic second commandment. The Protestant tenth commandment about coveting is broken into two distinct commandments in the Catholic version, one dealing with the neighbor's spouse and one with the neighbor's property—thus bringing the number to ten. Virtually all versions of the commandments in the public square give the Protestant version. Nor is this difference trivial: Protestant/Catholic strife has often focused on the issue of images, and many fine works of Catholic (and even of Anglican) art have been destroyed by Protestant "iconoclasts," or "image-smashers." The chapel of King's College, Cambridge University, is a particularly vivid reminder of the way in which image-smashing figured in the English civil wars: angels and saints with their faces bashed in are all around. A Catholic litigant coming before Judge Moore's court would not feel reassured or fully respected.

Imagine, now, some Hindu litigants coming before Judge Moore's court. (Hindu groups in America were active in the recent contest over the Ten Commandments: the Hindu American foundation filed an amicus brief on behalf of Hindus, Buddhists, and Jains in America, urging the Court to declare the Texas display unconstitutional.[76]) These litigants walk into the courtroom lobby and see the huge granite monument, which announces in large letters that they had better have no other gods but the one God of Jews and Christians. But these litigants recognize the divinity of many gods, including Rama,

Ganesha, Shiva, and many others. They cherish their religion, and, as first-generation American citizens, they are already feeling anxious about whether America recognizes them as full equals in the public square. Polytheism has often given Christians an excuse to discriminate against Hindus. The British routinely expressed their disdain for Hinduism, which Winston Churchill referred to as a "beastly religion." He also referred to the great religious/secular leader Mohandas Gandhi as a "half-naked fakir," and he repeatedly misrepresented the roles of Hindus and Muslims in the struggle against the Axis powers in the war, telling President Franklin Delano Roosevelt that Hindus were cowards and that all the work was being done by (monotheistic) Muslims. President Roosevelt's personal investigation showed this to be altogether false.[77] All this history is well known to the Hindu litigants, as part of their *apartheid* treatment by the British (who did not permit them to attend the same clubs, swim in the same pools, and so forth), and as part of what made the British indifferent to appalling violence inflicted on peaceful Hindu civilians by the British military. Many people really thought that worshippers of many gods were less than fully equal, and perhaps less than fully human.

To these litigants, who had hoped to find in America a respectful pluralism that their parents or grandparents did not find in British India, Judge Moore's monument announces that they are not equals. Not a traditional relic of some bygone time, but a newly minted and very conspicuous display, it expresses to them the statement that the Supreme Court of Alabama endorses Judaeo-Christian monotheism, including its derogatory view of polytheism. Nor is it simply the hypersensitivity of this imagined group of litigants that leads to such a conclusion. An "objective observer," acquainted with Judge Moore's many statements about his intent to show that the Judaeo-Christian God is the foundation of this nation's legal system, and acquainted with the history and values of Hinduism and its relationship to monotheism, would concur in their judgment: Moore wants to announce that the state supports Judaeo-Christian religion, and he also wants to announce, and does announce, that it does not support those who follow other gods.

No matter what our personal religious beliefs are, we can agree in seeking a legal system that is not biased, that is fully and truly fair to all litigants, no matter what their religion. The Moore monument compromises that fairness. I believe that when the issue is put this way, many Americans who dislike the mechanical idea of separation will agree that the monument ought to be removed. The Court, fortunately, has usually preferred equality language to separation language, although many nongovernmental organizations working on this issue have not.

The Moore case, I have said, is easy: the monument is alone, not accompanied by any other symbols of varied legal traditions. It stands in a prominent place in a building whose function is central to the equal and unbiased operation of government. It is huge, impossible to miss. It is new, so it can't be explained as something left over from the heritage of a more homogeneous time. Its introduction was accompanied by unequivocal statements of purpose.

So, nobody ought to object to Moses on the Supreme Court building. All Americans concerned with fairness ought to object to Judge Moore's monument. In the middle lie most of the cases that actually stir up controversy. As in *Lynch* and *Allegheny*, so too here: context is all. Moreover, wise judges might agree on an orienting framework, but (as in both of those cases) apply it differently to the case at hand. In approaching the recent decisions about the commandments, then, we have a twofold task: to commend an orienting framework as the best one for the cases, and to show how wise practical reason might apply it. I shall argue that the equality/endorsement framework is the best one for both of the recent cases, and I shall also argue that, when it is applied, the Kentucky displays are unconstitutional and the Texas monument is (probably) constitutional. One might agree with my framework, however, while reaching a different concrete decision, particularly about the Texas case, which is a very close call.

Two Kentucky counties posted large, readily visible copies of the Ten Commandments in their courthouses.[78] Challenged in court, they modified the exhibit so as to show that the commandments are Kentucky's "precedent legal code," citing the state legislature's acknowledgment of Jesus Christ as the "Prince of Ethics." They added several smaller displays of documents linked only by their inclusion of religious references. After another challenge, they revised the exhibits again, calling the new display "The foundations of American Law and Government Display." The version of the commandments in the new display is explicitly identified as the "King James Version" (that is, the Protestant version). The display explains that they have had a deep influence on the formation of our nation's legal thought. The other documents were various traditional American documents that were supposed to demonstrate the formative role of the Ten Commandments in America's legal tradition; not surprisingly, all were excerpted so as to highlight a religious theme, and most contained mention of (the Judaeo-Christian) God.

First of all, it has to be said that the claim that the Ten Commandments played a large role in forming the American legal order is very unconvincing. The secular commandments are so vague and general that they give no precise guidance for lawmaking. All legal orders prohibit murder and theft, and the commandments say nothing about a good or distinctive way of doing this. So they give no guidance for anyone wanting to establish a code of criminal law. The prohibition on adultery is not enforced by law today, although some such laws remain on the books. Although in this case it is more plausible to think that the commandment influenced our legal tradition, it is a part of it that has since been abandoned. "False witness" is a crime only when the person is under oath (perjury), or when the false statements amount to libel or slander. But the commandment seeks to prevent lying very broadly. It does not confine itself to the types of lying that our legal order prohibits, nor does it say anything about what sorts of lies are legally sanctionable and what sorts are not. Finally, coveting is a human vice that is very unfortunate, but that cannot be prevented by any legal order, since it takes place in the mind and heart. The cmmandment against it is of great ethical importance, but no legal importance.

So there is not a particularly good match between our legal tradition and the commandments, nor should we expect one, since the commandments were offered to the Hebrew people as guidance for pious moral thought and behavior, not as the foundations for a state. The historical sources of U.S. law are, above all, the British common law and, to a lesser extent, the tradition of Roman law. These systems are legal systems, and they handle the details with which a legal order must be concerned. Kentucky did nothing to make its case for the formative *legal* role of the commandments.

The history of the legislation establishing the displays, and of its various modifications in response to lower court pressure, clearly indicates a religious purpose, and a sectarian one at that, as the message that the state was seeking to express. Kentucky asked the Court to trivialize the inquiry into purpose, taking the state's word for it that the aim was purely historical and refusing to look at the entirety of the record. The Court decided the case by a 5–4 vote (Justices Souter, Stevens, Breyer, Ginsburg, and O'Connor in the majority, Justices Scalia, Thomas, Rehnquist, and Kennedy dissenting). Using the "endorsement test" as a further elaboration of the "secular purpose" requirement, the Court held that the displays did not have a secular purpose, and were therefore unconstitutional. They insisted that the secular purpose must be "genuine, not a sham, and not merely secondary to a religious objective," and that history must be used to ask about purpose. "Reasonable observers have reasonable memories, and the Court's precedents sensibly forbid an observer 'to turn a blind eye to the context in which [the] policy arose.'"[79] The "unstinting focus" on religious passages, which provided the only link among the documents, showed that the sectarian content of the commandments was paramount.

Both the opinion of the Court (written by Justice Souter) and Justice O'Connor's separate concurrence place enormous emphasis on equality. Repeatedly, they insist that government may not send some citizens the message that they are not fully equal, our tradition requires respect for all citizens. Repudiating the view expressed in Justice Scalia's dissenting opinion, which argues that the Establishment Clause permits government to favor monotheism and disfavor polytheism, nontheistic religion, and atheism (a section of the opinion that Justices Rehnquist and Thomas joined, but not Justice Kennedy), they reaffirm their commitment to full-fledged neutrality and equal respect. They also reaffirm their commitment to the "objective observer" as the right way to implement the endorsement test. And they insist that from the start, the Establishment Clause has required full-blooded neutrality in matters of religion, not simply nonpreferentialism in religious matters. "It is true," Justice O'Connor concludes, "that many Americans find the Commandments in accord with their personal beliefs. But we do not count heads before enforcing the First Amendment. . . . Nor can we accept the theory that Americans who do not accept the Commandments' validity are outside the First Amendment's protections."

McCreary County brings a welcome clarity of analysis to the difficult issue of the commandments. Not so *Van Orden v. Perry*, the case from Texas, which was decided at the same time.[80] The case is inherently more difficult as regards practical reason and line drawing. It could certainly have been handled, however, with the very same orienting theory. Unfortunately, this did not happen. Four Justices—Stevens, O'Connor, Ginsburg, and Souter—keep to the old analytical framework, affirming the key importance of equality and nonfavoritism (although Justices Stevens and Ginsburg also place unfortunate emphasis on separation), and these four all find the Texas display unconstitu-

tional. Justices Scalia, Thomas, Rehnquist, and Kennedy find the displays
constitutional, but of course they have all by this time, in various different
ways, rejected the equality-based analytical framework.

The key swing vote was cast by Justice Breyer. In his concurring opinion,
he introduces a new theory of the Establishment Clause: that its primary purpose is "to avoid that divisiveness based upon religion that promotes social
conflict, sapping the strength of government and religion alike." Civil peace
has traditionally been important, as a subsidiary consideration. But, as the
early settlers knew all too well, there can be a peace that is oppressive, denying
minorities equal respect. Justice Breyer, by failing to reaffirm the equality/en-
dorsement theory in addition to his own theory, leaves us with a disturbing
theoretical gap. Should we really say that a display that everyone likes and that
isn't stirring up trouble, because the offended minorities are too powerless to
make trouble, is for that reason constitutional? This seems to be a very bad
theory for an egalitarian nation to adopt.

Think of the Hindus, Buddhists, and Jains who joined the litigation, insisting that the display expressed the endorsement of Judaeo-Christian religion
and disfavored the Hindu religion.[81] Members of these religions are not very
numerous in America. A policy that favors monotheists and disfavors polytheists is certainly not going to lead to civil war. And, since the U.S. Hindu community is an unusually law-abiding community, such a policy would be utterly
unlikely to lead to rioting in the streets—unless monotheists start beating up
on Hindus, as happened to Jehovah's Witnesses after *Gobitis*. Does this mean
that it is all right to tell Hindus that they are not fully equal in the eyes of government? Again, we can't imagine peaceful Buddhists rioting because the Ten
Commandments disfavor them. But that surely does not make it all right to
send a message that these people are not fully equal citizens. So a threat to
peace doesn't seem to be necessary for an Establishment Clause violation. If
what Justice Breyer really means to say is that the Court should not say that a
violation is a violation when so doing would lead to violence, that is a different
claim, but is it correct? *Brown v. Board of Education* could have been expected to lead to violence, and it did. Should the Court therefore have maintained silence?

Often, moreover, a focus on violence will in and of itself favor majorities
and disfavor minorities, especially relatively powerful minorities. It's a safe bet
that a decision that shocks and upsets Christians will be more likely to lead to

widespread tumult than a decision that disfavors Buddhists or Hindus, simply because there are a lot more Christians in the U.S. Should the Court really build its theory of constitutional interpretation around such reasoning?

Justice Breyer's theory, then, seems ill considered and unconvincing. Surely it is not ready to replace the equality/endorsement theory, which has years of theoretical development and success behind it. At the very least, he might have supported that theory, as well as his own; that he did not do so is deeply unfortunate. As I shall argue, Justice Breyer was probably right on the merits of the particular case. But his reasoning, not very convincing in itself, has muddied the waters for the future, making it no longer clear that the equality theory is consistently endorsed in hard cases.

Now let's look at the case. For many years, a large number of monuments have stood on the grounds of the Texas state capital. At the time of the case there were twenty-one historical markers and seventeen monuments. These displays are typically donated by local groups, and are then set up in various places around the park. One of these is a six-foot-high monument of the Ten Commandments. It was donated in 1961 by the Fraternal Order of Eagles, a secular civic organization, with the expressed intent of discouraging juvenile delinquency and commemorating the Eagles' work with delinquents. The religious part of the Ten Commandments is highlighted: the words "I AM THE LORD THY GOD" appear in large letters at the monument's top. The text of the commandments presented was chosen by an interdenominational committee with Protestant, Catholic, and Jewish members. That fact, of course, does not guarantee that the text is acceptable to all or even most members of those religions, but it does show a good-faith effort.

Other displays in the park commemorate the heroes of the Alamo, fallen Confederate soldiers, voluntary firemen, the Texas Rangers, Texas cowboys, Texas children, Texas pioneer women, Pearl Harbor veterans, the Statue of Liberty, Korean War veterans, World War I veterans, disabled veterans, Texas peace officers, and a few others. If there is a common theme in all the displays, it might be said to be the history and ideals of Texas, as the state explicitly stated.

The plaintiff in the case was a local lawyer, Van Orden, who passed the monument routinely on his way to the state's law library, which is located in the park's supreme court building.

This is a truly hard case. On the one hand, there are some obvious differences between this monument and the Kentucky displays that work in favor of the former. The monument is surrounded by many others, and the common link, if any, is one of history and tradition. The monument was donated by a private organization, rather than commissioned by government, and, unlike the private donation of the crèche in *Allegheny*, it was not given special pride of place. It does stand on government property, but not alone, and not in a location of unique prominence. One can walk around the park and observe the different monuments. So Justice Stevens seems to be stretching when he writes, in dissent, that "God, as the author of its message, the Eagles, as the donor of the monument, and the State of Texas, as its proud owner, speak with one voice for a common purpose—to encourage Texans to abide by the divine code of a 'Judaeo-Christian' God."[82] Finally, the monument has stood there for forty-five years without controversy, so it can fairly be claimed that it has become a part of Texas tradition. Surely removing a monument in such circumstances is a far more aggressive judicial act than simply telling Kentucky it cannot proceed with its new program.

On the other hand, the location of the monument, though not uniquely prominent, is quite prominent, very near the state house. (So are the monuments to Texas children and pioneer women.) So people are very likely to come before it in doing business with the state. The park contains no celebrations of other religious or ethical traditions, or other sources of law. And it is difficult to find a convincing theme (as in *Allegheny*) to link the monument to its neighbors, beyond the bare reference to history and tradition. It's at least plausible to think that in accepting the donation the state is agreeing with the Eagles that the Judaeo-Christian religious/ethical code is important for the youth of Texas.

Reasonable people, applying the analytical framework I favor, can differ about this case. It is unfortunate that the framework itself, at this point, stands on shaky ground.

VI. The Tradition Under Assault

School prayer and public displays are difficult issues in a pluralistic society like ours. The rhetoric of "separation," applied without a deeper theoretical analysis, wrongly suggests that the goal of the Establishment Clause is to purify the public square of all reference to religion, in effect establishing secularism as the theory of government. Harping on the words "separation of church and state" has done a lot of harm to reasoned public debate in this area, because it obscures the important underlying issues and alienates people from one another. Separation is good, when it is good, because the fusion of church and state in question offends against other constitutional values, above all liberty and equality. The "endorsement test" makes good sense of all this, elaborating the foundational commitment to equality in the form of an applicable analytical framework. For quite some time, between roughly 1960 and 1991, a consensus existed around this framework. Even today, it may still prevail in particular cases, as in the Kentucky Ten Commandments case.

Gradually, however, the changing membership of the Court, combined with new scholarship on the religion clauses, has changed the landscape, threatening to remove much of the bite from the Establishment Clause. Most radical is Justice Thomas's theory that the Establishment Clause was never incorporated. This theory is as old at least as Judge Brevard Hand in the *Jaffree* case. Hand, however, took an untenable position when, as a lower court judge, he simply announced that the Supreme Court was wrong. It is quite a different thing when Justice Thomas asserts this theory. Justice Thomas has not gone all the way with extreme thinkers such as Janice Rogers Brown, who believes that none of the Bill of Rights applies to the states. Nonetheless, the threat to traditional American values is much keener in the area of establishment than in that of free exercise. States really do want to announce that theirs is a Christian, or perhaps a Judaeo-Christian, state. Alabama was doing that in *Jaffree*, as was Kentucky in *McCreary*. As I write the present chapter, the Republican platform of the state of Texas has just announced that America is a "Christian nation, founded on Judeo-Christian principles."[83] So there is a huge threat to equality coming from some of our states, and only incorporation has prevented us from being a nation of varying hierarchies. I have argued that Justice Thomas's historical argument is mistaken. Even if one does not agree with that contention, his position would require the rejection of a long and wide set of precedents, since incorporation has repeatedly been explicitly asserted in opinions since 1946. No other Justice, so far, is willing to pay this price. The importance of the underlying Madisonian goal of protecting the equality of citizens should lead to redoubled vigilance about the incorporation issue, when judicial candidates are examined.

The late Justice Rehnquist for many years espoused a different dissident theory, nonpreferentialism. I have argued against his historical analysis in

Chapter 3. By now, furthermore, we can also see that such a theory has little content, when applied to the diverse religious landscape of America. Repeatedly, we have seen that there is no religious language we could construct for a school prayer that is truly nonpreferential, given the growing importance of polytheism and nontheistic religion—although a moment of silence, undirected, seems like a fine way to encourage thoughtfulness and to permit prayer. In the area of public displays, nonpreferentialism also offers no helpful guidance. As even Justice Scalia has asserted, "If religion in the public forum had to be entirely nondenominational, there could be no religion in the public forum at all."[84]

More recently, nonpreferentialism has faded and a different theory, noncoercion, has taken its place as the preferred conservative alternative to the endorsement theory. Noncoercion says that only a coercive religious exercise can cause an Establishment Clause problem. Coercion may be defined generously: in *Lee v. Weisman*, Justice Kennedy found "indirect coercion" in the graduation prayer. In *Allegheny*, apparently expressing the same sort of view, he said that the government may "endorse," but it may not "proselytize"—so extremely forceful persuasion counts, for him, apparently, as a forbidden type of coercion. Justice Scalia seems to go along with this view, drawing a sharp distinction between funding issues, where taxation is inherently coercive, and the public display issue, where there (he believes) is no coercion.[85]

The noncoercion approach is often linked to originalism in constitutional interpretation, and its proponents often defend it by pointing to the many religious observances of the founders. Their historical argument is not very convincing. The debate about establishment, already in several states before the Founding and ubiquitously thereafter, objected to state endorsement of a church, even when that was not coercive.[86] As time went on, as I have argued in Chapter 1, the classic objection to the practice of establishment took the Madisonian form of focusing on endorsement and equality, considerations that are not addressed by a noncoercive policy. Moreover, it seems difficult to tell a coherent story about what the Establishment Clause supplies over and above what is already implicit in the Free Exercise Clause. As Justice Souter said, this theory would make the Establishment Clause a "nullity," supplying nothing beyond the Free Exercise Clause.

Whatever one's views about history, however, what is amply clear is that the noncoercion theory has been explicitly rejected by a whole string of precedents, precisely on the grounds that it would leave no distinctive contribution to be made by the Establishment Clause. (In that sense, adopting the noncoercion policy is not all that different in consequence from denying the incorporation of the Establishment Clause while acknowledging the incorporation of the Free Exercise Clause. Both moves require the rejection of a long tradition of precedent. Justice Scalia's theory looks like a quieter version of Justice Thomas's theory.)

Noncoercion, then, is not supported by history or precedent. More importantly, it does no justice to underlying goals and purposes that our Constitution rightly seeks to protect. Indeed, it invites flagrant violation of those goals. Noncoercion does not require nonpreferentialism. People who support the noncoercion test can, and do, favor quite blatantly sectarian monuments and displays, on the grounds that these are not coercive. As for school prayer, although Justice Kennedy thinks that the school context creates a special danger of coercion, that view is not shared by the other proponents of the noncoercion theory, who are not bothered by requiring quite sectarian prayers. Most shocking of all is Justice Scalia's recent declaration, in his dissent in the Kentucky Ten Commandments case, that it is fine for public displays and observances to favor the three major monotheistic religions and to disfavor others. "[I]t is entirely clear from our Nation's historical practices that the Establishment clause permits [the] disregard of polytheists and believers in unconcerned deities, just as it permits the disregard of devout atheists."[87]

Justice Scalia goes on to say that such a large majority are monotheists that there is really no problem about doing this: "The three most popular religions in the United States, Christianity, Judaism, and Islam—which combined account for 97.7% of all believers—are monotheistic." He cites the *Statistical Abstract of the United States*, 2004–2005, table 67, citing the U.S. Bureau of the Census as the origin of the data and not mentioning that it is simply publishing these data and did not gather them through the techniques used in the census.[88] (In fact the census is forbidden to ask questions about religion, and these data come from a separate telephone survey of a relatively small number of adults selected at random.) When one looks at this table, one finds, first of all, that the data are based on a survey conducted only in the forty-eight continental states, and then projected out to the fractions of the *total* U.S. population. In other words, Hawaii and Alaska simply do not count, and one would expect to find in both of these states an unusually large proportion of non-Christians: Native Americans in Alaska; Buddhists, Hindus, and others in Hawaii. Second, the survey asks for self-described religious identification, and it finds, in fact, that a total of 19.6 percent of Americans either give no religious affiliation or refuse to reply to the question. Third, the category of Christians is highly capacious, including Mormons, Quakers, Mennonites, and many other dissidents, many of whom would find difficulty with a monument to a specific version of the Ten Commandments (in *Mc-Creary*, the Protestant version). The total number of "Christians," Jews, and Muslims makes up only 78.6 percent of the *total* American population. Finally, the number of Muslims is almost equaled by the number of Buddhists; Hindus, who count as fewer in this survey, taken in 2001, have become far more numerous since then. According to the reputable academic survey, "Self-Described Religious Identification of U.S. Adult Population," at http://www.gc.cuny.edu/faculty/research_briefs/aris/key_findings.htm, 79.8 percent of Americans in 2001 were self-described Christians, 1.4 percent were Jews, and 0.3 percent Muslims; 8.4 percent declared themselves no religion/atheist/agnostic. Unitarians and Buddhists were as numerous as Muslims. According to the survey at adherents.com, another reputable organization, 76.5 percent are Christian, 13.2 percent nonreligious, 1.3 percent Jews, 0.5 percent Muslims, 0.5 percent Buddhists, 0.4 percent Hindus, 0.3 percent Unitarians, 0.5 percent atheists, and 0.4 percent agnostics. In terms of rate of growth, the fastest-growing religion in the U.S. is Hinduism, followed by Buddhism and Islam; the Baha'i and Sikh religions and New Age religion also have very high growth rates. (Christianity shows a slight decline, Judaism a more marked decline.) So it seems that Justice Scalia's numbers need further scrutiny. He omits the large, and growing, number of Americans who do not state a religious affiliation; he ignores Hindus while including Muslims, who are no more numerous. Hindus and Buddhists, rapidly growing segments of American society, are very upset about some displays that denigrate them, and we can be sure that Justice Scalia's theory would not seem to them one that respects their equality. Even Muslims, Jews, and Roman Catholics, moreover, would not approve of the Protestant version of the commandments, which is the one in question here.

But let's not rely on the numbers. The U.S. has never been a pure majoritarian democracy. It has been one that puts certain fundamental rights off limits to the majoritarian political process, protecting them for all citizens, prominently including small and powerless minorities. Roger Williams understood that even when no Muslims lived in North America, it was important to affirm and protect their equality. The numbers matter to public perceptions, but they really shouldn't affect the rightness of the theoretical analysis. Equality is a good thing to insist on, even when nobody is complaining.

How should we resolve the difficult dilemma raised by public displays and observances in a nation with a long religious history? The cases, on the whole, do a good job of applying a reasonable equality framework to a complicated subject matter. But there is need for one more further theoretical step. Repeatedly the cases have recognized that some religious language in our tradition is so deeply embedded and so relatively minor that we should not view it as constituting a constitutional violation. Examples are given, such as the use of chaplains in the U.S. Senate and the use of "In God We Trust" on our currency. But no criteria have been offered to help us decide when such references to God constitute an impermissible endorsement and when they do not.

In her opinion in the Pledge of Allegiance case, Justice O'Connor takes this further step—her last distinguished contribution to the theorizing of the Establishment Clause.[89] The case was never resolved, because a majority held that the plaintiff, Newdow, did not have standing to bring the case, since his custody of his minor daughter was disputed. Three of the Justices did, however, offer their own reasoning on the merits, and the new tests for permissibility appear in Justice O'Connor's opinion. I shall examine her application of her own theory to the pledge later, in Chapter 8. What concerns me here is the theoretical contribution.

Justice O'Connor makes it clear that this is not a theory of *de minimis* violations, violations too small for us to be worried about them. There are, she rightly says, no *de minimis* violations where fundamental constitutional rights are at issue. There are, however, cases in which the religious reference or language does not rise to the level of a violation. The reasonable objective observer, knowing the relevant facts of history, would rightly see these references as using religious language "for essentially secular purposes. One such purpose is to commemorate the role of religion in our history." This is what the Court has repeatedly called "ceremonial deism." She insists that we have to stick to the "objective" or "reasonable observer" test, because there is no reference to religion that won't offend someone somewhere, and we can't allow a "heckler's veto" to determine our constitutional rights.

Four criteria are suggested as good things to look for when we ask about traditional religious language. The first is *history and ubiquity*: how old is the reference, how well embedded in tradition, and how widespread? A reference is part of "ceremonial deism" when it has been in place for "a significant portion of the Nation's history" and when "it is observed by enough persons that it can fairly be called ubiquitous." The second is *absence of worship or prayer*: the observance should not demand that people join in an act of worship. The third criterion is *absence of reference to particular religion*. Here Justice O'Connor has difficulty delineating the criterion, since she recognizes that reference to "God" does refer to some religions and not others: she mentions Buddhism in particular. But she believes that a generic reference to God, when traditional from a time in history "when our national religious diversity was neither as robust nor as well recognized as it is now," can still be constitutional. The final criterion is *minimal religious content*. The reference should be "highly circumscribed," so that people who want to avoid it can easily do so.

These criteria are not the final word on this important question. They need more work, and they leave a lot of work yet to be done by wise practical reason. Nonetheless, they are extremely helpful in structuring a vague and unstructured terrain. No Justice has ever held that all references to God in our public life are unconstitutional. Even those who have been most attached to the language of church-state separation have at the same time insisted that some traditional references, of the sort mentioned by Justice O'Connor, are constitutional. But the absence of criteria has led the tradition to flounder here, giving rise to the perception that the Court really wants to uproot such references entirely from our public life.

As Justice O'Connor says, there are no constitutional violations too small to notice. There is no such thing as an injustice that is small; there are only injustices that affect a small number of people, a very different matter. Justice Scalia's most radical departure from our constitutional understanding is his suggestion that if the numbers are small, we needn't worry about exclusionary language. Oddly, Justice Breyer, usually understood to be part of the Court's "liberal wing," comes by a different route to what looks like a similar conclusion, in his insistence that the threat of violence is key to finding a constitutional violation.

Our tradition has always been a minority-respecting and minority-protecting one, in theory at least, if not always in fact. That means that a religious display or observance that a reasonable objective observer, aware of the role now played in our public life by Hinduism, Buddhism, and nonreligious people, finds demeaning and offensive is not small because the numbers of such people are (relatively) small. The question Justice O'Connor helps us press, however, is whether this reasonable observer would zealously prune all traditional references from our public life. To that question she cautiously answers "no," with helpful arguments. In Chapter 8 I shall return to this question, giving my own (very similar) answer.

7

AID TO SECTARIAN SCHOOLS

The Search for Fairness

There is no doubt that the parochial school, whatever may be its virtues, is the most important divisive instrument in the life of American children.

PAUL BLANSHARD, *American Freedom and Catholic Power* (1949)

[W]e must be careful, in protecting the citizens of New Jersey against state-established churches, to be sure that we do not inadvertently prohibit New Jersey from extending its general state law benefits to all its citizens without regard to their religious belief.

JUSTICE BLACK, *Everson v. Board of Education* (1947)

I. Parochial Schools: A Climate of Suspicion

Should tax money be used to assist sectarian schools? This issue looks easier to resolve than the issues of public religious displays and school prayer, because there is no doubt that taxation is coercive. Moreover, the issue of using tax money to support religion was one that the founders had exhaustively debated, leaving a clear record. We might, then, expect less divisiveness over the funding question than over our other two issues, which have a thinner historical track record and which do not always raise the issue of coercion. In a sense this has been true: a theoretical framework based on the idea of fairness has proven dominant in this area from 1947 until the present day, supplemented with other principles. Nonetheless, the search for fairness has proven unusually difficult, in part because an additional principle, the principle of separation of church and state as an end in itself, has muddied the waters, clouding analysis based upon the equality principle. At one point, in the 1980s, the Court's decisions showed such dedication to the value of separation that they appeared to compromise fairness. A more balanced and equitable view has gradually prevailed in recent years, though not without continued controversy.

Our last chapter identified a threat to the equality tradition from the religious right. Most of the controversial proponents of school prayer and religious displays were conservative Christians; the Justices who support some of their demands today are identified with conservative Christian values. The funding issue is very different. Opposition to a balanced centrist view on aid to parochial schools in the 1940s and after has come primarily from an anti-Catholic left, which has used the rhetoric of separation to defend an almost total exclusion of the parochial schools from the mantle of state protection. Even though today the anti-Catholicism that once swept over America has receded and has no defenders, as such, on the Court, the attachment to separation that the "new nativism" introduced still complicates the Court's thinking about the fairness principle. Distinguished left-wing thinkers such as John Dewey, Paul Blanshard, and Bertrand Russell, and left-wing journals such as *The Nation* and *The New Republic* (which was on the left at that time), did the legal tradition some harm by nourishing public suspicion of the "Americanness" of all Catholics, and of the parochial schools in particular.

A structural difference between the two sets of issues helps to explain this political difference. The issue typically raised by school prayer and public displays is the protection of individual conscience from a traditional establishment that, by endorsing the religion of the majority, sends a message of inequality. Liberals are typically protective of individual minorities in such circumstances. The issue of funding for the parochial schools, by contrast, involved, in the eyes of liberals, a huge global bureaucracy, the Catholic Church, which many saw as authoritarian and repressive. This power was suspected of trying to subvert the rights and liberties that Americans hold dear. In such circumstances, protecting the freedom and equality of individuals seemed to many to require preventing the Catholic Church from gaining dominance in American public life. Liberals who would fight for the equal rights of minority children in the public schools could be extremely punitive when it came to giving any public benefit to the parochial schools, which were seen as cradles of despotism.

Interestingly, and revealingly, despite the existence of a strong parallel movement to establish Jewish schools, which continues today, Jews were not singled out when people expressed opposition to the government funding of parochial schools. There are several reasons for the asymmetry. First and most important were the numbers: there never have been very many Jews in America, and Reform Jews, the largest group within that small number, have not on the whole sought alternatives to the public school system. Many Conservative Jews do not either. The very small numbers of children who attend Jewish schools have never seemed to Americans to pose a serious threat to public education, all the more since these schools do not form a system and are in that sense more like secular private schools. Second, Jews have rarely been major proponents of public funding, because Jews have typically seen the principle of separation of church and state as one that protects them. These reasons explain a good deal. The fear of Roman Catholics as a potentially destructive force in American politics, however, must be added as a third reason.

Anti-Catholic nativism, which had flowered between 1850 and 1880, had a second rebirth after World War I, a time when massive immigration was, once again, altering the face of American political life. The new nativism was not a populist anti-immigration movement like the old nativism. Its leaders were intellectual elites, particularly on the left. Philosopher John Dewey studied the Polish community of Philadelphia during the war; his graduate students wrote a report that stressed Polish Catholics' unquestioning obedience to a corrupt Catholic hierarchy.[1] Prominent Yale philosopher Brand Blanshard, who worked with Dewey's team while a graduate student, wrote a damning report about Catholic culture, saying: "It is a world which is simply not our world, a world in which independent criticism and disinterested science is and must remain unknown, a world which still abounds with the primitive concepts and fancies of the middle ages."[2] Such views were common, especially during Catholic Al Smith's doomed run for the presidency. A 1927 editorial in *The New Republic* spoke in language both alarmist and Deweyesque of a conflict, in America, between a culture "which is based on absolutism and encourages obedience, uniformity and intellectual subservience, and a culture which encourages curiosity, hypotheses, experimentation, verification by facts. . . ."[3]

Soon the alarm had a real target, since many Catholic bishops in the U.S. openly favored the rise of fascism in Italy and Spain, spoke in glowing terms of Mussolini's achievements, praised Franco, and failed to deplore fascist attacks on liberty. The popular "radio priest" Father Charles Coughlin, who used his program to fan the flames of anti-Semitism in the 1930s, became a handy symbol of what many Americans feared. (The Catholic hierarchy did not repudiate anti-Semitism until very recently, a particular achievement of the late Pope John Paul II.) It was all too easy to pin blame for the fascist leanings of leading prelates on the religion itself—despite the fact that Catholic intellectuals also played a prominent role on the side of antifascist liberalism. Philosopher Jacques Maritain, one of the leading drafters of the Universal Declaration of Human Rights, worked closely with Eleanor Roosevelt in that cause.[4] He also consistently defended the idea that Catholics should live alongside others on a basis of respect for pluralism and the related idea that the public political principles of a nation should be moral propositions that all the major doctrines could endorse. His ideas about religion and society are important antecedents of the view of liberal philosopher John Rawls, and we might also add that they resemble in many ways the views of Roger Williams.[5] Jesuit intellectual John Courtney Murray, who later became one of the leading architects of Vatican II, wrote strongly worded attacks on authoritarian and fascist currents within the church and defended the essential "Americanness" and liberalism of Catholic values.[6] So, while liberal intellectuals had some serious issues to worry about, they did not have good reason to impute fascist tendencies to Catholicism as a whole. (Indeed, the growing acceptance of Roman Catholics as equal citizens within modern democracies was itself a major factor in the gradual liberalization of the Church, and American Catholics in particular were a major force behind Vatican II.)

At the same time, controversies over public morality pitted liberal American academics against members of the Catholic hierarchy on issues of censorship and academic freedom. When Bertrand Russell was fired from City College in 1940 for his views on sexuality and marriage, he attributed his situation, plausibly, to Catholic political influence, including attacks on his "irreligious viewpoint" in leading Catholic periodicals and by Archbishop Francis Spellman.[7] Other religious leaders were also involved: indeed, Russell's primary opponent was an Anglican. On the other hand, more liberal Catholic prelates and intellectuals did not rise to Russell's defense. It was not unreasonable, then, for liberals to worry about the power of the Catholic hierarchy in American political life, and to think that the parochial schools might nourish pro-censorship attitudes. Many thoughtful people concluded: if the Supreme Court had said that sectarian schools must be permitted to exist, at least we could deny them even the smallest amount of public assistance.

In the wake of World War II, these anxieties did not diminish. One of the most influential books of the postwar period was *American Freedom and Catholic Power* by journalist Paul Blanshard, an editor of *The Nation* and a former philosophy graduate student of John Dewey (along with his twin brother Brand).[8] First published as a series of articles in *The Nation*, the book eventually sold 300,000 copies and was widely praised by liberal intellectuals, including Dewey, Russell, and Albert Einstein. A blistering indictment of the church and its fundamentally antidemocratic values, the book repeatedly reassures its liberal readers that its arguments are not linked to the bad prejudiced nativism of the past: Blanshard is purveying not hateful bigotry, but sound rational argument. But then repeatedly, in an ingenious rhetorical turnaround, Blanshard says, but after all, those people, however bad their motives, did get it right about the objectionable features of the Catholic hierarchy. "In fact," goes a typical passage, "the bigoted character of the source has tended to divert attention from a valid and important question."[9] So liberals, Blanshard repeatedly suggests, can feel good about their anti-Catholic fears, seeing them as the fruit not of yesterday's bigotry, but of today's clear-eyed reason. Under cover of this calm rational manner, the book purveys all the familiar tropes of anti-Catholicism. It dwells on the (allegedly) weird life of nuns, with their "unhygienic costumes and their medieval rules of conduct";[10] it stresses the stifling of their erotic instincts and an "attitude of piety and feminine subordination that seems utterly alien to the typically robust and independent spirit of American womanhood."[11] Much emphasis is also given to population growth among Catholics, as Blanshard contends that Catholics are "outbreeding" Protestants, particularly in the lower (and therefore allegedly more docile) classes. (Population panics have long been a device used by majorities to kindle suspicion of minorities.[12] They are common today in Europe, expressing many people's fear of a Muslim takeover.) And all of this is seen as part of a sinister "plan" that will end in the replacement of our Constitution by a new Catholic constitution. Blanshard imagines this text and gives us its first three articles, each with six to eight subsections. It will declare the U.S. a Catholic nation, put all education in the entire nation under the direction of the Catholic Church, replace current marriage laws by the Canon Law of the Catholic Church, and remove the First Amendment in its entirety. This "plan," he argues, is well advanced, thanks in large part to the existence of the parochial schools. "The Catholic hierarchy proposes to realize the Catholic plan for America by maintaining and increasing the present Catholic population, by expanding the Catholic schools with the aid of public money, and by infiltrating and penetrating non-Catholic organizations with faithful Catholic laymen who will act as consecrated missionaries for the Church."[13]

It is remarkable that Blanshard, a leading public intellectual, seems utterly unfamiliar with liberal Catholicism, as exemplified in the work of Maritain and Murray, but also in the leadership of figures such as Father Hesburgh at the University of Notre Dame. It is even more remarkable that he seems utterly ignorant of the long history of Roman Catholic thought, with its profound attachment to rational argument, its commitment to the teaching of critical thinking and debate. While some parts of Protestantism might justly be thought antireason, or interested in exalting faith above the use of the critical faculties, that charge cannot be made against Roman Catholicism, which consistently stresses the importance of developing one's own rational powers to the utmost *as a necessary element of a good religious life*. One can see this commitment in the curricular requirements of Catholic schools and colleges, which stress philosophy *in addition to and separately from theology*, and which consistently show respect for modern science. It seems very odd that someone initially trained in philosophy should appear to know nothing about Thomas Aquinas and his role in the Catholic tradition—but for the fact that (probably as a result of pervasive anti-Catholicism) the thought of Aquinas was rarely taught in philosophy departments of that era, and history of philosophy courses typically leapt from Aristotle, in the fourth century BCE, to

Descartes, in the seventeenth century CE. (Albeit a Catholic, Descartes rejected much in the Catholic philosophical tradition and began the alliance of philosophy with modern science of which Dewey was an heir. This skewed version of philosophy's history still dominates.)

Another large gap in Blanshard's knowledge is his apparent ignorance of Catholic education around the world. The Roman Catholic Church has been distinguished for many centuries, in many nations, for its commitment to educating poor children, both male and female. In India, most of the private schools are run by the Catholic Church, and these are usually, even now, of higher quality than the government schools. In the coastal state of Kerala, which had earlier contact with Roman Catholicism than most regions on account of the visits of Jesuit missionaries in the seventeenth century, the unparalleled literacy rate (99 percent in adolescents, both male and female, compared to a national average of 65 percent for males and 50 percent for females in all age groups) can be attributed, at least in part, to that state's Catholic tradition. More generally, in a national education system dominated by rote learning, the Catholic schools are the places where one would be most likely to be encouraged to think independently. So Blanshard's picture of Catholic education as a tool of despotic control was not supported, and could not have been supported, by any serious look at Catholic education in the various places where it has flourished. Nor do the Catholic schools of India proselytize. By all accounts I have heard from colleagues who attended such schools, the Catholic component is modest, and respect is shown for other religions. The Catholic Church has also often played a respectful role socially, intervening in religious violence between Hindus and Muslims and providing aid to victims of this violence. Blanshard mentions none of this.

Blanshard's recommendations for frustrating the Catholic "plan" for America focus on the role of the parochial schools, which he sees as places of mindless conformity, where impressionable young people learn not to think for themselves, and where nuns, ill educated and utterly controlled by the church, exemplify a medieval picture of women as "enjoy[ing] subjection and revel[ing] in self-abasement."[14] Frustrating Catholic efforts to secure public funding for these schools is essential, he argues, to the preservation of a free America. (Blanshard's next book, *Communism, Democracy, and Catholic Power*, argued that Stalinism and Catholicism were parallel and similar threats to the American democracy.[15]) He recommends confrontation and escalation as the only course that will preserve "basic liberties": "There are times when the highest duty of a citizen is to increase the tensions between social groups temporarily until the threat of the triumph of reactionary policies is past."[16]

The fear of a fascist or totalitarian takeover was intense at the time, and Blanshard's book influenced many political leaders, including Eleanor Roosevelt, who energized the opposition to a bill providing federal funding for the parochial schools for busing and other services; the bill was defeated in 1949.[17] It was not without reason that liberal Catholic theologian John Courtney Murray wrote about Blanshard's book as a leading example of the new nativism.[18] Murray assails Blanshard's monolithic and misleading picture of Catholic values. He then plausibly argues that Blanshard wishes to deny Americanness to any group who does not favor a secular attitude to life as the best one for democracy. (Blanshard once said that "any honest man" should repudiate religion altogether and become an atheist.[19])

In Chapter 5, we saw how the first flowering of American nativism, from 1850 to 1880, was connected to an early move to forbid the use of public money for religious institutions, in the Blaine Amendment and related proposals that sought to introduce the phrase "separation of church and state" into the Constitution. Separationist rhetoric expressed nativist zeal—though, as time went on, was also used to express more laudable equality values. In the post–World War II period, the new nativism also used "separation of church and state" like a mantra, and focused once again on the issue of funding, which seemed to liberals like an attempt by the church (a foreign power) to hijack the political process, forcing Americans to support an anti-American ideology.

The liberal thinkers who led the charge against school funding were conscientious citizens, deeply attached to America's traditions and values. They had some legitimate worries about the Catholic hierarchy. And yet, they painted with much too broad a brush, criticizing an entire religion and all its institutions and members, rather than criticizing particular individuals and trends. They were able to get away with this because they exploited the residual distaste that many elite Protestant Americans still felt at that time for people from Southern and Eastern Europe. Somehow, anti-Catholicism was one prejudice that it was all right to own in polite circles. Humor that would be totally repugnant were it directed against Jews or African-Americans was— and often still is—acceptable when it targets all Catholics as such. (Consider

Tom Lehrer's controversial song "The Vatican Rag," from 1965, which makes fun of the Mass, the confessional, and much else, under the pretext of criticizing herdlike obedience. I found this a very funny song, as did all my friends in college.)

The liberal attacks on Catholicism did not simply attack too broadly. John Courtney Murray was basically right when he said that these elites had distaste for the whole idea that God is supreme in human affairs. Dewey, Blanshard, and Russell were all atheist/humanists, who felt that religion itself was reactionary and that America's future required a secular scientific attitude that renounced all church authority, whether in public or in personal life. It's one thing to say that the Catholic Church should not presume to speak for all citizens of a pluralistic society, or to impose its own dogmas on people of other faiths in the public square. The liberal elite, however, did not simply say that. They really were saying (or, at least, many of them were saying) that we would like an America where people do not plan their lives around religious goals and ends, especially as mediated by church leaders. For them "separation of church and state" did not simply mean, let's be fair to all our citizens. It meant, let's keep this primitive medieval force at arm's length and allow it to have as little influence as possible over our common life. Separation, then, remained linked to a type of unfairness, or at least a tendency to unfairness. It didn't feel like that, since challenging the Pope felt very different from challenging Ellory Schempp or Chioke Jaffree. It felt like protecting the little guy (the "average American") from the bullying behavior of the big guy. But of course children in parochial schools are not powerful bureaucrats, and it was their future that was at issue. Catholic parents felt that the denial of all public benefits was an injustice to their children. The American majority tended to ignore that claim, in favor of focusing on the alleged danger of Catholicism for America. As John Courtney Murray wrote:

> When a large section of the community asserts that injustice is being done, and makes a reasonable argument to substantiate the assertion, either the argument ought to be convincingly refuted and the claim of injustice thus disposed of, or the validity of the argument ought to be admitted and the injustice remedied. As a matter of fact, however, the argument customarily meets a blank stare, or else [is answered by saying, in effect]: "We might be willing to listen to this argument about the rights of

Catholic schools if we believed that Catholic schools had any rights at all. But we do not grant that they have any rights, except to tolerance. Their existence is not for the advantage of the public; they offend against the integrity of the democratic community. . . ."[20]

That such a description of the state of the question could be written by one of the most thoughtful liberal intellectuals of the time shows how polarized the nation was, and how difficult it would very likely be to think well about what fairness to all citizens requires.

II. The Basic Principle: Neutrality as Fairness

In 1941 the state of New Jersey passed a law authorizing local boards of education to contract with carriers to provide transportation for schoolchildren.[21] They were required by law to give this money to all children attending any not-for-profit school. One local township did this through an arrangement with the local public transportation system: the rides of children on their way to and from school would be free of charge (parents would be reimbursed). A taxpayer sued, on the grounds that money raised through taxation was used to support the transportation of Catholic children to the parochial schools. (Nobody challenged the exclusion of children attending for-profit private schools, and that issue was not addressed, although the Court drew attention to it as a legitimate question.) The claim was that the law violated the Due Process Clause of the Fourteenth Amendment by taking citizens' property for a private purpose, and that it violated the Establishment Clause by using state power to support church schools. On both grounds, the Supreme Court found the law constitutional, though by a 5–4 vote: from the beginning, these funding cases are contested in a way that, initially, the prayer cases were not. I shall focus on the Establishment Clause argument.

The Establishment Clause, unlike the Free Exercise Clause, had not yet been formally declared to be incorporated, so that issue is addressed first. Justice Black reviews the history of opposition to religious establishment, focusing on the Virginia experience; he makes it clear that the prevailing view was that opposition to religious funding was necessary to protect complete and equal religious liberty. The Free Exercise and Establishment Clauses are "complementary,"[22] and both should be seen as applied to the states by the

Fourteenth Amendment. Justice Black now offers a famous and influential account of what the Establishment Clause means:

> The "establishment of religion" clause of the First Amendment means at least this: Neither a state nor the Federal Government can set up a church. Neither can pass laws which aid one religion, aid all religions, or prefer one religion to another. Neither can force nor influence a person to go to or to remain away from church against his will or force him to profess a belief or disbelief in any religion. No person can be punished for entertaining or professing religious beliefs or disbeliefs, for church attendance or nonattendance. No tax in any amount, large or small, can be levied to support any religious activities or institutions, whatever they may be called, or whatever form they may adopt to teach or practice religion. Neither a state nor the Federal Government can, openly or secretly, participate in the affairs of any religious organizations or groups and *vice versa*. In the words of Jefferson, the clause against establishment of religion by law was intended to erect "a wall of separation between church and State."[23]

Notice, then, that, whatever one thinks about the original meaning of the Establishment Clause, both at its founding and at the time of the Fourteenth Amendment, the first opinion that declares the clause incorporated, in 1947, explicitly understands the clause as a guarantor of various individual liberties. Nonpreferentialism is also denied: the clause, Justice Black writes, forbids the government to prefer religion to nonreligion.

Justice Black is fond of the language of separation—both in this passage and in the concluding paragraph of the opinion, which insists that "[t]hat wall must be kept high and impregnable."[24] Nonetheless, his actual reasoning about the New Jersey law depends on a neutrality/fairness principle, not on a mechanical application of the idea of separation. New Jersey cannot support religion, he writes, but it also is forbidden by the clause to "exclude individual Catholics, Lutherans, Mohammedans, Baptists, Jews, Methodists, Nonbelievers, Presbyterians, or the members of any other faith, *because of their faith, or lack of it*, from receiving the benefits of public welfare legislation." The opinion analyzes the fairness issue in a way that recalls analyses we have encountered under the Free Exercise Clause: a state cannot condition public benefits on a person's religious identity. Care must certainly be taken to protect New Jersey citizens against state-established churches, but care must also be taken "to be sure that we do not inadvertently prohibit New Jersey from extending its general state law benefits to all its citizens without regard to their religious belief."[25]

Justice Black now departs utterly (and wisely) from the separationist norm, when he observes that it would be utterly absurd to hold that the Establishment Clause requires the state to deny religious schools "ordinary police and fire protection, connections for sewage disposal, public highways and sidewalks."[26] Even crossing guards for student safety seem part of what the state can and should provide on a basis of equality to all. The First Amendment "requires the state to be a neutral in its relations with groups of religious believers and nonbelievers; it does not require the state to be their adversary. State power is no more to be used so as to handicap religions than it is to favor them."[27]

Justice Black now argues that the transportation funding provision is like these basic services, and not like state aid to religion, because it is given to citizens to help their children get to school, "regardless of their religion." The state is not paying money directly to the religious school; it is giving it to all parents, without discrimination, and the parents then choose the school. Here we glimpse two subsidiary principles that will later prove very valuable in applying the neutrality/equality framework to concrete cases: the principle of indirect aid (the money goes to individuals, not to the school), and the related principle of choice (the parents choose, as they are always entitled to do, where their children may go to school, and the money simply enables that free choice).

Why did Justice Black combine the reasoning he actually used (the neutrality/equality framework, combined with a focus on choice and indirection) with repeated assertions of the separation principle? These assertions muddy the waters, enabling the dissenters to claim with some plausibility that he has misapplied his own framework, since he doesn't come down in favor of what separation, as a value on its own, would seem to require. As far as I can see, the separation language does no argumentative work in the opinion; it is mentioned rather like a *mantra* that is expected to make the opinion rhetorically acceptable.

Acceptable to whom? Justice Black was once a member of the Ku Klux Klan. Philip Hamburger has shown that Black actively participated in Klan activities, including some anti-Catholic activities,[28] and that the Klan gave him important backing in his early political campaigns. Clearly in this early period Black did use the language of separation to indicate anti-Catholic sentiments. Hamburger contends that by the time of *Everson*, Black's views had not changed, but his tactics had. Hamburger's account of the *Everson* opinion ascribes to Black a truly Machiavellian strategy. Black's real aim, Hamburger argues, was to get the Court to agree that "the separation of church and state" was the right principle to apply to such cases, since that would ultimately further his anti-Catholic ends. Knowing that he could not announce those ends publicly, however, he craftily planned to insert the separation theory in a case in which he would "reach a judgment that would undercut Catholic criticism. Black expected that his disarming conclusion would lead Catholics to think that they had succeeded in staving off the practical consequences of separation."[29] Hamburger presents no evidence for such devious intentions, and imputing such motives to a Justice whose service was long and honorable seems inappropriate without such evidence. In any case, Hamburger's argument is unconvincing, given Black's consistent thoughtfulness and impartiality on the whole range of church-state issues—including his role in striking down Protestant prayer in the school prayer cases, where he always joined the majority—and, in *Engel*, wrote the majority opinion that influenced all subsequent arguments in the area. In general, Hamburger is too ready to move from the true claim that separation language was often linked to anti-Catholicism to the false claim that anyone who uses this language is using it for (overt or covert) anti-Catholic purposes. Moreover, Hamburger simply neglects the fact that Black's actual argument in *Everson* does not use the idea of separation, but, instead, the idea of neutrality. Separation language is merely decorative. It is Justice Rutledge's dissenting opinion that really relies on separation as an interpretive theory.

What seems more plausible is that Black argued the case as he thought it best to argue it on the merits, using the idea of neutrality/equality, the idea that he found uppermost in his reading of the Madisonian history—but the phrase "separation of church and state" still attracted him, and he still wanted to use it, whether just because he liked it or also because he had a large audience that would expect him to use it. The language spins like an idle wheel, and so one could hardly see Black as foisting a bad analytical framework on the Court, since it isn't an analytical framework at all. What one might say, however, is that his words gave encouragement to those who did want to use separation as an independent analytical framework, and that this, over the years, has done damage to analysis.

The *Everson* dissenters neglect the neutrality idea and focus on separation, so their analysis does not really match up with Black's analysis in the majority opinion. They do, however, ask some good questions about the facts. The transportation program, they insist, is not quite like the sewer and police examples, because, without it, the Catholic children would still get to school just as safely, and on the very same public buses. They would simply have to pay for their rides. So it would appear, they argue, that the state is giving financial support to the project of getting them to the parochial school, rather than just making available a safety-related service.

This is not a compelling argument, however, because it neglects the fact that a public benefit cannot constitutionally be conditioned on religious membership. Now of course they can always say that the public schools are open to all children, so it is only the choice to attend a parochial school that is being penalized. But the choice to send one's children to a parochial school is a deep part of many Catholic parents' religious commitments, and it is a constitutionally protected choice. At that time, moreover, the Protestant nature of the public schools had caused the church to instruct all Catholic parents to send their children to parochial schools; doing so, then, was an important part of fulfilling one's religious commitments. So it does seem that conditioning the transportation benefit on a decision not to attend parochial school is comparable to denying Mrs. Sherbert her unemployment compensation because she observed her religion conscientiously. Here's where the Free Exercise Clause and the Establishment Clause touch hands, with equality the connecting link. Nobody is saying that the Establishment Clause *requires* New Jersey's program, so the Establishment Clause analysis is not the same as the Free Exercise analysis in *Sherbert*. Similar values, however, are involved. The case is not totally obvious, and competent judges, applying Black's neutrality standard, could differ on the merits. The dissenters, however, got carried away with the idea of separation and failed to ask the most pertinent questions.

III. The Search for Separation

Everson announced a neutrality principle. It also implicitly acknowledged that this principle is not sufficient, but must be supplemented with other considerations, for example the directness/indirectness of the aid, and the issue of choice. What would have been very good would have been to elaborate these criteria further, gaining a progressively clearer analytical vantage point for the resolution of difficult school funding cases. This, however, did not happen. The neutrality principle did get a welcome further development in other areas of law, especially in *Walz v. Tax Commission*,[30] where the Court upheld the constitutionality of the New York policy of exempting from taxation a broad group of nonprofit organizations, including churches. The Court held that it was important that the benefit went to a broad class of institutions that included both the religious and the nonreligious, the suggestion being that the exemption treated them all equally, favoring neither the religious nor the secular members of the group. (In a later case concerning a Texas tax exemption for religious periodicals, the program was declared unconstitutional because only religious magazines got the benefit, but the Court suggested that it might have been all right had there been some neutral classification by subject matter—for example, ideas about the meaning of life—and all religious and nonreligious periodicals addressing that topic had received the exemption.[31]) So neutrality as fairness to both religion and nonreligion did not disappear from the Court's concern with funding. In the fraught area of aid to sectarian schools, however, the idea of separation virtually took over, leading to results that seemed in some cases quite unfair to individual children, until the position of Justice Rutledge in *Everson*, rather than the nuanced position of Justice Black, more or less carried the day.

Trouble began with *Lemon v. Kurtzman* in 1971.[32] This case is famous for its articulation of the influential "*Lemon* test," which became the analytical framework for a whole generation of analysis. This "test," as we've seen, was not new: two-thirds of it was taken verbatim from the *Schempp* decision. It was the new third part that was going to do damage.

First, the statute must have a secular legislative purpose; second, its principal or primary effect must be one that neither advances nor inhibits religion; finally, the statute must not foster "an excessive government entanglement with religion."[33]

The "entanglement" prong, as the quotation marks show, was not strictly new: it had been mentioned in *Walz*. It was, however, new to the school issues, and it imported, in effect, the separationist norm that Justice Rutledge, but not Justice Black, favored as an analytical key in *Everson*. The "secular purpose" and "secular effect" prongs work well in the context of thinking about schools and school aid, especially when further articulated, as they later were, in terms of Justice O'Connor's endorsement test. "Entanglement," however, is a very vague standard, given the ubiquity of government in modern life. It suggests, at least, that it can only be satisfied by the sort of relentless exclusion of religious institutions from all public benefits that *Everson* disfavored.

The *Lemon* test was never meant by its author, Justice Burger, to be used in a mechanical way. Indeed, he stressed that "[o]ur prior holdings do not call for total separation between church and state; total separation is not possible in an absolute sense . . . Judicial caveats against entanglement must recognize that the line of separation, far from being a 'wall,' is a blurred, indistinct, and variable barrier depending on all the circumstances of a particular relationship." Nor did the case itself generate division on the Court: all agreed that the programs in question in the case, in which the states of Rhode Island and Pennsylvania directly subsidized a portion of the salaries of teachers in sectarian schools, were badly designed and would lead to no end of trouble. Because the entanglement prong had been introduced, however, analysis became lazy, falling back on that alone and not inquiring further into the issue of neutrality and the related issues of directness and choice (though directness was at least mentioned in Justice Brennan's concurring opinion). We end up having no clear idea what "excessive entanglement" is, and this would lead to real problems in cases where the program in question was more sensibly designed.

By 1984, the separationist position of Justice Rutledge had virtually (if temporarily) triumphed over the more sensible position of Justice Black. Two cases decided in that year, *School District of Grand Rapids v. Ball*[34] and *Aguilar v. Felton*,[35] marked the high-water mark of the Court's commitment to separationism in school funding. Because it was the latter that was later overruled, and because its facts were much more persuasive, truly dividing the Court even at that time, I shall focus on the latter.

New York City was using some federal funds it received under a Title I program to pay the salaries of teachers expert in remedial reading and mathematics who moved from school to school in the city offering instruction in these subjects—including some instruction on the premises of parochial schools. The program focused on low-income children who were also educationally deprived, recognizing that "poor academic performance by disadvantaged children is part of the cycle of poverty."[36] Instruction was offered on parochial school premises only after other strategies for reaching those students, for example offering the remedial instruction at the nearest public school, had been tried and found unsuccessful.[37] In many cities it was logistically feasible to transport the children to public school premises, but in the case of some 20,000 children, that was not feasible.[38] There had been no complaints alleging that the teachers were indoctrinating the students with religious ideas and values. By a vote of 5–4, the program was declared unconstitutional. Justice Brennan, writing for the Court, was joined by Justices Marshall, Blackmun, Powell, and Stevens; Justices Burger, White, Rehnquist, and O'Connor dissented.

The Court did not deny that the program had a legitimate secular purpose; it did not even conclude clearly that the primary *effect* was the advancement of religion, although doubts were expressed in this area. Under the prong of "excessive entanglement," however, the program was struck down. Three worries were expressed. First, there might be subtle indoctrination after all, and this could be avoided only by constant monitoring that would create the problem of state control over religious institutions. Second, the use of state money for instruction within the premises of a religious institution created a "symbolic union" of church and state. Third, by relieving the parochial schools of budgetary responsibility for remedial education, it indirectly helped them offer religious instruction.[39]

As all the dissenting Justices argue, the issue of indoctrination is a very weak one, because the money subsidized a type of technical remedial training to which religious instruction would be utterly irrelevant, and because the teachers, expert in that technical area, move from school to school, regardless of personal religious affiliation. Experience, moreover, had shown that this problem did not arise.[40] Indeed, as Justice O'Connor observes, if there is such a great danger of religious indoctrination in this case, this danger must exist in any case where teachers who have personal religious beliefs teach in any school, since they can always introduce their beliefs. If these programs require constant monitoring, as the Court insists, then probably all schools require monitoring all the time. And, as Justice Rehnquist insists, this creates an impossible "catch-22" for all such programs: either they will not include monitoring, which is held to pose a danger of religious indoctrination, or they will have it—creating, in the majority's view, an impermissible intrusion of the state into people's religious lives and practices.[41]

The "symbolic union" of church and state, a concept articulated by Justice Brennan with reference to Justice O'Connor's "endorsement test," is a much more serious worry: if the state is seen to foster the parochial schools, this may create an impermissible endorsement. However, in this case, where the state simply announces that it will subsidize remedial reading and math education for all low-income children with educational problems, it does not seem likely that this danger would prove real. (Other programs, such as the one at issue in *Lemon*, really did have this problem.) Justice O'Connor concludes that the "objective observer" would say that the actual and perceived effect of the program is that "impoverished schoolchildren are being helped to overcome learning deficits, improving their test scores, and receiving a significant boost in their struggle to obtain both a thorough education and the opportunities that flow from it." Had the majority relied on the endorsement test rather than the vague "entanglement" criterion, it would have been difficult to find the program constitutionally flawed.

Even the relief of funds that could then be used for religious purposes, an apparently more plausible argument, is a "tenuous" effect at best, given that Title I provides that funds may be used only "to provide services that otherwise would not be available to the participating students."[42] In other words, what would happen without Title I is that needy children would simply not receive intensive remedial instruction.[43]

Recognizing the weakness of any claim of impermissible effect, the Court relied entirely on the entanglement idea. As Justice O'Connor convincingly argues in her dissenting opinion, this prong creates confusion and can lead to the invalidation of programs that are perfectly defensible. The "entanglement" standard is inherently very vague, and it had not been developed in a coherent way. And yet, in this case it was used to invalidate a program with a long track record of success and with no complaints lodged against it that could be countenanced under the other two prongs, as articulated through the endorsement test. For the 20,000 children whose opportunities are affected, "the Court's decision is tragic. The Court deprives them of a program that offers a meaningful chance at success in life, and it does so on the untenable theory that public school teachers (most of whom are of different faiths than their students) are likely to start teaching religion merely because they have walked across the threshold of a parochial school."[44]

Justice Brennan was a very distinguished jurist, and he clearly did not harbor the sort of anti-Catholic bias that animated many people who spoke on the issue. Indeed at that time, and for some time before and after, he was the only Catholic on the Supreme Court, a factor that might possibly have led him to bend over backward not to appear to show any undue favor to the parochial schools (which he himself did not attend). His unfortunate reliance on a separationist principle, however, did lead to an unduly inquisitorial attitude to instruction in the parochial schools and, thence, to the invalidation of a type of aid that may be extremely valuable for society's most vulnerable children. The aid probably could have been defended as constitutional using *Everson*'s neutrality criterion, supplemented with some further standards. This case would be revisited.

IV. Disability Cases: Return to Neutrality

Aguilar marked the extreme point of separationism. Shortly thereafter, the Court began a return to the *Everson* emphasis on neutrality, understood in terms of the underlying norm of fairness. It is not surprising that this return began in the area of disability education. Students with disabilities need forms of aid that their schools are not always able to provide and that the government often arranges to provide. If those government programs were limited to children with disabilities who attended a public school, that would seem extremely unfair: by exercising their constitutionally protected choice to attend a sectarian school (a choice that Catholic families could see as a religious requirement), the student forfeits support that may be essential to academic success. In *Witters v. Washington Department of Services for the Blind*,[45] in a rare unanimous decision, the Court upheld the claim of a young ministerial student with a serious eye condition, who had applied for vocational rehabilitation assistance under a Washington state program. The fact that he would use the aid at a Christian college, the Court agreed, did not constitute impermissible aid to religion. It was his choice to use the aid that way, and that choice did not "confer any message of state endorsement of religion."[46] Here the Court used the neutrality/fairness framework: the aid is available to all who meet certain criteria, independently of religion or nonreligion. They then supplemented it with two other Eversonian principles: the aid is "indirect," given to the individual rather than to the institution, and it is mediated by the choice of the individual.

The principle of directness was very likely motivated by a reluctance to put state money in the hands of religious institutions, but it is not a terribly helpful principle, since a program could put money directly into recipients' hands and yet have conditions attached that did not give these recipients much choice about how to use the money. The principle of individual choice seems more promising, since it is a way of ensuring that all qualified individuals are similarly treated, and that all have both religious and nonreligious options. Not surprisingly, it is that principle that has proven long-lived, and has done important work in sorting out some divisive issues that arose subsequently.

In 1993, in a similar case, the Court upheld the claim of James Zobrest, deaf since birth, who, under the Individuals with Disabilities Education Act, requested a sign-language interpreter to accompany him to classes at a parochial high school in Tucson, Arizona.[47] The Court of Appeals for the Ninth Circuit held that providing him with such an interpreter would violate the Establishment Clause. A majority of the Court disagreed. The vote was 5–4, but largely because a group of the Justices felt that the case should be remanded because the constitutional issues were not necessary to its resolution. Once again, the majority opinion relied on the idea of neutrality: because the IDEA framework provides benefits neutrally to any child with a disability, allowing Zobrest the interpreter does not create a financial incentive to choose a religious school.[48] "[G]overnment programs that neutrally provide benefits to a broad class of citizens defined without reference to religion are not readily subject to an Establishment Clause challenge just because sectarian institutions may also receive an attenuated financial benefit."[49]

Disability cases are strong ones for a neutrality framework, because it seems grossly unfair that a student with a disability should not get urgently needed special assistance just on account of his or her choice to attend a parochial school. In addition, the specialized nature of the aid makes particularly implausible the usual presumption of suspicion that all instruction on the premises of a religious school may involve religious indoctrination. The sign-language interpreter is not teaching anything; she is simply translating what is said by others. Only "antiquated notions of 'taint'" would make us think that such a translator would be smuggling in religious material. "James's parents have chosen of their own free will to place him in a pervasively sectarian environment. The sign-language interpreter they have requested will neither add to nor subtract from that environment."[50] Once again, then, choice is a crucial subsidiary principle.

These cases made inroads on behalf of a return to neutrality, but they did not overrule any of the separationist cases. One further disability case, although it went against the religious plaintiffs, attracted widespread public attention, giving rise to much dissatisfaction with mechanical and extreme separationism. This was *Board of Education of Kiryas Joel Village School District v. Grumet*, in 1994.[51] The Satmar Hasidim are a conservative Orthodox Jewish sect who typically run their own private schools and do not use the public schools. Like any community in America, however, they have children with mental and physical disabilities whose educational needs cannot be met in the usual classroom setting. Under the Individuals with Disabilities Education Act, all children with disabilities are entitled to "free suitable" education, at public expense, in the "least restrictive environment possible," whether that be through inclusion in a regular classroom with special assistance or through separate education. The Satmar initially sought to have special-education teachers visit their private schools. This was denied, because it was thought to be an unconstitutional form of aid under *Aguilar*. They attempted, next, to send these children to the public schools. However, this simply did not work. It is difficult at the best of times to integrate children with mental and physical disabilities into a public school classroom: the danger of stigma and teasing is great, and was certainly greater in 1994, when "mainstreaming," and IDEA itself, were relatively new, and classroom teachers did not receive standard training in dealing with children with disabilities. But now imagine that the children, many already bearing obvious physical signs of difference related to their disabilities, arrive wearing the black hats, the long locks of hair, and the other identifying marks of the Hasidim. As we might expect, their "weirdness" stood out doubly, making them a double butt of jokes and taunts. Moreover, the unfamiliar atmosphere, for children who only knew the traditional community life of the Hasidim, made it far more difficult than it otherwise would have been for these children to settle into the new classroom. A Satmar child with no disabilities would have a hard enough time coping with the unfamiliar; these children, with disabilities including Down syndrome, deafness, and emotional disorders, could not do so.

Being well-off and politically influential, the Satmar then sought aid from the state legislature, which permitted them to set up their own public school district, a district only for Satmar children with disabilities, which would then have access to federal funds under IDEA. The borders of the school district were those of the village, so it was in principle possible that the district would include non-Satmars in the future. At the time, however, it was a district consisting of Satmar families only. So it was this arrangement that the Court was considering: that of a public school district drawn, *de facto* if not *de jure*, along religious lines, to benefit a religious group. Unsurprisingly, and rightly, they found this arrangement unconstitutional, since it involved government's delegation of its power to run an agency of government (a school district) to a religious group as such. The fact that the whole problem arose from the rigidity of the *Aguilar* framework, however, did not escape the attention of the Court, and Justice O'Connor called openly for *Aguilar* to be overturned:

> The Religion Clauses prohibit the government from favoring religion, but they provide no warrant for discriminating *against* religion. All handicapped children are entitled by law to government-funded special education. If the government provides this education on-site at public schools and at nonsectarian private schools, it is only fair that it provide it on-site at sectarian schools as well.
>
> I thought this to be true in *Aguilar* . . . and I still believe it today. The Establishment Clause does not demand hostility to religion, religious ideas, religious people, or religious schools . . . It is the Court's insistence on disfavoring religion in *Aguilar* that led New York to favor it here. The Court should, in a proper case, be prepared to reconsider *Aguilar*, in order to bring our Establishment Clause jurisprudence back to what I think is the proper track—government impartiality, not animosity, toward religion.[52]

Separationism was not going to depart without a struggle—as we see in Justice Stevens's concurring opinion, which, in a manner that I am tempted to call Blanshardesque, reproves New York for "affirmative support[ing] a reli-

gious sect's interest in segregating itself and preventing its children from associating with their neighbors." Like Blanshard, Stevens wants all Americans to
assimilate, and he is skeptical of any sectarian separation that would "increase[e] the likelihood that they would remain within the fold, faithful adherents of their parents' religious faith."[53] It would appear that Justice Stevens has
not managed to envisage precisely the situation of a child with Down syndrome, or Asperger's syndrome, or even deafness, in a strange new school environment—even though the documents in the case spoke of "panic, fear, and
trauma."[54] These children will be lucky if they get to the point of joining their
parents' tradition, and a zealous focus on prying them loose from it seems unduly harsh. The disability aspect of the case, so central to the plight of the Satmar parents and children, escapes Justice Stevens's notice because he is so
intent on the idea that religious conformity is a bad thing. This is the old cen-
ter-left of the Blanshard era speaking, and it does not seem to me to speak
fairly of and about religious Americans.

V. A "Variable Barrier": Pursuing Fairness

The neutrality framework made progress in the early 1990s, in two cases that
concerned financial support for religious speech. These two cases were very
different from the earlier neutrality cases, since they concerned not the permissibility of the subsidy, but whether it was actually *required* in certain circumstances, on neutrality grounds. Nonetheless, they do give the concept of
neutrality significant development. In *Lamb's Chapel v. Moriches*, argued under the Free Speech Clause and not the Establishment Clause, the Court
found unconstitutional a school district's policy of allocating space to various
student groups but excluding those with a religious viewpoint.[55] Two years
later, in *Rosenberger v. University of Virginia*,[56] the Court addressed a policy at
the University that aided only those student groups that qualified as "contracted independent organizations," but denied that status to religious organizations. Aid was extended by paying bills directly, so no money was actually
given to the student organizations. The basic argument in the case was a free
speech argument—the denial of funds to groups with a religious viewpoint is
impermissible "viewpoint discrimination." The Establishment Clause issue
was raised as a potential obstacle on the other side: would aiding the religious
group alongside the others violate the Establishment Clause? A neutrality-

based analysis, however, sufficed to show that there was no constitutional problem. Justice Kennedy asserts, referring to *Everson*, that the neutrality framework is central to dealing with such cases: a program has to benefit all citizens without regard to religious belief. He writes: "We have held that the guarantee of neutrality is respected, not offended, when the government, following neutral criteria and evenhanded policies, extends benefits to recipients whose ideologies and viewpoints, including religious ones, are broad and diverse." Using student fees to aid a broad range of student groups is utterly unlike a tax levied for the support of a church or churches. The wide range of aided groups, furthermore, made it clear that government was not endorsing the viewpoint of the religious organization. Indeed, Justice O'Connor stresses in her concurring opinion, withholding support would be to treat people differently based on their religious choices, sending "a message of hostility to religion." The fact that the university pays the bills incurred by the group, and thus aid is not directly given to the religious group, is a further significant factor in making the program constitutional.

Justice O'Connor had invited rethinking of *Aguilar*, given a suitable case. In 1997, considering the same New York program in *Agostini v. Felton*,[57] the Court overruled *Aguilar* and most of its companion case, *Grand Rapids v. Ball*, by a 5–4 vote, emphasizing the neutrality framework. What makes New York's remedial program acceptable, the Court argues, is the fact that it helps all children who qualify for remedial instruction, using neutral secular criteria based on family income and academic disadvantage, criteria that neither favor nor disfavor religion. The fact that the instruction is in some instances offered on-site in a parochial school is not sufficient to invalidate the program, given its manifest neutrality. Justice O'Connor, writing for the majority, explicitly states that the Court has by now discarded the presumption of suspicion that the Court had previously used in assessing teaching activities on the premises of a sectarian school: the presence of a public employee on those premises no longer is seen as inevitably leading to indoctrination. Nor does the presence of such an employee on sectarian school property necessarily create an objectionable symbolic link between government and religion.[58] The remedial teachers in this case are no more to be seen as indoctrinating their students than is the sign-language interpreter: they supply a specialized skill, which is now made available to all students without regard to their religion. The program creates no incentive to undertake religious instruction, and sends no message that government favors religion, since its recipients are identified on a neutral basis.

Neutrality is not by itself sufficient for constitutionality. It needs ancillary principles. Justice O'Connor passes over indirectness and focuses on the criterion of independent individual choice, which seems in any case to capture the meaningful aspects of indirectness. She focuses on *Witters*, where the grant for vocational education was seen as similar to a paycheck given to an individual. Similarly, the New York program benefits "all children who meet the eligibility requirements, no matter what their religious beliefs or where they go to school."[59]

I have described choice as an additional principle, but it can be argued that a focus on choice is actually entailed by neutrality, if understood as an expression of an underlying norm of fairness. What would be deeply unfair would be for government to support some religious institutions that it selects, singling them out for favor. If, however, the government gives a benefit to individuals (selected by some neutral criteria), allowing them to choose to use that benefit at a religious institution, that is, by contrast, an attractive way of showing equal respect for each person's conscience. Each citizen equally gets the benefit, whether the individual is religious or secular, headed for a religious school or a public school. Indeed, to withhold benefits from some individuals, simply on the grounds that they prefer a religious school, would seem to be to violate that equal respect.

Four Justices dissented, and yet it is important to see that the disagreement is not wide. (Some of these issues are clarified in a later case, *Mitchell v. Helms*, where Justice Souter supplies a useful summary of the state of the question.)[60] A majority of the Court agrees with Justice O'Connor that it is impermissible for government to advance or aid religion, or to send a message endorsing religion.[61] A majority also agrees with her that government provision of "universally general welfare benefits"[62] is fine. They agree, further, that the neutrality of the aid is necessary for constitutionality, but not, by itself, sufficient.[63] (Although several of the other Justices appear to favor a laxer rule, a majority of the Court clearly holds, at this point, that individual choice is also essential.) Whether a benefit is close enough to "universally general welfare benefits" to be acceptable must, Justice Souter argues, be a function of the "purpose and effect of the challenged law in all its particularity."[64] That interpretive principle would seem to command majority support. There is deep division about whether the indirect/direct distinction is important, but most of the Justices agree that individual choice is important.

The *Agostini* opinion makes real progress, moving away from the unhelpful strict-separationist framework, and yet articulating some principles that could supplement the key neutrality principle and limit its scope. Analytical conflicts have not been utterly removed, and yet the Court is closer to analytical consensus than it has been at any recent time, and perhaps not since *Everson*, when the split between neutrality and separation was already marked. The Court shows vestiges of separationism, especially in the thought of Justice Souter and Justice Stevens. A centrist group, however, has convincingly brought the focus around to the fairness issue, supplemented with the issue of individual choice—important because choice negates the perception that government itself is endorsing the religious use of its funds.

VI. Vouchers and Scholarships

School vouchers are a scary topic to many Americans. On this topic many people who would judge Paul Blanshard's views extreme and inflammatory become Blanshardian, fearing a religious takeover of education and the demise of our common schools. The issue is genuinely difficult. Homeschooling requirements are so lax in most states that the idea of the public schools as linchpins of a common culture has already been very much undermined. If, in addition, religious parents could get government money to send their children to religious schools, a further exodus from those schools could be expected.

At this point in our history Americans probably have relatively little fear of the parochial schools, which have shown their academic quality over the years, and which have also extended their benefits, in many cases, to non-Catholic children in the inner city. If Blanshard's book were to be written today, it would probably have a different target: the evangelical movement, which seems interested in radical changes to scientific education, and which has also challenged the very teaching of respect for diverse groups, as we shall see in Chapter 8. Most Americans can see by now that Roman Catholicism is a highly pro-reason religion, which favors and teaches independence of mind and which accepts modern science. Catholics have shown themselves happy to teach a curriculum that overlaps substantially with that of the public schools. In fact, the most consistent support for the teaching of critical philosophical thinking in American college education comes from the Roman Catholic colleges and universities.[65] Parochial schools are feared in the voucher context, insofar as they are, only because they are so numerous, so that state support for them seems to promise radical changes in the role of the public schools. The things that Blanshard worried about—not learning to think critically, not learning science—are more genuine fears, it would seem, in thinking about evangelical schools or homeschooling. People plausibly fear that an evangelical takeover of the public schools would eviscerate their commitment to scientific reason, and that the flight of evangelicals from the public schools would not be very good either, leading to an alternative system that could not be relied on to acquaint students with the need to show respect for diverse religious and secular traditions. (Of course, reasonable curricular requirements could always be imposed, but states have proven unwilling to do this with homeschooling, and they probably would not do better with a rival school system.)

The public schools are a very important part of American life. They bring children together from diverse backgrounds, and they impart values essential for citizenship in a pluralistic society. They are threatened in lots of ways: by insufficient support from cities struggling with myriad problems, by the preference of many well-to-do parents for elite private schools, by the easy availability of homeschooling. Indeed, if people start worrying about the loss of a common culture only when they hear talk of vouchers, one might reasonably reply that this train has already left the station, in that the laxity of homeschooling requirements already allows parents who don't like diversity to exit the public schools, without virtually anything in the way of oversight or solid curricular requirements. It would have been good if more parents had paid attention to that issue earlier, putting pressure on their states to include substantial requirements bearing on citizenship in their homeschooling requirements. (Even then, lack of exposure to diversity in the classroom itself poses a problem for citizenship.) There can be little doubt, however, that a universal voucher program (a program open to any parent who requested such money) would create still further trouble, and would very likely lead to the death of the public schools, in at least some places.

On the other hand, the case that has been made for vouchers is that they are not necessarily bad for the public schools, because choice improves educational quality. If parents really can choose, then they can exit from a failing public school system, helping their own children; and this will also send a message to the public schools that they need to shape up. This is a reasonable argument, particularly in the inner-city context, although data as yet are inconclusive. Given the well-known failures of many, if not most, inner-city public schools, experimenting with vouchers in limited contexts seems like an intelligent strategy—at least until we have reliable information about how well they work. We cannot begin our arguments on this issue from a baseline that presumes that the public schools are all right as they are, for that is simply not true.

As in *Aguilar*, so with this issue: fairness to poor children seems very important. We know that rich children who don't like the quality of the public schools have other options. Poor children often don't—and this creates a vicious cycle, as the fact that the public schools are increasingly populated largely by poorer children can lead to further neglect and erosion of quality.

The state of Ohio created a scholarship program to assist families living in any school district that is under state control as the result of a federal court order. These are failing school districts, and the only one that was covered by the law at the time of the challenge was the Cleveland City School District. That district has been one of the worst in the nation for some time. In 1995, a federal district court declared a "crisis of magnitude" and placed the entire district under state control.[66] So we are dealing with a situation in which students who are too poor to exit from the system are being deprived of equal opportunity.

The purpose of the law was that of "providing educational assistance to poor children in a demonstrably failing public school system."[67] Aid is conditioned on financial need, and parents may spend the aid wherever they choose to enroll their children. If they choose to remain in the local public school, the scholarship supports extra tutorial assistance. If they choose to enroll in parochial or other private schools, the grant pays part of tuition costs. (Over 80 percent of private schools in Cleveland are religious.) If they choose an independent "community" public school or a magnet school, they may use it to go there. If the school is private, the family will have to copay some portion of the tuition; if it is a magnet school, or a local public school, they will not. So the system does not create a financial incentive to choose a religious school. However, in fact, 96 percent of the participating families chose to send their children to parochial schools. The question before the Court was whether this program violates the Establishment Clause. By a 5–4 vote, the Court held that it did not. Justices Rehnquist, Scalia, Thomas, Kennedy, and O'Connor were on one side; Justices Souter, Breyer, Stevens, and Ginsburg on the other.

For the majority, following *Agostini*, the key issues were neutrality plus private choice. The program puts money into the hands of all parents who meet the income qualifications, without regard to religion. Parents then choose to attend the school they prefer. The fact that a large proportion choose to attend a parochial school is by itself not legally significant, since the program demonstrably creates no financial incentive for them to make that choice, and indeed creates an incentive in the other direction.

Justice Souter, in dissent, expresses concern that perhaps the parents had no real alternative. If that were really so, then there would be a constitutional problem: the program would be pushing parents in the direction of the parochial schools. But if we look behind the numbers and ask why such a large proportion of parents chose parochial schools, the reason is probably that they were fed up with the public schools, didn't trust the magnet school or "community school" (since some of them did not have better test scores than the public schools[68]), or found them inconvenient geographically, and/or didn't like the educational orientation of the private schools. Some of the private schools had experimental philosophies that might be educationally unfamiliar to the low-income parents making the choice (for example, Montessori schools), whereas the conservative pedagogy of the parochial schools was familiar and appealing.

The record indicates, then, that parents did have reasonable nonreligious options. (No student was turned away from a nonreligious private school for reasons of cost, for example.) It seems likely that for many parents, religion did not even play a very important role in the selection: the parochial schools have been educating non-Catholic children from the inner city for a long time now. (Similarly, when parents in India send their children to a Catholic school, they are usually thinking of quality, and view the religious affiliation as a slight disadvantage.) If the program used genuinely neutral criteria and provided genuine choice, then it should not be judged unconstitutional on account of its effects.[69] It is surely to be regretted that suburban public schools refused when invited to join the program; their participation would have added to the menu of secular options for parents, even granted the well-known difficulties of busing. Nonetheless, the facts do not show that the parents had no choice.

Zelman is a genuinely difficult case. It is not like *Agostini*, because the benefit is not a specialized support of one specific educational function, but a general tuition benefit, which supports all the educational purposes of the chosen school.[70] Even if one agrees that neutrality and choice are the twin criteria to be applied, reasonable people can differ in applying them to these very convoluted facts.[71] The dissenters raise some very important additional points. They worry that taxpayers are being forced to support a religion that they do not endorse, the classic Establishment Clause problem.[72] They worry that the nondiscrimination requirements imposed on participating schools involve illegitimate state control over religious institutions.[73] They worry about the danger of social conflict.[74] All these are very serious worries.

Reasonable people, applying the analytical framework I have endorsed (which the Court today expresses, in this context, as neutrality plus choice), might, then, worry about the specific features of the program, whose neutrality is less clear-cut than that of the disability programs and the remedial programs at issue in *Aguilar/Agostini*. It would be a good thing, however, if we could agree that the framework is legitimate and that the problem is in applying it to the facts. The Court today lacks such a clear agreement on guiding principles—although its differences in this area are far less sharp than they are in the areas of school prayer and public displays. Separationist language is no longer bandied about as sufficient to resolve a constitutional problem; fairness and choice are agreed to be key criteria, even if not all of the Court believes them decisive. We can hope, then, for increasing agreement, or at least for reasonable disagreement, about what types of funding are permissible.

The cases we have considered so far concern permissibility; they assess the acceptability of a particular type of funding that has already been put in place. *Rosenberger* did use the neutrality principle to require the university to fund the religious periodical on a basis of equality, but that was a mixed speech-religion case, and the requirement side of it came from the speech argument; the religion clause part simply held that neutral aid did not constitute an Establishment Clause violation. We still are unclear, then, about how far states may adopt programs that seem to violate neutrality in some respect. A disturbing recent case on this question was *Locke v. Davey* in 2004.[75]

The state of Washington established a scholarship program for academically gifted students. In accordance with the state constitution, students may not use the scholarship to pursue a devotional theology degree. Joshua Davey won such a scholarship and chose Northwest College, a private Christian college affiliated with the Assemblies of God. He planned to pursue a dual major in business administration and devotional theology. He was told that he could not receive his scholarship if he persisted in this plan. He claimed that the policy violated his rights under the Free Exercise Clause of the First Amendment.

So this case was argued as a Free Exercise case, not an Establishment Clause case. Under the post-*Smith* understanding of Free Exercise, the state did not have to show a "compelling" state interest to justify its "substantial burden" on Davey's free exercise of religion. It only had to show that there is no egregious violation of neutrality, as there was in the Santeria case. The Court held that in fact the violation was not that egregious, and Davey lost by a 7-2 vote. As Douglas Laycock writes of the outcome, "The Court struggled for decades to find a middle ground that would permit some funding for religious institutions but not too much. Its new middle ground is to permit most funding but to require hardly any. This position maximizes government discretion and judicial deference, but it threatens religious liberty."[76]

Davey's case looks very strong. The policy is not treating him fairly. If he had majored in business administration alone—or in fashion design or in advertising, or indeed anything else—he would have been able to use his scholarship. The only major he was not able to elect, and keep the money, was theology. This looks like a punishment, meted out to him because of the character of his religious beliefs. And, as Laycock emphasizes, it involves a lot of government control over people's religious choices, something that the religion clauses surely disfavor.

Legally, the case is indeed a hard one under the Free Exercise Clause, in its current weakened form. Prior to *Smith*, Davey would very likely have won. Even after *Smith*, it is far from clear that the violation of neutrality is really any less egregious than in the Santeria case, for surely animus is directed toward theology, as it was toward the Santeria worshippers. Does the policy pose an Establishment Clause problem? The Court has so far been reluctant to interfere in states' funding decisions, speaking only when spoken to. This policy is a cautious one in a pluralistic society, but it may be unwise. The same neutrality/choice framework that is used to permit the various forms of state aid to religion that are currently permitted suggests that the state is unfair to Davey when it tells him that his is the only choice that it will not fund. He is being denied equal standing in the political community.

Significantly, Justice Scalia, who was responsible for narrowing the reach of Free Exercise accommodation, dissented, holding that the state's interest was not strong enough to justify the burden on Davey. (Interestingly, he looks for, and fails to find, a "compelling" interest, the very standard he had opposed in *Smith*.[77]) He worries about an era in which public secularism will lead to unfair treatment of religious people. "What next? Will we deny priests and nuns their prescription-drug benefits on the ground that taxpayers' freedom of conscience forbids medicating the clergy at public expense? . . . When the public's freedom of conscience is invoked to justify denial of equal treatment, benevolent motives shade into indifference and ultimately into repression."[78] These concerns are legitimate. One only wishes, however, that Justice Scalia had had them in 1990, when, instead, he insisted that religious groups will typically lose out in majoritarian politics and that this is not a constitutional problem.

Davey remains a difficult case, since one could easily envisage difficulties down the road, particularly in the already divisive voucher area: some would surely claim that a different result in *Davey* entails that vouchers for attendance at religious schools are constitutionally required, and the Court may have had that potential problem in mind when deciding the case.[79] On balance, however, Davey's case was strong, and the voucher issue could have been distinguished in a variety of ways. Both liberals and conservatives, then, can conclude *Davey* was wrongly decided. In fact, however, because liberal groups in civil society are still overwhelmingly committed to the principle of separationism, Laycock was quite isolated among liberal advocates (not, however, among liberal academics) in his amicus opinion on Davey's behalf.[80] The separationism that has caused such difficulty over the years, in the delicate area of state funding, still plays its part in impeding genuine fairness.

Accepted to Harvard Law School, Joshua Davey was already enrolled there as a one-L when his case was argued before the Court in 2003. He graduated in 2006, having been a managing editor of the *Harvard Law and Public Policy Review*. Quite a few of the students I taught at Harvard in spring 2007 in a course on religion and the First Amendment remembered him as an impressive fellow student. Despite his legal setback, then, Davey is on the road to success. That fact, however, does not make his case less disturbing.

How much should the Court interfere with state funding decisions that seem burdensome or unfair on grounds of religion? What type of state interest should be required to justify a policy that is manifestly not neutral? How far should the courts turn over such important issues, involving claims of fairness, to the democratic process? An important next challenge for the equality framework would be to revisit the relationship between free exercise and establishment with these questions in view.

8

CONTEMPORARY CONTROVERSIES

The Pledge, Evolution, Imagination,
Gay Marriage, Fear of Muslims

*Absolute liberty, just and true liberty, equal and
impartial liberty, is the thing that we stand in
need of.*

JOHN LOCKE,
A LETTER CONCERNING TOLERATION

*That our selves and all men are apt and prone to
differ it is no new Thing in all former Ages in all
parts of this World in these parts and in our
deare native Countrey and mournful state of
England. . . . To try out Matters by Disputes and
writing is sometimes Endles. To try out Argumts by
Armes and Swords is cruell and merciless.*

ROGER WILLIAMS,
LETTER TO THE TOWN OF PROVIDENCE
(AUGUST 31, 1648)

I. Equal Liberty of Conscience Today

The tradition we have explored is ongoing. Each of its strands continues to generate debate. An analytical framework based on the ideas of equal respect and equal standing in the political community has the potential to help us further, as we confront some of our time's most divisive questions.

It is difficult to predict the issues on which either public debate or the Court will focus over the next decade or so, where the religion clauses are concerned, but five issues in this general area stand out as focal points of public controversy. The Pledge of Allegiance, addressed by the Court in *Gobitis* and *Barnette*, has once again become topical, the emphasis this time being on the status of the words "under God." That question came before the Court in 2004, but the case was not decided because a majority of the Justices held that the plaintiff did not have standing to bring the case on behalf of his daughter.[1] Probably at some future date another case testing the constitutionality of "under God" will arise, and perhaps the Court will hear it. In the meantime it would be good to have a wide, informed, and calm public debate about the words and their relationship to our constitutional tradition.

As we have seen, the public schools have long been a battleground where groups contend to insert their preferred religious doctrines and observances. The school prayer issue seems dormant for now, but two other educational issues are very much alive. The teaching of evolution in the schools, religiously controversial since the early years of the twentieth century, has once again been contested, this time by recent attempts in many states to insert "Intelligent Design" as an alternative to evolution in the high school science curriculum. Those proposals have been challenged as illegitimate attempts to establish a particular religion. The evolution question rests, ultimately, on scientific facts, and on the precise definition of scientific concepts such as "theory" and "testable." It is therefore one that expert scientists must continue to address, and this book cannot offer an exhaustive account of it. We can, however, at least try to understand the constitutional aspects of the question and sketch an attractive approach.

At the same time, other more humanistic aspects of the typical public school curriculum are also under fire as religiously burdensome: those that expose students to other ways of life, ask them to imagine those lives, and fail to instruct them that these other ways are incorrect. We cannot tell what the next challenge will be along these lines, but a 1987 case from Tennessee shows us the issues that are on people's minds and maps out an attractive response.

Our nation is currently undergoing considerable division and upheaval over the morality and legality of same-sex relations, and particularly over the issue of same-sex marriage. Although this is not an issue that can be directly approached through the religion clauses, there may be something we can learn about this issue by pondering the history of religion in our nation.

Finally, in much of the world people are currently in a state of panic over Muslim immigration and the alleged threat posed by observant Muslims to traditional ways of life. To the great credit of the United States and its tradition of respect for visible expressions of difference, there has not been a widespread outbreak of anti-Muslim feeling here, and public leaders have strongly discouraged any facile equation between terrorism and Islam. In Europe, by contrast, an atmosphere of suspicion and fear has led to much intolerance and disrespect, and leading politicians are voicing a demand for imposed homogeneity that seems misguided from the viewpoint of the approach that I have been recommending. By ending with a study of these phenomena, we will be able to see how the equal-respect tradition has steered us well, and how its absence in Europe has left politics prone to panic.

II. "Under God": The Pledge, Present and Future

Many public school districts in America require daily recitation of the Pledge of Allegiance. At this point, school authorities know that they have to permit an exception for any child who conscientiously objects to participating. Moreover, *Barnette* by now commands not just grudging acceptance, but widespread approval. Most Americans think it very bad to force children to make statements that offend their conscience.

What, however, about the timid child, or the child who has reasonable worries about stigma and peer pressure? The history of the pledge and of the related school prayer issue makes it obvious that nonparticipation often comes at a cost. If Ellory Schempp was greeted with outright persecution for reading from the Quran, we can expect that children who refuse to say the pledge—whether they stand in silence, sit, or leave the classroom—will be courting the hostility of teachers, administrators, and, perhaps most clearly, their fellow

students. The whole point of the pledge, in the mind of its original support-
ers, was to put all Americans on record as supporting patriotism, and to inculcate the value of patriotism by a daily required exercise in the schools. From
the point of view of these concerns, the nonparticipating child is bound to
look at the very least weird and not fully American, at the worst subversive and
threatening.

Lee v. Weisman recognized the coercive role of peer pressure, and this
problem, studied in famous experiments by Solomon Asch, has been prominently recognized in recent studies of the Holocaust and of the social importance of dissent.[2] It is clear that even adults are highly vulnerable to peer
pressure, to the extent of being willing to say things that they know to be false,
and to do things that are terrible.

At the time of *Barnette*, the children involved objected to the pledge because it asked them to swear loyalty to an entity other than God, which their
faith did not permit them to do. Although Jehovah's Witnesses were not the
only Americans who had such conscientious objections, the other concerned
groups were relatively small. It seemed at the time that arranging exemptions
for a small number of children was feasible without undue stigmatization and
upheaval. When the words "under God" were added to the pledge in 1954,
the whole issue suddenly became much more complex.

At this point, many new groups of Americans acquired conscientious
grounds for objection to the daily recitation: atheists, agnostics, believers in a
detached God who does not take a direct interest in human affairs, believers in
a God who looks for right conduct and thus does not take a particular interest
in Americans over Russians just because Americans (many of them) believe in
God and Russians (many of them) are atheists, believers in a plurality of gods,
believers in religions that do not assert the existence of a God. Hindus, Buddhists, Jains, Sikhs, Unitarians, and some types of Jews and Christians now
have conscientious grounds for objection.

Indeed, the more one thinks about what "one nation under God" means,
the more religious people it excludes. As a Reform Jew, I hold that God loves
truth and righteousness, and that these values can be imagined as residing in
an ideal community—rather like Immanuel Kant's "kingdom of ends." I also
believe, however (again, with Kant), that no actual nation instantiates them adequately, and that, in consequence, no actual nation enjoys God's sponsorship. Merely recognizing God's existence cuts no ice: what interests God is

the committed pursuit of justice. So I myself would object to the pledge on such grounds and would now not want to recite it, although in high school I did so, not having thought very much about religious matters. I don't think that America is "under God" any more than Israel, or India, or Britain, or Germany, or Syria, or, for that matter, the Soviet Union in the 1950s is "under God": all nations should strive for right conduct, and if they do what is just, God will approve their actions. But God doesn't play favorites: God loves justice, peace, and righteousness, and doesn't single out a particular nation, flawed as all nations are flawed, for special loving protection. Or so I hold. But at the time, the phrase (introduced by the Knights of Columbus) was clearly intended to show why the U.S. was superior to godless communism. Well, one could argue convincingly that it is in fact superior, but that argument would have to be made, and the mere fact that the U.S. is a nation of believers (on the whole) certainly does not make it a nation of righteous believers.

Maybe "under God" means "subject to God's judgment," not "enjoying God's favor and protection." That is not what the people who introduced the words meant by them, on the whole, since most believers think that all human beings are subject to God's judgment, but the whole point of the language was to introduce a distinction between the U.S. and the Soviet Union. This, however, is a reading through which someone like me might attempt to reconcile the disharmony between the pledge and my beliefs. Still, this leaves many Jews on the outside: those who, like many leaders of Reform Judaism through the centuries, have denied the existence of a personal God and who have conceived of God as a force of rationality and order in the cosmos, in the manner of Spinoza. Isaac Meyer Wise, one of the greatest leaders of Reform Judaism in America, was a Spinozist, and he could not have accepted the pledge in its current form.

Even if we did have a situation in which the theological views of all Jews and Christians were consonant with reciting the pledge, which we don't, that would hardly deal with the legitimate grievances of Hindus, Buddhists, Unitarians, agnostics, atheists, and others. It's important to notice, then, that it is not simply a matter of excluding nonbelievers, and that the issue cannot be solved by retreating to a nonpreferentialist version of the Establishment clause. Lots of believers, and more every day (as Hinduism and Buddhism continue to grow), have cogent objections to the morning ritual. It states that America is a monotheist nation with a particular type of theistic conception, and this statement, in turn, entails the further statement that they are not fully equal to those monotheists in the public square. There is bound to be stigma in this, particularly in the light of the history of the demonization of Hindu polytheism in India by British monotheists, a history that the "reasonable observer" would be sure to learn.

At this point we might try to say that the pledge, while sectarian, is voluntary, and does not coerce anyone. Certainly it is a good thing that after *Barnette*, recitation of the pledge cannot be made mandatory. The question is whether this disposes of the constitutional question. Justice Kennedy, as we've seen, has prominently emphasized a coercion-based theory of the Establishment Clause. His theory of the Establishment Clause, however, is unconvincing, for surely an establishment issue can be present even when an observance, or a display, is utterly noncoercive, as Justice O'Connor's endorsement test has repeatedly emphasized.

Even if we liked the coercion theory, however, it would not help rescue the pledge, at least not if we accept Justice Kennedy's analysis of *Lee v. Weisman*. If the suggestion that one ought to stand during someone else's reading of a graduation prayer is viewed as coercive, on the grounds that peer pressure and fear of stigma are coercive to young people, the pledge is surely much more coercive. The children involved include far younger children, and the act of not reciting, while other children are reciting with their hands over their hearts, is more conspicuous than the act of nonparticipation in the graduation prayer—even if one thought that sitting down was the only way to express nonparticipation. Justice Thomas, in his opinion in the pledge case, helpfully recognized that under *Lee v. Weisman* the words "under God" are unconstitutional. His radical solution was to deny the incorporation of the Establishment Clause and to throw out a whole series of precedents. If we are not ready to accept his doctrine, we should still accept his reading of *Lee* and the problem it poses for the pledge.

There is one remaining way out, and this is to say that the pledge is one of those traditional historic ceremonies that does not create a problem because it is part of "ceremonial Deism" and simply expresses our historical tradition. In her opinion in the pledge case, Justice O'Connor plausibly points out that some manifestations of religion in our public life can be defended along such lines. (The Court has often said similar things.)

Some references to God may indeed be defensible in this way: the use of "In God We Trust" on our currency, the "God Save this Honorable Court"

that opens the sessions of the Supreme Court. These ceremonial manifestations of religion may bother some people. And yet, they have been around for
a very long time, and perhaps we now accept them as part of our history rather
than as containing any devotional message. Or so Justice O'Connor's argument goes.

Let's now look at Justice O'Connor's four criteria for saying that a traditional observance does not constitute a constitutional violation. And let's
compare "In God We Trust" to the pledge. Although Justice O'Connor her-
self tries to argue that the pledge is all right under her criteria, I think we'll see
that this argument is unconvincing.[3]

First, Justice O'Connor mentions *history and ubiquity*: the questionable
item must have been in place for "a significant portion of the Nation's history."
This criterion is important because it seems right to be more forgiving about
something that is a historical relic than about something contentiously introduced in recent times. Here "In God We Trust" looks very different from "under God" in the pledge: the former has been in place since right after the Civil
War, the latter only since 1954. "Reasonable observers have reasonable memories," Justice O'Connor once said, and many living Americans remember the
sudden change in the pledge, as well as the debate surrounding it, which was
highly theistic in content, stressing the need to get Americans to stand behind
a symbolic affirmation of our difference from "godless communism."

Second, she mentions *absence of worship or prayer*: there is a difference,
she says, between asking someone to join in a ritual observance and simply
making a statement that doesn't ask people to affirm anything. Here "In
God We Trust" looks pretty good: we pass money around all the time without thinking of ourselves as endorsing that sentiment, and it would take a
real haggler (of the sort that Justice O'Connor spoke when she mentioned
the possibility of a "heckler's veto") to be very upset about the presence of
time-honored words on the coins we use. The pledge is of course entirely
different: impressionable children are being asked to join in a ritual observance that is an affirmation of God as well as of country. The whole point of
the pledge was that it was an act of quasi-worship, suited to inculcate strong
patriotic emotions in young children. The whole point of adding the language of God was to make those same children think that we (unlike the Soviet Union) are in a nation that is protected by God. *Barnette* has sufficiently
established that the recitation is not devoid of affirmation: that's why the

children had a legitimate grievance. Now the affirmation includes religious affirmation.

The third criterion, and an important one, is *absence of reference to particular religion*. As we've seen, it's virtually impossible to construct a religious reference that is not somehow particular, and Justice O'Connor acknowledges that the pledge is indeed particular, excluding Buddhists, Hindus, and others. She then retreats to the position that it derived from a time "when our national religious diversity was neither as robust nor as well recognized as it is now." I find this unconvincing. First of all, the numbers of people who accept a divergent religion should not decide the constitutional question. Second, the reason there were not many Hindus here until recently was that immigration law kept them out by restricting immigration quotas to the proportion of the population that a given national origin occupied in 1895; this imbalance was rectified only by the Immigration and Nationality Act of 1965.[4] So it seems doubly churlish to keep people out unfairly and then to say, "Because we succeeded in keeping you out for so long, we don't have to take your religious sensibilities into account." Third, there were lots of agnostics, atheists, Reform Jewish Spinozists, Deists, Unitarians, and others who could not endorse the religious conception of the pledge all along. Moreover, there can be little doubt that the movement to add "under God" to the pledge was connected to a desire to denigrate most of these people, as fellow travelers with "atheistic communism." ("Ceremonial Deism" is an odd name for a ritual affirmation that a Deist would be very reluctant to endorse, since Deists think of God as a rational causal principle but not as a personal judge and father.)

What about "In God We Trust"? Well, it has in principle the same problem, but it was not introduced with intent to exclude and denigrate, and the fact that it does so much better on the first two criteria seems to me to suggest that the third criterion might be waived in that case. The criteria are not supposed to be necessary conditions of acceptability, just good things to look for.

Finally, *minimal religious content*: the reference must be "highly circumscribed" and easy to avoid. On this count the pledge does well enough, if one imagines that children who object could simply drop those two words, while reciting the rest. We do have the *Lee v. Weisman* worry, however, again in this case: if what the objector wants to do is to make it clear that she doesn't go along with the ritual as the majority practice it, she will have to do something more than silently omit two words. She will have to ask for an excuse, or stay seated, and this will make the pledge every bit as onerous as the prayers that were rejected in the whole string of school prayer cases. If the defender of "under God" now says that the words don't mean anything much, have no content, she has the history of the addition of the words to contend with: for people felt that they were very important and had significant religious content. Moreover, defenders of the pledge today argue that it does have substantial content.[5]

Here again, "In God We Trust" seems on stronger ground: most people don't think of it as religious at all, and are able to use the currency without noticing it.

We should agree with Justice O'Connor and the entirety of the tradition that I've described: there are traditional references to religion in our public life that should not be pruned away and that pose no constitutional problem. It is extremely doubtful, however, that the pledge, in its current form, is among them.

Given public feeling on the issue, it would cause a national crisis were the Supreme Court to say that the words "under God" are unconstitutional. If we adopt Justice Breyer's theory of interpretation, then, we can find a way round the problem: a test of constitutionality is whether deciding the other way would threaten civil peace. This principle seemed, and seems here, unfortunately ad hoc, favoring majority beliefs and making a virtue of convenience. As an account of the meaning of the religion clauses, Breyer's conflict principle should be rejected. Nonetheless, one might reach the conclusion that the Supreme Court ought to hold off in this case by a different route—for example, one might introduce considerations of judicial modesty and caution, arguing that, for institutional reasons, judges should usually be reluctant to cause a national crisis. If there is uncertainty about the correct way of proceeding in such a momentous case, it is probably wise for the Court to avoid the issue as long as possible—hoping that, in the meanwhile, greater public understanding of Hinduism, Buddhism, and other related religions, as well as a greater appreciation for conscientious moral atheism and agnosticism, will undermine the perception that the opponents of the pledge are all dangerous subversives. From the vantage point of these practical concerns, it was extremely unfortunate that the case that went to the Supreme Court was brought by an outspoken atheist who openly scoffs at religious belief. It was a good thing that the Court was able to find a way around the case, by holding that Newdow did not have standing, since he did not have custody of his daughter.

It was also basically good for Justice O'Connor to do what she did, misapplying her own analytical criteria: it is much better to have the analytical framework right and make a mistake about this or that case than to veer to a new analytical framework that is on balance weaker (as Justice Breyer did in the Ten Commandments case).

On July 19, 2006, the U.S. House passed, by a vote of 260–167, a bill removing jurisdiction, in the matter of the words "under God" in the pledge, from the federal appellate courts and the U.S. Supreme Court. This move is deeply to be regretted, because it undermines judicial independence and the very idea of the separation of powers. Proponents seem to be pursuing their immediate goal in a way that neglects the larger long-term structural issues the bill implicates. Fortunately, a companion bill in the Senate is likely to fail.[6]

How can we make progress on this divisive issue? First of all, we simply need to talk about the issue and its history far more than we do, and members of affected minority religions need to get involved. It would be good if all Americans understood the history of "under God" in the 1950s, and understood, as well, the reasons many believing Americans, as well as nonbelievers, have for being troubled by the words. The participation of the Hindu and Buddhist communities in the recent Ten Commandments case is a welcome sign for the future. Hindus sometimes duck away from challenging monotheism, and can even represent themselves, at times, as quasi-monotheists, because they are tired of being pilloried for their polytheism and, as new immigrants in a vulnerable position, they desire respectability. It would be wonderful if they would tell Americans frankly that they worship Rama and Shiva and Ganesha and other gods, and that the pledge refers to a monotheistic conception that denigrates them. Buddhists, whether immigrants or American converts, should also join this conversation, explaining that theirs is a genuine religion and yet recognizes no God. Confucianists, Taoists, and others should enter the debate as well. It would also be very helpful if more Jews and Christians who hold views that render the language of the pledge problematic would say forthrightly what these reasons are.

Meanwhile, we need to talk more about Justice O'Connor's helpful criteria and how they apply in a wide range of cases, refining the criteria themselves, adding to them if new helpful criteria can be found, and saying more about how many of them need to be present in order for a religiously divisive practice to be constitutional.

This national conversation is not taking place. One reason is the reluctance of many dissident religions to get involved in public discussions of their dissident conceptions, for fear of stigma for themselves and their children. That is why it ended up being an atheist who brought the famous case, a fact that proved very bad for public understanding of the issues. The pledge, as I've argued, is offensive to many believers, as well as to atheists. Most Americans, however, currently think that only atheists have a problem with it.

Another reason the conversation is failing, more problematic still, is the reliance of American liberals on the language of "separation of church and state": because they think it's self-evident that "under God" violates "separation" and is bad for that reason alone, many liberals don't bother to investigate the deep inequalities and hierarchies that it constitutes. Let's, then, try speaking the language of equality and endorsement, and see how far we can get.

III. Debating Evolution

One of the most divisive issues of the early twentieth century was the teaching of evolution in the public schools. Religious fundamentalism, though relatively new,[7] had become influential in some parts of America by the 1920s. Fundamentalists believe that the account of Creation in *Genesis* is literally true, and that, therefore, it cannot be correct to think of human beings as having gradually evolved from other animals. Human life was directly created by a special act of God.

Many believing Jews and Christians do not read *Genesis* this way. Throughout history, a common mode of interpretation—and the dominant one in Jewish and Christian theology—has been one that treats biblical texts as containing multiple layers of meaning, frequently allegorical or metaphorical. Practices of allegorical reading of scripture are nothing new, not in the least connected with skepticism or agnosticism. In Jewish tradition they are extremely old indeed, and it is probably not possible to give them an original date. One well-known example is the Passover Haggadah, where a variety of metaphorical and nonliteral interpretations of biblical text are offered by famous rabbis, some of them very serious, some apparently jocular. Much of the humor in the traditional Seder derives from the play of interpretive speculation, and the rabbis evidently liked to joust to see who could come up with a more elaborate metaphorical reading (or a larger number of plagues!). In

Christianity, the practice of nonliteral reading appears to begin with Jesus himself, who offered parables to his audience, asking them to read them nonliterally for the ethical lessons they contained. Many have plausibly thought that the example of Jesus gives them an invitation to read biblical texts nonliterally.

At any rate, the new religion soon exhibited a proliferation of allegorical readings, many under the influence of Philo Judaeus, the Hellenized Platonist Jew who lived during the first century BCE and the first century CE, and whose interpretive strategies were influenced by techniques of allegorical reading developed in ancient Greek Stoicism. (The Stoics believed that texts of many sorts contained hidden lessons illustrating the rational nature of the world; notoriously they applied these techniques to some very unpromising texts, including a pornographic painting, just to show how powerful those techniques were.) Throughout the history of Christianity and Judaism, metaphorical reading is commonplace, and it would be utterly mistaken to think that the tradition of either religion is committed, as a whole, to a fundamentalist literal reading of scripture. Believers differ over which elements of the text may be read nonliterally and which may not; much of Jewish and Christian theology is concerned with such matters. But only a small proportion of Christians, and virtually no Jews, attempt a literal reading of the entirety of scripture.

Nonliteral reading says, "This text is sacred, but it may mean something very different from what it at first seems to mean." By the nineteenth century (though really such movements, too, begin in antiquity, historicist reading of religion being quite familiar in Greece in the sixth and fifth centuries BCE), another position is common: one, namely, that says that "this text, sacred in inspiration (composed by people genuinely inspired by God), was written down by human beings, using the ideas of their time, and much of it, whatever derives from the imperfect ideas of those times, is not sacred or binding." That is the dominant attitude toward text in Reform Judaism, though some interpreters go further, utterly denying the sacredness of the nonethical parts of the Bible. Similar attitudes are common in Christianity as well. The nineteenth century saw a cultural explosion of historical accounts of Jesus' life, in influential writings, for example, by David Strauss (1808–1874) in Germany and Ernst Renan (1823–1892) in France. Both Strauss and Renan rejected some aspects of traditional religion (for example, the belief in the literal truth of miracles), but both remained believers of a sort, while also suggesting that there was a moral core to Jesus' teaching that could be shared by those who did not share its theological premises.[8] Today, much of mainstream Christianity follows the lead of these scholars, accepting the idea that Jesus' ethical teachings may be the basis for interreligious dialogue among people whose theological commitments are diverse.

At this same time, critical biblical scholarship began to dissect the Bible into different strata, arguing that the texts that have come down to us represent various later conflations and editions of heterogeneous earlier texts. This view was so standard in mainstream Protestantism by the time I went to college in the 1960s that we were all required to learn it in our required Bible class, taught (at Wellesley College, founded by Protestants, though by then nondenominational) by a Protestant minister.

The creation story (or, really, stories) in *Genesis* has long been one of the prime candidates for allegorical reading. Augustine and many other great Christian thinkers have offered allegorical readings of it, and historicizing thinkers have connected the story to surrounding cultural paradigms. So by the time Charles Darwin's theory appeared on the scene, there was nothing intrinsically shocking to religious sensibilities about the idea that Creation took millions of years, or that the species appeared gradually, by evolution one from another, even though Darwin himself may have thought so. Even the Thirty-Nine Articles of the Church of England, which were used as a kind of "test oath" for academics until the 1870s, and which required one to affirm belief in many fine points of Christian theology (the nature of the Trinity, for example), contain nothing relating to a literal understanding of the biblical creation story. Darwin shocked many people because he upset what they had unreflectively thought, and they reacted by adopting anti-Darwinian forms of biblical literalism; but the religions most common in Europe at the time already had ample room for his views.

The American fundamentalist movement was different. Fundamentalism began to gather steam at the end of the nineteenth century (long after the publication of Darwin's *Origin of Species* in 1859), as a reaction to historicizing readings of scripture, and became a movement to reckon with only in the early twentieth, under the influence of the Moody Bible Institute and related preachers. In 1925, influenced by fundamentalist arguments, the state of Tennessee made it illegal for a public school teacher "to teach any theory that denies the story of the divine creation of man as taught in the Bible, and to teach instead that man has descended from a lower order of animals." A teacher of

Darwin's theory probably should have maintained that he was not violating that law. Teaching Darwin's theory does not deny the biblical story (although it does suggest that one would need to read it nonliterally), nor would any good evolutionary biologist teach that human beings descend from "a lower order of animals." If one respects animals as dignified parts of the world, this very language is quite insulting. In any case, an evolutionary biologist doesn't see animals that way.

In the famous "Monkey Trial," high school teacher John T. Scopes was convicted of violating the law and fined one hundred dollars.[9] His conviction was reversed on a technicality by the Tennessee Supreme Court,[10] so the case was never reviewed by the U.S. Supreme Court; the law remained on the books. The Scopes trial was a national circus, pitting Clarence Darrow and the ACLU against William Jennings Bryan, who agreed to help the prosecution. Bryan, a diehard opponent of evolution, once said, "All the ills from which America suffers can be traced back to the teaching of evolution. . . . It would be better to destroy every other book ever written, and just save the first three verses of *Genesis*."[11]

Although Bryan was a complex character, whose opposition to evolution was motivated in part by his concern about eugenics and forced sterilization, such remarks helped to convert the trial into a test of intellectual freedom. The play and film *Inherit the Wind* have made these issues famous.[12] Most Americans know that Darrow, frustrated in his effort to call expert scientists to the stand to testify about the theory of evolution, called Bryan as an expert on the Bible, and put his literal reading of *Genesis* to the test. (As a child I played one of the Tennessee children in a summer stock production of the play, learning the whole script by heart in my passion for the theatre. My father played one of the professors who never got to testify. Prejudiced against Jews, he was annoyed that his character's name was that of a Jewish philosopher, Dr. Walter Aaronson, "one of the most brilliant minds in the world today.") The play portrays the trial as a victory for Scopes and a loss for Bryan—although it also clearly prefers Darrow's sensitive respectful agnosticism (at any rate, as depicted in the script) to the scoffing of the character who represents H. L. Mencken.

After *Scopes*, only two additional states, Arkansas and Mississippi, passed anti-evolution laws; but the teaching of evolution did not spread rapidly. Indeed, the high school science curriculum remained very underdeveloped until the Cold War era, when Soviet progress in space and missile technology led to a massive push to upgrade science education.[13] The controversy over evolution then revived, and it has not died down since.

The battle has had three phases, and a good understanding of our situation today requires understanding how each phase has led to and shaped the next.[14] In the first phase, laws prohibiting the teaching of evolution were struck down as incompatible with the Establishment Clause. In the second phase, the opponents of evolution sought not a prohibition but only the teaching of Creationism alongside evolution. When that attempt also failed, the anti-evolution movement regrouped and developed a more scientific-looking alternative, Intelligent Design. This recent theory has just begun to be tested in the courts.

The first phase culminated in the case of Susan Epperson, a biology teacher in Little Rock, Arkansas.[15] Epperson had graduated from the College of the Ozarks, where her father was a professor of biology. She said that her parents "both are dedicated Christians who see no conflict between their belief in God and the scientific search for truth. I share this belief." Married to an Air Force officer who was part of a missile crew stationed at the Little Rock Air Force Base, she began teaching in the Little Rock schools.[16] The new edition of a standard textbook had introduced a tentative, generalized reference to evolution. Epperson believed that she had a responsibility to acquaint her students with this theory, as she later testified,[17] but she also believed that it clashed with Arkansas' anti-evolution law (worded similarly to the Tennessee law in Scopes's case). At the request of the Arkansas Education Association, she agreed to challenge the law in court, "because of my concept of my responsibilities both as a teacher of biology and as an American citizen."[18]

The law was challenged on several grounds, one being its vagueness, which left science teachers unclear about what they could and could not teach. It might have been struck down on that basis, and four of the Justices argued that this would be the right legal argument, using the Due Process Clause of the Fourteenth Amendment. Five, however felt that the Establishment Clause was implicated, and Judge Abe Fortas wrote a majority opinion to that effect, saying that the law violates the required "governmental neutrality between religion and religion, and between religion and non-religion." It was clear, he said, that a sectarian conviction about divine creation was the reason for the law. Such religious views may be taught historically, as "part of a secular program of education," but the state may not prefer them, as would be the case if a teaching perceived to conflict with them were to be banned.

Opponents of evolutionary theory eventually regrouped, enunciating a view known as "scientific creationism" and arguing that this view ought to have equal time with evolution in the schools. They promoted legislation in a variety of states with the purpose of mandating "equal time." One such law was, again, in Arkansas. The ACLU promptly challenged it, recruiting top scientists to explain evolution. The state, unable to find convincing scientific testimony on its side, presented expert testimony about "cometary seeding" (the view that life on Earth was "seeded" by comets that delivered genetic material to Earth from interstellar dust in outer space) with such poor results that leading religious figures denounced the state attorney general as a closet ally of the ACLU.[19] Judge Overton, in federal district court, declared the law unconstitutional, saying that it had neither a valid secular purpose nor a primarily secular effect.

There remained Louisiana's "Balanced Treatment for Creation-Science and Evolution-Science in Public School Instruction" act, which forbade schools to teach evolution unless "creation science" was also taught and given a balanced treatment. In 1987, this law was struck down by the U.S. Supreme Court, by a 7–2 majority. Justice Brennan, writing for the majority, used the *Lemon* test and found that the law did not have a valid secular purpose.[20] The weakness of the scientific evidence for "creation science" was a great problem for its proponents. In further lower court decisions, stickers placed in textbooks in several states, warning that "this textbook contains material on evolution" and saying that "evolution is a theory, not a fact," were also ordered removed, on the ground that it is an Establishment Clause violation to single out evolution from among all the scientific theories that are taught, as if it is in some way uniquely controversial. (The Georgia warning sticker case is still being contested.)

Evolutionary biology is not uniquely controversial, not among scientists. In fact, in the scientific community, it is not controversial at all. Its main claims have long been overwhelmingly supported by evidence. As biologist Jerry Coyne writes, evolution is both theory and fact. "Theory," as scientists use the term, does not mean a "guess" or a "hunch." It means a unifying account that is testable by observations, that has survived a good deal of such testing, and that makes confirmable predictions about new cases. (Of course, in the case of evolution, given the millennia it takes for change to occur, most of the actual confirmation comes from new archaeological discoveries that bear out what the theory says we should expect to find.) "Theory" contrasts with "fact" or observation only in the sense that theory is overarching, bringing a variety of data into a perspicuous pattern. In this sense gravity is a theory, the account of the atom is a theory. Evolution is as well established as these other theories. The reason that laws banning the teaching of evolution, or urging "equal time" for a religious account, have not stood up to scrutiny is that there is no scientific reason for singling out evolution for challenge, so the purpose must be a religious purpose. Creation science wore this purpose on its face, and was easily rebutted.

Recently, the opponents of evolution have paid more attention to the canons of scientific explanation and have produced a more intellectually so-phisticated version of creation science—that is "Intelligent Design," or ID. Its negative claim is that certain gaps in the evolutionary record show weaknesses in evolutionary theory. Unfortunately for ID, some of the gaps to which atten-tion was directed have by now been filled in a way that strongly supports evo-lution, through new fossil evidence.[21] ID's principal positive claim is that some instances of "irreducible complexity" in nature are best explained not by evolution but by the positing of a superior intelligence or "master intellect" who created these life-forms. Although proponents do not name this intelli-gence, and often assert that it might be a space alien or some other entity quite unlike God, it is perfectly clear that the theory is actually a descendant of cre-ation science, and that it has deep religious roots.[22] Its proponents are some-times forthright about their religious goals: in raising funds for an ID textbook, *Of Pandas and People*, one ID proponent writes, "[W]e have to in-undate [young people] with a rational, defensible, well-argued Judeo-Chris-tian worldview. FTE's carefully researched books do just that." A document known as the Wedge Document, developed by leading ID proponents, speaks of the goal of the ID movement as replacing science as currently practiced with "theistic and Christian science."[23]

ID, as has often been noted, is not exactly new: indeed the argument from design goes back at least to Thomas Aquinas, and had wide currency in nine-teenth-century responses to Darwinism, the only difference being that these older arguments don't use biochemistry, and they do name God as the (super-natural) creator.[24] ID has had somewhat more success than creation science—

in part because of President Bush's support,[25] in part because its proponents argue more carefully and have better academic credentials than their earlier counterparts.

In October 2004, the Dover, Pennsylvania, school board (after a lot of debate) passed a resolution saying: "Students will be made aware of gaps/problems in Darwin's theory and of other theories of evolution including, but not limited to, intelligent design. Note: Origins of Life is not taught."[26] A month later, the school board clarified its intentions in a press release, announcing that, beginning in January 2005, teachers would be required to read the following statement to students in the ninth grade biology class at Dover High School:

> The Pennsylvania Academic Standards require students to learn about Darwin's Theory of Evolution and eventually to take a standardized test of which evolution is a part.
>
> Because Darwin's Theory is a theory, it continues to be tested as new evidence is discovered. The Theory is not a fact. Gaps in the Theory exist for which there is no evidence. A theory is defined as a well-tested explanation that unifies a broad range of observations.
>
> Intelligent Design is an explanation of the origin of life that differs from Darwin's view. The reference book, *Of Pandas and People*, is available for students who might be interested in gaining an understanding of what Intelligent Design actually involves.
>
> With respect to any theory, students are encouraged to keep an open mind. The school leaves the discussion of the Origins of Life to individual students and their families. As a Standards-driven district, class instruction focuses upon preparing students to achieve proficiency on Standards-based assessments.

All eight science teachers in the high school protested in a letter saying, "intelligent design is not science. It is not biology. It is not an accepted scientific theory."[27] They asked to be excused from reading the statement, saying that to do so would "knowingly and intentionally misrepresent subject matter or curriculum." School administrators actually read the statement to all the ninth grade classes, while the teachers and some students left the room.[28] The administrators added the statement, "There will be no other discussion of the issue and your teachers will not answer questions on the issue."[29]

Not surprisingly, the case ended up in court, in the Federal District Court for the Middle District of Pennsylvania. Weeks of expert testimony on both sides were offered. On December 20, 2006, Judge John Jones issued a 149-page opinion declaring the school board's policy unconstitutional. The opinion is very impressive on a number of fronts. Judge Jones really tried to acquaint himself with the scientific issues, and he understood what witnesses were saying, to the extent that he was able to form an independent well-reasoned judgment, arguing that ID is not science, but a thinly disguised religious viewpoint. He also marshaled the evidence about ID's founding and the various religious statements of its founders in a convincing way, creating a helpful public record.

Particularly impressive, though less discussed in the media, is Judge Jones's legal reasoning. He argues, first, that the endorsement test is an essential part of a good inquiry about whether a policy has a secular effect. He marshals the Supreme Court and Third Circuit precedents very convincingly, showing that endorsement, introduced as a way of articulating both secular purpose and secular effect, has had lasting and central importance in the second area above all. (In the end, Judge Jones concludes that ID fails on both "secular purpose" and "secular effect," though he connects the endorsement test more closely to the "effect" prong.) He then goes further, studying the various versions of the endorsement test to see what criteria for his own analysis they suggest. He comes to the conclusion that the "reasonable observer," in this case, needs to be, in effect, two distinct observers. The Third Circuit has indicated that in cases dealing with schools, the point of view of a reasonable objective high school student needs to be considered, but, he argues, it is also important to consider the reaction of a reasonable observer who is a member of the adult community. In both cases, this observer is imagined as one who knows the history of the challenged policy, the history of the community, and "the broader social and historical context in which the policy arose."[30]

So, as Judge Jones sees it, the questions to be asked are, first, whether the imaginary reasonable student observer (who might not be identical with any real-life student) would judge that the policy shows school system favor for a religious viewpoint; and, second, whether the reasonable adult observer would form a similar judgment.

On both counts, Judge Jones answers in the affirmative: the policy is reasonably perceived as one that advances a sectarian religious viewpoint. The objective observer would know that ID evolved from earlier creationist teaching and would be aware that the account of "gaps" in evolutionary theory problematizes that theory alone among scientific theories, simply because it is religiously contested. The observer would also know the documents that show the orientation and aims of the proponents of ID to be religious in nature. The observer would understand that ID introduces supernatural causation, and is thus outside the realm of science as science has been understood for centuries. ID has failed to publish in peer-reviewed science journals, to engage in research and testing, to undergo scientific scrutiny, and, in general, to form part of the scientific community.[31] For all these reasons, the observer would conclude that the ID policy constitutes an endorsement of religion by the school board.

The case will not be appealed, because new elections for school board resulted in the defeat of the pro-ID members and the election of a group who oppose the ID policy. It seems likely, moreover, that the thorough and unequivocal nature of Judge Jones's opinion has removed ID from the political map for some time. The issues it raises, however, have not disappeared, and probably will not disappear for some time. Can our equality-based perspective supply anything that will assist public debate in this divisive area?

First, it would be good if public debate could dispel those objections to evolution that are based on misunderstanding. If people understand what scientists mean by "theory" and how theories, evolution included, are tested and supported, that would by itself be progress. (An excellent permanent exhibit for children at Chicago's Field Museum, called "Evolving Planet," does this very simply, in language that grade school children can easily understand, apparently without controversy.) At the same time, people should become acquainted with the massive evidence supporting evolutionary theory as contrasted with ID.

Next, it would be good if that misunderstanding about "a lower order of animals" could also be removed. Evolutionary biologists are not teaching that human beings evolved from something base or disgusting. Indeed, Darwin loved life in all its forms, and had respect for the complex cognitive capacities of animals as simple as the flatworm.[32] Nor does anything in evolutionary biology prevent us from holding that human beings have dignity and that this dignity ought to be respected. Darwin's theory, by stressing the continuity between human life and the lives of some nonhuman animals, does strongly suggest that we might look and see whether this dignity is not also present in animal life, but it never suggests disrespect for human life. Americans will continue to argue about what human dignity is and how it is related to natural properties of various sorts of creatures. Those controversies, however, are to a large extent independent of scientific controversies, in the sense that a range of subtly different ethical positions are compatible with the scientific evidence.[33]

It would also be good if opponents of evolution did not associate it with irreligiosity. Proponents of evolution have a wide range of different views, theistic, nontheistically religious, agnostic, and atheist. Religious people have many ways of making sense of the totality of their beliefs, and have since modern science began. Accepting Darwin's theory is incompatible with accepting certain types of Protestant fundamentalism. It is not incompatible with Judaism or Christianity per se—in the sense that there are many nonliteral versions of the origin of life in Judaism and Christianity that are fully compatible with evolutionary biology—and, as I have said, most traditional forms of Judaism and Christianity happily accept nonliteral interpretation.

On the other side, it would be great if scientific people who are themselves atheists would not speak dismissively or condescendingly about religion, suggest that religion is only for dummies, or even suggest that religion is basically a source of strife and bad behavior. There are many sources of strife and bad behavior in human life. Religious extremism has sometimes been one of them, but so has atheistic political extremism, as in various violent Marxian regimes and the basically atheistic regime of Nazi Germany. So, too, has the extremism of profit, as in the violence of capitalist colonialism. The violence of men against women is one of the most long-lived and pervasive types of violence in human history, and it appears to have little to do with religious, political, or even economic ideologies, since its religious versions are continuous with their cultural origins, and religion has shown at least as great a capacity for self-reform as have its surrounding cultures.

There is much more to be said about how it happens that religious doctrines that internally favor peace so often lead to violence against one's neighbors, but this phenomenon probably has much more to do with universal human frailty, and with the mobilizing power of ideologies, than with anything specific to religion or religions. It would be best if all people could focus on combating bad behavior wherever it arises, rather than smugly suggesting that if we were all atheists, the world would be a more peaceful place. The history of Marxism certainly did not support that contention.

To be a successful nation, our nation, like all modern nations, needs science, and science undiluted, science as it meets the highest standards of scientists and scientific journals. Our children need to learn science undiluted, and the incursion of religious viewpoints into this sphere is unfortunate. It seems fine, and in fact valuable, for children to learn about different religious viewpoints in courses on history and culture. To substitute a religious viewpoint for science is to jeopardize our future. With Judge Jones, however, I would emphasize a further point: it is also unfair. To require a religious teaching in the science curriculum is to give a governmental endorsement to the religious doctrine of a single group.

IV. Imagination and Difference in the Classroom

I have said that the public schools can and must teach values that lie at the heart of our political principles. A further aspect of making democracy stable is the inculcation of attitudes that provide the emotional underpinning for those principles. We see this emotional formation happening all the time. Schoolchildren learn to love the history of the civil rights struggle and the people who fought it. They celebrate the birthday of Martin Luther King, Jr., a major national holiday that conveys a strong message: racism is bad and equal respect and inclusion are good. They listen to King's emotive rhetoric in the "I Have a Dream" speech, and they learn to identify with those sentiments. If they are shown images of George Wallace and other leading segregationists, they are taught not to identify with those examples. Some of them might put on a play about Rosa Parks, learning how racism feels through the experience of stigma and apartness. Others might tell the stories of their own ancestors' struggles with slavery. Similar exercises take place with disability, with gender, with the majority's relationship to other racial and ethnic minorities. The classroom strongly encourages the use of imagination to come to grips with the variety of people who live together in our country.

Where religion is concerned, government may not express a particular message, as it does with race. But it still may teach *about* religious difference and its history; it still may acquaint students with the wide range of religions that exist in America today; and it still may convey as truth, and as a principle worthy of love, the principle of equal respect for conscience. It may also emphasize the importance of understanding the diversity of America and the need of all Americans for acknowledgment of their equality.

In all of this teaching, the imagination is of central importance. A constitution is only words on paper. What makes it live in a young person's life is the ability to imagine diversity and to see equal humanity in strange and unfamiliar shapes. The humanity of another human being is an easy thing to deny, and equal humanity is even easier to deny. When you look at a strange shape before you, what is it that tells you that this shape is that of a full-fledged equal human being, rather than that of a member of an inferior primitive group, or a godless uncivilized tribe, or even a lifeless machine? As Roger Williams indicates in the poem that is my epigraph, pride makes it easy for us to be stingy with our attributions of humanity, and it takes a real imagination to see beneath the Indian's strange garb, customs, and language a person equal in worth to oneself. It was not very long ago that a large proportion of Americans thought that African-Americans were an inferior race. People with a wide range of disabilities are still treated as inferior every day. A humanoid face and form don't seem sufficient to guarantee the presence of an equal human soul within, not so long as people find it convenient to avoid the attribution of equal humanity.

This tendency to deny can be overcome—if people learn to imagine the presence of humanity in another. But people don't cultivate their imaginations enough. Often they simply are unable to imagine that a shape in front of them has an inner life similar to their own. As time goes on they may come to have an active stake in denying that. Novelist Charles Dickens suggested that the absence of this cultivation of imagination was a central factor in the callous treatment of the poor in his time: people learned to see them as inputs into economic formulae, no more individual, no more different from one another than "ants and beetles passing to and from their nests."[34] Was it, then, any wonder that industrialists and politicians treated workers as cogs in a machine, rather than as human beings with minds and hearts?

The task of educating the imagination of difference, the imagination that sees equal humanity behind difference, is a very important part of primary education.[35] Children learn that ability easily, as soon as they can talk, if not before. The minute they can ask the question, "Twinkle twinkle little star, how I wonder what you are," they are in the realm of imagination, and this realm is cultivated, through childhood, by stories of all sorts.[36] As time goes on, the stories get more and more sophisticated, as children learn to put themselves into the shoes of people good and bad, black and white, old and young. Ethnic, religious, and national differences often have particular attraction for young children curious about the world they are in, and many first-rate books for children focus on these differences. It is absolutely standard practice for primary educators to develop this focus on difference in ways that connect it to the diversity that our nation contains, which may or may not be fully represented in the classroom.

For some believing Christians in our nation, this exercise of imagination is sinful. It is a kind of magical thinking, and magic is bad. What is good is strict obedience to the literal word of the Bible. It is a little difficult to know whether this can be an internally coherent position. The Bible does not contain instructions about how its lessons are to be applied to a wide range of situations that people encounter in real life, so even living by the Bible usually requires using one's imagination to connect scriptural text to daily reality. Nor does the Bible give instructions for daily life in the twentieth century, which contains many situations and entities that did not exist in biblical times. So it would appear that to apply it to new circumstances one must rely on imagination. Jesus, as I've said, requires nonliteral reading of the audience who hear his parables, so even reading the Gospels literally requires us to think metaphorically. Moreover, when a child grows up in a family with good ethical beliefs, she still needs to learn that her mother and father are not just looming shapes that, like robots, minister to her interests, but individual human beings with minds and hearts, and needs similar to her own. The end of narcissism, and the beginning of true morality, require such acts of imagination.

I am inclined to think that evangelicals who speak ill of imagination do not mean to condemn its every application, for otherwise how could they teach their children that their aggression inflicts pain on others, a lesson that seems to lie at the core of all real morality? It isn't self-evident that the screams and cries of a person who has been assaulted are really pain, the way you and I feel it. (As brilliant a person as seventeenth-century philosopher René Descartes held that the yelps of animals being vivisected were not real pain, but only reflex motions.) But let us put this objection to one side and consider what the denial of imagination means for citizenship.

In a famous 1987 case called *Mozert v. Hawkins*, a group of evangelical parents in Tennessee, led by Bob Mozert and Vicky Frost, took issue with a new collection of elementary reading books that their school district had ordered. They had many objections, finding in the books various things that seemed to violate their fundamentalist creed. They didn't like mention of boys cooking, which seemed to break down traditional gender roles. They didn't like mention of the historical achievements of outstanding women. They didn't like the word "comrade," which they thought a communistic word. They didn't like alleged hidden messages in the text that seemed to them to endorse Satanism. They argued that the texts promoted Hinduism, because they thought that Hinduism was connected to the themes of mental telepathy, evolution, and other themes they discovered in the texts and found objectionable.

Among the hundreds of objections they mentioned, however, paramount was an objection to exposing their children to "other forms of religion and to the feelings, attitudes and values of other students that contradict the plaintiffs' religious views without a statement that the other views are incorrect and that the plaintiffs' views are the correct ones."[37] This objection appears to have been twofold. First, they objected to mention of religions with a content different from their own, without denunciation of that content. Second, they objected to stories mentioning the imagination, since they thought that these stories encouraged a belief in witchcraft or demonic possession. For example, a section called "Seeing Beneath the Surface," which referred to the use of the imagination as a way of seeing things not visible to the physical eyes, was held to be "related to an occult theme." Vicky Frost said that it is sinful to "use imagination beyond the limits of scriptural authority."

Interestingly, the parents did not object to the idea of "critical reading," which was taught along with the books: students were asked not just to read and internalize, but to evaluate what they read. Parents admitted that "critical reading is an essential skill which their children must develop in order to succeed in other subjects and to function as effective participants in modern society."[38] It is rather difficult to see how the practice of critical reading could be sharply separated from the aspects of the reading series to which the parents took exception. Nor is it easy to square this concession with the fundamentalism they elsewhere espoused: Vicky Frost said that the Bible "is the totality of my beliefs."[39]

The parents tried to arrange exemptions for their children from the mandatory reading classes. When alternative arrangements eventually broke down, their children still refused to attend the reading classes, and were eventually expelled from school. The parents went to court, claiming that the reading requirement imposed a substantial burden on their religious free exercise.

In *Battleground: One Mother's Crusade, the Religious Right, and the Struggle for Control of Our Classrooms,*[40] journalist Stephen Bates paints a vivid portrait of the plaintiffs and of the diverse outside groups that eventually arrayed themselves on the two sides of the case. He suggests that some reasonable accommodation might have been reached, under which the children would have read from an alternative set of books, had both sides, after a certain point, not been so rigid and bent on control. The story he tells casts doubt on this contention, since the objections of the parents are so numerous and so wide-ranging that it is difficult to imagine any group of elementary school reading texts that would not be found objectionable in some respect. Very likely if there were a series that seemed better along some important dimensions (feminism, for example), parents would waive their other objections for a while. Such an accommodation, however, would probably be temporary at best, and unstable.

When one considers the religious views that Vicky Frost and Bob Mozert held, it does appear that the reading books imposed a burden of some sort on their religious free exercise, since their religion is one that mandates nonexposure to different views and nonuse of the imagination to think about other people's and groups' experiences. They made it clear that a brief mention of some other view might be acceptable, but "if the practices of other religions were described in detail, or if the philosophy was 'profound' in that it expressed a world view that deeply undermined her religious beliefs, then her children 'would have to be instructed to [the] error [of the other philosophy].'"[41] On the other hand, as the idea of "substantial burden" has been developed throughout our tradition, mere exposure to a view does not constitute a burden. No student complained of having been required to affirm a belief or disbelief in any idea or practice in the readers. So, although one can understand the plaintiffs' idea that exposure was contaminating, mere exposure cannot constitute a "substantial burden" as the religion clauses have standardly been interpreted. Chief Judge Lively argues convincingly that other cases in the tradition all involve some element of "compulsion to engage in conduct that violated the plaintiffs' religious convictions." Mrs. Sherbert was not merely exposed to the view that Saturday is not the Sabbath: she was penalized for holding that it was. Free Exercise violations always involve, in this way, an element of coercion.

Because no substantial burden (in the sense relevant to our legal tradition) was found, the Court did not need to ask whether the state had a compelling interest (the relevant standard in 1987, before *Smith*). Nonetheless, Chief Judge Lively speaks in an illuminating way of the importance, for democracy, of exposure to diverse views:

> The Supreme Court has recently affirmed that public schools serve the purpose of teaching fundamental values "essential to a democratic society." These values "include tolerance of divergent political and religious views" while taking into account "consideration of the sensibilities of others." The "tolerance of divergent . . . religious views" referred to by the Supreme Court is a civil tolerance, not a religious one. It does not require a person to accept any other religion as the equal of the one to which that person adheres. It merely requires a recognition that in a pluralistic society we must "live and let live." If the Hawkins County schools had required the plaintiff students either to believe or say they believe that "all religions are merely different roads to God," this would be a different case.[42]

Judge Kennedy, in her concurrence, mentions similar facts as reasons why there is a compelling state interest—even though that issue did not have to be reached, in her view, since no burden was found.

Judge Lively's distinction between "civil tolerance" and "religious tolerance" (a distinction with a long philosophical pedigree) has particular importance. Recall that we said that the common ground on which citizens live together, sharing political institutions, has a moral content, but not a metaphysical or specifically religious content. That is why it can be endorsed by citizens who hold many different religious views. The proposition that all religions are roads to God is a controversial theological proposition that many religions in our society cannot endorse. Many believers, then, cannot accept religious or theological toleration, and a public endorsement of that theological view would endorse some religious teachings and disendorse their own. Civil tolerance is what we have called equal respect for conscience: it is an attitude of respect for persons, who may be in error, but who are entitled to be considered as free and equal members of the political community. It is the type of tolerance (I prefer "respect") that Catholic philosopher Jacques Maritain spoke of in a passage discussed in Chapter 1:

> There is real and genuine tolerance only when a man is firmly and absolutely convinced of a truth, or of what he holds to be a truth, and when he at the same time recognizes the right of those who deny this truth to exist, and to contradict him, and to speak their own mind, not because they are free from truth but because they seek truth in their own way, and because he respects in them human nature and human dignity and those very resources and living springs of the intellect and of conscience which make them potentially capable of attaining the truth he loves.[43]

Now we are in a position to understand better what Maritain is after. He wants a society that extends liberty to all its citizens' consciences—not on the ground that their views are correct, since many believe that their neighbors' views are incorrect, and we need to show respect for their convictions, but on the ground that we respect them as human beings and beings whose consciences are striving after understanding. Maritain is responding, here, to an opponent who has claimed that toleration in a liberal democracy must always be based on skepticism and that this skepticism is unacceptable to believing Christians. Maritain, with Roger Williams, says no, it is based on respect for their consciences. Accepting the principle of civil toleration does not burden the conscience of the believer, because it does not ask him to qualify his belief or to affirm that his neighbors are not in error.

Why is exposure to differing views important for civil tolerance? Why can't schools simply say, and repeat, "All of you are equal citizens, entitled to equal liberty of conscience"? Perhaps for some children that thin teaching would be sufficient—children who already understand the fact of pluralism in their society and who have been encouraged in attitudes of respect. Imagine, however, children who are brought up at home to think that only their own view is good and that other views are *evil* (not just wrong). For such children, it will be difficult to arrive at the attitude of equal respect. Even the acknowledgment of basic humanity in another is an achievement, not something we can take for granted. Seeing as equal another who might easily be treated as lower, not fully human, requires getting to know the other a bit, listening to the other's story. Understanding does not guarantee acknowledgment, but ignorance is a virtual guarantee of nonacknowledgment, in a climate of polarization and mistrust. When, through reading, children are acquainted with other views as views that real human beings hold, when they understand these different stories as, each, the story of a person, they have an easier time recognizing the humanity of the people around them who hold such views, views that initially might surprise or repel them. Gradually, they come to see these different people as having similar faculties of conscience and striving, as people trying to make sense of life. That way of seeing others is a crucial linchpin of religious liberty.

Think of the similar case of people with disabilities. When children met children with disabilities in the past, unequipped with any understanding of their stories, they often let the weirdness of the appearance of a child with Down syndrome, or cerebral palsy, put them off, so that they started thinking, "These are not real human beings like me." Today, in any good classroom in which these children participate, teachers try to get the "normal" children to understand what the lives of children with disabilities are like—not only so that they will be more sensitive in lots of concrete ways, but, more importantly, so that they will be able to think of these children as full-fledged individuals, each with a life history and a set of desires and strivings. Jews, fundamentalists, Hindus, Native American believers—all these and many others have similarly been treated as weird aliens and denied human recognition. Learning about the views and lives of others is a way of undoing those denials.

The Supreme Court refused to hear *Mozert*, so it remains binding law in the Sixth Circuit, persuasive law in other circuits. The issues it raises may come before the Court in some form at a later date. When and if they do, we need to think carefully about what democracy requires. Today it is all too common to focus on the scientific and technical abilities that the public schools impart and to neglect the foundations of democratic citizenship. *Mozert* is a good reminder of some of these abilities, and their importance for a shared future in a nation of increasing religious diversity.

V. Fearing Strangers: Same-Sex Marriage

No issues in our time are more divisive than the political and legal issues surrounding the standing of gays and lesbians in U.S. society. Sodomy laws have now been declared unconstitutional,[44] as have a range of state initiatives that block local efforts to protect gays and lesbians through antidiscrimination legislation.[45] These decisions, however, remain controversial. The controversy over same-sex marriage, meanwhile, becomes ever more intense, as one state (at present) makes same-sex marriage available, as three others offer civil unions, and as many more have passed or are currently debating laws or state constitutional amendments defining marriage as the union of one man with one woman. Can the framework we have worked out to think about religious fairness help us in this delicate area?

First of all, are the issues religious issues or not? Certainly a common justification offered for policies denying gays and lesbians equality in marriage and other areas of public life is a religious reason, namely, the prohibition on homosexual acts in *Leviticus* (20:13, where males are forbidden to "lie with a man as with a woman"). Sometimes this textual appeal is combined with appeal to a shared moral/religious tradition. We might, then, regard a set of commitments about the status of gays and lesbians as a part of many people's religious views, and consider whether the religious clauses have any bearing on what the state ought to say.

The idea that denying gays and lesbians a variety of public privileges under law is an essential part of Judaeo-Christian religion, something without which religion suffers a substantial burden, is, put just that way, unconvincing. There are so many parts of the Bible that believing Jews and Christians do not seek to enforce as public law: prohibitions on idol worship and heresy, for example, which cannot be enforced as public law because of the religion clauses themselves. There are also many biblical prohibitions that, in the modern era, strike most people as an implausible basis for public law: few, for example, would support general laws forbidding intercourse during a woman's menstrual period or laws forbidding tattooing, even though observant Jews impose these prohibitions on themselves. To my knowledge nobody supports laws making fortune-telling illegal, and yet it is as strongly denounced in the Bible as homosexuality—indeed more so, since same-sex relations are mentioned only once, whereas consulting fortune tellers and mediums is mentioned repeatedly in *Leviticus* 19–20, and they are singled out for a particularly gruesome mode of death, by stoning (20:27). Cursing one's father or mother is assigned the death penalty in *Leviticus* 20, shortly before the list of sexual offenses in which same-sex acts figure; and yet nobody is proposing enforcing that prohibition through public law. Same-sex acts, moreover, are treated in *Leviticus* exactly the way adultery is treated (20:10), and few Jews and Christians, however pious, still support criminal penalties for adultery.

Then there is the matter of greed, sharp dealing in business, withholding the wages of one's laborers (*Leviticus* 19:13), putting obstacles in the way of people who are deaf or blind (19:14), failing to give aliens exactly the same treatment that the native-born receive (19:34), and failure to help the poor. Such sins of retentiveness and egoism are mentioned far more often in the Bible than is homosexual conduct (which, as I've said, is mentioned just once). Some of them may be good grounds for public law, part of an overlapping consensus based on equal respect, since violations in these areas harm others and violate their rights. But these biblical texts are ignored in the debate about gay rights. Jews and Christians do not seek legal action against the greedy on account of the long tradition of biblical denunciation, and they certainly do not all line up behind laws mandating equal treatment for aliens. One might then wonder why homosexuality is singled out for special attention: one might at least pose the question whether the motives for singling it out are pure religious motives or some mixture of fear, shame, and disgust that would not bear close scrutiny. We can also see that people are far more eager to target others, especially a relatively powerless minority, than they are to work on their own sins and errors, so (among heterosexuals) greed gets little attention and homosexuality gets a lot of attention.

Even were there some people who sought the implementation of the entirety of *Leviticus*, the Roger Williams tradition that we have defended tells such people that they must stop short when acting on their religion threatens the equal standing of others in the political realm. It has never been our tradition's view that religious freedom entitles citizens to act on and enforce any and every commandment of their religions, where those commandments impact the rights of others.

Is the sinfulness of homosexuality even a shared religious tenet? We also need to confront the inconvenient fact that the Judaeo-Christian religions differ greatly in their understanding of the tradition concerning homosexuality. The well-known sentence in *Leviticus* is difficult to interpret. What does it mean to say that men shall not lie with a man as one would with a woman? Scholars agree that the sentence does not say anything about females, thus nothing about same-sex conduct among them (which, in antiquity, was usually not regarded as similar to or classified with same-sex conduct among males). Most, moreover, think that the male acts it forbids do not include all same-sex sexual acts. (One view, strongly suggested by the text, is that it forbids only active, insertive male-male acts.) But suppose it did condemn all same-sex acts, or is read nonliterally so as to do so: what then? Most Judaeo-Christian denominations do not read everything in the Bible ahistorically. They ignore some prohibitions (e.g., on fortune-telling) as the legacy of another era, and they consider only a part of what they read as lasting moral insight applicable to their own time. For example, most denominations now accept female clergy, although earlier they believed that a literal reading of scripture forbade female clergy. These changes have happened very rapidly. When I was a teenager I wanted to be an Episcopal minister, and I was told by my local minister, in 1964, that this change was impossible and would simply never happen. Women began to be ordained as Episcopal priests in 1974; in 1976 their ordination as both priests and bishops was officially sanctioned. In 2006, Katherine Jefferts Schori, only six years younger than I am, was chosen as the first female presiding bishop of the Episcopal Church.

Change, then, is an ongoing fact of life in every religion. Differences of opinion concerning the morality of homosexual conduct and its implications for the ordination of clergy and the institution of marriage are intense within more or less every Judaeo-Christian denomination, even more than they are across the denominations.[46] One thing one can see clearly is that there is no single Judaeo-Christian position on such questions.

Even in the fraught area of marriage, the Judaeo-Christian tradition at present exhibits great diversity. Reconstructionist and Reform Jews both permit and perform same-sex marriages; they were joined in December 2006 by Conservative Jews, who permit commitment ceremonies without calling them "marriage." Reform Jews, indeed, have actively lobbied against the recently defeated constitutional amendment to ban same-sex marriage. Unitarian/Universalists accept same-sex marriage and have also lobbied against the proposed constitutional amendment. It is well-known that the issue of same-sex conduct and partnership has divided the Anglican Communion worldwide, as the Protestant Episcopal Church of the United States, having consecrated an openly gay bishop living in long-term partnership with another man, has refused to back down. (The church's recent selection of Jefferts Schori as presiding bishop has only added fuel to the fire, since some member churches in the Communion do not accept female bishops.) Presbyterians and Methodists also have widely publicized battles over this set of issues. Roman Catholics have less widely publicized battles.[47] One could say, looking at the picture overall, that many religious Americans support a variety of gay rights measures, including the right to same-sex marriage. Indeed, the largest organized group of Americans that supports and practices same-sex marriage is probably the Reform Jewish community. Agnostics and atheists, meanwhile, are also divided. So this issue can hardly be cast as one that pits the religious against the nonreligious.

Given these facts, what connection might the religion clauses have with the legal issues facing gays and lesbians? It seems difficult to imagine any Free Exercise claim in this area. George Reynolds's religion required, or at least very strongly urged, polygamous marriage, so he had a not implausible Free Exercise claim when the state arrested and imprisoned him for his conduct. Reynolds did not even claim or argue that the state ought to have extended to his plural marriages all the same protections that it gave to monogamous marriages; he was interested only in avoiding prosecution. So even if one holds, as I do, that *Reynolds* was badly argued and very likely wrongly decided, it does not establish a right, on religious grounds, to the state's *recognition* of one's religious marriage. No denomination I know of, moreover, requires same-sex marriage or holds it to be a necessary part of good religious life. And now that sodomy laws are a thing of the past, gays and lesbians face no criminal penalty for contracting religious marriages and living together as married couples (although they continue to suffer many civil disabilities by comparison to heterosexual couples married by the state). So they are not in Reynolds's position, although at one time they were closer to it. They do not, then, appear to have a plausible Free Exercise claim.

The Free Exercise Clause might come up on the other side, if an institution that discriminates against gays and lesbians, or forbids same-sex dating, were threatened with loss of its tax exemption and cited reasons of religion in its defense. Bob Jones University, which forbade interracial dating on religious grounds, claimed a Free Exercise right to do so and still keep its government-granted tax exemption.[48] The university lost the tax exemption: the Court granted that there was a substantial burden to religious free exercise, but that the state had a compelling interest in removing government support for racial discrimination. One can imagine a parallel case arising in the area of same-sex dating: an institution forbids it on religious grounds, the government removes its tax exemption, and the institution goes to court, citing the Free Exercise Clause. This, however, would simply not happen: it is just unthinkable that any government, at this time in our history, state or federal, would even think of denying a tax exemption to an institution because of this type of discrimination. Even blatant sex discrimination has never been targeted: Catholic universities whose statutes require that their president be a member of a particular order of priests, hence a male, have not lost their tax exemptions, although the case for taking them away seems comparable to the case for removing Bob Jones University's tax exemption. But if we do not have a consensus about the urgency of eradicating sex discrimination, we certainly have no such public consensus about discrimination against gays and lesbians. This hypothetical case, then, would simply never get started, unless and until we enact some form of national nondiscrimination legislation for sexual orientation, and probably long after that. The fact that such a legal situation will not arise does not show, however, that it should not arise. In that sense, there is at least a potential Free Exercise issue, though one that would only be triggered by a type of government action that is at present unthinkable.

The Establishment Clause might seem more promising, for many people see the current restrictions on same-sex marriage as a de facto establishment of a Christian or Judaeo-Christian norm. But a case that claimed a right to marriage for gays and lesbians on Establishment Clause grounds would be extremely weak. As I've argued, these limitations on marriage are not particularly characteristic of Judaism and Christianity, at least in their present form; they are things with regard to which Judaism and Christianity are deeply divided, and nonreligious America is also deeply divided. Nor is there any religion that strongly promotes same-sex marriage, though many permit it.

Moreover, the state has always chosen definitions of marriage and family that favor some traditions and disfavor others, without any apparent constitutional problem under the religion clauses. During the heyday of anti-Catholic panic, for example, definitions of family reflected a preference for the Northern European norm of a small nuclear unit living in a single-family home, rather than for the larger extended families dwelling together that are more characteristic of Catholic Southern Europe.[49] And yet a challenge to these definitions on Establishment Clause grounds would have been very weak, because these family styles are part of ethnic tradition, not religious devotion.

But if the issue of sexual orientation is not really a religious issue, or, at any rate, not an issue to be handled under the religion clauses, is there some other way in which these clauses can help us think through our divisions over these issues? I believe that this book's historical narrative does put us in a position to think critically about some aspects of our current situation.

We have seen that people are very fond of establishing orthodoxies that favor themselves, and attempting to enforce those orthodoxies by law. In times of stress and insecurity, things get worse, and unpopular people get targeted as the agents of Satan in our midst. What happened to dissenters in Puritan Massachusetts happened to Mormons, Roman Catholics, and Jehovah's Witnesses, as each entered the public consciousness. Unpopular because of the strangeness of their behavior, they became handy targets of what one can only call projected panic. Dissident sexual behavior always makes these panics worse. Mormon polygamy did not cause anti-Mormon feeling (which had elicited violence even before polygamy was instituted), but it added fuel to the fire, as salacious antipolygamy novels focused on the alleged promiscuity and hyperfertility of Mormon men. Catholic sexuality was also a central focus of the anti-Catholic panic, as genteel pseudo-moral pornography portrayed convents and monasteries as places of wild sexual indulgence, and as political propaganda inspired fear of a Catholic takeover on account of the allegedly hyperfertile nature of the Catholic family.

Such sexual panics are a common part of religious discrimination and animosity in today's India. A major factor fueling Hindu violence against Muslims is, once again, a panic about a population takeover, as Muslim families are alleged to be hyperfertile on account of the alleged prevalence of polygamy.[50] Narendra Modi, the governor of the state of Gujarat who orchestrated that state's pogrom against Muslims in 2002, and whose visa to enter the United States was revoked because of his record of fomenting religious violence, campaigned for reelection, after the pogrom, on the slogan, "We are two and have two; they are five and have twenty-five"—meaning that Hindu families are monogamous and have only two children, whereas each Muslim man has four wives and twenty-five children. In reality, the rate of polygamy is about the same for Hindus as for Muslims, around 5 percent, although polygamy is illegal for Hindus and legal for Muslims. Polygamy in Islam has always been an option for the wealthy and has never been widely practiced. Nor do population data bear out the fear of an alleged population explosion.[51] Nonetheless, fear of Muslim sexuality not only fueled the panic in general, it also inspired horrifying acts of sexual revenge, in which Hindu males circulated hate literature fantasizing about the rape and torture of Muslim women and then performed such acts, killing, very likely, around a thousand women, who were often raped and then tortured, with large metal objects inserted into their bodies, before being incinerated.

A common pattern runs through these cases. In all, the majority imputes to the minority a dissident sexuality that is depicted as indulgent, hypersexual. It then uses this fear of the allegedly oversexed "other" to fuel a more general animosity toward this other's dissident religious practices and refusal to assimilate. This same pattern is prevalent in antigay propaganda. Gay men are repeatedly depicted as addicted to promiscuous sex and as sapping the vigor of the community by their alleged debauchery. Already in 1950, Lord Patrick Devlin, opposing the Wolfenden Report's recommendation that consenting same-sex acts be decriminalized, compared homosexuality to drug addiction and argued that a nation in which either of these practices was publicly tolerated would soon lose its moral spine and be unable to answer a call to arms such as Winston Churchill's call for "blood, sweat, and tears."[52] The fear of gay male sexuality is so widespread in our society, and so widely regarded as normal and reasonable, that numerous courts have even held that a noncoercive sexual advance by a gay man is a "reasonable provocation" to homicide, meaning that such circumstances can earn the defendant a reduction from murder to voluntary manslaughter.[53]

We cannot doubt, then, that there is a lot of panic about gay sexuality and that it is used to rationalize, and to fuel, violence against both gay men and lesbians, which is disturbingly widespread in our society.[54] So there is at least a very strong structural similarity between the situation of gay men and lesbians (especially gay men) in America and the situation of Muslims in India and of Mormons and Roman Catholics in nineteenth-century America. Sexual panic is a thread running through all these cases, and in all cases the aggression it prompts is moralized and rationalized by reference to religious and ethical factors. Gay panic is not exactly a religious panic of the sort we described in Chapter 5, but it is disturbingly like those panics. Indeed, when I teach the history of these nineteenth-century panics, I find that students naturally turn to the contemporary panic over sexual orientation as a parallel, seeing gays and lesbians as the contemporary group who are closest to being in the position of

Mormons and Catholics in the 1870s. (This is a particularly disturbing thought for our many Mormon students, since they believe that their ancestors were grievously wronged, but they have also been brought up to be extremely intolerant of same-sex acts and even same-sex desire. One poll at Brigham Young University showed that a large proportion of students there think that people of same-sex orientation should be expelled for the orientation alone, even if they do not have sex with anyone, a position far more punitive than the official position of the church.)

Even if the issues of same-sex rights and same-sex marriage are not religious issues, then, we can gain a critical perspective on them by thinking about the history of religion in our country. From the seventeenth century onward, the fear of strangers has led insecure Americans to try to establish hierarchies that subordinate an unpopular group, and this fear has often taken the form of imputing to the group a diseased, or hyperaggressive, sexuality.

Now of course this is one part of the debate over same-sex marriage, not the whole. And yet it does appear to be a salient aspect of the public campaign to restrict same-sex marriage. In the congressional debates over the Defense of Marriage Act, fears of the collapse of civilization were frequently invoked, and one speech, by Senator Byrd of West Virginia, even compared America to Babylon, about to topple like that unfortunate city if it did not impose restrictions on same-sex marriage.[55] The idea that heterosexual marriage is damaged by allowing same-sex couples who want to marry to do so is an idea hard to understand without invoking fear-inspired ideas of stigma and taint. Surely, if one were to ask seriously why heterosexual marriage is ending in divorce more often than formerly, and what could be done about that, one would not turn in this direction before considering many other explanatory factors (the greater labor force participation of women combined with ongoing sex discrimination in child care and housework; the absence of low-cost marriage counseling, drug and alcohol treatment, and psychiatric treatment; the longer life span, since marriages actually last about as long as they did before, only people are living past them). Nor would one conclude that the best remedy for the problems of heterosexual marriage was the exclusion of same-sex couples who value and seek the institution, at least before considering many more obvious remedies, such as subsidized counseling, drug and alcohol treatment, and subsidized child and elder care. So the nature of the debate does suggest that irrational ideas of stigma and taint are fueling panic.

Many people have sincere religious convictions that require them to forgo same-sex acts and to hold, within their own religious communities, that same-sex marriage should not be practiced there. Not all reasons for opposing same-sex marriage are based on irrational fear. But the reasons that are not based on fear do not look like public reasons, part of the shared ethical space we inhabit together; they look like theological reasons that are inside the private domain of the religions in question. Some religions hold this, but other religions (and/or other branches in the same religion) don't agree. So the religious reasons not to favor same-sex marriage look very like the religious reasons not to get a tattoo, not to eat pork, not to go to a fortune teller: these are commandments internal to a particular sect or sects. Certainly they are obligatory for the members of these sects, but they cannot be made public law without extruding the religious into the public domain in an impermissible way. We do not think that Jews and Muslims have reason to make the eating of pork illegal for everyone, simply because it is religiously off limits to Jews and Muslims. Same-sex marriage looks like it could well be this sort of issue: a good source of specific religious reasons, but not of public reasons. (Note that we think other people ought to have the right to eat pork and shellfish even though there is no religion that makes the eating of pork required, so the availability of pork doesn't depend on a Free Exercise accommodation; it just depends on the absence of a good public reason against the eating of pork. Similarly, the fact that no religion requires same-sex marriage does not mean that there is no case for its public availability: the case does not turn on an idea of Free Exercise accommodation.)

Some people do offer purported public reasons against recognizing same-sex marriage. One such reason that is not very strong is that by admitting such marriages the state would thereby be endorsing "the gay lifestyle," and thus insulting sincere believers for whom it is sinful. Certainly the state uses many considerations when it decides which marriages to recognize, as it does when it defines the family, but moral approval has never been salient among these interests. If moral approval were conveyed by allowing two people to marry, we would have a different regime of heterosexual marriage from the one we currently have, where wedding licenses may be obtained more or less on demand and there is no inquiry at all into the character of the parties, their history of drug or alcohol addiction, and so forth. Most religions do engage in serious inquiry before they marry heterosexual couples, precisely because, in those religions, marriage does connote a degree of moral approval. This has never been true of state marriage. Nor is it true of the public definitions of family that have prevailed in different times and places. When the state decides which groups deserve the title "family"—for example, only nuclear households, or also extended networks of relations—is is considering quite a few state interests—including, prominently, interests in attracting certain classes of immigrants—but moral approval is not what it is all about. If grandparents are recognized as parts of "family" by one state and not another, that is not because one state thinks grandparents good and the other thinks them bad. Both, probably, think that they are good; they just have a variety of financial and other interests that affect their decision.[56]

If this endorsement argument is weak, what about other arguments that at least look like public reasons? We might try to maintain that the opposition to same-sex marriage is not like the religion-based panics we have studied, if we can locate such arguments. Arguments do not always wear their true purpose on their face, nor are courts required to take them at face value. Laws against miscegenation paraded in a religious and moral dress, but the Supreme Court ultimately held that they were nothing but a device to shore up "White Supremacy."[57] We might, however, try to argue that the desire to pass laws against same-sex marriage is different. What, for example, about the view that marriage ought to retain its traditional link with procreation?[58]

Unfortunately, this argument goes either too far or not far enough. The state has never sought to limit marriage to those who wish to procreate or who are able to procreate. Religions may impose such further limits if they choose, through commandments peculiar to that religion, but the traditional public concept of marriage has opened marriage to the infertile as well as the fertile, and, very conspicuously, to those who are too old to procreate as well as those in childbearing years. So if the (putatively) public argument does any work, it entails excluding such couples from marriage. Moreover, same-sex couples can and do have and raise children, whether by adoption or through artificial insemination or by raising the biological children of one member of the pair. So it just isn't true that the state's interest in children is not served by the recognition of same-sex marriages.

Suppose, then, we rephrase the nature of the state interest, saying that it is an interest in supporting couples who plan to have children that are the biological children of the two people. Again, this argument goes either too far or not far enough. Heterosexual couples have always been able to adopt children, to rear children from a prior marriage, and to use artificial insemination, so a restriction of marriage to those who plan to have biological children that are the children of both partners would impose drastic limits on heterosexual marriage. Nobody is even suggesting that we should impose any of these new limits. But if we don't exclude such heterosexuals, then the argument doesn't exclude same-sex couples either.

The failure to suggest such limits for heterosexual marriage suggests that the people who proffer the marriage-for-procreation argument don't really mean what they are saying, that the restriction on same-sex marriage is not supported, in actuality, by this plausible-seeming public argument but, rather, by fear that the heterosexual institution will somehow be defiled or tainted. And this fear does lie close to the fears that underlay laws against miscegenation, which the Court held to be based merely on the desire to establish "White Supremacy."

Other moral arguments against same-sex marriage suffer from similar problems. If one speculates that same-sex marriages are more unstable, or bad for children, and uses that speculation as an argument against legal recognition of same-sex marriage, one will first of all have to contend with the lack of empirical evidence for such theses, and indeed the presence of counterevidence. (Here we should be reminded of the suspect empirical claims made about Mormon polygamy, by people who had never seriously studied the difficulties endemic to heterosexual monogamy as then practiced.) Asserting something despite evidence against it is a likely sign of prejudice. Moreover, one will need to grapple, as well, with the fact that we do not refuse marriage rights to people who seem flaky or uncommitted, who have had bad records of fidelity or seriousness in previous marriages, or who have shown evidence of being bad parents. (Britney Spears had no difficulty marrying.) Once again, then, the opponent of same-sex marriage, if sincerely committed to a consistent ethical principle, must conclude that we should drastically limit access to heterosexual marriage. If this conclusion is not drawn, then the argument, once again, looks like a fancy dress for something like "White Supremacy."

In short, we seem to have some reasonable intrareligious arguments for not permitting same-sex marriage *as a part of that religion*, but no plausible public arguments that can be shared by all citizens. What we have, instead, is what Justice Kennedy talked about in *Romer v. Evans*: a lot of "animus." Talking

about the referendum in Colorado that deprived only gays of the right to propose and campaign for local nondiscrimination laws, he said that "the amendment seems inexplicable by anything but animus toward the class it affects; it
lacks a rational relationship to legitimate state interests."[59] This seems just as
true in the same-sex marriage area as in the area of discrimination law. To allow mere animus to prevail in the political process, he continued, is the most
naked and direct sort of violation of the very idea of the equal protection of the
laws. "It is not within our constitutional tradition to enact laws of this sort."[60]

Same-sex marriage is not, as such, a religion clause issue. Nonetheless,
thinking about the fear of strangers that has marred our history in the area of religion has heuristic value for our reflections about same-sex marriage. The current antigay panic expressed in the virulent crusade against same-sex marriage
is comparable to the panics that have beset us in the religion area, and is, indeed, our nearest analogue, in today's United States, to those lamentable panics. Thinking about this history, then, gives us ample food for critical reflection.

VI. Fearing Strangers Again: The Alleged Muslim Threat

Large groups of new immigrants frequently generate panics, particularly in
times of general insecurity, and particularly if the new immigrants have a visibly
different set of customs and religious observances. The arrival in Europe of
new immigrants from Islamic nations has generated a crisis of major propor-
tions, comparable to the panics we studied in Chapter 5. The United States
and Europe have both suffered from Islamic terrorism. In the U.S., however,
despite some highly regrettable individual instances of assault against peaceful
Muslims, and despite the undoubted existence of religion-based profiling in
airports and other places of surveillance, there has been no massive public out-
cry against U.S. citizens, residents, and visitors who are Muslims; no public demand that they renounce their distinctive articles of dress; and no claim that
their visible difference from others, should they refuse to dress "like everyone
else," means that they are somehow threatening or disloyal. Most people seem
to grasp the distinction between terrorists, who are criminals, and peaceful
Muslims, and they do not, on the whole, suspect someone of being a terrorist
simply because of being a Muslim—perhaps not nearly as much as they suspect
someone of being a criminal because of being African-American.

Indeed, what is both striking and reassuring is the lack of First Amendment litigation over the religious rights of Muslims in America. The one salient case involved a genuinely difficult issue. A Florida woman wanted to have a driver's license photo taken while her face was covered (except for the eyes).[61] Her husband strongly supported her request. When her license was suspended for her refusal to remove her veil, she went to court on First Amendment grounds (supported by the ACLU), and lost. Here is a case where it seems entirely reasonable for the religious interest to lose. A "compelling state interest" certainly does require good identification photographs. In the future, a full-face photo will probably be unnecessary for identification, since the new recognition technology focuses on the eyes alone. At this point, the new technology is not widely available, and so, for the time being, the woman should be given the opportunity to have the photo taken by a female photographer in a secluded place. In any case, the prominence and isolation of this truly difficult case show the basic sanity of the U.S. situation concerning Muslim dress and other visible signs of Muslim difference.

I am generalizing, and all generalizations have exceptions. I am also reporting on how things are in early 2007, and this is not necessarily how they will be in the future. As we can see, the United States is not immune to violence generated by panic over the presence of strangers in our midst. So far, however, we have something to be proud of.

What might explain this absence of panic? From the beginning of our reaction to 9/11, U.S. leaders carefully insisted, in public pronouncements, that we must and would distinguish Islam, a religion worthy of respect, from people who try to hijack it for criminal ends. We can also point to the heterogeneity of the origins of U.S. Muslims, many of whom are African-American converts, and many of whom come from the Indian subcontinent—neither of these origins being at all easy to link to the idea of an Arab Muslim monolith bent on the destruction of democracy.

I believe, however, that some credit for the absence of violence is due to the very tradition that I have been describing, a tradition that regards religious conscience as precious and worthy of respect, and worthy of respect even when it enjoins conduct that refuses assimilation. If people want to wear religious articles of dress, that has been their right ever since the Quakers and the Mennonites and the Jews dressed strangely. If they seek accommodations from general laws on a religious basis, that again has been seen to be their right ever since Jews were exempted from testifying on their Sabbath and Quakers from taking off their hats in court. Our tradition has wisely seen that coercive assimilation involves a threat to conscience. By now we have deeply internalized this idea, so that it would seem to most Americans weird and tyrannical to tell someone that they can't dress in a different way, or observe other commandments of their religion—in the absence of a compelling state interest.

Not so in many of the nations of Europe. In the eighteenth century, when the Jews sought to gain civil rights, a very common attitude was that they could have civil rights only if they would dress like everyone else and eat like everyone else and marry like everyone else. Conspicuous signs of their separateness—the yarmulke, the observance of dietary laws, separatism in marriage—seemed like signs that the Jews did not want to be full citizens of the polity, and full and equal citizenship was understood to mean giving up those marks of difference, which, of course, didn't mean living in a neutral way; it meant living in a Protestant (or, depending on the locale, Catholic) way. This was anti-Semitism—less violent and more polite than the anti-Semitism of the twentieth century, but anti-Semitism all the same.

The reasons for this difference between the European and the American traditions are many and complex. One reason was surely that the Americans had experienced the European way and didn't like it. Another was that there was no real majority religion in the U.S., at least at the level of sects within Protestantism, so all the different "seekers" had to find a way to live together. A third reason was that European nationalism has typically relied on ideas of blood, soil, and belonging to define nationhood, whereas America's self-conception as nation has, like India's, been political: a set of democratic commitments, not a single ethnic style, is what holds us all together.

For a variety of reasons, then, Europe has typically sought ethnic and stylistic homogeneity in the public square, and has viewed any divergence from the dominant style as threatening. Any group that does not seem ready to fit in looks subversive. This role was played by the Jews in the eighteenth century and is played by Muslims today. Like Jews, Muslims are not ready to give up their traditional religious attire simply because the majority thinks it weird. Some choose to assimilate, but others do not. Because a substantial number do not (and no doubt this number is much larger than it otherwise would be, because people are reacting angrily to the demand for homogeneity), these people are understood by many Europeans of the majority tradition to have made a statement against the *political* culture of the nation into which they have immigrated. This (alleged) statement, as summarized by one educated, mild-mannered person of my acquaintance, is, "Let's f*** the West." (Not just "F*** the West," which might simply express dismissiveness, but "Let's f*** the West," which sounds like an aggressive project.)

Here are some of the legal issues that have arisen in Europe, issues that, had they arisen in the U.S., would surely trigger a First Amendment challenge. In France, it is illegal to wear large and conspicuous articles of religious dress in the public schools. The Muslim headscarf and the Jewish yarmulke are explicitly prohibited, along with "large" Christian crosses. This policy looks fair on its face, but of course it is not fair, because many Jews and Muslims believe the forbidden articles to be religiously obligatory, whereas no Christian is obliged to wear a large cross. (Moreover, even if it were fair, it allows too little liberty: the right solution to a problem of unequal liberty cannot be to level down, denying liberty equally to all.)

In Holland, a bill making the Muslim burqa (full garment covering the body and all of the face but the eyes) illegal has been introduced into the legislature.[62] The bill has been defended on the grounds that society will work well only if people can see one another's faces as they pass one another in the street.[63]

In Britain, leading politicians, including Tony Blair, former prime minister, and Jack Straw, former foreign secretary (now leader of the House of Commons), have announced, similarly, that they do not want Muslim women to cover their faces, because this threatens social harmony. "Communities," Straw told the BBC, "are bound together partly by informal chance relations between strangers, people being able to acknowledge each other in the street or being able to pass the time of day." He suggested that these recognitions are not possible if the face is covered.[64]

Related issues have arisen in law. A Muslim girl whose (publicly financed) school permitted a salwar kameez (a loose trouser suit), but did not permit the more modest "jilbab" (which does not cover the face, but does cover the body and head more modestly), asked to wear the jilbab, saying that she felt that it was required by the religious demand for modesty, now that she was an adolescent. Denied by the school, she went to court. She won her case at the lower court level, but the House of Lords reversed, finding in favor of the school.[65] Meanwhile, in Croydon, outrage swirls over a new policy that allows Muslim men certain hours when they can swim without women present, wearing a modest form of full-body covering, and that allows Muslim women separate hours when they too may swim covered without the opposite sex present.[66] The complaint is that the facilities are for all, and yet at prime hours they are unavailable to the many non-Muslim families who used to use them.

Let's begin with the burqa. When it snows in Chicago, we pull our wool hats down over our eyes and wrap our scarves around our noses and mouths. Along the streets we go, greeting one another by a gleam in the eye or a wave of the hand. Then we go home, sit in front of the TV, and watch our favorite group of eleven men—mine being the Chicago Bears—face down another group of eleven, the faces of all more or less totally obscured by their helmets and faceguards. We love them nonetheless for that, and we acknowledge them as our fellow citizens. Dutch people, too, cover their faces when they skate in the cold, and have even been known to wear ski masks with cutouts, when they compete in distance skating events. Dutch people, too, watch with passion athletes whose faces are covered (skiers, skaters, and many others). Dutch people, too, go to dental hygienists and surgeons who cover their faces for hygienic reasons. Despite the covering, these people are among our most trusted professionals.

So the idea that face covering makes trust and social cohesion impossible is quite ridiculous. The eyes, as they say, are the windows of the soul. It's one thing for the Florida court to argue that we need some identification document that shows more than the eyes. That, given current technology, is a not unreasonable position. What is unreasonable is to say that civil encounters among citizens require showing the full face. Moreover, even when a covered face seems initially strange or out of place, people get used to it very quickly. For some weeks, because of allergenic dust from construction in the university building where I work, I wore a surgical mask during my student office hours (as at other times). Students quickly learned that eyes are the main points of contact in a human relationship, and soon they were not only relaxed in the presence of the mask, they were annoyed at me for not offering them one too.

The burqa poses no problem that normal Chicago winter gear and surgical masks do not pose. So what is going on when people focus on it as a threat to a common culture and seek to ban or limit it? It seems fairly evident that what is really going on is a fear of difference and strangeness, fear of a nonmajoritarian lifestyle that refuses to assimilate. Jack Straw was at least honest when he concluded that the burqa is "such a visible statement of separation and of difference," and was objectionable on that count alone.[67]

Suppose we imagine these cases transferred to our U.S. legal tradition. The French ban on the headscarf and the yarmulke in the public schools would surely not survive a First Amendment challenge, even under the current post-*Smith* regime. The policy not only imposes a "substantial burden" on people's religious free exercise, it is also not even neutral, burdening Jews and Muslims in ways that Christians are not burdened. The "small crosses" that Christians are allowed to wear show us that the majority can get a dispensation to wear devotional articles belonging to that religion; not so the minority. I tentatively conclude that even Justices Scalia and Alito would find a First Amendment problem, following the analysis of neutrality in *Lukumi*, *Fraternal Order of Police*, and *Gonzalez v. O Centro Espirita Beneficente Uniao do Vegetal* (the hoasca case). Even if a problem of denominational preference were not found, the law clearly burdens religious people in a way that nonreligious people are not burdened, and would be objectionable for that reason alone.

Similarly, the Muslim schoolgirl would clearly get to wear her jilbab. To require her to wear something that she thinks religiously immodest, a violation of her religious obligation, is surely to impose a substantial burden on her free exercise of religion. Before *Smith*, the inquiry could just end there, since there is not the ghost of a plausible "compelling state interest" on the other side. (Not even the most ardent defenders of the status quo, in the U.S., have ever maintained that an interest in homogeneity, all by itself, supplied the state with a compelling interest![68])

Post-*Smith*, the inquiry is harder. We would need to know a good deal about what other exemptions from the school uniform are permitted, on what sorts of grounds. But it seems likely that some sort of neutrality problem would emerge. Certainly no child from the majority religion is being told that she cannot satisfy her religious requirements, and that, combined with the sheer reasonless meanness of the denial (which is not defended by any serious interest beyond the sheer interest in homogeneity), seems to me to give the girl a very strong case, even in the present legal regime. Certainly the fact that the salwar kameez is acceptable to mainstream Muslim belief (the main point made by the Law Lords in overturning the lower court decision) would cut no ice in America, used as our tradition is to a bewildering proliferation of sects and subsects. Conscience, not the dominant group, is the measure.

The fact that the pre-*Smith* (or RFRA-based) tradition has no trouble with this case is a strong point in its favor, since the conscience-based claim is strong, and we really do not need to come up with a case where someone else gets an exemption from the uniform policy in order to see how oppressive the regulation is, and how weak the interests supporting it.

As to the Croydon swimming pool, the accommodation was granted through democratic processes, so there is no need, in fact, for courts to be involved, unless the grousing of the British tabloid press leads to a change in the policy. Suppose, however, the accommodation had been denied and the Muslims had taken the town to court to ask for an accommodation. Under the pre-*Smith* regime, they would have a good argument, though the outcome would not be utterly clear. The Muslims could not argue that the denial of special hours in the swimming pool was in and of itself a substantial burden to the free exercise of their religion. Swimming is not religiously required. They could, however, base their argument on an equality claim: by being denied a means of swimming in the town pool that was consistent with their religious requirements, they were being treated unequally, and that inequality itself could constitute a burden (as in *Sherbert*). The town (if it opposed the request for accommodation) would probably base its claim on the administrative difficulty of setting aside special hours for different groups with their different requirements. The fact that these special hours actually worked (despite griping and complaining) shows *us* that such a claim would not be very strong. In the imaginary case before us, however, that could not yet be known, and it would not be too surprising if the imaginary court denied the Muslims' claim. The facts before us show, however, that the denial would not have been well grounded. Courts often think accommodations more administratively difficult than they actually prove to be once people bite the bullet and make the allegedly difficult change.

In general, we can see that the equality tradition asks the right questions in this difficult area, questions about how to weigh the state's strongest interests against the very weighty interest in respect for conscience. If we approach these difficult cases from the point of view of the tradition's key concepts, we prompt an inquiry into the basis of equal citizenship that itself serves to defuse panic and promote respect. The very discussion promotes a sense of respect for difference. By contrast, the current approach in Britain, in France, and in some parts of Holland—where there is a public demand for the subordination of conscience to homogeneity—works in just the opposite way. The very conversation is framed so as to fuel panic, since people are told that others who insist on looking different are *ipso facto* subversives. The debate also expresses disrespect for fellow citizens, since their conscientious claims are not given very much weight when they are asked to drop them simply for reasons of homogeneity, with no compelling state interest.

The United States has deep problems to face in the area of religion and equality. My first four examples show us grappling uneasily with issues that divide people and inspire fear. Especially in the area of same-sex marriage, fear runs deep and mutual respect is difficult to find. Many other nations have progressed further on this issue than we have. Nonetheless, at least on our fifth issue, a very important one for the world's future, it seems that Europe might gain something useful by studying the colonial experience. (India, another former British colony, also provides a useful example of learning to live with people who look different and who will not renounce their difference.) As the *Times of India* comments, discussing the recent British statements, the current European policy "puts visually-distinct, culturally-differentiated immigrants on notice," expressing not the universal values of toleration and respect, but the less admirable sentiment that "Hell is other people."[69]

In short, learning to live with others on terms of mutual respect does not mean what Blair seems to think it means, namely an entirely one-sided duty on the part of immigrants to "integrate," until they look and act like everyone else—meaning, of course, the Protestant majority. Mutual respect imposes duties that are themselves mutual: the duty for each and every person to allow each and every person, majority and minority, a space for conscience to unfold itself, even in ways that are strange and surprising—so long as they violate no compelling state interest and respect the equal rights of others.

9

CONCLUSION

Toward an "Overlapping Consensus"?

Boast not proud English, of thy birth and blood,
Thy brother Indian is by birth as Good.
Of one blood God made Him, and Thee and All,
As wise, as faire, as strong, as personall.

ROGER WILLIAMS, *A Key into the*
Language of America (1643)

Almost four hundred years ago, Americans embarked on a bold experiment in religious equality. For much of the world's history, governments had imposed a single religious orthodoxy on all citizens, marginalizing or subordinating those who believed, or practiced, differently. This intolerance of religious difference was particularly pervasive in the Western traditions of Europe. India boldly instituted religious toleration in the second century BCE when the emperor Ashoka, himself a convert to Buddhism from Hinduism, promulgated policies of toleration and respect. These values were subsequently eclipsed by less tolerant policies, but toleration enjoyed a revival and extension under some of the Moghul (Muslim) rulers of India in the seventeenth century. The emperor Akbar, in particular, instituted far-reaching official policies of religious equality that extended respect to all the diverse religions of a large empire, encompassing many more human beings, and more religions than Ashoka's ancient policies. Akbar's court poet, the great mystic Kabir, described himself as a child of both Allah and Ram.

Meanwhile, the Muslim-governed Ottoman Empire had its own policies of divided religious sovereignty that, while less ambitious than the Indian experiment in coexistence, represented a major step toward harmony and respect. Under the so-called millet system, which was in place for centuries, each ethnoreligious community enjoyed considerable autonomy in matters of religion, and was even permitted separate courts and some separate taxation. The central government undertook to protect difference. This experiment was less far-reaching than India's in that people of different creeds were deliberately not asked to form a shared government: peace was kept by separation. Nonetheless, a single federal government did link, and protect, all communities.

In Europe, however, these cases remained relatively unknown and certainly were not imitated. (It is an odd misconception of many Americans and Europeans that religious toleration is a value particularly associated with the European Enlightenment. In reality, Europe was a latecomer to the debate; moreover, the first great European theorist and practitioner of toleration, well before the Enlightenment, was actually Roger Williams, an American.) The Peace of Westphalia in 1648, which ended the bloody wars of religion, instituted only a limited type of toleration, namely the concession that each state would decide on its own dominant religion and that states would not go to war to impose their religion on a different state. This policy did nothing for religious minorities within each state: it permitted each state to carry out internal religious repression. (By this time Rhode Island's experiment was well under way, and Roger Williams's major work had been in print for four years; Pennsylvania soon embarked on a similar path.)

Without established precedents and paradigms from their European heritage, the American colonists set out to live together. At first, many believed that coexistence would have to be Westphalian: each colony would repress dissent within, and they could then coexist with colonies who had different types of religious establishment. Soon, however, with Rhode Island and the Middle Atlantic colonies taking the lead, internal toleration began to spread, and it became evident that civil peace did not require the repression of religious dissent. As colonists traveled for business or for education, they learned about other ways of life: recall James Madison's encounter with the religious freedom of Pennsylvania, through a friendship made at Princeton. The moral imperative to respect the individual conscience, always strongly felt in colonists who had taken the risk of crossing the ocean to follow their own conscience's call, gradually generated a demand for the protection of religious liberty everywhere. As time went on, the idea of equality, always powerful in people most of whom began American life as minorities fleeing from dominating majorities, increasingly infused the idea of liberty: liberty was not true or full liberty unless it was equal liberty.

Equal liberty of conscience is a hard thing to create, a harder one to keep. The colonists gradually learned more and more about the institutions and practices that were required to protect it. Religious establishment came under fire early on, as the colonists understood that even benign liberty-protecting establishments did not really protect fully equal liberty, or show respect, more generally, for the equality of citizens in the public realm. Though many grasped this abstract point, however, agreement could not be reached at the time of the Constitution's drafting to make this norm binding against the states. Nonestablishment was already the trend. All state establishments had come under fire on grounds of equal standing, and some had already succumbed to the forces of equality. Influential defenders of state establishments simply did not want the federal government telling them what to do in a matter of such great importance. Even at the level of federal government, where nonestablishment commanded an overwhelming consensus, the analysis of what nonestablishment required remained imperfectly developed, as the framers worked on some issues (taxation) more than on others (public displays and ceremonies). The Constitution wisely set down some highly general goals and values, rather than extensive rules, leaving further interpretation to later generations.

Within fifty years of the Founding, it was generally agreed that religious establishment was inimical to citizens' equality, and state establishments became a thing of the past. By the time the Fourteenth Amendment applied the Bill of Rights to the states (or, by the time to which that incorporation was later dated, whether or not it was clearly intended at the time the Fourteenth Amendment was passed), it was perfectly clear that the Free Exercise Clause was to be understood as a guarantor not just of liberty, but also of equal liberty. And it was clear, furthermore, that the Establishment Clause was to be read as

Madisonian, forbidding governments from endorsing a particular religion over other religions, or religion over nonreligion, in such a way as to create ranks and orders of citizens, in-groups and out-groups. The application of these ideas to concrete cases remained to be worked out, but the broad analytical framework was set.

The nineteenth century, however, did not see the flowering of equal respect that these theoretical developments might have seemed to promise. The rapid influx of new types of citizens caused public sentiment and, in many instances, public policy to be far less Madisonian than it had been at the time of the Constitution, an era of relative homogeneity. Panics involving people with strange and apparently threatening religions—Mormons, Jehovah's Witnesses, and, above all, Roman Catholics—threatened the tradition of equal respect, in some cases making a hollow mockery of its high ideals. Suppose reasonable observers with all the relevant historical knowledge, hearing that this book's purpose was to defend "America's tradition of religious equality" against attacks and dangers, asked themselves what era the book would be most likely to be about. In what era, they ask, did that tradition endure the most alarming attacks? Very likely, given their knowledge of history, they would select the period between 1840 and 1925 (or, 1840 and 1945, to include the panic over patriotism that marred the period leading up to World War II). Madison's era did not see mass lynchings of religious dissidents, or violent attempts to deny a whole religious group equal political and civil liberties. The late nineteenth century did. Difficult though our own time is, it is well to remember that we are not beating small Catholic children because they won't make a Protestant affirmation in the public schools, or killing Jehovah's Witnesses in the streets because they conscientiously refuse to say the Pledge of Allegiance, or decreeing that Mormons who believe all the tenets of their religion may not vote. We have made some progress, and it is likely that we won't choose to go back to that dark time.

These panics against the different were a shameful blot on our history of protecting religious liberty. Their legacy, however, was positive: Americans achieved, gradually, a new depth of insight into their own founding document and its principles, articulating ever more precisely an analytical framework, based on its central ideas, that could be applied to the bewildering range of cases that the growing size and reach of government brought before the courts. Ideas of reasonable accommodation were worked out in the Free Exercise area, with increasing attention to nontraditional religions and their demands. Ideas of equal respect and nonendorsement, articulated early on in the area of funding, and associated above all with Madison's conception of democracy, were brought to bear on the controversial areas of school prayer and public displays.

These insights were not utterly stable: they were, and are, under threat both from a conservative traditionalism that Madison knew well and from an antiseparationism that would have been new to him. One might more accurately call this latter position pseudo-liberal, since it slights the classic liberal value of equality. The search for fairness is still a work in progress, and some of these alternative positions enjoy considerable influence. Nonetheless, some of the equality tradition's main lines have been worked out well.

America today contains a religious diversity unparalleled in its history. Religions that Roger Williams merely imagined (Islam, varieties of "pagan" polytheism) are now increasingly common among us. Nontheistic religions such as Buddhism, Taoism, and Confucianism, polytheistic Hinduism and its Jain and Sikh offshoots—all are rapidly growing on account of a more evenhanded immigration policy that began in the 1960s, when earlier restrictive immigration policies were altered. This change in immigration policy has had a great impact on the religious makeup of the United States, ending the virtual prohibition of immigration from the Indian subcontinent and considerably expanding the possibilities for immigration from Asia generally.

Increasing religious diversity is also the result of diversification from within. Native American religion, which Protestants long tried to wipe out, did not die, and is enjoying a resurgence. The variety within Protestantism and the distance between its more conservative and its more evangelical denominations is huge. The Mormon Church, once persecuted, is now an established part of our religious and political landscape, and numbers of Mormons continue to grow. Roman Catholicism has become the largest single denomination in the nation, and itself contains great diversity of opinion. Quakers, Mennonites, the Amish, Jehovah's Witnesses, and many others, once persecuted, are now at least nominally included as members of our constitutional consensus with equal standing. Although some of the growth in numbers of Buddhists involves diversification from without, through immigration, many Buddhist Americans are converts—as, of course, are many Islamic Americans in the African-American community. Furthermore, the number of Americans who do not mention a religious identification is substantial, though it does not approach the proportion who had no church affiliation at the time of the Founding. The presence of agnostics, atheists, and people who are seeking truth for themselves in their own nontraditional way is now acknowledged as a big fact in our political life, and these people too are recognized as equal citizens, nominally at least.

The new diversity is not well understood. Many Americans, for example, think that all or most Muslims are Arabs, and are unaware that the three largest Muslim nations in the world are Indonesia, Pakistan, and India; in terms of the Islamic influence in the U.S., South Asia is of particular importance, if we separate the highly influential Black Muslim churches as, in effect, a different religion.

Many Americans, again, don't realize that there are many genuinely religious people who do not recognize a Supreme Being. They know the names of Buddhism, Confucianism, Taoism, and Unitarian Universalism, but they do not realize that these religions are nontheistic. Many also don't know that there are varieties of familiar religions, Christianity and Judaism, that do not acknowledge a personal creator God. All these facts have significance for our public debates about religion and the law, and yet our systems of education have not succeeded in getting them across to our citizens. Our constitutional principles need further refinement to meet the challenges that this new diversity poses, and this refinement will require, in turn, a public conversation in which citizens tell one another about their own ways of making sense of life and listen respectfully to things that they initially find strange or even offputting. This conversation will go better if education at all levels does better at conveying basic facts about the different religions that are present in our society.

The attack on America's tradition of religious equality, as we have seen, is ongoing. It has been with us, in a variety of different guises, from the very moment that there was such a tradition. The values that this attack, in its many forms, exemplifies (fear of the strange, a love of hierarchy, a desire to lord it over others) are probably older than the equality tradition itself. In each era of human history, it would seem, the value of equal respect for all human beings needs to be reforged and reestablished, in reaction against easier and more prevalent customs of unequal regard that have deep roots in human psychology. Just as Seneca struggled to win a hearing for the equal worth of each person's moral capacity, in a Rome riven by distinctions of class and faction, so too the American colonists who favored equal liberty of conscience had to struggle against more prevalent practices of "soule rape," in which a religious orthodoxy was imposed on the consciences of minorities. We have the great good luck to live in a nation that has taken the principle of equal liberty of conscience to heart in its founding document. But history shows us that constant vigilance is required lest this value be narrowly and partially construed, or misapplied in ways that favor hierarchy.

The attack on religious equality, in short, is never-ending, and the battle for equal respect needs to be refought in each new era. People will try to establish their religious superiority to others as long as the sin of pride exists, which is to say as long as human life is anything like the life we know. No doubt the ways people will find to lord it over others will keep on changing and evolving, so we can't be sure past remedies are a good guide, in detail, to present problems.

At one level, the attack on equality comes from within the human mind and heart, and must be fought there, as each person seeks to attain a respectful common life with others and to defeat the overweening demands of "the great God Selfe." Beating back the internal attack on equality is a task that must be waged by each citizen, with the help of families and whatever voluntary groups individuals and families join to search for ethical goodness. Often, as Kant observed, groups help support the fragile moral faculties—though care must always be taken to watch out lest the support system becomes, itself, a new source of hierarchy.

Law in a liberal democracy cannot do a whole lot about this daily struggle in the mind and heart. It can't tell people that they have to respect one another; it can't make them join a church or an ethical group to work on their ethical problems; and it cannot penalize them for being merely indifferent or selfish, or even intolerant, unless that selfishness leads them to violate the rights of others.

Law, however, does matter. First of all, good laws and institutions set limits on people's ability to act on their intolerant and inegalitarian views. And even when the idea of religious equality has to be interpreted by courts in subtle ways, those interpretations do effect significant changes in people's lives. Mrs. Sherbert, and others like her, now have their unemployment compensation. Catholic children do not have to recite Protestant prayers in the public schools. Children who wish not to recite the Pledge of Allegiance do not have to do so. The Ten Commandments are gone from the courthouses of McCreary County.

Beyond these very concrete results, law also has great symbolic and expressive value. Even when the decisions of legislatures and courts do not have a very wide practical effect, they do make a statement, and the story we have been following has really been the story of such statements, some on target and some erring in one or more respects, as fallible courts try to figure out how to translate the general idea of equal liberty of conscience into concrete reality. This tradition of statement-making itself has continually been under attack, as political currents try to push the Court into a position that is not equality-affirming. Beating back this continual set of attacks (which come, as we've seen, from both the left and the right) does not require perfect virtue and wisdom, but it does require a careful intellectual vigilance and a keen awareness of the pitfalls that our tradition, like any great tradition, has encountered in the past.

A constitutional tradition, then, however fine, must not lapse into overconfidence. The general principles and goals that it protects must continue to be applied anew, as people find new ways to flout them. This requires both analytical clarity and wise practical reason, as a decent analytical framework is first adjusted or extended and then applied to the cases. (Often this will not happen in discrete stages: often an insight about a new case proves the occasion for a retooling of the analytical framework.)

Roger Williams issued a challenge to the new colonies: that they find, and learn to inhabit, a shared moral space, without turning that space into a sectarian space that privileges some views over others. This same challenge was issued in the late twentieth century by John Rawls, when he argued that people who hold different religious and secular "comprehensive doctrines" can live together on terms of equal respect only if they can form an "overlapping consensus," agreeing to share a "freestanding" ethical conception in the political realm, and agreeing, at the same time, to forgo the search for the dominance of any one comprehensive doctrine over the others. A Rawlsian "overlapping consensus" is not simply a way of staving off strife, a mere *modus vivendi*: people sign on to it because they approve of the values that it embodies, as values suited to a common life among people who differ about ultimate ends and who are not likely to come into agreement anytime soon. Like Williams, Rawls starts from the idea of equal respect and shows that only a political conception that separates certain key moral/political values from religious ideas will appropriately preserve that all-important value. Separation is not a starting point. It is a conclusion of an argument that begins elsewhere.

Citizens themselves will rarely separate their understanding of the political conception from the comprehensive doctrine they love. They usually will see the point of the political values in terms of the other values in their comprehensive doctrine, and this is fine. They do, however, respect their fellow citizens as fully free and equal, and this sets limits on the ways in which they will seek to enact that more comprehensive understanding. When they inhabit the shared space of moral/political principle, then they will not seek to make it a Protestant space, or a Hindu space, or an atheistic space. They will seek principles, and applications, that are truly fair to all.

Why? Not because being a Protestant, or a Hindu, or an atheist is not important to them; not because they do not teach these values to their children and love them as their own best hope in a confusing world. They recognize, however, that the space they share with others is a space of diverse opinions about ultimate matters, and they respect the springs of conscience in their fellow citizens that lead them to diverse conclusions by diverse routes, even when they find these routes and these conclusions profoundly mistaken.

We embarked on the path toward overlapping consensus almost four hundred years ago. We still haven't reached the goal. As Roger Williams's "Truth" puts it, "Deare Peace, Habacucks Fishes keep their constant bloody game of Persecutions in the Worlds mighty ocean."[1] And Americans, albeit in a less overtly violent form than in some previous eras, have not altogether ceased to favor "a Tenent whose grosse partialitie denies the Principles of common Justice, while Men waigh out to the Consciences of all others, that which they judge not fit nor right to be weighed out to their owne" (BTY 498). Some want to post the signs of their religion in courthouses and schoolrooms. Others want all schoolchildren to pray in terms that advance their own religion. Still others want to deny religious citizens who choose sectarian schools some protections that the nonreligious routinely get.

Americans have done pretty well in forging a political order that exemplifies equal liberty of conscience. Given human frailty, however, we always need vigilance lest backsliding occur, and we always need wise citizens—including judges—who can think well about how to realize this value in changing circumstances, as part of a political overlapping consensus that is, let us hope, fair and respectful as a whole.

Recall, however, that Truth and Peace have a sister, Patience, whose company is both delightful and necessary. Patience is not imagined as tuning out, or relaxing her concentration on the ground that all is well. Peace and Truth know that all is not well: we live in a world where, on balance, human beings behave pretty badly, and this means that we live in a world that needs good laws and persistent hardworking attempts to make them better. Like the Indians whom Williams knew and admired, Patience sits still and listens hard. Her waiting is a form of highly focused attention. Vigilant, hardworking, and modest, interested in really hearing what other people have to say, Patience is, we might say, the tutelary spirit of the law, the attentiveness and respectfulness that make vague abstract principles into a concrete reality by which we can seek to live together.

ACKNOWLEDGMENTS

This book is the book of a philosopher who has taught these issues as philosophical issues for some time. I owe gratitude to philosophers with whom I have talked, over the years, about equal respect and its relationship to religion: above all, to Charles Larmore and Paul Weithman and, more recently, Daniel Brudney and Josef Stern. Long before those conversations, in the early 1980s, I was privileged to be at Harvard while John Rawls was drafting the material that later became *Political Liberalism*. Both Rawls's presentation of his ideas as they developed and my own work on that book as I've taught it in recent years have influenced my thinking a great deal. So too have the shrewd comments of my philosophy graduate students, including Jeremy Bendik-Keymer, Chad Flanders, Jeffrey Israel, Jennifer Johnson, Ryan Long, and Micah Lott. Thomas D'Andrea introduced me to the ideas of Jacques Maritain and especially to his important essay on "Truth and Human Fellowship," whose ideas have been important to me here.

This is also, however, a book about the law, and I have taught these issues as legal issues to law students. Here I am deeply grateful to Michael McConnell, who allowed me to sit in on his class in 1995–1996 and who talked with me often about the issues. More recently, I am grateful to Andrew Koppelman, Adam Samaha, and Cass Sunstein for illuminating conversations. Koppelman has been especially kind, reading more than one draft of many chapters, and giving me extensive comments. Students in my class on religion and the First Amendment at the University of Chicago also helped me with comments on the manuscript, especially Joseph Callister, Sloan Speck, and Brad Romney. During the final stages of revision, I was similarly helped by the acute comments of my class at Harvard Law School.

I presented two chapters of the book at a legal theory workshop at Northwestern University, and received very impressive written comments from the law students who attended, as well as oral comments from Koppelman and Steven Calabresi, the faculty coordinators. Chapter 2 was presented as a lecture at a memorial conference for Philip Quinn at the University of Notre Dame, as a Foerster Lecture at the University of California at Berkeley, as a law student talk at the University of Chicago, and as faculty workshop papers at Harvard Law School and Columbia Law School. I am grateful to the audiences there for their helpful questions and challenges, and especially to Robert Merrihew Adams, whose thoughts about these issues over the years have greatly informed my own. In the final stages of revision, I presented three lectures based on the manuscript at The University of Pennsylvania as a Templeton Lecturer, and was lucky enough to have as my commentators Samuel Freeman, Solomon Katz, and Kok-Chor Tan, to whom I'm extremely grateful for the high quality of their criticisms.

As I revised the manuscript, I owe thanks to the various people who read my draft and offered me comments: to Daniel Brudney, Joseph Callister, Jerry Coyne, Andrew Koppelman, Charles Larmore, Brian Leiter, Ryan Long, Michael Kremer, Martha Minow, Brad Romney, Adam Samaha, Sloan Speck, Geoffrey Stone, Bill Stuntz, Cass Sunstein. Heidi Mueller and Zoe Robinson were exemplary research assistants, who participated actively in the shaping of the argument. I'm also grateful to my agent Sydelle Kramer and my editor Bill Frucht for believing in the project and helping me get started.

My work on the book during a year of leave was supported by the University of Chicago and the Spencer Foundation, and I owe particular gratitude to Michael McPherson, the president of that foundation, for arranging an ideal setting for quiet reflection and for his ongoing interest in my work.

In quite a different way, I owe thanks to people in my own religious community with whom I have talked about ideas over the years, in particular to my rabbi emeritus, Arnold Jacob Wolf, a great teacher and a notoriously cantankerous interlocutor, but also to the rabbi with whom I studied for conversion in 1969, Rabbi Solomon Weinberger, and to the entire Nussbaum family, who introduced me to a tradition of argument that was different from the one in which I was raised. More recently, I'm grateful to my colleagues at our university's Hillel, who helped me organize symposia on civility and on interreligious marriage, particularly to Josef Stern, Daniel Brudney, David Rosenberg, Michael Fishbane, Richard Strier, and Paul Mendes-Flohr. To everyone on the Hillel board, I'm grateful for their indulgence toward a board member who invariably ducks out when budgetary matters are discussed.

Philip Quinn was my colleague at Brown University from 1983, when I was hired, until his departure for a chair at the University of Notre Dame in 1985. He remained my friend until his tragically early death in 2004 at the age of 64. A distinguished scholar of philosophical and religious ethics, he wrote eloquently on moral dilemmas, on the role of religion in American public life, and many other related questions (as well as doing fine work in the philosophy of science). Although not an observant Catholic, he sought out the atmosphere of a Catholic university because he felt that the issues he cared about got more respect and attention there than they did in the secular academy. At Notre Dame, despite his shy unassuming manner, he was a dominant philosophical presence. He was also a quietly effective leader of the liberal wing of the faculty, as he worked for better treatment for the campus women's group and, especially, for a nondiscrimination policy on sexual orientation—which was overwhelmingly supported by the faculty, but denied by the administration and the trustees. Elected chair of the Philosophy Department by his colleagues, Phil then refused the position, publicly stating that for him to negotiate with the administration in that role either would cause him to drop his active opposition to administration policy on sexual orientation, which would violate his conscience, or would cause the department to forfeit administration support, which would be unwise.

Phil and I worked together closely when I was writing *Cultivating Humanity*. He prepared a report that I used as background for the section on Notre Dame in my chapter "Socrates in the Religious University," and he set up many appointments for me with people at Notre Dame who had widely varying views on campus issues. Thus I owe to him whatever understanding I have of the Catholic tradition of higher education. I also worked with Phil in the American Philosophical Association, where, as a past president, he served for several years as chairman of the National Board. He was an exemplary citizen of every institution to which he belonged. His soft-spoken voice, his humor, and his unflagging commitment to reason made many people's lives better in many different ways.

Phil was known for the view that liberal philosophy had often slighted the claims of religious citizens. His April 1994 Presidential Address to the American Philosophical Association's Central Division addressed this theme, on which he had differences with John Rawls that influenced Rawls in his last years as he rethought his position about the proper limits of religious discourse in public life. I hope that Phil would have found this book deeply respectful of religious commitment and religious citizens. I am sure he would also have found a lot to argue about. When I heard that his

ACKNOWLEDGMENTS

cancer had taken a very sudden turn for the worse, I sent a message via two friends in South Bend that I would like his permission to dedicate my future book to him. Because his consciousness failed rapidly, I never got to visit him in the hospital, and the friends never had a chance to ask him my question. So I am just hoping that my idea would have met with his approval. Even more, I wish that we could have talked about the ideas and arguments.

NOTES

1 Introduction: A Tradition Under Threat

1. *Board of Education v. Barnette*, 319 U.S. 624 (1943).

2. For references, see Chapter 3.

3. *McCreary County, Kentucky v. ACLU*, 545 U.S. (2005), Scalia, J. dissenting.

4. *Washington Post* online, Tuesday, August 2, 2006.

5. *Elk Grove Unified School Dist. v. Newdow*, 542 U.S. 1, 49–54 (2004). See detailed discussion in Chapters 3 and 4.

6. *Torcaso v. Watkins*, 367 U.S. 488 (1961).

7. "Committee Hearing Reinforces Case Against Confirmation of Janice Rogers Brown," http://www.pfaw.org.pfaw.dfiles/file_257.pdf.

8. Dennett, "The Bright Stuff," *New York Times*, July 12, 2003, op-ed.

9. Daniel Dennett, *Breaking the Spell: Religion as a Natural Phenomenon* (New York: Viking, 2006).

10. *Elk Grove v. Newdow*, above.

11. See Chapter 8.

12. Letter of 1989, quoted in *Religion and the Constitution*, ed. Michael W. McConnell, John H. Garvey, and Thomas C. Berg, 1st ed. (New York: Aspen, 2002), p. 54.

13. A full discussion of my religious conversion, and my views, can be found in Nussbaum, "Judaism and the Love of Reason," in *Philosophy, Feminism, Faith*, ed. Ruth E. Groenhout and Marya Bower (Bloomington: Indiana University Press, 2003), pp. 9–39.

14. *Sherbert v. Verner*, 374 U.S. 398 (1963).

15. *County of Allegheny v. ACLU*, 492 U.S. 573 (1989).

16. Maritain, "Truth and Human Fellowship," in Maritain, *On the Use of Philosophy: Three Essays* (Princeton: Princeton University Press, 1961).

17. To my knowledge, the first (by quite a few years) was Martin Meyerson, president of the University of Pennsylvania from 1970 to 1981.

18. De Tocqueville, *Democracy in America*, Volume II, chapter 1.

19. Of course there are other reasons for recommending it, such as the fear of anarchy in interpretation.

2 LIVING TOGETHER: THE ROOTS OF RESPECT

1. Throughout I reproduce Williams's spellings, which are not terribly distracting, but not his frequent use of italics, which seem intrusive to readers unaccustomed to seventeenth-century style.

2. Hugo Grotius, *On the Law of War and Peace* (*De Iure Belli ac Pacis*), 1625. Grotius was an Arminian. His vulnerable situation at the French court may partially explain his reticence about internal toleration.

3. See Perry Miller, *Orthodoxy in Massachusetts 1630–1650: A Genetic Study* (Cambridge: Harvard University Press, 1933).

4. Actually, the tribes in the immediate area were peaceful; when they were treated with respect they were extremely helpful. They did, however, encounter aggression from the Pequot Indians; Williams assisted the Narragansett tribes in those conflicts.

5. Roger Williams, *The Correspondence of Roger Williams*, ed. Glenn La Fantasie (Providence: Brown University Press, 1988), vol. I, p. 15. Hereafter the works of Williams will be cited as follows: the correspondence, as C I and C II, followed by the page number in each case. *The Complete Writings of Roger Williams* (New York: Russell and Russell, 1963), in seven volumes, will be cited as CW followed by the volume number and page number. However, since most citations to the *Writings* are to the *Bloudy Tenent of Persecution* (1644), which is in volume III, and to the sequel, *The Bloudy Tenent Yet More Bloudy* (1652), references to these works will be made as to BT (followed by page number) and BTY (followed by page number).

6. C I.345.

7. *A Key into the Language of America*, Williams CW vol. 1, p. 47. Williams tells us that he focuses on the Narragansett dialect, and that the work is an "implicit dialogue" (p. 29) with the native inhabitants. See further treatment of the *Key* in Andrew Delbanco, *The Puritan Ideal* (Cambridge, MA: Harvard University Press, 1989), p. 166.

8. See Delbanco, *The Puritan Ideal*.

9. See John Demos, *Entertaining Satan: Witchcraft and the Culture of Early New England* (New York and Oxford: Oxford University Press, 1982).

10. Ibid., p. 209.

11. London: Hannah Allen, 1647. Cotton standardly spells "tenet" in our modern way, Williams with an additional "n." Some extracts from Cotton's writings appear, along with other material of great interest, in *The Puritans: A Sourcebook of Their Writings*, ed. Perry Miller and Thomas H. Johnson, volume 1 (New York: Harper and Row, 1938).

12. Cotton's "Mosaic Code" was found too illiberal in Massachusetts, but was adopted by the New Haven community. Later on, Yale University became a haven for those who believed that Harvard had erred by tolerating Anglicans on its faculty and in its student body.

13. Data are given in Demos, *Entertaining Satan*.

14. See Demos, *Entertaining Satan*.

15. For data and analysis, see Demos, *Entertaining Satan*.

16. Demos, *Entertaining Satan,* p. 157.

17. Rhode Island did record one civil suit for slander, where the putatively slanderous charge was of witchcraft; Connecticut had 8, and Massachusetts 17. All these data are from Demos, *Entertaining Satan,* p. 11.

18. It cannot be proven that Locke read Williams, since he does not mention whom he is reading, even in correspondence; but Williams is a prominent part of a literature on the topic with which Locke was certainly familiar. I am grateful to Quentin Skinner for correspondence on this point.

19. Mark Howe, *The Garden and the Wilderness* (Chicago: University of Chicago Press, 1965), p. 6.

20. See Michael W. McConnell, John H. Garvey, and Thomas C. Berg, *Religion and the Constitution* (New York and Gaithersburg: Aspen Law and Business, 2002), pp. 56-57.

21. Delbanco, *The Puritan Ideal,* p. 168.

22. See Delbanco, *The Puritan Ideal,* pp. 165-166, with citations from *Key.*

23. Urbana: University of Illinois Press, 1998. See also his excellent earlier article, "Roger Williams and the Foundations of Religious Liberty," *Boston University Law Review* 71 (1991), 455-524, which contains an excellent account of Williams's relationship to Locke. An earlier theoretical treatment that valuably stresses the theme of equality and impartiality in Williams's writing is Edward J. Eberle, "Roger Williams's Gift: Religious Freedom in America," *Roger Williams University Law Review* 4 (1998-1999), 425-486. Another good treatment, though brief and not comprehensive, is Philip Hamburger's treatment in *Separation of Church and State* (Cambridge, MA: Harvard University Press, 2002), pp. 38-45.

24. Among good biographical studies of Williams, see W. Clark Gilpin, *The Millenarian Piety of Roger Williams* (Chicago: University of Chicago Press, 1979); Edwin S. Gaustad, *Liberty of Conscience: Roger Williams in America* (Grand Rapids: William B. Eerdmans, 1991); Perry Miller, *Roger Williams: His Contribution to the American Tradition* (Indianapolis: Bobbs-Merrill, 1953).

25. C I.358.

26. C I.379.

27. I am grateful to Mark Goldie and Quentin Skinner for correspondence on this point.

28. He does, however, often use phrases of Latin, and at times expects his audience to know a Latin quote. Thus, for example, in a letter of 1635 (C I.30), he cites the famous phrase from Ovid, *tempora mutantur et nos mutamur in illis* ("times change and we change with them"), a phrase that the otherwise estimable editor declares to be "an anonymous Latin epigram" (31).

29. See R. Helmholz, "Bonham's Case, Judicial Review and the Law of Nature" (discussing Coke's use of natural law argumentation in this famous case), working paper presented to the University of Chicago Law School Work in Progress Workshop, July 2006. One striking example of Coke's use of natural law argumentation is in *Calvin's Case* (1608), in which he cites both Aristotle and Cicero (whom he calls by his middle name, Tully) as sources for his natural law doctrine: see *The Selected Writings of Sir Edward Coke,* ed. Steve Sheppard (Indianapolis: Liberty Fund, 2003), pp. 195-196.

30. See the detailed account in C I.12–23, "Editorial Note."

31. C II.610.

32. C II.535, 541.

33. For example C II.534, complaining about the refusal of the English to pay his emissary: "These very Barbarians when they send forth a publike messenger they furnish him out, they defray all paymts, they gratifie him with Rewards, and if he prove lame and sick and not able to returne, they visit him and bring him home upon their shoulders (and that many Scores of miles) with all Care and Tendernes."

34. In 1730 a synagogue was founded in Manhattan.

35. C II.616. "Matie" is Williams's abbreviation for "Majesty."

36. C II.617.

37. C II.423–424.

38. C I.340.

39. C I.33–40.

40. BTY 440.

41. C II.586.

42. See Maritain, *The Rights of Man and Natural Law* (Washington, DC: Catholic University of America Press, 1951), ch. 4, and *The Rights of Man and Natural Law* (Chicago: University of Chicago Press, 1943). See also Mary Anne Glendon, *A World Made New: Eleanor Roosevelt and the Universal Declaration of Human Rights* (New York: Random House, 2001).

43. C I.338.

44. For a similar reworking of the Stoic position, see my "The Worth of Human Dignity: Two Tensions in Stoic Cosmopolitanism," in *Philosophy and Power in the Graeco-Roman World: Essays in Honour of Miriam Griffin*, ed. G. Clark and T. Rajak (Oxford: Clarendon Press, 2002), pp. 31–49.

45. See Nussbaum, "Kant and Stoic Cosmopolitanism," in *Perpetual Peace*, ed. J. Bohman and M. Lutz-Bachmann (Cambridge, MA: MIT Press, 1997), pp. 25–58.

46. For those who read Kant as holding that our capacity for self-legislation is the source of moral principles, as well as the source of moral worth, there will be a difference at this point between Kant and Williams, since Williams plainly believes that moral truths are true independently of human choice. Those who find this element of Kant's position extreme or implausible will find that there is no analogue to it in Williams.

47. Cambridge, MA: Harvard University Press, 1971.

48. Rawls, *A Theory of Justice*, p. 207.

49. Ibid., p. 587.

50. Expanded paperback edition (New York: Columbia University Press, 1996).

51. Unfortunately, I never asked Rawls whether he knew Williams, since I myself did not read Williams's work until after Rawls's death. (The works are hard to find; a good popular edition is badly needed.) He certainly knew thoroughly, and taught, Hobbes, Locke, Rousseau, and Kant. He was also familiar with modern religious thought, for example the views of John Courtney Murray, that can be said to be in Williams's spirit. Finally, although he never wrote about the religion clauses, he knew a lot about the U.S. constitutional tradition.

52. BT 221.

53. Locke, *A Letter Concerning Toleration* (Amherst, NY: Prometheus Books, 1990), pp. 43–47, 69.

54. Ibid., p. 33.

55. Ibid., p. 59.

56. Rousseau, *On the Social Contract*, in *Jean-Jacques Rousseau: The Basic Political Writings*, trans. Donald A. Cress (Indianapolis: Hackett, 1987), Book IV, chapter VIII, p. 226.

57. Rawls, *Political Liberalism*, pp. 36–37, and the constructive argument that follows.

58. Personal conversation with Richard Strier, Department of English, University of Chicago.

59. See Timothy Hall's excellent treatment of this issue.

60. On the "freestanding" basis, see Rawls, *Political Liberalism*, pp. 10–13; on overlapping consensus, pp. 133–172.

61. BTY 501.

62. W. Clark Gilpin, *Millenarian Piety*, p. 1.

63. *Key*, I.134.

3 PROCLAIMING EQUALITY: RELIGION IN THE NEW NATION

1. Smith is of course not the only philosopher to have such ideas: John Locke's account of the mind as *tabula rasa* had already had wide influence. But we should remember that the Scottish Enlightenment was particularly important in the education of Americans—Madison, at Princeton, in particular.

2. Gordon S. Wood, *The Radicalism of the American Revolution* (New York: Vintage Books, 1991).

3. *Wallace v. Jaffree*, 472 U.S. 38 (1985).

4. See Anson P. Stokes and Leo Pfeffer, *Church and State in the United States* (New York: Greenwood Press, 1975), pp. 23–24. Their divergent estimates come from W. W. Sweet, "Church Membership," *Dictionary of American History* (one in eight) and from Harold Davis, "Religion, American," *Dictionary of American History* (one in 20–25). A more recent study suggests 17 percent in 1776: Roger Finke and Rodney Stark, *The Churching of America, 1776–2005* (New Brunswick: Rutgers University Press, 2005), at pp. 22–23 and ch. 2. To some extent, these low numbers might reflect rural isolation, but Americans have never required large numbers to begin a congregation. So it would seem that the more likely explanation is Protestant "seeking"—many were like Roger Williams, not happy with any organized orthodoxy.

5. Cicero rejected Stoicism in epistemology, allying himself with a moderate skepticism. In ethics, his views are very close to those of the Stoics, with subtle differences; in political thought, those differences become unimportant.

6. Wood, *Radicalism of the American Revolution*, p. 103.

7. These poetic dramas include *The Adulateur* (1772), *The Defeat* (1773), and *The Group* (1775); the British governor appears in the first two under the name of Rapatio, or "Plunderer." Warren later published all her dramas in a book that she dedicated to George Washington. Warren is an ancestor of my mother, whose maiden name was Elizabeth Warren.

8. See David Sedley, "The Ethics of Brutus and Cassius," *Journal of Roman Studies* 87 (1997), 41–53. Sedley argues convincingly that Brutus was not a Stoic, as is sometimes supposed, but a closely related type of Platonist, who rejected the quietistic strain in Stoic politics and insisted that political instability is worse than lawless tyranny. His "audition question" to the prospective conspirators, as reported by Plutarch, aims to uncover their views on this point.

9. Cato is the hero of Lucan's *Pharsalia*.

10. See Plutarch's account, and the analysis in Sedley.

11. See Nussbaum, "Kant and Stoic Cosmopolitanism," in *Kant's Perpetual Peace*, ed. J. Bohmann and M. Lutz-Bachmann, and "Human Dignity and Political Entitlements," in *Human Dignity and Bioethics: Essays,* ed. A. Schulman (Washington, DC: Government Printing Office, 2007), commissioned by the President's Council on Bioethics.

12. See Wood, *Radicalism of the American Revolution,* p. 240.

13. Pettit, *Republicanism: A Theory of Freedom and Government* (New York and Oxford: Oxford University Press, 1997).

14. In his excellent paper "On Noncoercive Establishment," *Political Theory* 33 (2005), 812–839, Daniel Brudney argues that this sort of concern about alienation from the polity can be upheld against a mild and noncoercive establishment only if one believes that citizens' connectedness to or intimacy with the polity is very important. If one does not believe that, one will not have a good basis for objecting to that sort of establishment. Brudney's argument is valuable, but I do not believe that the position of the American founders is best reconstructed in the language of alienation and intimacy (a language Brudney derives from Marx). It is, instead, best reconstructed in terms of equal respect and equal dignity, and one does not need to believe that connectedness is a very important value in order to find an affront to minority dignity in government statements that a given religion is preferred.

15. See Wood, *Radicalism of the American Revolution,* p. 221.

16. Ibid.

17. See Nussbaum, *The Clash Within: Democracy, Religious Violence, and India's Future* (Cambridge, MA: Harvard University Press, 2007).

18. See McConnell, *Religion and the Constitution,* p. 37.

19. See ibid., and Hamburger, *Separation of Church and State,* p. 97.

20. Quoted in McConnell, *Religion and the Constitution,* p. 24.

21. Data are from Leonard W. Levy, *The Establishment Clause: Religion and the First Amendment* (New York and London: Macmillan, 1986), pp. 1–62.

22. See McConnell, *Religion and the Constitution,* p. 23; Philip Kurland, "The Origins of the Religion Clauses of the Constitution," *William and Mary Law Review* 27 (1986), 839–861, at 845; Douglas Laycock, "'Nonpreferential' Aid to Religion: A False Claim About Original Intent," *William and Mary Law Review* 27 (1986), 875–923, at 916.

23. See Levy, *Establishment Clause,* p. 64.

24. Hamburger, *Separation of Church and State,* p. 76.

25. Ibid., p. 96.

26. Ibid., p. 99.

27. Ibid., pp. 96–97.

28. Quoted in Levy, *Establishment Clause,* pp. 5–6.

29. A. E. Dick Howard, "James Madison and the Founding of the Republic," in *James Madison on Religious Liberty,* ed. Robert S. Alley (Amherst, NY: Prometheus Books, 1985), pp. 21–34, at 21.

30. Robert S. Alley, "Introduction," in *James Madison on Religious Liberty,* p. 13.

31. Irving Brant, quoted in Alley, p. 13.

32. See Roy Branson, "James Madison and the Scottish Enlightenment," *Journal of the History of Ideas* 40 (1979), 235–250; Samuel Fleischacker, "Adam Smith's Reception Among the American Founders, 1776–1790," *William and Mary Quarterly* 59 (2002), http://www.historycooperative.org/journals/wm/59.4/fleischacker.htm.

33. Quoted in Howard, "James Madison and the Founding," p. 23.

34. Kenneth Clark, "Madison and Slavery," http://www.jamesmadisonmus.org/textpages/clark.htm.

35. Letter of January 24, 1774, quoted in Alley, p. 48.

36. Ibid., letter of March 4, 1774.

37. Ibid., p. 46, letter of December 1, 1774.

38. Letter of January 24, 1774, p. 47.

39. Letter of May 15, 1818, Alley, p. 80.

40. See McConnell, *Religion and the Constitution,* p. 59.

41. See McConnell, *Religion and the Constitution,* pp. 59–60, and M. McConnell, "The Origins and Historical Understanding of Free Exercise of Religion," *Harvard Law Review* 108 (1990), 1409, 1443–1444, 1462–1463.

42. From full version of the *Memorial and Remonstrance* in McConnell, *Religion and the Constitution,* pp. 63–68.

43. See Philip Kurland, "The Origins of the Religion Clauses of the Constitution," *William and Mary Law Review* 27 (1986), 839–861, at 847.

44. For a more detailed account, see McConnell, *Religion and the Constitution,* pp. 71–79.

45. McConnell, *Religion and the Constitution,* p. 80.

46. Madison, cited in McConnell, pp. 84–85.

47. Amar, *The Bill of Rights* (New Haven: Yale University Press, 1998), pp. 32–45, 246–257.

48. Ibid., p. 40. He cites Jefferson, in an 1804 letter: "While we deny that Congress have a right to control the freedom of the press, we have ever asserted the right of the States, and their exclusive right, to do so." Madison, in 1800, concluded that "liberty of conscience and freedom of the press were *equally* and *completely* exempted from all authority whatever of the United States."

49. *School District of Abington Township v. Schempp,* 374 U.S. 203 (1963), concurring opinion by J. Brennan.

50. Kurt T. Lash, "The Second Adoption of the Establishment Clause: The Rise of the Nonestablishment Principle," *Arizona State Law Journal* 27 (1995), 1085–1154.

51. Amar, *Bill of Rights,* p. 254, although he holds that it really does not matter all that much whether we incorporate the Establishment Clause, since the relevant issues can be taken care of by combining the Free Exercise Clause with the Equal Protection Clause (p. 254).

52. Amar, so far as I can see, makes no parallel argument: he simply stresses the obvious fact that many people sought the protection of state establishments. Since, however, he stresses this same fact with regard to speech and press, he never succeeds in demonstrating the asymmetry between the Establishment Clause and the other clauses that he apparently intends to demonstrate. In both cases, incorporation would remove from the states a power that many sought to grant them through the limited wording of the original amendment: the power to control speech and press in the first case, the power to declare an established church in the second (see pp. 32–45).

53. Here I follow the excellent argument of Douglas Laycock, in "'Nonpreferential' Aid to Religion: a False Claim About Original Intent," *William and Mary Law Review* 27 (1986), 875–923.

54. Laycock, "'Nonpreferential' Aid," p. 878.

55. See Laycock, p. 881.

56. Ibid., pp. 882–883.

57. Thus Rehnquist's position cannot be that the drafting history is simply irrelevant, since he relies heavily on a tiny part of it.

58. See also the excellent treatment of this issue in Laycock.

59. See Laycock, "'Nonpreferential' Aid," p. 914.

60. Here I am agreeing with Laycock, pp. 914–915.

61. On Thursday, July 10, 2007, Rajan Zed, Hindu chaplain of the Indian Association of Northern Nevada, became the first Hindu to deliver the Senate's opening prayer. Zed spoke at the invitation of Democratic Senator Harry Reid of Nevada, not as part of an organized diversity program. Several Christian demonstrators were ejected when they tried to disrupt the prayers, calling it an "abomination." (See "US Senate Opens with Hindu Prayer," http://www.rediff.com/news/2007/jul/12zed.htm). A Muslim opening prayer was delivered by African-American leader Wallace D. Mohammed, son of Elijah Mohammed, in 1992.

62. "As the government of the United States of America is not in any sense founded on the Christian Religion—as it has in itself no character of enmity against the laws, religion, or tranquility of Musselmen—and as the said States never have entered into any war or act of hostility against any Mehomitan nation, it is declared by the parties that no pretext arising from religious opinions shall ever produce an interruption of the harmony existing between the two countries."

63. See Hamburger, *Separation of Church and State*.

4   THE STRUGGLE OVER ACCOMMODATION

1. Pericles' famous "Funeral Oration" is given in Thucydides' *History of the Peloponnesian War*. It may or may not be an accurate version of what Pericles said.

2. See *Cutter v. Wilkinson*, 709 U.S. (2005), n. 5.

3. 494 U.S. 872 (1990).

4. When this chapter was in the final stages of revision, Kent Greenawalt's magisterial *Religion and the Constitution. Volume 1: Free Exercise and Fairness* (Princeton: Princeton University Press, 2006) was published. I was therefore unable to draw on it in

fashioning my own argument, and I can here only indicate in several footnotes areas of the book that relate to my argument. On the whole, Greenawalt's analysis is broadly consistent with mine, although it is more open-ended and plural-valued, focusing less on equality as a central goal, and suggesting that different approaches may be justified in different areas of the law—that the draft, for example, should be treated differently from the case of drug laws. I will indicate some of our most salient differences at various points, but on the whole the book is a wonderful treatment of the issues.

5. Michael McConnell, "The Origins and Historical Understanding of Free Exercise of Religion," *Harvard Law Review* 103 (1990), 1409 ff., extract in McConnell casebook, pp. 103–112. On the history see also Greenawalt, *Religion and the Constitution*, pp. 11–22.

6. Philip Hamburger, "A Constitutional Right of Religious Exemption: An Historical Perspective," *George Washington Law Review* 60 (1992), 915 ff.

7. McConnell, cited in casebook, p. 109.

8. McConnell, casebook, p. 111.

9. Ibid.

10. See McConnell, casebook, p. 112.

11. See *In re Estate of May*, 305 N.Y. 486, 107 N.Y. S. 2d 170 (1953). The New York Court of Appeals held valid an uncle-niece Jewish marriage by two residents of New York that was lawfully celebrated in Rhode Island.

12. We should not, however, accept the eccentric reading of Amar, *The Bill of Rights* (New Haven: Yale University Press, 1998), pp. 42–43, where he argues that "prohibiting the free exercise of religion" really means "prohibiting 'the free exercise of religion'"—in other words, he argues that the clause rules out only laws that explicitly state that their purpose is to curtail religious expression, not other laws that do so without saying that this is what they are doing.

13. *Stansbury v. Marks*, 2 Dall. 213 (Pa. 1793).

14. Quoted in McConnell, casebook, p. 124.

15. Ibid., pp. 129–130.

16. *Simon's Executors v. Gratz*, 2 Pen. & W. 412 (Pa. 1831).

17. The case was complex, because the area in question was predominantly Roman Catholic, as was the municipal council that passed the law (see McConnell, casebook, pp. 86–87).

18. *Permoli v. New Orleans*, 44 U.S. (3 How.) 589 (1845).

19. *Cantwell v. Connecticut*, 310 U.S. 296 (1940).

20. *Everson v. Board of Education*, 330 U.S. 1 (1947); see Chapter 7.

21. *School District of Abington Township v. Schempp*, 374 U.S. 203 (1963), concurring opinion by J. Brennan.

22. See district court opinion summarized in *Wallace v. Jaffree*, 472 U.S. 38 (1985).

23. *Chicago Tribune*, Saturday, July 8, 2006, p. 6.

24. Until very recently immigration from nations with large numbers of members of these religions has been tightly controlled.

25. See J. Douglas's concurring opinion.

26. Greenawalt recognizes the importance of equality issues, but he treats them as supplemental to the ideas of substantial burden and compelling state interest (*Religion*

and the Constitution, p. 228). I am arguing that this approach is misleading. For another article that makes the prominence of equality considerations in Free Exercise jurisprudence plain, see William P. Marshall, "What Is the Matter with Equality? An Assessment of the Equal Treatment of Religion and Nonreligion in First Amendment Jurisprudence," *Indiana Law Journal* 75 (2000), 193–217. Two more general articles by Greenawalt are also helpful: "How Empty Is the Idea of Equality?" *Columbia Law Review* 83 (1983), 1167–1185, and "'Prescriptive Equality': Two Steps Forward," *Harvard Law Review* 110 (1997), 1265–1290.

27. 366 U.S. 599 (1961).

28. On burden, see also Greenawalt, *Religion and the Constitution,* p. 207.

29. See also ibid., p. 215.

30. *Thomas v. Review Board,* 450 U.S. 707 (1981); *Hobbie v. Unemployment Appeals Commission,* 480 U.S. 136 (1987); *Frazee v. Illinois Dept. of Employment Security,* 489 U.S. 829 (1989).

31. *U.S. v. Lee,* 455 U.S. 252 (1982).

32. *Goldman v. Weinberger,* 475 U.S. 534 (1986).

33. *Bob Jones University v. United States,* 461 U.S. 574 (1983).

34. *Bowen v. Roy,* 476 U.S. 693 (1986); *Lyng v. Northwest Indian Cemetery Protective Assn.,* 485 U.S. 439 (1988).

35. Green, "Liberal Legislation and the Freedom of Contract," *T.H. Green: Lectures on the Principles of Political Obligation and Other Writings,* ed. Paul Harris and John Morrow (Cambridge: Cambridge University Press, 1986), pp. 194–212.

36. Adam Smith, *The Wealth of Nations,* 1st ed. 1776 (Indianapolis: Liberty Fund, 1981), p. 787.

37. The fathers were active in the case, the mothers not.

38. Amy Adamczyk, John Wibraniec, and Roger Finke, "Religious Regulation and the Court: Documenting the Effects of *Smith* and RFRA," *Journal of Church and State* 46 (2004), 237–262.

39. *Swann v. Pack,* 527 S. W. 2d 99 (Tenn. 1975).

40. I owe a great debt in this section to Garrett Epps's excellent book on Smith and his case, *To an Unknown God: Religious Freedom on Trial* (New York: St. Martin's Press, 2001). See now also Carolyn N. Long, *Religious Freedom and Indian Rights: The Case of Oregon v. Smith* (Lawrence: University of Kansas Press, 2005).

41. See Epps, *To an Unknown God,* p. 57.

42. See Jacob T. Levy, "Indians in Madison's Constitutional Order," *James Madison and the Future of Limited Government,* ed. John Samples (Washington, DC: Cato Institute, 2002), pp. 121–133.

43. Epps, *To an Unknown God,* p. 9.

44. Ibid., p. 8.

45. Quoted in Epps, *To an Unknown God,* p. 14.

46. Ibid., p. 15.

47. Ibid., p. 17.

48. Ibid., pp. 18–19.

49. Ibid., pp. 41–42.

50. Ibid., p. 46.

51. Ibid., p. 60; see Long, *Religious Freedom,* pp. 4–16, on the history of peyotism in Indian rituals.

52. The difference may well be one of dosage: LSD does not produce hallucinations in small doses.

53. Epps, *To an Unknown God,* p. 62.

54. According to Long, *Religious Freedom,* p. 6, there is now evidence that peyote can help people overcome alcohol abuse.

55. Epps, *To an Unknown God,* p. 65.

56. Ibid., p. 95.

57. Ibid., p. 110.

58. See Long, *Religious Freedom,* pp. 16–17.

59. See Epps, *To an Unknown God.*

60. See ibid., p. 125–129.

61. Ibid., pp. 154–155.

62. Ibid., p. 155.

63. *Employment Division v. Smith,* 494 U.S. 904 (1990).

64. Ibid.

65. Ibid., p. 905.

66. See McConnell, "Free Exercise Revisionism and the Smith Decision," *University of Chicago Law Review* 57 (1990), 1109–1153; "A Response to Professor Marshall," ibid. 58 (1991), 329–332; and also "Freedom from Persecution or Protection of the Rights of Conscience? A Critique of Justice Scalia's Historical Arguments in *City of Boerne v. Flores," William and Mary Law Review* 39 (1998), 819–847.

67. *Smith,* pp. 878–879.

68. 310 U.S. 586 (1940).

69. Ibid., p. 884.

70. Ibid., p. 876.

71. Ibid., pp. 881–882.

72. Ibid., pp. 883–884.

73. Ibid., p. 897.

74. Ibid., p. 886.

75. Ibid.

76. Ibid., pp. 902–903.

77. Ibid., pp. 901–902.

78. Ibid., p. 903.

79. Ibid., p. 908.

80. Ibid., p. 909.

81. See Adamzcek *et al.,* "Religious Regulation and the Court."

82. For this language, see also McConnell, casebook, p. 180.

83. *City of Boerne v. Flores,* 521 U.S. 507 (1997).

84. Long, *Religious Freedom,* pp. 277–279.

85. Epps, *To an Unknown God,* pp. 252–257.

86. See, for example, *Chalifoux v. New Caney Ind. School Dist.,* 976 F. Supp. 659 (S. C. Tex. 1997).

87. *Church of the Lukumi Babalu Aye v. City of Hialeah,* 508 U.S. 520 (1993).

88. *Fraternal Order of Police v. City of Newark*, 170 F. 3d 359 (3d Cir. 1999).

89. See Douglas Laycock, "Theology Scholarships, the Pledge of Allegiance, and Religious Liberty: Avoiding the Extremes but Missing the Liberty," *Harvard Law Review* 118 (2004), 155 ff., esp. 211–212 and nn. 368–373; Angela C. Carmella, "State Constitutional Protection of Religious Exercise: An Emerging Post-*Smith* Jurisprudence," *Brigham Young University Law Review* 1993.

90. *Cutter v. Wilkinson*, 544 U.S. 209 (2005).

91. *Gonzales v. O Centro Espirita Beneficente Uniao do Vegetal*, 126 S. Ct. 1211 (2006).

92. www.supremecourtus.gov/oral_arguments/argument_transcripts/04-1084.pdf.

93. McConnell's casebook suggests this line, and McConnell has favored it at least at times.

94. Actually, neither of these philosophers was a pacifist; Kant held a form of "just war" theory, and Thoreau's well-known act of civil disobedience arose from specific objections he had to the war against Mexico.

95. William Marshall, "In Defense of *Smith* and Free Exercise Revisionism," *University of Chicago Law Review* 58 (1991), 308–328; Marshall, "What Is the Matter with Equality? An Assessment of the Equal Treatment of Religion and Nonreligion in First Amendment Jurisprudence," *Indiana Law Journal* 75 (2000), 193–217; Christopher L. Eisgruber and Lawrence Sager, "Why the Religious Freedom Restoration Act Is Unconstitutional," *New York University Law Review* 69 (1994), 437–476; "Congressional Power and Religious Liberty After *City of Boerne v. Flores*, *Supreme Court Review* 3 (1997), 79–139.

96. For one of the best legal attempts, using this two-pronged approach, see *Malnak v. Yogi*, 592 F. 2d 197 (3d Cir. 1979).

97. *State v. Hodges*, 695 S. W. 2d 171, 171–172 (Tenn. 1985); see discussion in Marshall, "Equality," p. 193 n. 101.

98. Another problem raised by Koppelman is the issue of subjective commitment to something that is serious but evil: Hitler, for example, may have experienced his policies as nonoptional in this way. We can add that, as Lincoln said in the Second Inaugural, southern slaveholders did advance religious justifications for slavery, in some cases, no doubt, sincerely. This, however, is not the problem Koppelman takes it to be, since we can admit such claims as genuinely religious and defeat them at the next stage, when their holders propose to do harm to others or to violate other constitutional norms. The racist dating policy of Bob Jones University was held to be a genuine expression of religious commandment, but the Court held that a compelling interest in the eradication of racism justified discontinuing the university's tax exemption.

99. See *Malnak v. Yogi*.

100. Koppelman, forthcoming.

101. In that way, Williams's view is similar to my political "capabilities" view, as developed in *Women and Human Development* (Cambridge: Cambridge University Press, 2001), see chapter 3 on religion, and *Frontiers of Justice* (Cambridge, MA: Harvard University Press, 2006).

102. For such cases, see Marshall, "Equality," p. 193.

103. On the sincerity problem, see also Greenawalt, *Religion and the Constitution*, p. 110.

104. For a profile of Seeger, see Peter Irons, *The Courage of Their Convictions* (New York: The Free Press, 1988), 153–178.

105. *U.S. v. Seeger*, 380 U.S. 163 (1965).

106. Irons, *Courage*, p. 175.

107. *Welsh v. United States*, 398 U.S. 333 (1970), at 341, 343.

108. Ibid., 344.

109. Greenawalt proposes using a different standard for draft cases and cases involving drugs, giving more latitude for accommodation in the former type of case (see chapter 4 and 5). While there is a pragmatic case to be made for such case-by-case determinations, the enunciation of this difference as a legal principle makes me nervous, and Greenawalt nowhere, so far as I can see, offers a justification for the asymmetry. The structure of the book, which moves through each subject area separately, makes it possible for him to avoid comment on this difficult issue.

5   Fearing Strangers

1. I follow the account of the incident in John T. McGreevy, *Catholicism and American Freedom: A History* (New York: W. W. Norton, 2003), pp. 7–9; the citation is from p. 8.

2. I draw throughout this chapter on the sociological literature about "moral panics," which I analyze in my *Hiding from Humanity: Disgust, Shame, and the Law* (Princeton: Princeton University Press, 2004), chapter 5. The classic work is Stanley Cohen, *Folk Devils and Moral Panics* (New York and London: Routledge and Basil Blackwell, 3rd ed. 2002, original edition 1972).

3. See David Brion Davis, "Some Themes of Counter-Subversion: An Analysis of Anti-Masonic, Anti-Catholic, and Anti-Mormon Literature," *The Mississippi Valley Historical Review* 47 (1960), 205–224.

4. See McGreevy, *Catholicism and American Freedom*, and the excellent analysis in Philip Hamburger, *Separation of Church and State*.

5. Jon Krakauer, *Under the Banner of Heaven: A Story of Violent Faith* (New York: Random House, 2003). Krakauer is known for writing about mountaineering, and appears to have no credentials in the area of religion.

6. See Seth Perry, "Why Is It So Hard to Talk About Mormons?" *Sightings*, January 26, 2006, online publication of the Martin Marty Center, University of Chicago.

7. Ibid.

8. *Cultivating Humanity: A Classical Defense of Reform in Liberal Education* (Cambridge, MA: Harvard University Press, 1997), chapter 8.

9. For a good example of analysis from this point of view, see Bryan Waterman and Brian Kegel, *The Lord's University: Freedom and Authority at BYU* (Salt Lake City: Signature Books, 1998).

10. I am indebted to the following research papers, all submitted by University of Chicago law students in the fall of 2006: Joseph Callister, "Revisiting *Reynolds*: A Legal Defense of Mormon Polygamy"; Brad Romney, "The Wonderful World of Mormon Polygamy." (Callister got his undergraduate degree from BYU, Romney from the University of Utah.) I am also indebted to Sloan Speck, "'Under the Control of a

Theocratic Despotism': Mormon Polygamy, National Power, and the Supreme Court, 1860–1890." (Speck, unlike Callister and Romney, is not a member of the LDS church.)

11. I am grateful to references on this point in Joseph Callister's paper.

12. For Smith's early problems with the law, see Edwin Brown Firmage and Richard Collin Mangrum, *Zion in the Courts: A Legal History of the Church of Jesus Christ of Latter-day Saints 1830–1900* (Urbana and Chicago: University of Illinois Press, 1988), pp. 48–50.

13. Richard Lyman Bushman, *Joseph Smith: Rough Stone Rolling* (New York: Knopf, 2005), p. 72.

14. Joseph Callister points out to me that this explanation does not account for the presence in the text of Near Eastern names and religious practices that were unknown both to Smith and to the world at large at the time.

15. All quotes are from Bushman, *Joseph Smith*, pp. 3–4.

16. See Firmage and Mangrum, *Zion in the Courts*.

17. See Richard S. Van Wagoner, *Mormon Polygamy: A History* (Salt Lake City: Signature Books, 1986), pp. 1–3.

18. Bushman, *Joseph Smith*, pp. 549–550 on the legal complaints; on mob violence, pp. 222–230 (Missouri), pp. 356–370 (western Missouri), pp. 532–550 (Illinois).

19. For this list I am indebted to Van Wagoner, *Mormon Polygamy*, p. 3.

20. Ibid., p. iii.

21. Ibid., p. 4.

22. See Bushman, *Joseph Smith*, p. 491; Van Wagoner, *Mormon Polygamy*, pp. 4 ff.

23. Van Wagoner, *Mormon Polygamy*, pp. 6–10.

24. Ibid., pp. 23, 35, 38.

25. Bushman, *Joseph Smith*, p. 443.

26. Van Wagoner, *Mormon Polygamy*, pp. 89–91.

27. See Callister, pp. 6–7.

28. Callister, "Revisiting *Reynolds*," pp. 7–8, Van Wagoner, *Mormon Polygamy*, p. 90.

29. Bushman, *Joseph Smith*, p. 493.

30. See Sarah Barringer Gordon, *The Mormon Question* (Chapel Hill: University of North Carolina Press, 2002), pp. 96 ff., Bushman pp. 491–492, Van Wagoner, pp. 94–100.

31. Van Wagoner, *Mormon Polygamy*, p. 98, cf. Gordon, *Mormon Question*, pp. 96 ff.

32. Van Wagoner, p. 94.

33. Ibid., p. 103.

34. See ibid., p. 92.

35. See Nancy Cott, *Public Vows: A History of Marriage and the Nation* (Cambridge, MA: Harvard University Press, 2000), p. 7.

36. See Ibid., pp. 106–107.

37. *The Subjection of Women* (1869), ed. Susan Moller Okin (Indianapolis: Hackett, 1988), p. 33: worse because, at least as Mill sees it, slaves have the right to refuse intercourse, if not always the political power. The wife lacks even the right. Mill also notes that slaves may own at least some property, whereas wives can own none (p. 32).

38. *Bradwell v. Illinois*, 83 U.S. (16 Wall.) 130 (1873).

39. See Gordon, *Mormon Question*, pp. 29–54.

40. From Alfreda Eva Bell, *Boadicea*, quoted in Gordon, p. 47.

41. Even as astute a critic of prejudice as Mill takes it for granted that most domestic violence is committed by lower-class men.

42. From a presentation at the New Orleans Academy of Sciences in 1861, quoted in Van Wagoner, 106.

43. Gordon, *Mormon Question,* p. 55.

44. Van Wagoner, *Mormon Polygamy,* p. 107, Firmage and Mangrum, *Zion in the Courts,* pp. 130 ff.

45. From *Congressional Globe* 1860, quoted in Firmage and Mangrum, *Zion in the Courts,* p. 134.

46. Quoted in Van Wagoner, *Mormon Polygamy,* p. 109.

47. Firmage and Mangrum, *Zion in the Courts,* p. 147.

48. Van Wagoner, *Zion in the Courts,* p. 110.

49. Gordon, *Mormon Question,* p. 114.

50. Ibid., p. 114.

51. Ibid., p. 115.

52. See summary in *Reynolds v. U.S.,* 98 U.S. 145 (1874), at 148–150.

53. Ibid., pp. 145, 153.

54. *Crawford v. Washington,* 541 U.S. 36 (2004).

55. Ibid., pp. 167 168.

56. Ibid., p. 168.

57. Ibid., p. 162.

58. Ibid., p. 166.

59. Ibid., p. 166. See Cott, *Public Vows,* p. 114.

60. Firmage and Mangrum, *Zion in the Courts,* pp. 155–156, Cott, *Public Vows,* pp. 115–116.

61. Cited in Cott, *Public Vows,* pp. 114–115.

62. Ibid., p. 115.

63. Ibid., noting that Lieber did eventually leave the South for New York out of the conviction that slavery is wrong.

64. See Gordon, *Mormon Question,* pp. 156 ff.

65. Ibid., pp. 164, 181.

66. See *Davis v. Beason,* 133 U.S. 333 (1890), oath as excerpted in McConnell, p. 142.

67. *The Late Corporation of the Church of Jesus Christ of Latter-day Saints v. United States,* 136 U.S. 1 (1890).

68. Eric Larson, *The Devil in the White City* (New York: Crown, 2003).

69. The story of both men's roles in the flag movement and the writing of the pledge is told with excellent scholarship in Richard J. Ellis, *To the Flag: The Unlikely Story of the Pledge of Allegiance* (Lawrence: University Press of Kansas, 2005), to which I am greatly indebted. A more hagiographical, indeed gushy, version of Bellamy's life is given by Margarette S. Miller in *I Pledge Allegiance* (Boston: The Christopher Publishing House, 1946), and *Twenty-Three Words: The Life Story of the Author of the Pledge of Allegiance as Told in His Own Words* (Portsmouth, VA: Printcraft Press, 1976), the latter being a fictionalized autobiography of Bellamy whose subtitle means words that Miller has invented, words such as "I possess a driving will and a forceful nature that always aided me in the life I sought" (1).

70. Ellis, *To the Flag*, pp. 10–11.

71. Ibid., pp. 8–9.

72. See Ellis, *To the Flag*.

73. Ellis, *To the Flag*, p. 32.

74. Quoted in ibid., p. 32.

75. See the shrewd analysis in ibid., pp. 46–47.

76. Ibid., pp. 50–58. See also David R. Manwaring, *Render Unto Caesar: The Flag-Salute Controversy* (Chicago: University of Chicago Press, 1962), pp. 3–7. See also the briefer account of the case and the profile of Lillian in Peter Irons, *The Courage of Their Convictions* (New York: The Free Press, 1988), pp. 15–35.

77. Manwaring, *Render Unto Caesar*, pp. 9–10.

78. Ellis, *To the Flag*, p. 83.

79. Ibid., p. 84.

80. The analysis focused on pacifism: they interpreted the pledge as entailing the willingness to fight for one's country.

81. See Manwaring, *Render Unto Caesar*, p. 11.

82. Ellis, *To the Flag*, p. 85.

83. Ibid., p. 86.

84. Ibid., pp. 86–88, Manwaring, *Render Unto Caesar*, p. 13.

85. Ellis, *To the Flag*, p. 87.

86. Ibid., p. 88.

87. Shawn Francis Peters, *Judging Jehovah's Witnesses: Religious Persecution and the Dawn of the Rights Revolution* (Lawrence: University Press of Kansas, 2000), p. 30.

88. Wikipedia, "Jehovah's Witnesses."

89. Peters, *Judging Jehovah's Witnesses*, p. 35.

90. *Cantwell v. Connecticut*, 310 U.S. 296 (1940).

91. J. S. Conway, quoted in Peters, *Judging Jehovah's Witnesses*, p. 25.

92. Online extract from pamphlet *Jehovah's Witnesses*, published by United States Holocaust Memorial Museum. The museum offers oral histories and other resources for the study of this period.

93. Ellis, *To the Flag*, pp. 92–101; Manwaring, *Render Unto Caesar*, pp. 56–80.

94. Peters, *Judging Jehovah's Witnesses*, p. 20.

95. Ibid., p. 26.

96. Ibid., pp. 27–28.

97. Ellis, *To the Flag*, p. 97, Peters, *Judging Jehovah's Witnesses*, p. 36.

98. Peters, *Judging Jehovah's Witnesses*, p. 36.

99. Lillian writes her points as a numbered list, mentions the Biblical texts by number only, and stresses the constitutional as well as religious arguments. Billy writes a long discursive paragraph, quotes the relevant biblical texts, and mentions his love of his country.

100. Peters, *Judging Jehovah's Witnesses*, p. 39.

101. Ibid., p. 40.

102. Ibid., p. 40.

103. Ibid., p. 41. On this phase of the case, see also Manwaring, pp. 86–106.

104. Peters, *Judging Jehovah's Witnesses*, p. 46; Manwaring, pp. 106–117.

105. Manwaring, *Render Unto Caesar*, 114.

106. Ibid., ch. 6, esp. pp. 121–123, 132.

107. *West Virginia Board of Education v. Barnette*, 319 U.S. (1942), at 646.

108. Peters, *Judging Jehovah's Witnesses*, p. 52.

109. Ibid., p. 53.

110. Ibid., at 593.

111. Ibid., at 595.

112. Ibid.

113. Ibid.

114. Ibid., at 601.

115. Ibid., at 604–605.

116. Stone here alludes to *U.S. v. Carolene Products*, where his own opinion had mapped out the approach to different levels of judicial scrutiny that has since become dominant in issues relating to race and sex.

117. Ibid., 607.

118. See Peters, *Judging Jehovah's Witnesses*, chs. 3 and 4; Manwaring, ch. 8.

119. Peters, *Judging Jehovah's Witnesses*, pp. 73–74.

120. Ibid., pp. 80–81.

121. Ibid., p. 81.

122. Ibid., p. 85.

123. Ibid., ch. 6.

124. Ibid., pp. 113–123.

125. Manwaring, *Render Unto Caesar*, ch. 7, pp. 148–162; Manwaring criticizes the legal reasoning of many of these criticisms, but from a shaky and badly defended viewpoint: he seems to think that there is no precedent for accommodations against laws of general applicability, and he suggests, wrongly, that there is a lot of support in the precedents for a *Reynolds*-style denial of accommodation.

126. Manwaring, *Render Unto Caesar*, pp. 153–154.

127. Peters, *Judging Jehovah's Witnesses*, p. 237; the quotation is from Black, who said, "Felix mesmerized us."

128. Peters, *Judging Jehovah's Witnesses*, pp. 235–236.

129. *West Virginia Board of Education v. Barnette*, 319 U.S. 624 (1942), at 638.

130. Ibid., 642.

131. Ibid., 641.

132. Irons, *Courage of Their Convictions*, p. 35.

133. See Hamburger, *Separation of Church and State*, p. 202.

134. See Hamburger, *Separation of Church and State*, p. 215; Davis, "Some Themes of Counter-Subversion," p. 216; McGreevy, *Catholicism and American Freedom*, p. 12.

135. McGreevy, *Catholicism and American Freedom*, p. 12.

136. Ibid., p. 26.

137. Hamburger, *Separation of Church and State*, p. 206; McGreevy, pp. 13, 33.

138. McGreevy, *Catholicism and American Freedom*, p. 22.

139. Ibid., pp. 28–29.

140. Hamburger, *Separation of Church and State*, p. 209.

141. McGreevy, *Catholicism and American Freedom*, pp. 49–57.

142. Ibid., pp. 34–35; Hamburger, *Separation of Church and State*, pp. 193–251.

143. See, for example, Hamburger, *Separation of Church and State*, p. 207; McGreevy, *Catholicism and American Freedom*, chs. 1–3, on the complex debates with Catholicism at this period.

144. Davis, "Some Themes of Counter-Subversion," p. 208.

145. McGreevy, *Catholicism and American Freedom*, p. 64.

146. Hamburger, *Separation of Church and State*, p. 408.

147. McGreevy, *Catholicism and American Freedom*, p. 38.

148. *Pierce v. Society of Sisters*, 268 U.S. 510 (1925).

149. Hamburger, *Separation of Church and State*, pp. 296 ff.

150. McGreevy, *Catholicism and American Freedom*, p. 91.

151. Hamburger, *Separation of Church and State*, p. 298.

152. Ibid., pp. 392–393.

153. Quoted in ibid., p. 392 n. 3.

6   The Establishment Clause: School Prayer, Public Displays

1. *Everson v. Board of Education*, 330 U.S. 1 (1946).

2. *Texas Monthly v. Bullock*, 489 U.S. 1 (1989).

3. For our topic, this inclusiveness is crucial, since it is crucial to extend religious freedom to include people with mental disabilities. (If they are unable to exercise it, due to the nature of their disability, then my approach recommends guardianship, but not the withdrawal of rights.) On this see *Frontiers of Justice*, ch. 3, and also "Human Dignity and Political Entitlements," in *Human Dignity and Bioethics: Essays*, ed. A. Schulman (Washington, DC: Government Printing Office, 2007), commissioned by the President's Council on Bioethics.

4. 403 U.S. 602 (1970).

5. Ibid., 614.

6. *Loving v. Virginia*, 388 U.S. 1 (1967).

7. See Laycock, discussed in Chapter 3.

8. *Pierce v. Society of Sisters*, 268 U.S. 510 (1925): states can require "that certain studies plainly essential to good citizenship must be taught, and that nothing be taught which is manifestly inimical to the public welfare" (534).

9. *Schempp*, p. 208 n. 3.

10. *Engel v. Vitale*, 370 U.S. 421 (1962), at 430.

11. See Justice Brennan's historical account in his concurring opinion in *Abington School Dist. v. Schempp*, 374 U.S. 203 (1963), 269–273.

12. Ibid., 272.

13. Ibid., 273.

14. *Engel v. Vitale*, 422.

15. Ibid., 438.

16. Ibid.

17. Ibid., 425.

18. Ellery Schempp, "The Democratic Way," Sermon at the First Parish in Bedford Unitarian Universalist, February 1, 2004, http://www.uubedford.org/sermons/Schempp-TheDemocraticWay.htm.

19. Ibid., 426–429.

20. Ibid., 429–430.

21. Ibid., 431.

22. Ibid., 428.

23. Ibid., 424 n. 2, citing the opinion of the trial court.

24. Ibid., 434.

25. Ibid., 435.

26. *Schempp*, 205.

27. Ibid., 209, citing expert testimony from a scholar of Judaism.

28. Ibid., 210, citing expert testimony from a scholar of Christianity.

29. He cited confusion with the name Elroy, and admiration of the mystery writer Ellery Queen and Unitarian minister William Ellery Channing. I will refer to him as "Ellory" when talking about the early period and "Ellery" when talking about his career in general.

30. Schempp, sermon.

31. Edward died in November 2003, at the age of 95; Sidney died in June 2004, at the age of 91.

32. *Schempp*, 208–211.

33. Ibid., 214 n. 6.

34. Ibid., 215, quoting from an unpublished opinion by Judge Alonso Taft.

35. Ibid., 222.

36. Ibid., 225.

37. Ibid., 223.

38. Ibid., 222.

39. See the profile in Peter Irons, *The Courage of Their Convictions* (New York: The Free Press, 1988), pp. 355–378.

40. *Wallace v. Jaffree*, 472 U.S. 38 (1985), at 45. For Chioke's reaction, see Irons, *Courage of Their Convictions*.

41. Ibid., 23.

42. Ibid., 41 n. 3.

43. Irons, *Courage of Their Convictions*, p. 363.

44. Ibid., p. 363.

45. *Wallace v. Jaffree*, p. 41.

46. Irons, *Courage of Their Convictions*, p. 378.

47. Ibid., pp. 58–59.

48. Ibid., p. 61, quoting *Lynch v. Donnelly*, 465 U.S., at 690–691.

49. Ibid., p. 69.

50. Ibid., p. 73.

51. *Brown v. Gilmore*, 258 F. 3d 265 (4th Cir. 2001).

52. *Lee v. Weisman*, 505 U.S. 577 (1992).

53. Ibid., 581.

54. Ibid., 581–582.

55. Actually, the citation reads "American Jewish Congress *et al.*," but it is not stated who the others are.

56. *Lee v. Weisman*, 588.

57. Ibid., 593.

58. Ibid., 621

59. Ibid., 623, quoting Jefferson.

60. Ibid., 627.

61. *Lee v. Weisman*, 598 (J. Blackmun, concurring).

62. *Lynch v. Donnelly*, 465 U.S. 668 (1983).

63. Ibid., 679, quoting *Lemon*.

64. Ibid., 687.

65. Ibid., 690.

66. Ibid., 691.

67. Ibid., 692.

68. Ibid., 691.

69. *Allegheny County v. Greater Pittsburgh ACLU*, 492 U.S. 573 (1988).

70. Ibid., 608.

71. Ibid., 626, O'Connor, J., concurring.

72. Ibid., 626.

73. Ibid., 585.

74. "Ten Commandments Judge Removed from Office," CNN.com, Friday, November 14.

75. See *McCreary County v. ACLU of Kentucky*, 545 U.S. 844 (2005), majority opinion section III A: they "unmistakably rest even the universally accepted prohibitions (as against murder, theft, etc.) on the sanction of the divinity proclaimed at the text's beginning."

76. Brief for the Hindu American Foundation and Others, Representing the Interests of Hindus, Buddhists and Jains, as Amici curiae in Support of Reversal, in *Van Orden v. Perry*.

77. See my *The Clash Within: Democracy, Religious Violence, and India's Future* (Cambridge, MA: Harvard University Press, 2007).

78. *McCreary County v. ACLU*.

79. Ibid., p. 3, quoting *Santa Fe Independent School District v. Doe*, 530 U.S. 290, 315.

80. *Van Orden v. Perry*, 545 U.S. 677 (2005).

81. Amicus brief section I.B., entitled "The Effect of the Ten Commandments Monument on Followers of the Non-Judeo-Christian Religions Is to Signal an Endorsement of Particular Religious Views."

82. *Van Orden v. Perry*.

83. Texas GOP: no church-state split, Saturday, July 8, 2006.

84. *McCreary*, dissent, 10.

85. See *McCreary* dissent.

86. See detail in Douglas Laycock, "'Noncoercive' Support for Religion: Another False Claim About the Establishment Clause," *Valparaiso University Law Review* 26 (1991–1992), 37–69, focusing on South Carolina and Virginia.

87. *McCreary*, p. 10.

88. Statistical Abstract of the United States: The National Data Book, U.S. Department of Commerce, 124th Edition, 2004–2005.

89. *Elk Grove Unified School District v. Newdow*, 542 U.S. 1 (2004).

7   Aid to Sectarian Schools: The Search for Fairness

1. See discussion in McGreevy, *Catholicism and American Freedom*, p. 169.

2. Brand Blanshard, *The Church and the Polish Immigrant*, no publisher given, 1920, quoted in McGreevy, p. 169.

3. McGreevy, *Catholicism and American Freedom*, p. 170.

4. See Mary Anne Glendon, *A World Made New: Eleanor Roosevelt and the Universal Declaration of Human Rights* (New York: Random House, 2001).

5. See Maritain, *The Rights of Man and Natural Law* (Washington, DC: Catholic University of America Press, 1951), ch. 4, and *The Rights of Man and Natural Law* (Chicago: University of Chicago Press, 1943). When he was very young, in the 1920s, Maritain was briefly sympathetic with Charles Maurras's ultraconservative movement Action française, but he soon became disillusioned with conservative antidemocratic Catholicism.

6. See his important book *We Hold These Truths: Catholic Reflections on the American Proposition* (New York: Sheed and Ward, 1960).

7. McGreevy, *Catholicism and American Freedom*, p. 174.

8. Boston: Beacon Press, first edition 1949, second edition 1958; my page numbers are those of the second edition.

9. Blanshard, *American Freedom and Catholic Power*, p. 302.

10. Ibid., p. 88.

11. Ibid.

12. For population panics as a trope of subordination, see Mohan Rao, *From Population Control to Reproductive Health: Malthusian Arithmetic* (Delhi: Sage, 2005). Rao discusses British rhetoric about the Irish, Indian Hindu rhetoric about Indian Muslims, and other examples. See ch. 6.

13. Blanshard, *American Freedom and Catholic Power*, p. 306.

14. See p. 88.

15. Blanshard, *Communism, Democracy, and Catholic Power* (Boston: Beacon Press, 1951).

16. Ibid., p. 337.

17. For Blanshard's influence in this matter, see his Wikipedia biography.

18. Murray, "Paul Blanshard and the New Nativism," on line at http://www.georgetown.edu/users/jlh3/Murray/1951a.htm.

19. *New York Times* obituary, January 30, 1980.

20. *We Hold These Truths*, p. 18.

21. *Everson v. Board of Education*, 330 U.S. 1 (1947).

22. Ibid., 15.

23. Ibid., 15–16; Jefferson's phrase is cited from *Reynolds v. United States*, not the most propitious precedent.

24. Ibid., 18.

25. Ibid., 16.

26. Ibid., 17–18.

27. Ibid., 18.

28. Hamburger, *Separation*, pp. 422–434, 461–478.

29. Ibid., p. 462.

30. 397 U.S. 664 (1970).

31. *Texas Monthly v. Bullock*, 489 U.S. 1 (1989).

32. 403 U.S. 602 (1971).

33. Ibid., 612–613, citing *Walz*.

34. 473 U.S. 373 (1984).

35. 473 U.S. 402 (1984).

36. Ibid., 422.

37. Ibid., 423.

38. Ibid., 431.

39. These criteria are set out in *Grand Rapids*, decided earlier, and are referred to in *Aguilar*, so it isn't entirely clear that they are worries associated with entanglement only, and not also with secular purpose, which was found lacking in the *Grand Rapids* program.

40. 473 U.S. 424 (1984).

41. Ibid., 420–421.

42. Ibid., 425, O'Connor, J. dissenting.

43. Ibid.

44. Ibid., 431.

45. 474 U.S. 481 (1986).

46. Ibid.

47. *Zobrest v. Catalina Foothills School District*, 509 U.S. 1 (1993).

48. Ibid., 10.

49. Ibid., 8.

50. Ibid., 13.

51. 512 U.S. 687.

52. Ibid., 717–718.

53. Ibid., 711.

54. Ibid.

55. 508 U.S. 384 (1993).

56. 515 U.S. 819 (1995).

57. 521 U.S. 203 (1997).

58. Ibid., 223–224.

59. Ibid., 205.

60. 530 U.S. 793 (2000).

61. See 242.

62. *Mitchell v. Helms*, Souter, J. dissenting, I.B.

63. Ibid., 253, and see Justice O'Connor's concurrence in *Mitchell v. Helms*, which is the controlling opinion because it is narrower than the plurality opinion authored by

Justice Thomas, which she criticizes for its implication that neutrality is a sufficient condition for constitutionality.

64. *Mitchell v. Helms*, Souter, J. dissenting, I.B.

65. See Nussbaum, *Cultivating Humanity: A Classical Defense of Reform in Liberal Education* (Cambridge, MA: Harvard University Press, 1997).

66. *Zelman v. Simmons-Harris*, 536 U.S. 639, 644.

67. Ibid., 640.

68. Ibid., 674.

69. Ibid., 670, O'Connor, J. concurring.

70. See dissent, 695.

71. See 696 ff.

72. Ibid., 711.

73. Ibid., 711–713.

74. Ibid., 715–717, and Justice Breyer's separate dissent, 717–729.

75. *Locke v. Davey*, 540 U.S. 712 (2004).

76. Laycock, "Theology Scholarships, the Pledge of Allegiance and Religious Liberty," *Harvard Law Review* 118 (2004), 155–246.

77. *Davey*, 730.

78. Ibid., 734.

79. I am grateful to Adam Samaha for this suggestion.

80. Laycock, "Theology Scholarships," p. 159.

8 CONTEMPORARY CONTROVERSIES: THE PLEDGE, EVOLUTION, IMAGINATION, GAY MARRIAGE, FEAR OF MUSLIMS

1. *Elk Grove Unified School District v. Newdow*.

2. Asch's experiments are discussed in detail in both Christopher Browning, *Ordinary Men: Reserve Police Battalion 101 and the Final Solution in Poland* (New York: HarperCollins, 1992), and Cass R. Sunstein, *Why Societies Need Dissent* (Cambridge, MA: Harvard University Press, 2005).

3. See also Laycock, "Theology Scholarships," who similarly likes her criteria but not her application of them to the pledge.

4. See my *The Clash Within: Democracy, Religious Violence, and India's Future* (Cambridge, MA: Harvard University Press, 2007), ch. 9.

5. See Laycock, "Theology Scholarships," discussing a number of interpretations by believers.

6. Associated Press, July 19, 2006.

7. The book *The Fundamentals: A Testimony of the Truth*, after which the movement was named, was published in 1910–1915 (see McConnell, casebook, 656, and Irons, *The Courage of Their Convictions*, p. 210).

8. Strauss's *Leben Jesu* was published in 1835. (It was later translated into English by George Eliot.) Strauss had studied both with Hegel and with the Christian philosopher Schleiermacher, but, since he clearly preferred Schleiermacher's intensely religious orientation to Hegel's, his book was strongly denounced by the Hegelians. Renan's *Vie de*

Jésus was published in 1865. Although the work was controversial at the time, Renan soon became a pillar of the establishment. He continued to write influential works on the history of Christianity, and in 1892, shortly before his death, delivered as a lecture the highly influential "What Is a Nation?", which argues, *inter alia*, that nationhood must not be defined in religious terms, not even in terms of a generalized Christianity or a still more generalized religiosity, because each person has the right to the free exercise of religion or nonreligion.

9. *Scopes v. State*, 154 Tenn. 105 (1927).

10. *Scopes v. State*, 289 S. W. 363 (1927).

11. Quoted in Irons, *The Courage of Their Convictions*, p. 210.

12. The play, written by Jerome Lawrence and Robert E. Lee, opened in 1955; the film, starring Fredric March and Spencer Tracy, opened in 1960. Both play and book are fictional and contain numerous departures from the actual trial, but some essential issues are conveyed very powerfully.

13. See McConnell, casebook, p. 657.

14. The best brief review of the issues is Jerry Coyne, "The Faith That Dare Not Speak Its Name: The Case Against Intelligent Design," *The New Republic,* August 22 and 29, 2005, pp. 21–33, with an outstanding discussion of the scientific issues involved.

15. *Epperson v. Arkansas*, 393 U.S. 97 (1968). Peter Irons's *The Courage of Their Convictions* profiles Epperson on pp. 207–230.

16. Irons, *The Courage of Their Convictions*, p. 208.

17. Ibid., p. 212.

18. Ibid., p. 210.

19. *McLean v. Arkansas Board of Education*, 529 F. Supp. 1255 (E. D. Ark. 1982); see Irons, *The Courage of Their Convictions*, p. 216.

20. *Aguillard v. Edwards*, 482 U.S. 578 (1987).

21. See Coyne, "The Faith That Dare Not Speak," p. 23.

22. See ibid., p. 23, and *Kitzmiller v. Dover Area School District*, 26–29.

23. *Kitzmiller v. Dover*, pp. 28–29.

24. See summary of expert testimony in *Kitzmiller*, 24.

25. *Washington Post* online, August 2, 2005. Bush said that "both sides ought to be properly taught . . . so people can understand what the debate is about."

26. *Kitzmiller v. Dover Area School District*, Memorandum Opinion of Judge Jones, December 20, 2005.

27. Coyne, "The Faith That Dare Not Speak," p. 21.

28. Ibid.; *Kitzmiller v. Dover*, 45.

29. *Kitzmiller v. Dover*, 45.

30. Ibid., 16.

31. Ibid., 89.

32. He contrasted the flatworm with the sphex wasp, which simply goes through a programmed routine, no matter what environment it is in; by contrast, the flatworm responds to changes in environment and modifies its behavior accordingly. For a fine discussion of Darwin's work on this question, see James Rachels, *Created from Animals: The Moral Implications of Darwinism* (New York: Oxford University Press, 1990).

33. For my own view about dignity, see my "Human Dignity and Political Entitlements," in a volume prepared by the President's Council for Bioethics and edited by Adam Schulman, forthcoming.

34. Dickens, *Hard Times*.

35. See the longer treatment of these themes in Nussbaum, *Poetic Justice: The Literary Imagination and Public Life* (Boston: Beacon Press, 1995).

36. The nursery rhyme example is from Dickens's *Hard Times*: see my discussion in *Poetic Justice*.

37. *Mozert v. Hawkins County Board of Education*, 827 F. 2d 1058 (1987).

38. Ibid., opinion of Chief Judge Lively, I.A.

39. Ibid., I.B.

40. New York: Simon and Schuster, 1993.

41. Ibid.

42. Ibid., citing *Bethel School District v. Fraser*, 478 U.S. 675 (1986).

43. Maritain, "Truth and Human Fellowship," see ch. 1.

44. *Lawrence v. Texas*, 539 U.S. 559 (2003).

45. *Romer v. Evans*, 517 U.S. 620 (1996).

46. See the essays gathered in *Sexual Orientation and Human Rights in American Religious Discourse*, ed. Saul Olyan and Martha Nussbaum (New York: Oxford University Press, 1998).

47. See the essays by James Hanigan, Charles Curran, and Margaret Farley in Olyan and Nussbaum.

48. *Bob Jones University v. United States*, 461 U.S. 574 (1983).

49. See Martha Minow, "All in the Family," in David Estlund and Martha Nussbaum, eds., *Sex, Preference, and Family* (New York: Oxford University Press, 1997).

50. See my *The Clash Within: Democracy, Religious Violence, and India's Future* (Cambridge, MA: Harvard University Press, 2007), ch. 6.

51. See Mohan Rao, *From Population Control to Reproductive Health: Malthusian Arithmetic* (New Delhi: Sage, 2004), whose findings are discussed in my chapter.

52. Devlin, *The Enforcement of Morals* (London: Oxford University Press, 1965), discussed in my *Hiding From Humanity: Disgust, Shame, and the Law* (Princeton: Princeton University Press, 2004).

53. See Nussbaum, *Hiding*, ch. 3.

54. See Gary David Comstock, *Violence Against Lesbians and Gay Men* (New York: Columbia University Press, 1991).

55. See the detailed discussion of the debates in my *Hiding*, ch. 5, pp. 256–258.

56. See Martha Minow, "All in the Family," in David Estlund and Martha Nussbaum, eds., *Sex, Preference, and Family: Essays on Law and Nature* (New York: Oxford University Press, 1997).

57. *Loving v. Virginia*, 388 U.S. 1 (1967).

58. See Andrew Koppelman, *Same Sex, Different States* (New Haven: Yale University Press, 2006).

59. *Romer v. Evans*, 621.

60. *Romer v. Evans*, 633.

61. See "Judge: Woman Can't Cover Face on Driver's License," CNN.com Law Center, June 10, 2003.

62. "Netherlands Considers Ban on Wearing Islamic Cloak," *Chicago Tribune*, November 18, 2006, p. 13.

63. See my article on this issue, "Fearing Strangers," translated into Dutch as "Boerkaverbod komt voort uit irrationele angst" ("The Banning of the Burqa Comes from Irrational Fear"), *NRC Handelsblad* (The Netherlands), December 5, 2006.

64. "Official Lifts Diplomacy Veil to Chide Muslim Custom," *Chicago Tribune*, October 7, 2006.

65. "Muslim Girl Wins Battle to Wear Traditional Dress in School," *Times Online*, March 2, 2005; "Law Lords Overturn School Uniform 'Jilbab' Ruling," *Times Online*, March 22, 2006.

66. "'Muslim Only' Pool Outrage," *The Sun* online, December 8, 2006; "You Can Swim, But You Have to Wear Muslim Dress," *Daily Mail* online, December 9, 2006.

67. Quoted in "Official Lifts Diplomacy Veil."

68. The military is, as always, an exception.

69. Rashmee Roshan Lall, "Hell Is Other People," *The Times of India*, Monday, December 11, 2006.

9   Conclusion: Toward an "Overlapping Consensus"?

1. BT 424. Williams here, in a footnote, cites Habakkuk I:13, 14: "Wherefore lookest thou upon them that deal treacherously, and holdest they tongue when the wicked devoureth the man that is more righteous than he? and makest men as the fishes of the sea, as the creeping things, that have no ruler over them?"

INDEX

INDEX OF CASES